Constructing (In)Competence
Disabling Evaluations in Clinical
and Social Interaction

Constructing (In)Competence
Disabling Evaluations in Clinical and Social Interaction

Edited by

Dana Kovarsky
University of Rhode Island

Judith Felson Duchan
State University of New York at Buffalo

Madeline Maxwell
University of Texas at Austin

LEA

LAWRENCE ERLBAUM ASSOCIATES, PUBLISHERS
1999   Mahwah, New Jersey   London

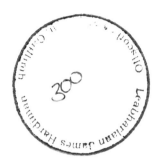

Lawrence Erlbaum Associates, Inc., Publishers
10 Industrial Avenue
Mahwah, NJ 07430

Cover design by Kathryn Houghtaling Lacey

Library of Congress Cataloging-in-Publication Data

Constructing (in)competence : disabling evaluations in
clinical and social interaction / editors : Dana Kovarsky,
Judith Felson Duchan, Madeline Maxwell.
 p. Cm.
ISBN 0-8058-2590-8 (cloth : alk. paper)
ISBN 0-8058-2591-6 (pbk. : alk. paper)
 1. Communicative disorders—Diagnosis—Social
aspects. 2. Communicative disorders—Diagnosis—Psychological aspects. 3. Therapist and patient. 4. Impression
formation (Psychology) 5. Disability evaluation.
I. Kovarsky, Dana. II. Duchan, Judith F. III. Maxwell,
Madeline M.
 RC428.8.D57 1998
 616.85'5075—dc21   98-24197
                                       CIP

Books published by Lawrence Erlbaum Associates are printed
on acid-free paper, and their bindings are chosen for strength
and durability.

Printed in the United States of America
10 9 8 7 6 5 4 3 2 1

Contents

Part I   Introduction

1 Evaluating Competence in the Course of Everyday   3
Interaction
Judith Duchan, Madeline Maxwell, and Dana Kovarsky

**Part II   Hidden Factors Influencing Judgments
of Competence**

2 "I Used to Be Good With Kids." Encounters Between   29
Speech-Language Pathology Students and Children With
Pervasive Developmental Disorders (PDD)
Robert Stillman, Ramona Snow, and Kirsten Warren

3 Slipping Through the Timestream: Social Issues of Time   49
and Timing in Augmented Interactions
D. Jeffery Higginbotham and David P. Wilkins

4 How Opposing Perceptions of Communication Competence   83
Were Constructed by Taiwanese Graduate Students
Carol Jorgenson Winkler

5 The Social Competence of Children Diagnosed With   111
Specific Language Impairment
Terry Irvine Saenz, Kelly Gilligan Black, and Laura Pellegrini

6 Deaf Members and Nonmembers: The Creation of Culture   125
Through Communication Practices
Madeline Maxwell, Diana Poeppelmeyer, and Laura Polich

7 Spiraling Connections: The Practice of Repair In Bektashi   149
Muslim Discourse
Frances Trix

Part III   Diagnosis as Situated Practice

8 Good Reasons For Bad Testing Performance: 171
The Interactional Substrate of Educational Testing
Douglas W. Maynard and Courtney L. Marlaire

9 An Afro-Centered View of Communicative Competence   197
Toya Wyatt

10 Reports Written by Speech-Language Pathologists: 223
The Role of Agenda in Constructing Client Competence
Judith Felson Duchan

11 Revelations of Family Perceptions of Diagnosis   245
and Disorder Through Metaphor
Ann M. Mastergeorge

12 The Social Work of Diagnosis: Evidence for Judgments   257
of Competence and Incompetence
Ellen L. Barton

Part IV   Intervention as Situated Practice

13 The Construction of Incompetence During Group Therapy   291
With Traumatically Brain Injured Adults
Dana Kovarsky, Michael Kimbarow, and Deborah Kastner

14 Social Role Negotiation in Aphasia Therapy: Competence,   313
Incompetence, and Conflict
Nina Simmons-Mackie and Jack S. Damico

15 The Social Construction of Language Incompetence   343
and Social Identity in Psychotherapy
Kathleen Ferrara

Author Index   363

Subject Index   369

INTRODUCTION

Chapter 1

Evaluating Competence in the Course of Everyday Interaction

Judith Duchan
State University of New York at Buffalo

Madeline Maxwell
University of Texas at Austin

Dana Kovarsky
University of Rhode Island

1. Mr. H: . . . I'll take along a camera. Speech-Language Pathologist: **Very good, Walter.**
2. Pediatrician: **Have you heard the term "cerebral palsy" before?** Father: Cerebral . . . Pediatrician: Cerebral palsy. Father: Yeah. Mother: That's what he has. Father: Oh, I know that—
3. **My tall and graceful cypress. . . .**

The boldfaced elements in the snippets of talk just presented can be interpreted as evaluative. The first example (from Kovarsky, Kimbarow, & Kastner, chap. 13, this volume) is an explicit evaluation of a client's previous response. The issuer, a speech-language pathologist, intends the recipient, Mr. H., to interpret her expression as an evaluation of his response. The second example (from Barton, chap. 12, this volume) is a less direct one in which a pediatrician is revealing an evaluation by underestimating the knowledge of a family as she explains to them what they already know. The third evaluation is even less transparent. It was interpreted by the recipient as a validation of her competence in speaking Albanian—competence that had been previously placed in question (Trix, chap. 7, this volume). This is a book about ways that evaluations, such as the three just cited, are achieved. It is also about how evaluations can impact on one's notions of competence (and incompetence)[1] and ultimately how they affect an individual's notions of self-identity.

This idea that one's identity is tied directly to evaluative contexts experienced in everyday life differs from the more traditional view of identity as a single, fixed, encapsulated entity. The ideas and findings of the authors in this text support the conceptualization of identity as a flexible system that can include a multiplicity of selves, that can be brought to bear on the moment, and that can be influenced by what happens in the moment. Our view follows that of Kenneth Gergen (1994) in psychology and Donal Carbaugh (1988, 1994, 1996) in speech communication. Carbaugh (1996) commented: "Identities [are] something created and subjected to particular conversational dynamics. . . . From this vantage point the question 'who am I?' depends partly on 'where I am,' 'with whom I am,' and [material and symbolic] resources that are available to the people there" (pp. 213–214).

Support for the construction of a flexible, situated identity is provided by Trix (chap. 7, this volume) in her description of how her identity as a learner of Albanian was altered when native speakers of that language began to tease her about a language mistake she made. On one occasion a group of women laughed when Trix used the Albanian term *long* to refer to her height, rather than using the more appropriate term *tall*. It was the women's reaction to that occasion that engendered in Trix feelings about her limitations as a speaker of Albanian. These feelings of incompetence increased throughout the day when the women continued to laugh among themselves at her "mistake." Trix's view of herself as incompetent was reversed later when her mentor referred to her as a tall and graceful cypress. Trix may well have experienced the different evaluations, one from the women and the other from her mentor, as both being valid views of her competence as a speaker of Albanian.

There are instances described in this volume in which acts of evaluation are closely tied to feelings of belongingness. Judgments of incompetence, in their most severe form, can lead to threats of expulsion from a social community. The subjects in Maxwell, Poeppelmeyer, and Polich's study (chap. 6, this volume), who are deaf, commonly experience alienation in interactions with hearing peers. Similarly, the subjects in Higginbotham and Wilkins' study (chap. 3, this volume), who use augmentative communicative systems, experience ostracism by partners because they are unable to meet the temporal or social demands expected by oral communicators. In these cases, the interactants who are ignored may view themselves as

---

[1]*Competence* is used in this chapter to refer to the overall domain ranging from least (incompetent) to most competent.

disabled (incompetent) communicators. Alternatively, those same interactants may view themselves as different, but competent, communicators
and their partners as rude or ignorant about their differences. The choice
is similar to that of a person from a different social or ethnic community
who is treated as gauche or ignorant (see Maxwell et al., chap. 6, this
volume, for a clear statement of how those who are deaf are faced with a
choice of identity as disabled or as culturally different).

Even though the contributors to this volume hold various views of competence, they come to the same conclusion: Competence judgments per-
vade, influence, and grow out of ordinary social interactions. The studies
presented here can be described together within a single multicomponential framework. The framework depicts evaluations of competence taking
place as participants assume a particular, situated view of the interaction.
Participants take a position, one of a *situated self*, from which they interpret
what is going on and gauge how they and others are doing (see Carbaugh,
1988, 1993, 1994, 1996, for a detailed view of this position).

The research in this volume on the construction of competence builds
on the findings of other researchers who have been working within a
variety of theoretical frameworks and using a variety of methodologies.
Ethnomethodologists have, for example, studied ways authors design their
talk for their audiences (see discussions of "recipient design" in Maynard,
1992; Sacks & Schegloff, 1979; Schegloff, 1979). Cognitive scientists have
investigated how one's theory of another's mind pervades social interaction
(Astington, Harris, & Olson, 1988; Frye & Moore, 1991; Wellman, 1990),
and systemic linguists have examined the communication resources available to language users to convey an "attitude" (Halliday, 1961, 1967–1968;
Halliday, McIntosh, & Strevens, 1964) or "appraisal" (Eggins & Slade, 1997;
Martin, 1992).

The situated viewpoint expressed in this book has perhaps the strongest
affinity with that of Dell Hymes (1974) in his depiction of communicative
competence. In Hymes' view, a speaker draws on a variety of resources in
deciding "when to speak, when not, and as to what to talk about with
whom, when, where, [and] in what manner" (p. 177). A speaker, as depicted by Hymes, is thereby seen as being situated and as drawing on a
variety of resources in the course of communicating. Although Hymes did
not focus directly on evaluation, his view of communication is easily extended to one laid out here—individuals, when evaluating others, use
evaluative resources available in the language and cultural practices of
their community.

These various scholarly approaches all lead to the view that participants
in interactions are continually tracking what is going on. Those engaged
in interactions convey their attitudes about their own and their partners'

contributions in a variety of ways—a raise of an eyebrow, a change in intonation or timing, an evaluative statement, even a nonresponse in contexts in which a response is required. In this situated view, competence judgments are continually being constructed and negotiated.

Evidence that tracking is ongoing and pervasive comes from studies and observations of people aligning with or making accommodations to one another as they interact (Coupland & Coupland, 1991; Giles & Coupland, 1991; Kendon, 1985). Communicators of all ages and abilities can be observed initiating activities to fit their view of their interactants. They may suggest activities through nonverbal means, or they may verbally raise different topics with different partners. Their initiations depend on judgments they make about their interactants' knowledge and interests. Speakers' initiations are responded to differently, depending on the recipients' construal of their partners' experiences, language background, or overall capability. When recipients show signs of incomprehension, speakers repeat themselves, simplify the original message, slow it down, and provide additional background, basing their repairs on judgments about what is causing their partners' confusion. All of these activities are based on the results of tracking one another's competence in the course of face-to-face interaction.

Competence judgments also occur in non-face-to-face contexts, such as when someone writes a report about a third party. The author of the report also takes on the perspective of a situated self, assuming a particular point of view, drawing from particular background knowledge, and constructing a view that becomes situated in the discourse of the report (Duchan, chap. 10, this volume; Ward & Duchan, 1996).

Many of the evaluations described in this book are part and parcel of the institutionalized practices between partners. Clinicians are socialized to evaluate the competence of their clients. Teachers assume the role of evaluator when they engage in teaching students. The evaluations of clinicians and teachers, whether positive or negative, can be empowering, resulting in a sense of self as competent; or evaluations, even if they are positive, can lead to the creation and maintenance of disabled identities— feelings of being sickly, deficient, incapable, powerless, incompetent.

This book, in sum, is designed to make a case that competence is created and evaluated in the course of situated interactions and that the evaluations are important in the construction of social identities. This chapter outlines a framework for examining how competence is socially constructed from everyday experiences. This framework also provides a way for us to present what the different authors in this book have to say about the effects of evaluations on the individuals' emerging judgments of their own competence.

CONSTRUCTING COMPETENCE IN INTERACTION

Because social interactions are rich and complex, a framework for studying and thinking about how competence is constructed in the course of social interactions must be rich and complex. We offer the following multicomponential rendition of competence construction:

A situated self draws from a variety of communication resources to evaluate competence from some position, occasioned by something, about something, in comparison with a set of expectations, and with potentially long-lasting and profound effects.

The framework as just described contains six dynamic and highly interactive constructs:

1. Communication resources.
2. Evaluating competence from some position.
3. Occasioned by something.
4. About something.
5. In comparison with something.
6. With potentially long-lasting and profound effects.

Each contributes to our understanding of how competence gets constructed, and each is discussed in various ways by this volume's authors.

Communication Resources for Expressing Evaluation

Evaluations in their most explicit form are conveyed in a statement such as that found in employee performance evaluations, in school lessons, or in therapy sessions: "You are doing a good job." But evaluations do not always occur as overt speech acts; they may also be covert, as when someone arches an eyebrow or when someone passes up an obligatory turn at talk: "How do you like my new car?" (no response) (Pomerantz, 1988). Even when individuals are not part of an ongoing interaction, they can interpret their position as one in which they have been excluded or ostracized—and thus as a very strong negative evaluation (Higginbotham & Wilkins, chap. 3, this volume; Maxwell, Poeppelmeyer, & Polich, chap. 6, this volume).

One way to discover how evaluations get constructed is by looking at the evaluative tools available in the linguistic or semiotic system being used by the participants. These tools are the communication resources that comprise a person's potential communication repertoire. Hymes used the term *repertoire* to describe resources that are used by members of a particular community and those that are used by particular speakers who participate in one or more "ways of speaking" (Hymes, 1974, p. 199). We examine some of the linguistic and nonlinguistic resources that are available to Americans communicating evaluations in English (see also Eggins & Slade, 1997).

Linguistic Elements Associated With Evaluation

Lexical Choices. One obvious way to convey evaluations is through the use of evaluative terms such as good–bad, lousy–fantastic, sloppy–careful, stellar–plebeian, a keeper–a loser, and so on. These lexical items may appear syntactically as *nominals* (nouns, noun phrases) or as *modifiers* (adjectives and adverbs). *Epithets* (nouns such as "brat" or "shithead") are also primary candidates for evaluating others' performances, along with *interjections* ("abso-fucking-lutely," "run like shit"). Some less obvious lexical elements used for evaluations are *general terms* that serve to undercut straightforward descriptions and thereby show value-laden equivocation ("sort of responsive"; "pretty bright"), and nonliteral, *metaphoric language* used to understand and translate the effects of high-impact evaluative contexts (Mastergeorge, chap. 11, this volume).

One of the characteristics of evaluative terms is their implied dichotomous structure. Thus one can interpret assertions containing evaluative terms as *implicatures* (Grice, 1975). Calling one thing good may be heard as implying that another thing is bad. A compliment issued today may be heard as an indicator that criticism was withheld in bygone days.

Preposed adverbials not only take on meaning by virtue of the lexical interpretation, but also by their placement and pronunciation in a contrastive context (Biber & Finegan, 1988). The following phrase containing a preposed adverbial, "essentially," can be read as a deprecating statement because of its placement at the beginning of a sentence, and even more so if there is extra stress placed on the second syllable: "*Essentially* it's a review of old literature." This is in contrast with the phrase: "It's essentially a review of old literature," which may be interpreted as describing a happy discovery after having looked for old literature. Other preposed adverbials such as "well," "but," and "actually" also can be interpreted as a signal for a negative evaluation when placed at the beginning of a conversational turn.

Evaluation can also be encoded through strategic use of *verbs*. "His proposal thrilled her" is rightfully interpretable as a positive evaluation since it is encoded in the verb as a positively valued emotional reaction.

Grammatical and Discourse Resources. Consider the parent who regards his or her child's coloring and says: "Staying within the lines is really hard, isn't it?" or "Try harder to stay inside the lines" or "You're not supposed to color outside the lines" or "It looks messy when you go outside the lines" or even "I think it's boring to stay within the lines." All these are interpretable by the parent and child as evaluations. The interpretations will depend on the history of the partners and the context in which the comments are issued. The comments may also be treated at face value—as meaning what they say—or they may be seen as ironic, and intended or interpreted in ways that are exactly opposite from their literal meaning.

The opposition between surface and intended meanings is signaled by the occurrence of unexpected grammatical and discourse devices. Grammatical formality can be evaluative, if one is not expecting it; and displays of familiarity or deference can be evaluative if the footing fosters another expectation (see Goffman, 1981, chap. 3). The use of passive voice or other forms of indirectness is also interpretable as evaluative and as resulting from someone's reluctance to make direct, evaluative threats (Scollon & Scollon, 1995). Consider, for example, the parent who turns from the phone conversation with a friend to ask the children to stop what they are doing. Such an insertion sequence, if issued as a direct command, is abrasive unless it is an emergency. Parents often substitute a mitigated request form using conditional modals ("would you") or presequences ("Honey, Mama's on the phone. Be quiet.") to soften the force of the directly issued request and thereby convey respect (Ventola, 1987).

Paralinguistic Signals and Movements Associated With Evaluation

Timing, Repetition, Intonation, and Movement. Participants in communicative interactions carry out their activities within a carefully organized temporal system. They move and talk in synchrony, matching or contrasting their contributions along dimensions such as rhythm, tempo, and rate (Clark, 1996; Higginbotham & Wilkins, chap. 3, this volume). Clark has labeled these temporal patterns as leading to a temporal imperative. Successful communication requires the participants to display their meanings and understandings to one another in a timely way. Violations of such temporal dictates can be and often are interpreted as evaluative. A temporal delay in responding can be seen as reticence or incompetence. Movement asynchrony can be interpreted as a negative judgment about the previous content or as a signal of nonalignment (Scheflen, 1964), as can a comment made too late (Robillard, cited in Higginbotham & Wilkins, chap. 3, this volume).

The expressions of attitudes are often conveyed through manipulations of repetition, loudness, and pitch, in addition to timing. Using such devices can serve to highlight particular content, thereby placing extra value on it (Labov, 1972; Tannen, 1989; Tench, 1996).

Movement of the body also offers key resources in the evaluation process. Physical distance and orientation of the body, the use of gestures and eye gaze, and moving in or out of synchrony with another's temporal beat can all be interpreted as evaluative. For example, an extra few inches of distance between members of a dyad can be seen as a signal that the partner is annoyed. An especially powerful evaluative signal is conveyed by mutual eye gaze. Avoiding eye gaze or meeting eye gaze can express a disapproval (see Stillman et al., chap. 2, this volume). Neck rolls (Wyatt, chap. 9, this volume), eye rolls (Maxwell & Kovarsky, 1993), and other such movements have been shown to have powerful evaluative effects.

Employment of Resources Evaluating Communication

How does it come about that a communicator uses certain resources to convey evaluative content or to interpret others' evaluations? It would be a fruitless enterprise to try to discover which particular resources are associated with which particular evaluations. This would be a problem for the following four reasons:

1. Evaluative resources do not occur singly, but often are used in combination with one another. Lexical selection, repetition, and increase in pitch, intensity, and rate may show evaluative outrage: DON'T YOU EVER EVER DO THAT AGAIN!

2. Resources are not isolable from their context, but take on meanings beyond that offered by the evaluative indicator itself. A nod can show approval in one context and reluctant acknowledgment or disapproval in another. Particular personal histories and expectations may lead interpreters to different renditions of the same evaluation

3. Interpreting evaluative elements involves the use of a hidden and fluctuating evaluative standard. For instance, the selection and interpretation of the evaluation elements will depend on one's knowledge of the other interlocutor. I may think you are shouting unless I know that you characteristically speak with greater intensity than most of the other people I know. If I know you to be "bossy" then I may evaluate your actions as benign—a manifestation of your "personality"—rather than negatively, as a violation of protocol or a sign of disrespect. A college student said that his brother could "demolish" him with a grunt that the rest of the class heard as an acknowledgment or clarification request. The intimate knowledge that interlocuters have may be unrecoverable by others (Kreckel, 1981)

4. Evaluations can be issued and interpreted in linguistic contexts that have no overt evaluative indicators. Some evaluations are delivered in such a way that partners can focus directly on the activity at hand without having to shift out of the activity frame to comment on how things are going. The interactions between the preschool children in the study by Saenz,

Gilligan, and Pelligrini (chap. 5, this volume) exemplify how tacit evaluations might be taking place. The two children in their study are vying for play space and use of toy train tracks. The interaction may engender different evaluative reactions, depending on the evaluator's construal of the event. The child who was there first may be seen negatively, as selfish, or positively as standing up for his or her rights. The outcome is also likely to yield different evaluative responses, depending on its interpretation: The victor may see it as a positive evaluation of his or her actions, the vanquished as a negative evaluation of the victor's and of his or her own actions.

. . . From Some Position. . . . The Stance of the Interactants

The authors in this book show how evaluations are issued and interpreted by interactants from particular positions. Participants in evaluations position themselves in relation to one another and in relation to what is going on. This notion of the positioned nature of talk is elegantly forwarded by Erving Goffman (1981) in his discussion of the role of *footing* in talk exchanges. Goffman described participants as positioning themselves interpersonally in different ways. They can have official status in the main encounter, as when a speaker and listener talk to one another—"a ratified position," in Goffman's terminology. Or participants may assume the position of unofficial bystanders or eavesdroppers. Goffman also illuminated, through examples, how participants in interactions are positioned relative to the situation. They organize their talk around the task at hand, shifting from social talk to work-related talk, to no talk at all. Goffman further discussed how talk is affected by one's position in the discourse event, differing if one is at the beginning, middle, or end of a talk encounter. Finally, Goffman spoke of varieties of authoring in which speakers can speak directly, introspectively, reportatively, or from the position of someone else.

Goffman's revelations about footing are easily translatable to the data on evaluative talk described in this volume. The issuers and recipients of evaluations are described within these pages as having assumed identifiable positions in relation to one another and in relation to what is going on. A number of chapters (e.g., those by Barton; Ferrara; Kovarsky et al; Maynard & Marlaire; Simmons-Mackie & Damico) involve studies of interactants who hold ratified participatory positions in the interactions being analyzed. They involve talk between therapists or teachers and their clients or students, with all parties recognizably positioned.

From within their ratified positions, participants in studies reported within these pages gear their exchanges to be in keeping with the presumed background information of their partners. Evaluators engage in what ethnomethodologists have called *recipient design* (e.g., Maynard, 1992; Sacks & Schegloff, 1979; Schegloff, 1979).[2] Of particular interest are those occasions in which the communication is incorrectly designed, resulting in an unintended negative evaluation (Simmons-Mackie & Damico).

A few authors in this volume describe evaluations that are expressed remotely rather than in the course of a face-to-face evaluation encounter (Duchan; Ferrara; Higginbotham & Wilkins; Mastergeorge; Maxwell et al.). The remote position for issuing or experiencing evaluations in these cases includes instances in which evaluations are made in writing or reading an evaluation report (Duchan), instances in which individuals feel ostracized from speech communities (Higginbotham & Wilkins; Maxwell et al.), instances in which family members are reflecting on the devastating impact of a previous evaluation (Mastergeorge), instances in which psychotherapists evaluate their clients' reports of previous events (Ferrara), and instances in which researchers comment on the potential impact of their subjects' talk (Ferrara).

Evaluations, like other communications described in Goffman (1981), are designed to achieve particular goals. For example, the authors of the diagnostic reports cited by Duchan (chap. 10, this volume) cast their descriptions of client's competence differently depending on what they are attempting to achieve. When authors write diagnostic reports, they are aiming to show the need for client services. To do so, they emphasize the negative side of their clients' performance. When writing progress reports to show a client's successes, the authors emphasize the positive aspects of their client's performance.

For many interactions described in these chapters, the evaluations are positioned in relation to a specifiable social role. Participants cast in the role of a clinician or teacher, for example, may feel compelled to evaluate someone's performance so as to keep track of how well the person is doing ("He got that one right," "That's better than yesterday") or to provide corrective feedback ("You need to work on that one"). Clinicians and teachers may also overtly or covertly evaluate their own adequacy ("I shouldn't have raised that issue").

The clinician and teacher, in keeping with their defined roles, engage in evaluations of clients or students. A client may take a clinician's evaluation as an indicator of competence in handling a particular item or task

---

[2]Schegloff (1979): "When social behavior is differentiated by reference to its recipient or target, investigators can hardly escape the importance that attaches to the processes by which identification of recipients is made. . . . (p. 25). We are just beginning to appreciate the degree of detail to which such differentiation—by 'recipient design' is applicable, but a sense of its range may be gleaned from considering that on the one hand the very occurrence or not of interaction may be contingent on it, and on the other hand, should conversation be entered into, the selection of words in the talk will be sensitive to it. . . ." (p. 26).

("I said that wrong") or as a more general indicator about overall competence for tasks of this type (e.g., "I'm inarticulate"; see Ferrara, chap. 15, this volume). Less often, the student may respond to a teacher's evaluation by interpreting it as an unfair correction or as inauthentic ("I really did OK even though she thinks I didn't"; see Higginbotham & Wilkins, chap. 3, this volume).

There are a few significant examples in this volume in which those evaluated do not conform to role expectations (Higginbotham & Wilkins; Simmons-Mackie & Damico). An augmentative system user, reported in Higginbotham and Wilkins, negatively evaluates his nurses. A client, described in Simmons-Mackie and Damico, criticizes her speech-language pathologist for failing to provide meaningful therapy.

An interesting third example of a role violation is described by Stillman et al. (chap. 2, this volume), who interviewed students in a speech-language pathology curriculum. The students revealed their feelings of incompetence in working with children who, because of their severe communication and social problems, did not interact according to the students' role expectations. In this case, the professionals in training did not blame the lack of interaction on their clients as would more experienced professionals (see Goode, 1994; Higginbotham & Wilkins, chap. 3, this volume; and Maynard & Marlaire, chap. 8, this volume, for a discussion of how professionals blame clients for interaction difficulties). Rather, these clinicians in training saw themselves as lacking in skill and as the source of the problematic social interactions.

An alternative to evaluations made from a single role-positioned view, particularly from the view of the expert, is one described by Ferrara (chap. 15, this volume). She cites a movement in psychotherapy under the influence of postmodernism that allows clients to take a much stronger role in the therapy discourse. Ferrara's alternative is one that empowers the client. Danforth (1997) provided an even broader possibility, advocating a postmodern approach to those labeled mentally retarded: "Professionals can ally themselves with labeled persons, their families, and loved ones in efforts to transform social constructions of deficiency and incompetence into relationship-based and self-based understandings of personal power and efficacy" (p. 101).

Goffman's notion of footing also allows for variability in evaluative stance. For example, he discussed alterations in footing based on whether the speaker is speaking directly ("Shut the window"), reflectively ("I said shut the window"), as an actor (Macbeth: "Shut the window"), or for someone else ("He said 'shut the window'"; Goffman, 1981, pp. 148–151).

Evaluations, as depicted in our situated framework, are emergent and variable, being made from highly fluid stances. Participants in interactions often create stances in their communication that relate to gender, age, musical taste, and religious feeling. Their relative positions and consequent evaluations based on such constructs can be manifested directly or indirectly. Mockeries are direct. Evidentials, forms that are used to cast information as doubtful, suspicious, or hearsay, are less direct.

Adverbs, when used as evidentials, can serve to soften or strengthen the stance toward information presented in an evaluation. The very presence of the adverb may signal the audience to treat the upcoming information from a particular stance and to evaluate it accordingly. The detached stance required of media newscasters provides them with the occasion to use adverbs such as "allegedly" to avoid prejudging a person as guilty. A reporter saying that "Andrew Cunanan allegedly killed Gianni Versace" may actually believe that Cunanan committed the act but wants the audience to evaluate the report (and reporter) and not to prejudge the case. The adverb "allegedly" in this instance creates an interesting complex evaluative situation in which the newscaster, in an effort to show that he or she is not being evaluative, is inviting the audience to evaluate the report as fair.

. . . Occasioned by Something. . . . How Evaluations Are Locally Determined

Evaluations grow out of the situations in which they occur. A telling example of this is offered by Robillard (Higginbotham & Wilkins, chap. 3, this volume), who described others saying "Not now" in response to his attempts to tell them something. Robillard uses a communication device to create messages, and thus takes a long time to get his ideas out. The result is that he and his partners cannot meet the ordinary time requirements of typical speech communication. When his interactants refuse to accept his efforts to communicate with them, they are levying the ultimate negative evaluation—telling him that his ideas are not worth waiting for.

There are chapters in this volume that contain evaluations issued in the course of clinical "lessons" (Kovarsky, Kimbarow, & Kastner; Simmons-Mackie & Damico). Lessons are events that are structured around evaluation exchanges. They contain three-part turns involving (a) a prompt or question from the teacher—a clinician in this case, (b) a response from the student, and (c) the teacher's evaluation of the student's response.

These explicit evaluations delivered as a third component of the exchange are also present in the testing situation as described by Maynard and Marlaire (chap. 8, this volume). They show that even when testers try not to evaluate a student's responses as a third slot in a prompt–response–evaluation exchange, they can succumb inadvertently to the evaluation imperative. These authors found that the test giver inadvertently altered what she said and did depending on the accuracy of the student's response. After correct responses the test giver said "Good" or proceeded to the next item, with no comment. After incorrect responses, the tester said "Okay" rather than "Good" and sometimes slowed down the tempo of the exchange.

Psychotherapists who follow traditional practices also evaluate throughout the therapy sessions. Ferrara (chap. 15, this volume) identified a variety of negative evaluations issued by the therapist. Her clinician complained about the ambiguity in his client's language (Therapist: "You use a lot of pronouns that I don't know *what* you mean. . . ."); asked the client to say things in a different way, as if not accepting her own renditions (Therapist: "Are there any other words that you could put on that piece . . . ?"); and focused on deficits through negative summary statements—what Ferrara calls "recycling communicative failure" (Therapist: "Poor communication. Heaps of blaming. Not recognizing what you *could* do. . . .").

It can be shown in data presented in this volume that all evaluations are influenced by what is happening in the here and now—even those evaluations that are made of people who are not present. The evaluations of clients in the diagnostic reports analyzed by Duchan (chap. 10, this volume) and the metaphoric descriptions of parents' responses to previous evaluations reported in Mastergeorge (chap. 11, this volume) are constructed in light of what is happening at the moment. Report writers design reports for an audience to achieve a particular agenda; parents use metaphoric language to translate a catastrophic experience for their naive audience.

Kovarsky and his coauthors (chap. 13, this volume) add another set of dimensions for understanding how evaluations are tied to the occasion in which they are issued. For example, they describe how theoretical models subscribed to by clinicians lead the clinicians to focus on client deficits. They also see the lack of shared knowledge between clinician and client and the institutional requirement that a client's progress be tracked as leading to gamelike activities in which performance is continually evaluated.

These examples, taken from everyday life contexts described in this volume, allow us to make the point that all evaluations are locally occasioned. Even for the evaluations that are of remote occurrences, the evaluator must be sensitive to the particular institutional, discourse, and pragmatic demands that occasion the issuance of the specific evaluation.

. . . About Something. . . . The Scope and Domain of Constructed Evaluations

The situated interaction framework exemplified by the studies in this book focuses primarily on how and where ideas of competence are generated. The authors look at what is happening during naturally occurring social interactions. Evaluations of specific performances during an event ("Great throw!") can be used by participants to build to more generalized ideas about how well individuals are doing across several occasions ("You're outdoing yourself so far in this game"), and from there to summary impressions about how well individuals did overall ("You played a great game"). Evaluations also can have an even more general scope, such as those describing performance for types of activities ("You're a great ballplayer") or those describing the overall competence of individuals ("You're a great athlete").

A particular occasion can serve to elicit evaluations at a variety of levels of generality. For example, the speech-language pathologist in Kovarsky, Kimbarow, and Kastner (chap. 13, this volume) evaluated her patients' particular performances (such as putting their "heads down on the table") as well as their general abilities (difficulties with "problem solving, thought organization, the ability to generate lists and . . . to organize to complete a task").

Furthermore, a particular evaluation may be issued as having a particular scope or focus and be interpreted by the recipient more or less broadly. For example, Jorgensen Winkler describes watershed experiences of her Taiwanese subjects (chap. 4, this volume) based on a particular comment by an evaluator.

Evaluations not only vary in scope, they also vary in what it is that is being evaluated—what we call the domain of the evaluation. The domains of evaluation described between the covers of this book vary widely. They include such diverse areas as sound blending (Maynard & Marlaire), attention (Kovarsky et al.), and speaking Standard English (Jorgensen Winkler; Maxwell et al.; Wyatt).

. . . In Comparison With an Expectation. . . . The Standard for Making Competence Comparisons

The studies in this book are of competence evaluations made about people who are in one way or another being judged as incompetent. Some of the studies are of normal people who are gaining competence in a selected domain. Trix, for example, describes her experiences under tutelage in Islam; Jorgensen Winkler describes the English-speaking competencies of Taiwanese immigrants; Stillman et al. describe the self-judgments made by college students in training to be speech-language pathologists; and Mastergeorge and Barton describe how adults respond to their children's disabilities.

The juxtaposition of studies of normal and abnormal learners in this volume provides a view of how standards and expectations influence evaluations. The subjects with diagnoses are cast in the subordinate role of patients, and the expectations and standards for evaluating performance are lowered. While interacting in such subordinating roles, subjects may be evaluated as performing well, but this notion of positively evaluated performance is highly constrained by virtue of their classification as people with problems. Their judged competence is couched in implicit conditionals. It is as if someone were saying: "You did very well, considering your limitations." The standard against which their performance is being judged is qualitatively different from that used for their counterparts who are seen as normal.

Besides leading to lesser expectations by professionals, judgments about the competence of those who have been diagnosed with a disability have an added feature. Those affected are also judged by professionals as more or less competent depending on the degree to which they follow the agenda of the professional and the degree to which they conform to the institutional practices that are prescribed for improving their competence. Barton (chap. 12, this volume) contrasts two members of different families whose children have attention deficit hyperactivity disorder; the first is treated by the professional as being competent, the second as incompetent. The difference between the two is based on the degree to which the family member buys into and complies with the view and agenda of the professional doing the evaluating.

... With Potentially Long-Lasting and Profound Effects. ...
The Possible Consequences of Situated Evaluations

Situated evaluations are shown by authors of these chapters to have differing effects. Some evaluations may have high impact effects, such as those that have diagnostic significance (Duchan; Maynard & Marlaire; Wyatt), or those that create a watershed change in people's views of their own or a family member's competence (Jorgensen Winkler; Mastergeorge). Other evaluations may have minimal impact, such as an "OK" following a correct response to an easy question in a domain of strength or an evaluation made outside the recipient's focus of attention (e.g., Simmons-Mackie & Damico's subject, who was evaluated during her efforts to change the topic).

Several authors in this volume make the case that it is not a single evaluation but the accumulated impact of multiple evaluations that can create long-lasting effects. The evaluations by the psychotherapist in the study by Ferrara, when viewed cumulatively, can create feelings of powerlessness. The evaluations implicitly conveyed when people are ostracized or ignored can be highly debilitating, such as those of hearing subjects in the presence of their deaf peers (Maxwell et al.), those issued by medical personnel in the presence of augmentative communication users (Higginbotham & Wilkins), and those made by children with autism when they failed to look at their student clinicians (Stillman et al.).

There is a healthy body of existing research showing the possible cumulative effect of evaluations on a person's notions of self-identity and on the person's performance in particular areas being evaluated. The research has been carried out within five different, yet related, frameworks: attribution theory (e.g., Weiner, 1974), expectancy theory (e.g., Rosenthal & Jacobson, 1992), labeling theory (e.g., Mercer, 1973), mindlessness/mindfulness theory (Langer 1975, 1979), and learned-helplessness theory (Seligman, 1975). Together, researchers working in these frameworks have shown that the classification of an individual can lead others to treat the individual negatively or positively depending on expectancies derived from the label. When the classification entails a lack of ability (a disability) or lesser competence, those classified eventually develop a lowered sense of self-esteem, a sense of helplessness, and a sense that they are not able to control what is going on. The expectancies thereby become self-fulfilling prophecies. Individuals who are labeled with a diagnosis feel more competent prior to their diagnosis than they did after being diagnosed. Interestingly, the reverse is also true. When labeled as having high potential, subjects (from mice to men) improve in their measured performance. They exhibit what has come to be called the "Pygmalion effect" (Rosenthal & Jacobson, 1992). In an interpersonal context, someone who is expected to lose his or her temper may be more likely to do so, someone expected to be brave may be more likely to be so. The situated interaction view would explain such changes as resulting from accumulations of evaluations and interpretations made on various occasions.

The data and interpretations of the authors of this volume, along with data from other paradigms, are taken as support of the situated interaction view. The authors show repeatedly and in various ways that judgments or displays of competence rely heavily on the conditions that prevail in particular occasions. They show that their subjects appear more or less competent depending on the objectives and worldview of the evaluators, on whether the person being evaluated shows compliance with professionals and institutional performance requirements, and on whether the evaluated person can meet the specific task requirements under which the judgments are being made.

These contextual factors are often ignored by professionals and scholars who are assessing, studying, or working to alter competence in others. The prevailing paradigm portrays competence as contained and circumscribed. In the "containment view" contextual factors are depicted as variables affecting competence rather than as central to the process of competence construction.

COMPETENCE AS CONTAINMENT

A prevailing view of competence, one that is countered in this volume, is that it can be located and measured in an individual in much the same way one would measure liquid in a container. People are described as "having" varying amounts competence. One's overall competence can range from minimal (incompetent) to considerable (expert, genius). Descriptors such as "high level" or "low level," "high functioning" or "low functioning," can be used to describe overall competence in the same way one would describe the level of material in a container. (See Lakoff & Johnson, 1980, for more detailed discussions of how the container metaphor has been used to depict aspects of the human mind.)

Social scientists, since Binet, have been hard at work creating standardized and reliable measures for judging amounts of overall competence. The measures add legitimacy to the container metaphor because they provide a way to quantify amounts of competence. Researchers and clinicians can now classify people in low-, normal-, or high-level competence groups, depending on the scores they obtain on a standardized test.

Competence testing, as traditionally carried out, has been aimed at discovering people's overall competence as well as their competence in particular domains. An individual can be found to have varying amounts of language knowledge, gross or fine motor skill, or social abilities. One very active area of competence research has been to discover how overall competence or components of competence might be increased. Another area of study is to determine how components of competence interact with one another. Researchers have made efforts to discover, for example, how language competence changes with different types of language intervention (see Howard & Hatfield, 1987; Weismer, 1991) and how language competence relates, say, to social competence (Fujiki & Brinton, 1994).

Many studies have been designed to control or manipulate components of competence, treating them as experimental variables. Sometimes components serve as control variables, others times as independent or dependent variables. The effects of mental age or language level on performance might, for example, be controlled by selecting subjects who fall within a restricted range of scores on an intelligence or language test. Or changes in a competence level might be measured before and after receiving training designed to enhance competence in a selected area. Effects of changes in one component (the independent variable) on another (the dependent variable) allow researchers to examine the relationships between components.

Competence tests have also come to be used as diagnostic measures to identify whether particular individuals need support to enhance competence of one type or another (see Maynard & Marlaire, chap. 8, this volume). Results from diagnostic evaluations have led to altered educational placement and programming for those who obtain scores significantly below what would be expected. For example, children found to have normal intelligence but below average reading, mathematical, or other academic ability, qualify for the diagnosis of learning disability.

Diagnosis is often the gateway to educational or therapeutic programs designed to increase competence in areas of identified deficiency. Some programs are loosely matched to general deficits. For example, individuals with traumatic brain injury or aphasia may be enrolled in a therapy program to enhance memory or attention, or to improve problem-solving abilities (see Kovarsky et al., chap. 13, this volume). Other programs have a more individualized focus, such as the psychotherapy approach described by Ferrara (chap. 15, this volume) that is closely tied to what the client chooses to talk about. Whatever the degree of individualization, many programs designed to enhance competence are grounded in the container view of competence, with the goal of the program being to increase or enhance a person's competence level.

The container metaphor fails to consider how competence is constructed by situated selves, in situated contexts. The data provided in this volume are intended to lend support to the situated interaction view—a view that allows us to see and understand how competence gets constructed, evaluated, and revised in the course of everyone's everyday life experience.

THE ORGANIZATION OF THIS VOLUME

This book is divided into three sections: the first related to nonobvious contextual factors that play a role in how competence is constructed; the second about the impact of diagnoses on judgments about competence; and the third on various sorts of competence evaluations that are made during therapy interactions.

Hidden Factors Influencing Judgments of Competence

The six chapters in the first section point to nonobvious and powerful factors affecting judgments of competence. They show (a) how violations of eye gaze (Stillman et al.) and temporality (Higginbotham & Wilkins) lead to negative judgments of competence; (b) the way different audiences can lead to different senses of ability (Jorgensen Winkler); (c) how the application of social rules can affect the way behavior is interpreted and evaluated (Saenz et al.); (d) how identity affiliations plays a role in self- and other evaluations (Maxwell et al.); and (e) how cultural practices can avoid embarrassment and save face (Trix).

Stillman, Snow, and Warren (chap. 2) start us off by discussing how violations of communicative expectancies for such things as eye gaze can affect competence judgments. Student clinicians summarizing their experiences with children who did not look at them showed how lack of eye gaze can have a devastating effect on judgments of competency. As one student put it: "I used to be good with kids. I expect to be good with kids. I assume children will be social and want to interact with me and be responsive to me. When it didn't happen, I felt like a failure" (p. 35).

Higginbotham and Wilkins (chap. 3) provide data to show similar devastating effects of violations of time expectations. Those interacting with communicators who used very slow technology to communicate sometimes refused to engage in communication with the device users or judged the communicators not the devices to be inappropriate or unworthy. One communicator described his nurse's attitudes as: "'I am the nurse from hell and do not try any of that communication shit with me'" (Robillard, 1994, p. 388, cited in Higginbotham & Wilkins. p. 63).

The critical role that different audiences play in the construction of competence is revealed in the chapter by Jorgensen Winkler (chap. 4). Her study chronicles the experiences of two Taiwanese women learning English as a second language during graduate school in the United States. Both women's views of their abilities in English varied with different audiences. These subjects' sense of their own competence was not found to be immutable, but changed over time as they experienced different evaluative situations. Jorgensen Winkler also points to the lasting role of particular evaluations, leading to dramatic alterations in a person's sense of competence.

In chapter 5, Saenz, Gilligan, and Pelligrini turn our attention to the importance of social rules and roles that are used to interpret ongoing events. They examine how two preschool children negotiate space and their rights to toys during a dispute. If the event is interpreted within the rule that children should share, the child who wants the toy is evaluated positively and the child who has the toy is evaluated negatively (refusing to share). However, if the event is interpreted as an example of protecting territorial rights, the child who refuses to share is seen as doing the right thing.

The relationship between self-identity and judged competence is dramatically displayed by the subjects with hearing impairment in chapter 6 by Maxwell, Poeppelmeyer, and Polich. These subjects describe being separated and alienated due to their being caught between hearing and deaf communities. As one person related, when describing adults who become deaf after they have developed language: "They lack both expertise in ASL and the experiences of growing up deaf. Many feel like outsiders in hearing and deaf communities" (Maxwell et al., p. 133).

In stark contrast to the rest of the chapters in this section, Trix (chap. 7) presents a situation in which the person in power works to avoid embarrassment and the lowering of self-confidence in his religious initiates. The spiritual leader of a Bektashi Muslim community in the United States responded to Trix's "mistakes" indirectly and much later, allowing her to save face and engendering in her strong feelings of competence.

Diagnosis as Situated Practice

The second section of this book examines contexts in which formal diagnoses of competence are rendered. Included are considerations of: (a) how the diagnostic test is a negotiated interaction, coconstructed by both tester and test taker (Maynard & Marlaire); (b) the importance of examining the ecological validity of the evaluation situation (Wyatt); (c) how agendas of the professional affect the way competence of the client is viewed (Duchan); (d) the emotional significance of a diagnosis for the family members and the person being diagnosed (Mastergeorge); and the impact of the family members' view of the "problem" on subsequent management of the problem (Barton).

The first of the five chapters in this section shows the misrepresentation of assessments based on a container view of competence. That is to say, tests that are designed to eliminate outside influences on the performance of the test taker fail to appreciate how futile it is to assume that the test taker can maintain a neutral stance. Maynard and Marlaire (chap. 8) show how responses on tests are actually negotiated achievements between examiners and test takers. Both partners evaluate and interpret the performance of the other through the test:

> we saw "mistakes" on the part of the clinician as well as the child, many of which appear not to stem from the inabilities or incompetencies of the clinician or the child, but precisely from the interactional competence they both exhibit. That competence resides in a set of skills through which they bring off official testing activities, such as providing a "stimulus" and a "response." (Maynard & Marlaire, p. 193)

The situated character of diagnosis becomes even more apparent in Wyatt's consideration in chapter 9 of evaluative procedures used to distinguish language differences from language disorders among speakers of African-American English. She begins with a review of previously reported biases in the assessment of children and a summary discussion of verbal-art forms in the African-American community. Wyatt then provides data regarding the language abilities of a 3-year-old boy during peer interaction, including one segment of spontaneous rapping. Based on these data, she argues that professional judgments of language disorders must involve the sampling of communicative abilities across "a wider range of culturally relevant discourse contexts" (Wyatt, p. 212).

Duchan (chap. 10) presents us with a picture of how the practices that are involved in describing a client's competencies have a strong effect on how those competencies get portrayed. She found that the competence statements in diagnostic and progress reports are influenced by the agenda of the report writer. In contexts in which report writers are making a case that the client needs intervention, clients are described negatively. In contexts in which report writers are emphasizing progress made by the client, the clients are described in positive ways.

The emotional impact of diagnosis on clients and their families is revealed in the chapter written by Mastergeorge (chap. 11). She describes the memories that caregivers and clients have of their reactions to first being diagnosed. The unusual prevalence of metaphors in their descriptions of their receipt of diagnostic news provides a view of their current understanding of the disability. The metaphors convey to the listener the powerful impact of that initial news. The descriptions of these reactions indicate how those involved in diagnoses must manage their conceptions of their own or their family members' abilities in light of the news.

In chapter 12, Barton shows the impact of not only the actual diagnosis but the understandings that are associated with that diagnosis. She shows that the parent who understands (and talks about) her child's disability, using the terminology and framework of the pediatrician, is seen by the doctor as more competent than the parent who did not. The judgments of the parents' competence strongly affected the degree to which the pediatrician and parents were able to collaborate when planning for the children's needs.

Intervention as Situated Practice

The final section of this book examines interactions in contexts of therapy—a speech event designed to improve the competence of those individuals receiving help. All three of the chapters in this section reveal interactional asymmetries between clinicians and clients and how the asymmetries affect the judgments being made of client competence.

In chapter 13, Kovarsky, Kimbarow, and Kastner examine group language therapy practices involving a speech-language pathologist and adults with traumatic brain injury. Analysis revealed how the institutional context for intervention, the agenda of the clinician, and the therapeutic activities all provide resources for the construction of client incompetence.

Simmons-Mackie and Damico (chap. 14) describe conflict talk between a woman with aphasia and a speech-language pathologist during a therapy session. The evaluative stance of the clinician, evidenced in part by her singular pursuit of responses she judged to be appropriate to her requests, leads her to overlook her client's requests to stop the activity.

Finally, in chapter 15, Ferrara examines how clients are disempowered during psychotherapy through the creation of an expert stance by the therapist, a commentary by the therapist on the proper use of language, and a recycling by the therapist of the client's communicative failure.

When taken together, the chapters in this volume should be considered as an initial exploration of how competence is socially constructed during

the course of everyday interactions. It is hoped that this book will stimu-
late future inquiry into how competence manifests itself and how identities get altered as a consequence. The ultimate hope is to design ways to
convert institutional and clinical practices that result in negative evaluations
and interactive dependencies to practices that are positive and more
empowering.

REFERENCES

Astington, J., Harris, P., & Olson, D. (Eds.). (1988). *Developing theories of mind.* New York:
Cambridge University Press.
Bakhtin, M. (1973). *Problems of Dostoevsky's poetics* (2nd ed.). (R. Rostel, Trans.) Ann Arbor,
MI: Artis. (Original work published 1929)
Biber, D., & Finegan, E. (1988). Adverbial stance types in English. *Discourse Processes, 11,* 1–34.
Carbaugh, D. (1988). Deep agony: "Self" vs. "society" in Donahue discourse. *Research on
Language and Social Interaction, 22,* 179–212.
Carbaugh, D. (1993). "Soul" and "self": Soviet and American cultures in conversation. *Quarterly
Journal of Speech, 79,* 182–200.
Carbaugh, D. (1994). Personhood, positioning and cultural pragmatics: American dignity in
cross-cultural perspective. In S. Deetz (Ed.), *Communication yearbook, 17* (pp. 159–186).
Newbury Park, CA: Sage.
Carbaugh, D. (1996). *Situating selves: The communication of social identities in American scenes.*
Albany: State University of New York Press.
Cazden, C. (1988). *Classroom discourse: The language of teaching and learning.* Portsmouth, NH:
Heinemann.
Clark, H. (1996). *Using language.* New York: Cambridge University Press.
Coupland, N., & Coupland, J. (Eds.). (1991). *Contexts of accommodation.* New York: Cambridge
University Press.
Crago, M., & Eriks-Brophy, S. (1994). Culture, conversation and interaction: Implications for
intervention. In J. Duchan, L. Hewitt, & R. Sonnenmeier (Eds.), *Pragmatics: From theory to
practice* (pp. 43–58). Englewood Cliffs, NJ: Prentice-Hall.
Danforth, S. (1997). On what basis hope? Modern progress and postmodern possibilities.
Mental Retardation, 35, 93–106.
Duranti, A., & Goodwin, C. (1992). Rethinking context: An introduction. In A. Duranti &
C. Goodwin (Eds.), *Rethinking context: Language as an interactive phenomenon* (pp. 1–42).
New York: Cambridge University Press.
Eggins, S., & Slade, D. (1997). *Analyzing casual conversation.* London & Washington, DC:
Cassell.
Ervin-Tripp, S. (1964). An analysis of the interaction of language, topic and listener. In J.
Gumperz & D. Hymes (Eds.), *The ethnography of communication* (pp. 86–102). Washington,
DC: American Anthropological Association.
Fishman, J. (1970). *Sociolinguistics.* Rowley, MA: Newbury House.
Frye, D., & Moore, C. (Eds.) (1991). *Children's theories of mind.* Hillsdale, NJ: Lawrence Erlbaum
Associates.
Fujiki, M., & Brinton, B. (1994). Social competence and language impairment in children.
In R. Watkins & M. Rice (Eds.), *Specific language impairments in children* (pp. 123–143).
Baltimore: Paul H. Brookes.
Gergen, K. (1994). *Realities and relationships: Soundings in social construction.* Cambridge, MA:
Harvard University Press.

Giles, H., & Coupland, N. (1991). *Language: Contexts and consequences*. Pacific Grove, CA: Brooks/Cole.

Goffman, E. (1981). *Forms of talk*. Philadelphia: University of Pennsylvania Press.

Goode, D. (1994). *A world without words: The social construction of children born deaf and blind*. Philadelphia: Temple University Press.

Grice, H. (1975). Logic and conversation. In P. Cole & J. Morgan (Eds.), *Syntax and semantics* (Vol. 3). New York: Academic Press.

Gumperz, J. (1962). Types of linguistic communities. *Anthropological Linguistics, 4*(1), 28–40.

Halliday, M. A. K. (1961). Categories of the theory of grammar. *Word, 17*, 242–292.

Halliday, M. A. K., McIntosh, A. & Strevens, P. (1964). *The linguistic sciences and language teaching*. London: Longmans.

Hanks, W. (1990). *Referential practice: Language and lived space among the Maya*. Chicago: University of Chicago Press.

Hanks, W. (1992). The indexical ground of deictic reference. In A. Duranti & C. Goodwin (Eds.), *Rethinking context: Language as an interactive phenomenon* (pp. 46–76). New York: Cambridge University Press.

Howard, D., & Hatfield, F. (1987). *Aphasia therapy: Historical and contemporary issues*. Hillsdale, NJ: Lawrence Erlbaum Associates.

Hymes, D. (1974). *Foundations in sociolinguistics: An ethnographic approach*. Philadelphia: University of Pennsylvania Press.

Jefferson, G. (1978). Sequential aspects of storytelling in conversation. In J. Schenkein (Ed.), *Studies in the organization of conversational interaction* (pp. 219–248). New York: Academic Press.

Kendon, A. (1985). Behavioural foundations for the process of frame attunement in face-to-face interaction. In G. P. Ginsburg, M. Brenner, & M. von Cranach (Eds.), *Discovery strategies in the psychology of action* (pp. 229–253). New York: Academic Press.

Kreckel, M. (1981). *Communicative acts and shared knowledge in natural discourse*. New York: Academic Press.

Labov, W. (1972). *Language in the inner city*. Philadelphia: University of Pennsylvania Press.

Lakoff, G., & Johnson, M. (1980). The metaphorical structure of human conceptualization. *Cognitive Science, 4*, 195–208.

Langer, E. (1975). The illusion of control. *Journal of Personality and Social Psychology, 7*, 185–208.

Langer, E. (1979). The illusion of incompetence. In L. Perlmutter & R. Monty (Eds.), *Choice and perceived control* (pp. 301–313). Hillsdale, NJ: Lawrence Erlbaum Associates.

Malinowski, B. (1923). The problem of meaning in primitive languages. In C. Ogden & I. Richards (Eds.), *The meaning of meaning* (pp. 296–336). New York: Harcourt, Brace & World.

Martin, J. (1992). *English text: Systems and structure*. Amsterdam: John Benjamins.

Maxwell, M., & Kovarsky, D. (1993). Values conflict in a diagnostic team. In D. Kovarsky, M. Maxwell, & J. Damico (Eds.), *Language interaction in clinical and educational settings, ASHA Monographs, 30* (pp. 60–67). Rockville, MD: American Speech-Language-Hearing Association.

Maynard, D. (1992). On clinicians co-implicating recipients' perspective in the delivery of diagnostic news. In P. Drew & J. Heritage (Eds.), *Talk at work: Interaction in institutional settings* (pp. 331–358). New York: Cambridge University Press.

Mercer, J. (1973). *Labeling the mentally retarded*. Berkeley: University of California Press.

Pomerantz, A. (1988). Offering a candidate answer: An information-seeking strategy. *Communication Monographs, 55*, 360–373.

Rosenthal, R., & Jacobson, L. (1992). *Pygmalion in the classroom: Teacher expectation and pupils' intellectual development* (2nd ed.). New York: Irvington.

Sacks, H. (1974). An analysis of the course of a joke's telling in conversation. In R. Bauman & J. Sherzer (Eds.), *Explorations in the ethnography of speaking* (pp. 337–353). New York: Cambridge University Press.

Sacks, H., & Schegloff, E. (1979). Two preferences in the organization of reference to persons in conversation and their interaction. In G. Psathas (Ed.), *Everyday language: Studies in ethnomethodology* (pp. 15–21). New York: Irvington.

Sacks, H., Schegloff, E., & Jefferson, G. (1974). A simplest systematics for the organization of turn-taking for conversation. *Language, 50*, 696–735.

Sapir, E. (1929). The status of linguistics as a science. *Language, 5*, 207–214.

Scheflen, A. (1964). The significance of posture in communication systems. *Psychiatry, 27*, 316–331.

Schegloff, M. (1968). Sequencing in conversational openings. *American Anthropologist, 70*, 1075–1095.

Schegloff, M. (1979). Identification and recognition in telephone conversation openings. In G. Psathas (Ed.), *Everyday language: Studies in ethnomethodology*, (pp. 23–78). New York: Irvington.

Scollon, R., & Scollon, S. (1995). *Intercultural communication.* Cambridge, MA: Basil Blackwell.

Seligman, M. (1975). *Helplessness: On depression, development, and death.* San Francisco, CA: Freeman.

Tannen, D. (1989). *Talking voices: Repetition, dialogue and imagery in conversational discourse.* New York: Cambridge University Press.

Tench, P. (1996). *The intonation systems of English.* New York: Cassell.

Ventola, E. (1987). *The structure of social interaction: A systematic approach to the semiotics of service encounters.* London: Frances Pinter.

Ward, P., & Duchan, J. (1996, November). *Information provided in language reports written by speech-language pathologists: Implications for computer-generated report formats.* Paper presented at the American Speech-Language-Hearing Association Convention, Seattle, WA.

Weiner, B. (1974). *Achievement motivation and attribution theory.* Morristown, NJ: General Learning Press.

Weismer, S. (1991). Child language intervention: Research issues on the horizon. In J. Miller (Ed.), *Research on child language disorders: A decade of progress* (pp. 233–241). Austin, TX: Pro-Ed.

Wellman, H. (1990). *The child's theory of mind.* Cambridge, MA: MIT Press.

Wolf, D. (1990). Being of several minds: Voices and versions of the self in early childhood. In D. Cicchetti & M. Beeghly (Eds.), *The self in transition: Infancy to childhood* (pp. 183–212). Chicago: University of Chicago Press.

Part II

HIDDEN FACTORS
INFLUENCING JUDGMENTS
OF COMPETENCE

"I Used to Be Good With Kids." Encounters Between Speech-Language Pathology Students and Children With Pervasive Developmental Disorders (PDD)

Robert Stillman
Ramona Snow
Kirsten Warren
Program in Communication Disorders
University of Texas at Dallas
Callier Center for Communication Disorders

INTRODUCTION

"I used to be good with kids" was a comment made by a graduate speech-language pathology student contrasting her prior experiences with children and her first assignment to provide therapy to a child with pervasive developmental disorders (PDD). The phrase effectively captures the bewilderment induced by children whose social and communicative behaviors are unfamiliar and incongruent with accepted notions about the ways young children interact. The following study explored the impact of the atypical interpersonal behaviors of children with PDD on students preparing for careers in speech-language pathology. It describes how behaviors that violate expectations lead to difficulties in establishing interpersonal relationships and can color one's personal and professional views. The study offers insight into difficulties experienced by speech-language pathologists in training and why, as professionals, speech-language pathologists may avoid some clients or be less effective with some clients than with others. Beyond these practical implications, the study also suggests that knowledge of the impressions children with PDD make and the images students construct of them may help explain why some developmental differences are ultimately more perplexing and challenging than others.

Pervasive developmental disorders is an umbrella term for several impairments, including autism, which are perhaps the most puzzling and intractable disorders of development. PDD is defined in the *Diagnostic and Statistical Manual of Mental Disorders*, 4th edition (DSM–IV; American Psychiatric Association, 1994), as "... severe and pervasive impairment in several areas of development: reciprocal social interaction skills, communication skills, or the presence of stereotyped behavior, interests, and activities. The qualitative impairments that define these conditions are distinctly deviant relative to the individual's developmental level or mental age" (p. 65). Although autistic disorder is the most familiar form of PDD, the classification of PDD also includes pervasive developmental disorder not otherwise specified (PDD-NOS). This particular diagnostic category includes children who exhibit impaired social and communicative skills and stereotyped behaviors, but who do not meet the full range of criteria necessary for a diagnosis of autistic disorder. In common usage, PDD usually refers to PDD-NOS (e.g., Grandin, 1995; Greenspan, 1992) and is used this way by participants in the study. Children diagnosed with PDD-NOS behave in ways that are qualitatively different from children with other developmental disabilities, but they show a broad range of abilities in communicating and establishing interpersonal relationships. In recent years, PDD-NOS has become a label of convenience for children exhibiting a variety of impairments in the social, communicative, and cognitive domains (Greenspan, 1992) and for children who are too young to accurately determine if they meet the criteria for a diagnosis of autistic disorder.

Research on autism and PDD has tended to focus on factors perceived to be internal to the individual. Thus, considerable effort has been devoted to the search for specific cognitive, social, and communicative deficits (e.g., Baron-Cohen, Leslie, & Frith, 1985; Fein, Pennington, Markowitz, Braverman, & Waterhouse, 1986; Mundy, Sigman, Ungerer, & Sherman, 1986; Wetherby & Prutting, 1984) or demonstrable organic pathologies (Courchesne, Townsend, & Saitoh, 1994; Dawson, 1994) associated with PDD. Despite this work, the source of the disorder remains unknown and PDD continues to be defined as an aggregate of observable behaviors each of which is perceived to be atypical or maladaptive. The reliance on behavioral characteristics in defining PDD raises the issue of the degree to which the disabilities associated with PDD are affected by an inadequate understanding of the communicative and social/affective behavior of these children. Frankel (1982) pointed out that in the typical interaction with a child with autism, true intersubjectivity or "mutual sense-making" does not exist. When the common code of language is missing or the language of one partner is clearly atypical (as in echolalia), the usual means of achieving intersubjectivity are lost. Without this common frame of reference, the adult often makes incorrect assumptions about the meaning of the child's behaviors (Frankel, 1982). This may precipitate significant misunderstandings that affect the course of their interactions. A prerequisite to effective interaction with children with PDD may be the ability to interpret accurately the meaning and intent of the child's nonlinguistic, echolalic, and social/affective signals. Because most people are not attuned to these forms of communication, nor do they consistently interpret them correctly, mutual understanding may be difficult to attain (Frankel, 1982).

Students entering the field of speech-language pathology are attracted to it in large measure because they perceive it as a "helping" profession. They tend to be motivated by a desire to assist others in overcoming obstacles and place a high value on interpersonal relationships. In fact, the American Speech-Language-Hearing Association (ASHA), the national professional organization of speech-language pathologists, stated in a recent recruiting manual: "To enter this career, one must have a sincere interest in helping people, . . . and the sensitivity, personal warmth, and perspective to be able to interact with the person who has a communication problem" (Chabon, Cole, Culatta, Lorendo, & Terry, 1990, p. A-6). The students in this study typically indicated in their graduate admission applications that a primary motivation for entering the field was to help others. They wrote of their desire to ameliorate or eliminate communication disorders, often sharing poignant stories of friends, relatives, or acquaintances who had been helped by speech-language pathologists. By placing students in a practicum with children who have PDD, the stage was set for some intriguing encounters between students who prize interpersonal relationships and wish to help, and children who may not welcome or appreciate their overtures.

METHODS

Participants were 36 speech-language pathology students enrolled in their first or second semester of graduate study. They were women, most of them in their twenties and with no children of their own. About half indicated a preference for future employment in positions serving children. All participants were enrolled in a clinical practicum (supervised practical experience in assessment of and interventions for persons with communicative disorders) and were assigned to a university based classroom program for preschool children with PDD. The program immersed students in all aspects of service delivery including assessment, preparation and implementation of treatment plans, and counseling of families. Students were assigned to, and served as the primary therapist for, one child for the entire semester. At the start of the semester, students participated in a 1-week inservice program where they were given general information about children with PDD and specific information about the children enrolled that semester. The inservice included observation of videotapes of the children and instruction in child-centered therapy. Students were taught ways to maximize communicative interactions in a variety of contexts and were instructed to use and respond to nonverbal as well as verbal communications.

Students spent four mornings a week mostly in one-on-one interactions with the child to whom they were assigned. There was no prepared curriculum for the program. Thus, students had considerable freedom but substantial responsibility for designing and implementing daily activities, and developing long-term intervention goals for the child to whom they were assigned. The intervention focus was on enhancing the children's communicative skills, and students were encouraged to select activities and contexts where productive communicative interactions were likely to occur. To better understand the communicative abilities of the children and to monitor progress, students conducted five or six standardized communication and language assessments over the course of the semester.

Students were videotaped once a week in an activity with their child. Each week, the students, under the guidance of a practicum supervisor, analyzed their videotaped interactions using a microanalytic coding system (Stillman & Williams, 1990). The coding system served as a framework for the students to identify the verbal and nonverbal behaviors they used to convey information and the communicative intention underlying each of their expressive acts. The students also coded the verbal and nonverbal expressions of the children. The purpose of the videotape coding was to assist students in understanding how and why they communicated with the children, and the "match" between their own expressions and the communicative abilities of the child.

Children in the program ranged in age from 18 months to 5 years, but were mainly in the 2- to 4-year range. The children were a distinctly heterogeneous group with regard to language, social, and cognitive skills. However, all had serious communicative impairments and all showed atypical social interactive skills. Most of the children had a prior diagnosis of PDD, although this was not required for admission to the program. In some cases, no formal diagnosis was available. However, a preadmission assessment confirmed that all children were appropriate for placement in a program for children with PDD.

The data for this study were collected through individual interviews and small group discussions. In addition, weekly videotapes of students interacting with the children were viewed by the researchers, sometimes in the company of the participating students. Interviews were conducted by peers employed as research assistants. Interviewers were instructed in nondirective interviewing techniques and in the use of probes to encourage expansions and clarifications. Most interviews lasted about 45 minutes, although some were much longer. Interviews were conducted in the first and last months of the semester and consisted of both open-ended questions (e.g., "Tell me about Joey?"; "What do you do with Joey?") and questions designed to elicit comments on specific topics (e.g., "How does Joey communicate?"; "What traits distinguish clinicians who are effective or ineffective with these children?"). Usually, 20 to 25 questions were asked. As themes emerged, additional questions were inserted in subsequent interviews in an effort to confirm or refute our evolving interpretations of the students' comments; and some questions were dropped when they appeared confusing to participants or yielded redundant responses. The participants were uniformly willing, in fact eager, to share their views and seemed candid in sharing their disappointments as well as their successes.

All interviews were audiorecorded and transcribed into a computer-based filing program. Informal group discussions including 2 or 3 students and the first author of this chapter were used to clarify, confirm, or reinterpret information emerging from analysis of the interview transcripts. Handwritten notes were taken during these conversations. Additional information was gathered during discussions with student clinicians as they viewed and described their videotaped interactions with the children, and in informal, unplanned conversations with the students. Videotaped viewing sessions were audiotaped and written notes were taken during or after other discussions and conversations. Interview transcripts and notes from the other discussions were analyzed for general themes and specific topics. Because the study was concerned with the students' thoughts and perceptions rather than their actual interactive behaviors, no effort was made in this study to match or confirm the students' comments with the videotaped observations of the students and children.

Coding of the transcripts was carried out by the authors of this chapter, who read the transcribed responses to each interview question and attached summary phrases to each response. The coders' summary phrases were either descriptive (eye contact, interaction with peers, lack of appropriate social feedback) or interpretive (social skills without language are better than language without social skills; feeling rejected by the child; being social makes you look better to others). The coding was sometimes carried out jointly, with several coders viewing and discussing portions of the transcripts displayed on a computer monitor. This was done primarily at the start of the coding phase in order to arrive at agreement in application of the coding categories and to generate new categories. However, it was not feasible to group-review all of the transcripts. Most transcripts were passed among the coders and serially evaluated. Each coder could then review, comment on, or add to the findings of the previous coder. Areas of disagreement were marked on the transcript and discussed at a later time. Where disagreements between coders could not be readily resolved, the particular segment of discourse was marked "ambiguous" and omitted from the results. When coding of the responses was complete, the codes were listed and sorted to reveal general themes and the topics that comprised the general themes. Specific instances, called "clippings," were then taken from the transcripts and notes and sorted under the theme and topic headings, using several large bulletin boards. A review of the clippings allowed us to confirm or modify the themes and topics extracted, using the initial code-sort.

RESULTS

The immense quantity of data and the broad range of issues that arise both in serving and learning to serve children with PDD and their families makes this very much a work in progress. But three general themes that have emerged are: "Normal Development Is the Standard," "Clinician Confidence," and "Relationships." In this chapter, we emphasize the results on the first and third themes, Normal Development Is the Standard and Relationships. The issue of Clinician Confidence, although clearly an issue in many of the students' comments, will be described more fully in future work. Examples of data from which the themes were derived are presented in this chapter as verbatim student comments. Their comments are interspersed with explanatory and interpretive statements. However, the clarity and cogency of most of the students' statements allow them to stand alone.

It is not surprising that the students selected normal development as the standard for judging children PDD. Most students had had considerable exposure to young children from babysitting and other paid and volunteer child-care work. As a result of their experiences, the students had acquired familiarity with and expectations for the social, play, and conversational abilities of young children; and they had developed a repertoire of skills in capturing children's attention, managing their behavior, and comforting or consoling them. Because the students' familiar role was mainly to keep the children entertained, happy, and safe, they usually enjoyed success in their interactions. Many, in fact, claimed a "knack" with children probably emanating from mutual affection, a feeling of being in control in interactions with children who were generally responsive and compliant, and the infrequent necessity to impose unwanted tasks or restraints. Some students, of course, had had prior experience with children with communicative impairments. But these were mostly children with relatively mild delays and disorders in the domains of expressive speech and language. Few students were prepared for the social interaction difficulties they were to encounter with children with PDD. It was not unexpected, then, as one student put it, that her first experience with these children "rocked my world."

Okay, this is how it is. This is the situation. It is not you just babysitting a normal kid like you used to, this is like . . . like M———'s different.

I worked in a day-care center, but those were all pretty normal kids. But it was a whole different thing because you could get them to attend and you could tell them things without their flying off the handle. . . . This is completely new for me, and baffling. But I think, on the other hand, I don't really know what's normal for kids. I mean, I do. I know what's textbook normal for kids, but some of these behaviors they don't talk about in textbooks.

I used to be good with kids. I expect to be good with kids. I assume children will be social and want to interact with me and be responsive to me. When it didn't happen, I felt like a failure.

Kids have always responded well to me, and I've always worked well with them. But the kids I've had exposure to have been normally developing children, so I have a feeling there could be a problem there. I may be expecting the same kind of reaction. And especially with these kids, you know, they don't look to other people for affection or stimulation or whatever.

I guess I expected a more reciprocal type thing, but I guess that's because that's what I've had with children, reciprocal type relationships. It was really frustrating and hard for me because he wasn't like any other child I'd spent time with. I mean, usually I can find something that the kid enjoys doing, but he was hard to engage.

I really thought "I don't know what I'm going to get from him" because he really wouldn't look at anyone, and he didn't want you to touch him. He didn't want you to pick him up so I really didn't know if I would get much of anything from him.

I think that overall it's going to be hard to relate to them, because there's going to be something there that's going to make it more difficult, whether you want to call it their disorder, or whatever it is, it's a barrier. And it seems like with the other kids I've worked with, there's always just this ease of—you know, you sit down and you play with them enough and they get to where they really like you, and it's real easy. You're friends. And especially if your goal is to make them happy, then they really like you.

The aforementioned comments relate the students' observations of differences between children with PDD and typically developing children, and the students' concern that their familiar ways of interacting with children will be unsuccessful. But the students' comments are clearly flavored by their impressions of whether the children like them or even care if they are around. This mingling of objective observation, clinical knowledge, and emotional reaction characterizes their comments throughout. The students know that children with PDD are different and that differences in the social-communicative domain are a defining feature of PDD. Nonetheless, they remain puzzled and disturbed by the children's apparent disinterest in or unwillingness to engage in reciprocal social interactions with them.

Among the factors that seemed most important in shaping the students' perceptions of the children were eye contact, focus on objects, and the extent to which the children's behaviors were atypical and unpredictable. All of these, of course, contribute to a diagnosis of PDD, but appeared to affect the students in a personal way. In particular, the presence and absence of eye contact was discussed extensively by all students. Eye gaze and gaze aversion are well-known and powerful social signals, having a multitude of culturally specific uses and meanings in adult–adult and adult–child interpersonal interactions (e.g., Brooks, Church, & Fraser, 1986; Grumet, 1983; Kleinke, 1986). In addition, eye gaze is reported to be a significant aspect of early communicative development. Thus eye gaze is considered one of the child's earliest and most potent means of regulating the behavior of others and contributes to the pacing of mother–infant interactions (Fogel, 1977; Kaye, 1982). Furthermore, with toddlers, the pairing of eye contact with nonverbal acts distinguishes intentional communication from other nonverbal behaviors (Bates, 1979).

For the students, the presence or absence of eye contact by the children seemed to play multiple social-communicative roles. For example, the absence of eye contact contributed to the students' sense that a child was avoiding you or "looking through you." It was an immediate indicator that there was "something wrong with the child." Eye contact was also a measure of a child's interest and attention, and whether the students were "getting through" to the child. Most importantly, eye contact indicated a child's interest in the student and was, perhaps, the students' most valued form of social feedback. Eye contact was typically described by students in all-or-none terms ("He makes good eye contact"; "He never makes eye contact") and contributed to the students' impressions of a child as sociable or nonsociable and influenced their view of the overall functioning level of the child. Students believed that the children could learn to make eye contact, and identified the acquisition of eye contact as an instructional goal. Eye contact, when observed in some children, was considered an indicator of emerging sociability and attachment by the child. In the following comments, eye contact (or its absence) is viewed as: defining autism, an index of functioning level, a measure of the effectiveness of interactions, a measure of progress of intervention, an essential nonverbal component of communication, and an indicator of sociability.

D——— is pretty classically autistic. He averts eye contact.

I would say that he is higher functioning than the other children in that he attends to you. His eye contact is great. There's no problem with the eye contact.

Someone in there had him one day and always thought he was higher level and she was like, "I didn't realize how he really doesn't make eye contact, and how much he does just take off, and not stay on task."

I would say he's probably the lowest functioning. For example, J———, he might look like he's lower functioning just because he's younger and he won't sit still during music, and he's running around on his tippy-toes, and he has some really strange behaviors, but he looks at you more. He makes eye contact.

He interacts very well with me. He has great eye contact. He doesn't try to avoid you.

I really enjoyed working with her. She really enjoyed being there. You know, she would look at me. And that was just the nicest thing, to actually have eye contact.

(How do you know when you are being effective?) When I've got him to look at me, and not just at my hands, but at my eyes or at my face. Whenever I get eye contact. I mean, I don't care what we're doing, if we're playing patty-cake, if we're playing hide-and-go-seek, if we're reading books. I mean anytime he looks at me and includes me in his activity.

He's expressing himself a lot more and using a lot more eye contact with me. I think he's doing pretty good.

If he has eye contact with me for five seconds during an activity and the next time we do it, he has it for ten seconds, that is progress. . . .

Another factor shaping the students' perceptions of the children was their concern about the children's attraction to certain objects and their perseverative actions and vocalizations, which seemed to render the students invisible. Students described the children as isolated and inaccessible, "in their own little world," and felt themselves excluded. It was as though their presence, at times, was of little consequence to the children. Students were also puzzled by the children's failure to respond to apparently salient environmental stimuli and noted the children's failure to "hear" verbal efforts to gain their attention.

His attention is pretty good to an activity. It's not to an individual.

If there is an object such as a ball or a toy, she interacts with the object, so then it's like I'm no longer there.

He can be right in front of me, and we're sitting at the table, but he's in his own world. He is just not hearing me.

When he's perseverating on something, when he goes off into his own little world, sometimes he'll just kind of stare off or he'll be having just kind of a gibberish conversation with himself, has his back turned, and puts himself in the corner or something so that he doesn't want to talk to anybody.

And a lot of time, like on the tricycles and stuff outside, he doesn't talk on them. And there's certain things where I know it doesn't work, and so we just don't even go on them anymore. Because it's like I'm not even there. He just kind of turns inward into his own little world.

He jargons a lot. He's in his own world at those points. He really is. And he'll jargon and jargon. He's absolutely not even hearing me, I don't think. My impression is that he does not hear me until at some point I get through and then he hears me.

. . . [he's] just kind of fixating on the wall or on a person, and even if I use gentle touch on his face or keep saying "C———, C———" right in his face, it's like I'm not even there.

He becomes fixated on a person or on an object or on just anything on the wall, and it's, I mean, you could knock-knock on his head and you cannot get through to him.

The students' impressions of the children were also shaped by the inconsistencies in the children's interests, moods, and behaviors. In some cases, the inconsistencies were viewed as puzzling or inexplicable. But in cases where there was a risk or history of violent or aggressive behavior, the students seemed to sense both a distance and a danger in the children and saw the children as driven by incomprehensible forces. The students expressed a sense of their own helplessness, as though whatever they did had no predictable or lasting effect.

You cannot predict what he is going to do, be it whether he's going to love doing something, or he's going to throw himself on the floor and have a fit for ten minutes.

He can be real responsive, real interactive, and then in the middle of it, just wander and go off into space, either actually physically walking and wandering off or he'll just look off and get stuck on something else.

Sometimes he'll just cry and I won't even know. I mean, out of the blue he'll be laughing and then he'll cry. And he laughs out of the blue sometimes, too. He's done that quite a few times where he'll have almost a wicked laugh and nothing is funny. Nothing has happened. I have no idea what's going on in his head.

It depends really on the kind of day he's having, because there's some days that he's in his own world, and doing self-stimulatory behavior, and running around, and I try everything every day to get him to pay attention to me, and there's some days that he will after a while, and there's some days that he won't.

And he has really good times and he does stuff where you're just like, "Wow, that's really great that he does that," and then he turns around three seconds later and he does something where you're just like, "Weird, what are you doing?"

I was kind of scared of him at first because he is so unpredictable, inconsistent, just his behavior is so bizarre. I was scared of what he was going to do next.

Some days he's really agreeable and some days he's really, really aggressive. Like he's been really aggressive lately with scratching and biting, and that scares me. Because I don't think I have the tools to deal with that.

. . . he seemed to have a few more violent tendencies than some of the others, and just has this look in his eye that he would just kind of, you know, hit you to death if he could.

One of the most striking aspects of the students' comments was the significance they placed on establishing relationships with the children. The students' statements regarding eye contact, object focus, and inconsistent behavior seemed overlaid by a general concern about their relationships with the children. The students wanted to be accepted and liked by the children and were disappointed, frustrated, or hurt when the children's attention or affection was not forthcoming. A strong positive relationship was regarded as a motivating force for both student and child in interacting and in joint participation in activities. Furthermore, a strong positive relationship was viewed as a hedge against public confrontations with the child or at least gave the student confidence that such confrontations would be short-lived. For these reasons, students seemed particularly eager for the children's appropriate displays of attention, friendship, responsiveness, and initiative. Students working with more social children described them in terms that suggest they noted the contrast between their children and others in the classroom. They emphasized their positive relationships with the children, discussed the children in warm and affectionate terms, and noted that the children liked and cared about them. These students described feeling included rather than excluded by the children and commented on appropriate displays of affection, such as hugging, and on the children's willingness to participate in an exchange of greetings and other conventional social routines. These students were aware of and sympathetic to students working with children who displayed less affection or did not establish positive relationships.

> I wasn't expecting such a friendly kid. We hit it off instantly. It was just so neat. We are so close, it is just so funny. And it's nice to have that relationship, seeing that the other clinicians—not that they don't have it, it's just that the kids aren't willing or aren't able to maintain a relationship like that. So he's really cute. I just love him to death.

> I have a real good relationship with him and he's real playful and real loving and real affectionate toward me, and friendly. So that's fun.

> Every morning he would come in and he would come to me to give him a hug. He had a lot of the social responses that are favorable, unlike a lot of the other children who are just like, "OK, I don't care if you're there." And he did care, for the most part. He really did. And that was kind of nice because you knew that he wanted you, so he wanted you to be part of whatever he was doing.

> I was really pleased with the way he responded to me and he would always come to me in the mornings and that was really fun, for him to be excited. And he would always say "Bye-bye, K———" and things like that in the afternoon. And I think he learned who I was. So I guess the relationship was the best.

> And just in the last couple of weeks, he's started hugging me sometimes. I've seen him hug his parents, and I thought it was wonderful, and that it would never happen [to me]. . . . But he will look at me and hug me sometimes, and that's been recent. And I feel like that's all good signs of how he's responding to me.

In contrast, students whose children were perceived as less social and who did not feel they had achieved a warm and affectionate relationship tended to attribute to the children a willful and selective disinterest in them. They interpreted the children's behavior, not as a global disinterest in social interactions, but as a personal rejection. They seemed to feel that despite their best efforts, they were excluded and rebuffed by children with whom they had anticipated affiliating and interacting.

> I've dealt with W———, and he just looked straight through me the whole time. I don't think he knew I was there.

> The minute he comes in, he'll just try to get into the closets and open objects, or get these little objects, and he'll have a little truck and he'll just look at the tire and just stuff like that. . . . I know there's gonna be absolutely no way that he'll include me. He just doesn't act like I'm there.

> Most of the time he'll just throw me away like I didn't even exist.

He just looks like he doesn't really like you, he doesn't want to be there, and he doesn't want to do anything with you.

For the most part of the day, he's not responsive to me and he doesn't listen to me, and he doesn't want me around, and he doesn't want to interact with me no matter how hard I try.

He'll never have eye contact with me or really care that I'm there. He'll never interact with me, basically. I've got to either hold him or do this or that. It's hard. It's just so hard.

The child's willingness to initiate contact with the student was judged to be very important. When asked to identify "transition signals," or indicators of the onset of a positive relationship, students cited child-initiated behaviors such as seeking out the student, voluntarily taking the student's hand, choosing that particular student when other adults were available, making eye contact, saying the student's name, showing the student something, and requesting that the student initiate or join in some activity that only they do together. Child responses to student-initiated interactions were considered less satisfactory indexes of a relationship than child-initiated behaviors directed toward the student, because initiations were interpreted as indicating the child's choice to be interactive. Responses by the child to the student were perceived as more obligatory and thus less indicative of the child's interest in the student. Students also alluded to a lack of feedback from the children, which appeared to be due to the absence of overt and consistent child displays of initiation, friendship, affection, and acceptance. Without these social features, which characterize typically developing children's relationships with familiar adults, the students seemed to acquire a negative view of the children and even expressed disinterest in serving them in a professional capacity.

Maybe it's just autistic children in general, but to me it's difficult to work with this type of child because you don't get that response back. You know with a normal child, especially just that hugging, just that emotional stuff—You don't get that reinforcement and it makes it difficult to work with him day in and day out.

I think probably anyone would say the higher-functioning kids are easier to work with, because you get more feedback.

. . . we're not getting anything from the kids. We're not getting any kind of reinforcement.

S——— could care less whether it's me or somebody else with him. I mean, he knows who I am, but I would guess I would rather have more of the personal attention. But that's not real common in these kids.

I think it's easier to work with the kids who are more responsive. I mean, that's the whole problem with some of these kids, is they're not responsive. Like M———. A lot of the time she's in her own little world. And it's just easier if they are responding. I think it takes a special person to work with a kid that's not paying attention to you. And at this point, I don't feel like I could do that.

In the following statements, students expressed a desire for the children to be more interested in establishing friendships with them. They seemed to see this as a responsibility of the child, as though the child were capable of establishing a relationship but chose not to engage or be responsive to the student. The students seemed to feel they were outsiders and wanted the children to feel closer to them.

I guess I'd like to have him engage more, I guess maybe socially. That means looking at me more, or responding in some way to what I'm saying or what he's doing. Maybe try to involve me in some sort of activity that he's doing.

I guess I would like him to become more comfortable with me, and eventually like me, maybe, and look forward to playing or whatever it is we do.

I would expect the child to be able to interact with me more easily, more comfortably. For us to get to know each other and for us to bond, just one-on-one.

The importance of the child's interest in the student was observed also when the students described the children's verbalizations. The children's verbal efforts to seek the student when needing assistance or to engage in conventional verbal exchanges were seen as indicators of the child's progress and of reciprocity in the relationship with the child.

He just doesn't communicate very well. You know, he doesn't ask for things or tell you if he's hurt or anything like that.

It was really refreshing to have him talk, say things back to me, and communicate with me, and ask me how am I doing; or what am I doing, and you can really interact so much more.

We'll be walking and all of a sudden I'll feel his hand in my hand. I'm not really reaching for him, but he's making that attempt. Or he'll ask me questions now, instead of before, when he needed help, he wouldn't ask me unless prompted. He would just try to do it himself and get frustrated. And now, after maybe two or three tries, he'll make eye contact and say, "G———, help?"

I think he uses my name a lot because he knows how excited I'll get.

At the end of the semester, students were asked to identify children in the program with whom they would most and least like to work. The following are key words and phrases used by students to describe the particular children they would select or avoid:

Select

Word	Phrase
affectionate	enjoys being there
social	provides feedback
expresses emotion	communicates
has personality	verbal
fun	normal behavior
cute	can see progress
compliant	rewarding
easygoing	higher-functioning
participates with group	interesting
interacts with peers	older
shows interest in student	

Avoid

Word	Phrase
tantrums	looks through you
lack of expression of emotion	difficult
not lovable	self-stimulatory behaviors
strange	severe impairments
aggressive	remote
violent	doesn't attend
no eye contact	extremely nonsocial

Based on the above lists, it appears that students would choose to work with children who participate in typical preschool activities, are sociable, expressive, and exhibit behaviors expected of children their age. They would avoid children who do not afford them feedback and with whom it might be difficult to establish a relationship. Thus, sociability, responsiveness, and the presence of typical interests and behaviors seem most important in the students' selection of children with whom they prefer to work.

DISCUSSION

Children with PDD are, by definition, impaired in reciprocal interaction abilities and communication skills, and may exhibit a variety of stereotyped interests and behaviors (*DSM–IV*). PDD, therefore, is a disorder in which both the ability to interact socially and to act in a socially appropriate manner are problematic. Graduate speech-language pathology students in their first clinical experience with children with PDD are greatly influenced and affected by the behavioral and interpersonal characteristics that define the disorder. Two factors seem responsible for the effect these children have on the students. First, students entering the field of speech-language pathology have a desire to help others and may assume that their clients wish to be helped. Perceived rejection of their efforts by the children may affect the idealistic view students hold of the profession and the confidence they have in their ability to effect positive change in their clients. Second, students enter the field with preconceptions about young children derived from previous successful experiences in interacting with children. The students' efforts to generalize this knowledge to children with PDD frequently eventuates in misunderstandings and frustrations similar to those reported by Frankel (1982). The assumption that kindness and affection should immediately yield a like response from the children reflects an apparent misunderstanding on the part of the students of the nature of PDD and the steps necessary to engender the children's trust.

One may be critical of the students' apparent naivete in expecting to be able to establish immediate rapport with the children or in anticipating positive feedback from them. Yet even Sacks (1995), in discussing his own encounter with a person with autism reveals a similar desire to be accepted and liked:

> I wanted to be liked by Stephen, or at least seen as a distinct person—but, there was something, not unfriendly, but de-differentiating in his attitude, even in his indifferent, automatic good manners and good humor. I had wanted some interaction; instead I got a slight sense, perhaps, of how parents of autistic children must feel when they find themselves faced with a virtually unresponsive child. I had still, in some sense, been expecting a relatively normal person, with certain gifts and certain problems—now I had a sense of a radically different, almost alien mode of mind and being, proceeding in its own way, not to be defined by any of my own norms. (p. 221)

The students' desire to establish interpersonal relationships with the children and to see the children as accessible and interested in them was a striking finding. Although it was not expected that students would approach children with PDD dispassionately, their feelings of rejection were greater than anticipated. It is tempting to conclude that what the students sought most from the children were behaviors the children, because of the nature of their disorder, were least able to provide. For example, eye contact was an issue of major concern. The students seemed to consider eye contact to be an essential social-communicative signal, and its absence was viewed as an expression of disinterest or rejection. Furthermore, children with unconventional eye contact were viewed more negatively than children whose frequency and timing of eye contact more closely approximated the students' expectations. The negative connotation attached to the failure to make eye contact is well recognized and has led some well-known behavior modification programs, which seek to "normalize" the behavior of individuals with autism, to focus on training eye contact as an initial intervention step (Lovaas, 1981).

Current research, however, has tended to show that the failure of children with PDD to show typical gaze behaviors is not volitional, but instead reflects cognitive or neurological problems underlying or co-occurring with PDD. For example, several lines of research suggest that children with PDD have difficulty coordinating eye gaze with other social, communicative, and object behaviors (Dawson, Hill, Spencer, Galpert, & Watson, 1990; Mundy, Sigman, Ungerer, & Sherman, 1986). Anecdotal evidence presented by Grandin (1995) supports the notion that simultaneous attention to several sensory channels is difficult for persons with autism. Furthermore, neuroanatomical abnormalities in the cerebellum (Courchesne, Townsend, & Saitoh, 1994) or the frontal lobe (Dawson, 1994) identified in persons with autism suggest a possible substrate for difficulties in a variety of domains that underlie social behavior, including eye contact, object/person coordination, and the ability to visually acquire information on others' emotional states. Although the students were not necessarily well versed in research regarding neurological correlates of PDD, they were certainly aware of neurologically based hypotheses regarding autism. Nonetheless, their own emotional reactions to the children's interpersonal behavior seemed to override their classroom-based knowledge regarding the disorder. For them, the lack of eye contact was a signal, if not a symbol, of the child's rejection of social interaction and disinterest in establishing an interpersonal relationship. In reverse, children who showed appropriate and consistent eye contact were viewed as friendlier, more responsive, and even more competent. Typical eye gaze behavior seemed to serve as a trigger for positive feelings from the students and served as a criterion for selecting children with whom they would prefer to work. It also influenced their evaluation of the children's prognosis.

It is the negative effects of atypical eye gaze, however, that are most troubling. Children who were perceived as failing to make eye contact were seen as less likely to progress and, if given a choice, students indicated that they would be less likely to select them for therapy. Some students even felt unable to work effectively with children who did not provide them feedback via eye contact. This suggests that students (and perhaps practicing speech-language pathologists as well) should examine their feelings and biases regarding eye contact. From the results obtained here, it appears that this particular deviation from typical child behavior has a disproportionate effect on the feelings of others and potentially a very real effect on the quality of therapy the children receive.

The other primary concerns of the students were the tendency for children to focus on objects in preference to, or to the exclusion of, people, and the children's atypical and unpredictable behaviors. Again, students tended to take these behaviors as personally directed and saw them as efforts by the children to exclude the students from their "world." Students were probably familiar with alternative explanations for the children's interest in objects—for example, Schuler's (1995) suggestion that this reflects one pole of an object-oriented versus person-oriented mode of thinking. They probably also recognized that the child for whom regulating the object world or regulating sensory input takes precedence over interacting with other people, is unlikely to develop relationships rapidly despite the students' best efforts and intentions. The students were probably also aware of the hypothesis that many atypical and apparently inconsistent behaviors of children with PDD reflect developmental discontinuities within and across the domains of communication, cognition, and social/emotional abilities (Schuler, 1995). However, for these students, prior knowledge of the causes and characteristics of autism seemed to be secondary to the emotional impact of the children on them. As one student put it, "No amount of preparation can prepare you for the first day the child walks through the door."

The premium students placed on positive interpersonal relationships and the preponderance of "isolating" compared to "engaging" behaviors among the children may have consequences for services to children with PDD. Students who were most pleased with their relationships with the children were those assigned to children who would most readily be described among this population as "social." Students assigned to children whose behaviors were more typical of autism tended to express greater frustration at their inability to get through to the child or to receive from the child the type of interest and affection they sought.

When asked to describe the characteristics that would lead them to seek or avoid a particular child, sociability factors predominated. This suggests that many students, if given a choice, would serve children whose social interaction abilities approximate those of typically developing children. Of course, the students were interviewed and observed very early in their graduate education, and some student attitudes and concerns may be attributed to immaturity and inexperience. However, previous work suggests that even experienced teachers and therapists are also deeply affected by a child's sociability and strive to elicit positive affect, teacher-directed behaviors, and indications of personal recognition by the children, even when these elicitations are counterproductive within the activity (Stillman, Williams, & Majors, 1991). Schuler (1995), too, has argued that clinicians serving persons with autism must ". . . examine their own levels of discomfort when common behavioral expectations and norms are violated" (p.

30). Thus there is the prospect that the attitudes, expectations, and feelings expressed by the students may be carried forward into their professional career.

CONCLUSIONS

This study has shown that students preparing for careers in speech-language pathology hold strong views regarding child sociability and would prefer to provide therapy to children who show typical social/affective behaviors. Thus child sociability may be a prime factor in attracting clinicians in training to particular clients. Students rely greatly on their interpretation of specific nonverbal acts, such as eye gaze behavior, object play, and unusual interests and attentional foci, in estimating the child's sociability. Some nonverbal behaviors, such as eye gaze, are imbued with intention and meaning that may not be warranted and may lead to generalizations that are counterproductive to effective therapy. The role of nonverbal behavior in therapy is often described only in terms of the identification and response to particular communicative acts (e.g., Siegel-Causey & Guess, 1989). However, for these students, some nonverbal behaviors seemed to elicit feelings of acceptance and rejection rather than communicate particular information. For student clinicians at this stage of their careers (and perhaps for others more experienced, too), the study shows that it is no easy task to overcome feelings of rejection caused by the children's impaired and atypical social interaction abilities, nor is it easy to accept the children's behaviors as indicators of a disorder rather than indicators of personal preference.

ACKNOWLEDGMENTS

We wish to acknowledge the contributions of Katherine Stanland, Fereshteh Kunkel, and Lara Baker to this study. We also thank Angela Linam, Allison Cook, and Amanada Owen for their assistance in editing and revising the chapter. Some of the data were presented at the annual meeting of the American Speech-Language-Hearing Association, in Orlando, FL, in November 1995.

REFERENCES

American Psychiatric Association. (1994). *Diagnostic and statistical manual of mental disorders* (4th ed.). Washington, DC: Author.

Baron-Cohen, S., Leslie, A. M., & Frith, U. (1985). Does the autistic child have a theory of mind? *Cognition, 21,* 37–46.

Bates, E. (1979). *The emergence of symbols: Cognition and communication in infancy.* New York: Academic Press.

Brooks, C. I., Church, M. A., & Fraser, L. (1986). Effects of duration of eye contact on judgments of personality characteristics. *The Journal of Social Psychology, 126*(1), 71–78.

Chabon, S. S., Cole, P. A., Culatta, R. A., Lorendo, L. C., & Terry, S. E. (Eds.). (1990). *Speech-language pathology and audiology student recruitment manual.* (Available from the American Speech-Language-Hearing Association, 10801 Rockville Pike, Rockville, MD 20852)

Courchesne, E., Townsend, J., & Saitoh, O. (1994). The brain in infantile autism: Posterior fossa structures are abnormal. *Neurology, 44,* 214–223.

Dawson, G. (1994). Development of emotional expression and emotional regulation in infancy: Contributions of the frontal lobe. In G. Dawson & K. W. Fischer (Eds.), *Human behavior and the developing brain* (pp. 346–379). New York: Guilford.

Dawson, G., Hill, D., Spencer, A., Galpert, L., & Watson, L. (1990). Affective exchanges between young autistic children and their mothers. *Journal of Abnormal Child Psychology, 18,* 335–345.

Fein, D., Pennington, B., Markowitz, P., Braverman, M., & Waterhouse, L. (1986). Toward a neuropsychological model of infantile autism: Are the social deficits primary? *Journal of the American Academy of Child Psychiatry, 25,* 198–212.

Fogel, A. (1977). Temporal organization in mother-infant face-to-face interaction. In H. R. Schaffer (Ed.), *Studies in mother-infant interaction* (pp. 119–151). New York: Academic Press.

Frankel, R. M. (1982). Autism for all practical purposes: A micro-interactional view. *Topics in Language Disorders, 3,* 33–42.

Grandin, T. (1995). *Thinking in pictures and other reports from my life with autism.* Garden City, NY: Doubleday.

Greenspan, S. I. (1992). Reconsidering the diagnosis and treatment of very young children with autistic spectrum or pervasive developmental disorder. *Zero to Three/National Center for Clinical Infant Programs, 13*(2), 1–9.

Grumet, G. W. (1983). Eye contact: The core of interpersonal relatedness. *Psychiatry, 46,* 172–180.

Kaye, K. (1982). *The mental and social life of babies: How parents create persons.* Chicago: University of Chicago Press.

Kleinke, C. L. (1986). Gaze and eye contact: A research review. *Psychological Bulletin, 100,* 78–100.

Lovaas, O. I. (1981). *Teaching developmentally disabled children: The me book.* Baltimore: University Park Press.

Mundy, P., Sigman, M., Ungerer, J., & Sherman, T. (1986). Defining the social deficits of autism: The contribution of non-verbal communication measures. *Journal of Child Psychology and Psychiatry, 27,* 657–669.

Sacks, O. (1995). *An anthropologist on Mars: Seven paradoxical tales.* New York: Vintage Books.

Schuler, A. L. (1995). Thinking in autism: Differences in learning and development. In K. A. Quill (Ed.), *Teaching children with autism: Strategies to enhance communication and socialization* (pp. 11–32). New York: Delmar.

Siegel-Causey, E., & Guess, D. (Eds.). (1989). *Enhancing nonsymbolic communication interactions among learners with severe disabilities.* Baltimore: Paul H. Brookes.

Stillman, R., & Williams, C. (1990). *Assessing forms and intentions of teacher communications.* Dallas: University of Texas at Dallas.

Stillman, R., Williams, C., & Majors, K. (1991, November). *Factors affecting communication between teachers and students with profound handicaps.* Paper presented at the meeting of the Association for Persons with Severe Handicaps, Washington, DC.

Wetherby, A., & Prutting, C. (1984). Profiles of communicative and cognitive-social abilities in autistic children. *Journal of Speech and Hearing Research, 27,* 364–377.

Chapter 3

Slipping Through the Timestream: Social Issues of Time and Timing in Augmented Interactions

D. Jeffery Higginbotham
Department of Communicative Disorders and Sciences
Center for Cognitive Sciences
State University of New York at Buffalo
Buffalo, NY, USA

David P. Wilkins
Cognitive Anthropology Research Group
Max Planck Institute for Psycholinguistics
Nijmegen, The Netherlands

In describing the tenor of their interactions, people who rely on means other than mouth-speech for face-to-face communication commonly bring up issues of time and timing. Sometimes the issues relate to how long it takes to get one's body to make all the movements needed to produce a coherent message. Sometimes it is an issue of how good certain interlocutors are in getting into synch with the speaker. Sometimes these issues concern interlocutors not having enough time or patience. Sometimes the issue is one of personal time management and how much time one can afford to spend in face-to-face interaction. Sometimes the issue concerns how and why different means and devices for communication are selected to meet the temporal demands of different contexts. And sometimes there's an issue surrounding normative understandings of the temporal flow of communication and how this can rob some individuals of the ability to say exactly what they want to say when they need to say it. Such concerns bring into sharp relief the fact that there is a significant number of distinct temporal threads that need to be jointly coordinated by all participants for each of them to feel that the interaction was not just a successful one but also a good one. If the joint communicative interaction is seen by one or the other party as a failure due to a temporal coordination problem, then there can be recriminations of communication incompetence that get launched in each direction. The primary aim of this chapter is to examine some of the distinct temporal threads that are attended to in the communicative interactions of individuals using alternative and augmentative means of communication, and to show how success or failure to meet in the same timestream can result in social evaluations of "competence" or "incompetence" in communication.

We are sympathetic with McDermott and Verenne's (1995) view that: "Disabilities are less the property of persons than they are moments in a cultural focus. Everyone in any culture is subject to being labeled and disabled" (p. 324). We find persuasive their thesis that culture—as an historically evolved pattern of institutions, practices, and values—is the agent that creates a them that is distinct from an us at the very same time it establishes that them and us are participants in one and the same cultural matrix, subject to the same institutional points of reference, and, in our discourse and daily activities, reliant on the same unexamined fabric of sociocultural givens. As Robillard (1994) has so eloquently shown, the "socially consensual order of conversation has a time order" and that time order is a sociocultural creation with its own normative givens, which prohibits the active participation of people, like himself, who are physically unable to produce mouth-speech. As Robillard (1994) states:

> The ordinary forms of conversational participation that generate and sustain a sense of agency are breached when the patient cannot communicate in socially consensual "real time." . . . delayed speech, through the use of an alphabet board, frequently leads to a host of interactional problems and mutual accusations about character. (p. 383)

This chapter expands on Robillard's notion of socially consensual "real time" and demonstrates, following McDermott and Verenne, that for augmented speakers the normative temporal threads (i.e., the standard time order) of communicative interaction in American English-speaking culture can have socially debilitating effects. It is hoped that a more detailed understanding of this problem can help overcome the hegemony of the institutionalized patterns of interaction and can empower people (both augmented speakers and their interlocutors) to find alternative time orders for communication that fit their needs and situation.

In this chapter we examine first some of the ways in which time and timing operate within face-to-face interaction, based on the recent work of Herbert Clark (1996). Then our attention focuses on individuals whose ability to produce mouth-speech and other conventional forms of communication is compromised by their physical disabilities; we examine the types of constraints on time and timing that these individuals and their interlocutors encounter when their interactions are augmented by various communication technologies. Through the scientific literature, first-person accounts, and an observational case study, we extend Clark's framework to the interactional problems faced by augmented speakers and their interlocutors.

TEMPORAL ASPECTS OF COMMUNICATIVE INTERACTION

In his recent major work, Clark (1996) argues that language use is a species of joint action. As such, language use cannot be reduced to autonomous actions of the individual participants, but has to be treated as a coordinated set of participant actions designed and deployed for jointly carrying out social activities. In such a perspective, time and timing issues have to be treated as issues that simultaneously involve speakers and addressees. Moreover, any problems in communication are located in the joint action, not in autonomous acts or individuals. To clarify this position, consider the following (Clark, 1996):

> Speakers' actions in talk aren't independent of their addressees' actions, or vice versa, and that goes for their problems as well. When speakers need extra time to plan an utterance, that isn't their problem alone. The time they need belongs to them and their addressees together, so they have to coordinate with their addressees on the use of that time. . . . Most problems in using language are *joint* problems, and dealing with them requires *joint* management. (p. 266)

When I am communicating, what I do in my time is also done in my interlocutor's time, and vice versa, and we both have to be aware of that fact; in Clark's apt phrasing, "time is doubly important" (p. 266). This leads to the proposal that the participants in any joint action, including language use, are subject to a constraint Clark (1996) calls "the temporal imperative" (p. 267): "In a joint action, the participants must provide a public account for the passage of time in their individual parts of that action" (p. 267).

Speaking (with ideal delivery) is the best public account participants can give of what they are doing with jointly shared time. For Clark, speaking covers any form of addressee-oriented signaling, not just speech. Thus, making a facial gesture or pointing to an alphabet board would constitute an act of speaking, and so would a public account of how the time is being used. However, once there is a pause there is no longer a public justification of actions. Similarly, when an individual constructs an utterance on an augmentative communication device in silence, the act is an individual one and in and of itself does not provide a public account of the passage of time—although when the utterance is played or displayed it does become a public account during the period it is issued.

People's behaviors in communicative interaction provide good evidence of their awareness of various aspects of the temporal structure and temporal constraints of joint actions. For instance, for English speakers, under the constraint of the temporal imperative, silent pauses are limited to about one second, after which one or the other participants will tend to speak, produce a nervous cough, or produce a filler like "um" or "uh" (Clark, 1996, p. 268). Building on the work of Sacks, Schegloff, and Jefferson (1974) and other conversational analysts, Clark (1996, p. 88) notes, "people are able to project entry and exit times in conversation with surprising precision," a point he associates with the idea that "people take it as common ground that mental processes take time" and have accurate heuristics for estimating processing difficulty. For example, if participants appear to be uncertain about what they want to say, then their addressees are likely to infer that processing time will take longer, and may demonstrate their recognition by commenting on the communication delay. Participants also order their contributions in time and deliver their contributions with the right timing, using constraints like the temporal imperative and heuristics like those grounded in processing time to guide them. Clark (1996) observes that "order in language use has been studied for a long time, but timing has not" (p. 171).

Yet another relevant temporal aspect in Clark's model relates to his position that language use is a form of participant coordination problem that requires continuous coordination of both content and process. Each participant in communicative interaction assumes that, in context, the problem of identifying the meaning and force of an utterance made by one of them has a unique solution that can be identified because there is sufficient available information. To arrive at that solution, speakers and listeners have to determine what participatory actions they expect each other to take, and they will deploy resources that signal what actions are expected. These resources, or coordination devices, rely on a principle that the ideal solution is the one that participants recognize as "most salient, prominent or conspicuous with respect to their current common ground" (p. 91). Clark (1996) reasons that, because communicative interchanges are a time-constrained sequence of coordination problems, the time needed to solve one of the component problems (the launching and interpretation of one utterance, for instance) must be immediate. He therefore proposes the immediacy premise: "In a coordination problem set by one of its participants in a time-constrained sequence of problems, the participants can assume that they can solve it immediately—with effectively no delay" (p. 69).

Participants in a conversation tend to bring with them convictions as to what knowledge, beliefs, and suppositions they share with their interlocutors. This is their common ground. As joint communicative interaction unfolds in time, the local immediate resolution of one communicative action will enter the common ground of the participants, and this will typically function as the basis against which a new coordination problem is resolved,[1] and so on until their larger joint project is accomplished. The coordination of *process* and *content* will be expected to be essentially synchronous, as will the timing of the addressee's processing in relation to a speaker's completion of an element of the utterance. Clark writes (1996):

> In conversation, then, addressees are expected to have completed their processing of a phrase roughly by the time speakers finish that phrase. The immediacy premise should hold for phrases of all sizes. At the level of single words, addressees should have completed hearing, identifying and grasping a word by the time speakers go on to the next word. At the level of intonation units, they should have understood what was meant in the current unit before speakers initiate the next one. If processing weren't roughly immediate, delays in one phrase would accumulate with delays in the next, making synchrony even more difficult down the line. (p. 88)

If we understand the immediacy premise correctly, then it would appear that there are a number of ways in which this premise could be compromised, meaning that participants would not assume immediacy and would encounter delays and other problems in the interaction. Some of these are listed below:

- If participant A believes that s/he does not know what participatory actions to expect of participant B, s/he will assume delays in interaction.
- If A is familiar with the body-based signals (coordination devices) of B, misunderstandings and delays in interaction will be assumed.
- If the participants diverge on their interpretations of what constitutes the current common ground, and especially what is salient within the common ground, then solvability will not be immediate and the immediacy premise will be compromised.
- If the online coordination of process is not essentially temporally synchronous with the coordination of content, then delays will be expected.

---

[1] This is essentially Clark's notion of "grounding." He writes (1996): "To ground a thing, in my terminology, is to establish it as part of common ground well enough for current purposes" (p. 221).

• If the addressee fails to comprehend a communicative element (or phase) produced by the speaker, then the successful processing of any larger constituent within which that element is contained may be compromised, resulting in delays and misunderstandings.

The interactional organization of mouth-speech communication is built to avoid and minimize interaction problems; participants adhere to the temporal imperative and exploit the immediacy principle to their communicative advantage. The sociocultural and psychological properties of conventional mouth-speech interaction afford relatively effortless and rapid production of speech and gesture. Turn taking and the exchange of speaking roles are commonly achieved nonproblematically with little or no temporal cost. If the current speaker realizes that his or her interlocutor needs additional information to aid comprehension, he or she can change the utterance-in-progress to meet the interlocutor's needs without noticeable communication delay. If a misunderstanding occurs, interactants share a wide variety of resources to mark and repair the communication problem immediately, again minimizing potential delays.

In augmented interactions, the communicators are faced with many of the potential communication problems noted above. In using media similar to written communication to perform face-to-face interactions, augmented speakers and their interlocutors are frequently unable to adhere to the normative requirements contained in the temporal imperative, but are under considerable interactive and social pressure to do so. As this chapter demonstrates, potentially disabling conditions arise from a complex of body, technology, and information-processing constraints in communicative interactions . These constraints help elucidate many of the interactional problems and unique adaptions found in augmented interactions. The crux of these problems are the issues of time and timing.

FIRST-PERSON ACCOUNTS

The preceding discussion begins to build a theoretical framework for examining time, timing, and the temporal requirements and constraints in communication and disability. These observations become all the more compelling when compared with the commentaries of augmented speakers about the impact of time and timing on their interactions and social relationships. The next two subsections of this chapter look at the comments of Creech (1992, 1996a, 1996b), regarding augmented interactions using a computer-based communication device; and Robillard (1994), concerning the use of a communication board for augmented interaction.

Creech

While Clark (1996) takes face-to-face direct oral speech conversations as the basis for his observations on language use, Richard Creech (1992, 1996a, 1996b) focuses on augmented communication. Creech himself is an augmented communicator, and though he has a master's degree in speech pathology, he considers himself not so much a speech pathologist as an augmentative communication specialist (Creech, 1992). Here we review some of the pragmatic principles and practical suggestions Creech has put forward with the aim of helping augmented communicators increase the quality of their communications in various settings. Because he believes that communication activity is a function of the interaction of motivation, effort, and time, it should not be surprising that time and timing issues are prominent in his work.[2]

To understand some of Creech's comments, it is important to know that he is addressing his comments to people who use augmented communication devices that are similar in design to the one he himself uses. That is to say, he presumes use of a computerized communication device, accessible by a keyboard or switch and equipped with synthesized speech output. Creech himself uses a head-mounted pointer to make selections. There are established routines for accessing stored vocabulary, and the user can also spell out words to be spoken. There is a screen display (often only intended for the user). Text to be spoken later can be stored ahead of time. In composing utterances online, there is an option to have words spoken as they are selected, or to wait until the entire utterance is finished before launching it into the discourse.

Creech's aim is to improve the communication of augmented communicators in interaction with both oral speakers and other augmentative speakers in dyadic and group settings. We can find in this work echoes of Clark's notion that communicative interaction is a joint activity with joint responsibilities and requiring joint management. With respect to what we might consider as personal time management constraints, Creech writes (1996b):

> Timing is a pragmatic that a polite augmented communicator is aware of and adapts his or her conversations around. By timing, I do not mean rate of speech. What I mean is being conscious of how much time the other person has to talk and adjusting the conversation accordingly.

Creech's sense of *timing* is not only about rate, but also concerns duration. Underlying such a pragmatic is the understanding that, from the

---

[2]He offers an equation concerning communication that reads as follows: "communication activity is equal to motivation, minus effort, divided by time" (1992).

perspective of the broader English-speaking speech community, utterance formulation on a communication device often takes considerable time. Creech (1996b) observes that "people can easily get to thinking of an augmented communicator as someone with whom they cannot have a conversation without it taking a block of their time," an attitude that can easily have the deleterious social effect of casting augmented communicators as communicatively incompetent. His practical advice for how "augmented communicators can be considerate of the other person's time" is as follows:

1. "If the other person is busy, use short and direct sentences, using words that are in communication device's vocabulary. . . . spelling words simply uses too much of the group's time"

2. "If a person is busy working on something, use 'Speech Off' and speak only after composing a complete thought"

3. "If the person stops what he/she is doing to listen, use immediate speech and speak each word as it is entered so that the person might be able to anticipate the sentence before you complete it"

Note that each of these three suggestions is sensitive to the context of the addressee and respects a general principle that the participatory acts of a communicator tend to be custom-designed to suit the context. In particular, we have a recognition that time is shared time and the actions taken to make the best use of each person's time will vary according to individual needs and circumstances. Creech appears overtly aware of his interlocutor's needs, making suggestions for altering the output method of the device to best meet his addressee's particular communication requirements given differing communication situations. For example, if we examine the third suggestion, we see that Creech is encouraging interlocutor co-construction of a message as a timesaving device. If the addressee is already attending, then giving him or her nothing to attend to runs one into the problem of Clark's temporal imperative—there is no public accounting of what is being done with the jointly shared time. By using immediate speech, the augmented communicator both works within the constraints of the temporal imperative and allows the interlocutor the chance to contribute to the temporal structure of the interaction through co-construction.[3]

From Creech's point of view, interlocutors also have responsibilities to tailor their behaviors to optimize the quality of the interaction. As has already been noted, it can be a laborious process for an augmented com-

---

[3]But, see the following section for an account of the sort of problems co-construction can lead to.

municator to construct an utterance, and Creech (1996a) writes: "If I can take the time and the energy to generate the message the other person has the time to listen and respond to that message." So, each participant has to be mutually considerate of time and situational constraints, and each has to be given the space to say what he or she needs to say. Thus, another of Creech's suggestions is to "take the time you need to say what you have to say" (1996a). He follows this up with the personal observation:

> there have been times when I did not take the time to communicate every-thing that I wanted to say because I didn't think that what I wanted to say was important and the other person was obviously busy, but now I realize that what I have to say is just as important as what anyone else has to say.

It happens all too often that augmented communicators overvalue the time of others in relation to the value of their own communicative desires and needs. The result may be that they do not communicate at all or keep their contributions as minimal and "practical" as possible. This again can lead to false perceptions and an underestimation of their actual commu-nicative competence (cf. Hoag, Bedrosian, Johnson, & Molineux, 1994). Creech's admonitions also exemplify a predominant dilemma for augmen-tative speakers. By taking enough time to communicate, do augmented speakers compromise their listeners' attention abilities or conflict with their time budgets?

In group (i.e., polyadic) settings, the problem of taking the time to say what one has to say can be compounded by the fact that the topic can change or advance before one of the participants has the chance to get his or her contributions to the topic out into the discourse. Augmented communica-tors may have a rapid method for signaling that they wish to comment on a particular issue, but during the time they are formulating their contribution other participants may have entered further information into the common ground and participants' attentions and understandings may have shifted, causing an extra processing load when a comment addressing an earlier point is launched. On this matter Creech (1996b) observes:

> What I do have is a quick communication marker signal-message stored under a two-icon sequence. This signal-message contains a 3-tone signal, followed by a 2-second pause, and the message, "I will comment on this; please continue talking while I prepare what I want to say." . . . *my feeling is that however long it takes for the augmented communicator to compose the message, it becomes the group's responsibility to remember the topic of the comment and to return to it when the augmented communicator makes his/her comment.* [italics added]

Thus, instead of conceiving of a contribution as mistimed or irrelevant to current context, Creech argues that it is up to all the interlocutors to keep a log that recognizes both the appropriate timing and relevance of the contribution. English-speaking augmented communicators are all too well aware of the brevity of the pauses with respect to which one times one's entry into conversation, and against which one has to guard so that the floor is not lost. Moreover, they are very conscious that there are conventional communicative means (coordination devices) for gaining and keeping the floor, but such conventions are often unavailable to them. Creech (1996b) notes that "often the pause between when one person stops speaking and another starts is so short that politely taking the conversation becomes next to impossible." With some humor he states (1996b):

> Everyone needs a way to signal that he or she has something to say. Most people can just raise a hand or quickly speak up during a pause in the conversation. If I were to try to signal the desire to speak by raising my hand, I would be likely to have a spasm and knock the person sitting beside me out of the chair. I find saying "excuse me" to be the most effective label that a speaker can add at the end of his or her sentence to get the floor again, and it's a lot safer than raising my hand. I have "Excuse me" encoded in my Liberator[4] so that it does not appear in the Liberator's display.

Thus Creech faces many of the same coordination problems facing all English-speaking communicators. In the case just discussed, he faces the problem of gaining (and/or keeping) the floor, and the temporal imperative is just one of several factors that place a constraint on the set of possible strategies he can use to solve the problem in a socially acceptable and explicit fashion. To the extent that socially conventional solutions to the problem are not available to individuals, due to physical differences, new conventions (new coordination devices) need to be formulated and recognized. In closing one of his presentations, Creech (1996b) appeals to his fellow augmented communicators by stating: "We must not be satisfied merely with being able to communicate; we must strive to communicate with excellence." As we have seen, he clearly believes that an understanding of time and timing is critical to that goal, as is the recognition that the onus is not only on augmented speakers to communicate with excellence but also on their interlocutors—be they mouth-speech communicators or other augmented communicators.

Robillard

Albert Robillard is a sociologist who has cast an analytic and self-reflective eye on the nature and quality of his communicative interactions with hospital care providers during his own three and a half months of hospitali-

---

[4]Creech's augmentative communication device.

zation (primarily in an Intensive Care Unit [ICU]) (Robillard, 1994). He has a neuromuscular disease, which manifested itself 6 years prior to the period of hospitalization he writes about. As a consequence of this neuromuscular disease, he cannot talk, but can carry on face-to-face interactions either through deliberate lip movements, which his interlocutor must be able to read, or through using an alphabet board. Concerning these two means of communication he writes (1994, pp. 383–395):

> This [i.e., lip movements for lip reading] is a slow process and does not match the real time order of natural conversation. Moreover, the number of people who can read my lip movements is highly limited. My lip movements are restricted, due to weak lip muscles, and it takes intensive training and exposure to be able to read my lips. . . . Otherwise, I have to communicate by using an alphabet board, an even slower process than lip reading. (p. 385)

With hospital staff his primary online communicative resource was his alphabet board if he was trying to address them directly. Alternatively, he could sometimes address staff through an intermediary who was acting as interpreter and was either reading his lips or his alphabet board. By and large, Robillard's attempts at online communicative interactions with the people responsible for his care were unsuccessful and unrewarding, and left him essentially disenfranchised from personal control over his own health care and treatment. He notes (1994) that:

> Not being able to conversationally influence most aspects of my experience in the hospital generated frustrations, resentments, and attributions about my intelligence, my motivations, and, equally from my perspective, about the intelligence, motivations, sensitivity, and the irrationality of the entire health care delivery system. (p. 386)

Failed joint actions generally stem from shared problems, but a common human reaction is to find fault with one or another of the participants. Robillard the analyst does not fall into this trap. In seeking to analyze the nature of the predicament he found himself in, he looked closely at the physical, social, and cultural aspects of his communicative interactions and identified relevant parameters of the shared conversational environment that influenced the quality of interactions.

Robillard emphasizes that the communication problems he encountered trace directly back to his bodily (muscular) constraints in the face of an institutionalized view of the "normal" rhythm of communicative interaction. It is due both to his neuromuscular disease and to conventional communication practice that he "cannot talk or communicate in anything approaching the social consensus of 'real time'" (Robillard 1994, p. 384).

He is well aware of the time and timing that underlie standard American
English conversational practice, but his body cannot "swim" in that time
stream. He states (1994):

> The institutionalized, naturalized, socially consensual order of conversation
> has a time order, a rhythm, that assumes an intersubjective coordination of
> physical human bodies. Having a body which could not inhabit this time
> order was a breach of the normalized conversational environment. (pp.
> 393–394)

This is not to be interpreted simplistically as being physically unable to
produce speech in real time, since, as we have already seen, time and
timing in interactive communication involve so much more than just
speech. Robillard makes it clear that the same bodily constraints that affect
his speech production also affect his body gestures, his gaze control, and
other potential body-based communicative resources, which might otherwise have been marshaled into use for directing and layering his own
communicative productions. Moreover, deployment of bodily resources,
such as visual attention, to operate a communication device can keep the
augmented speaker from being able to monitor the cues of his mouth-
speech interlocutor. For instance, employing an alphabet board requires
the user to maintain visual contact with the device, reducing the opportunity for visual monitoring of the interlocutor. This can lead the board
user to miss vital cues as to where interactions are breaking down, can
inhibit synchronous communication, and can lead to communication delay. Robillard (1994) writes about the problems that ensue: "Tied down to
looking at the spelling as it was written, I was usually unaware of the
behavioral signs of the need to respecify and was at a loss in formulating
a proper interpretational context" (p. 392). In addition, Robillard experienced difficulty with translators who couldn't merely read out his spellings
on an alphabet board. He states (1994):

> Because I could not talk while my translator was reading what I said, I
> frequently experienced gross editing of what I said. Sometimes the translator
> would refuse to say my thoughts. More frequently the translator would not
> be assertive and translate my thoughts at the proper spot in the conversation,
> choosing to wait, delaying my participation and leading to further out of
> context remarks. (p. 392)

So, while use of an alphabet board may require co-presence and co-par-
ticipation of participants and online generation of communicative acts, in
a very important sense it is not the normative form of face-to-face interaction: The interaction setting created by the device imposes severe re-

strictions on the augmented speaker's ability to play a successful role in the interaction.

Robillard distinguishes between the "socially consensual real-time" order embraced by the normative societal perspective of face-to-face interaction and basic to Clark's (1996) description of language use, and the temporal order manifest during his slow and labored alphabet board mediated interactions, which require the constant attention and cooperation of the interlocutor. Further, this alternative time order would often conflict with the time budgets of the medical staff, a situation that Robillard discussed as two different types of interaction problems.

First, physicians "operating under tremendous subjective time pressures" (Robillard, 1994, p. 386) would frequently generate interactions about his care or treatment. However, they would leave him with no other way to respond but by giving a nod "yes" or head shake "no," since any qualified answer he would try to give would fail, either because the physicians would not see themselves being addressed by Robillard's spelled out reply, or because they would leave before the conversation had come to a satisfactory conclusion. In their attempt to negotiate the situation:

> The physicians would suggest that I formulate what I had to say before they came. This suggestion left out the possibility to respond to any emergent conversation while they were in the room. It also assumed that I would remember what I wanted to say in conversational contexts long after the conversation had passed. (Robillard, 1994, p. 386)

Second, the "Not now" problem occurred when care providers would regularly determine the time when Robillard could and could not generate an utterance for them. Starting a production did not automatically give him control of the floor.

> "Not now" can take three avenues. The first is simply saying "Not now" when I am trying to speak. The second is when the party I am speaking to cuts me off by attending to another task, usually walking away in mid-sentence. The third possibility is when another interrupts my conversation, taking over the interactional focus. (Robillard, 1994, p. 391)

The avenues that Robillard lists above can happen in any face-to-face conversation. The "Not now" act is not a problem in and of itself, but presents a problem in relation to the frequency with which it occurred and the time and labor costs it incurred for Robillard. Because of the time it took for him to generate his utterances, interlocutors would often rank their time needs over his own. However, this loss of control of when he could speak effectively devalued both his time and labor and also brought into question the importance of his contributions. Moreover, interruptions and walking away in mid-sentence tended to generate a context in which the conversational thread was lost, meaning that a considerable physical effort would be needed to backtrack and reconstitute the background for the generation of the original utterance. This, in essence, is the third problem, the "out of context" problem. Robillard (1994) writes:

> It takes so much effort to spell out what I am saying I could not easily recycle the topic by saying "You know what we were speaking about a little while ago, the X topic." I could only, because of time and energy, speak directly to a former topic. This speaking out of context would generate many complaints and confusion. It would often break off further communication. (p. 391)

Robillard's production of utterances that were deemed to be out of context became the locus of attributions concerning his intelligence and common sense ("Are you crazy?"; "What the hell are you talking about?").

The situation of resuming a discontinued interaction provides a temporal conflict with no good solutions: If one spends the time and effort to provide the background needed to revive a failed communication, one faces the very real likelihood of running up against the "Not now" problem yet again (with a potential continuous loop effect). But if one generates a direct utterance on the premise that one's interlocutors will be able to remember the original context of the interaction after some time has past (and their attention has been directed to some other task), then one risks the possibility that the interlocutors cannot reconstruct the earlier context and instead judge the utterance to be out of context and inappropriate (and so reflective of a certain personality or turn of mind).

Although Robillard ran into these same general problems with all the hospital health care providers, this does not mean that the quality of the interactions was the same with all conversational partners. In fact, from an ethnographic point of view, one of Robillard's most important observations concerns the sociocultural factors that seem to be involved in distinguishing those individuals with whom he was able to carry out successful interactions from those with whom he had great difficulties interacting. Robillard observed significant differences between two groups of nurses; one group he terms "flying nurses" and the other he terms "authentic local nurses." Flying nurses were not native residents of the area of the hospital (Hawaii), but tended to come and work on 3- to 6-month contracts and then move on to work another contract at hospitals elsewhere. By contrast, local nurses were, like Robillard himself, long-term residents of the area, and most had been born, raised, and educated in the area. Critically, "none of the flying nurses would use the alphabet board" (Robillard, 1994, pp. 387–388). Those who tried soon became frustrated and stopped. The four people who consistently used Robillard's communication board all fell into the local nurse grouping. Moreover, they were all women; "no male nurses even attempted to use my communication board" (Robillard, 1994, p. 389).

In trying to explain these differences, Robillard makes a convincing argument for the role that closely shared cultural background can play in facilitating effective communication. Robillard and the local nurses belonged to many of the same cultural communities and shared particular inside information, whereas he had far less in common with the flying nurses. This had a profound effect on the tenor of communicative interactions. Local nurses could conversationally situate their patients as individuals sharing the same background assumptions and adhering to the same local social conventions. He elaborates as follows:

> Authentic local nurses could by glances, gaze, facial expression, vocabulary, syntax, cadence, dialect, body language, and topical reference conversationally locate themselves and the patients as members of and constrained by the same local culture and social structure. . . . There was a reciprocity of highly detailed knowledge which located me and them. I felt that they knew me as a unique situated individual. I felt I knew them as situated individuals. (Robillard, 1994, p. 388)

Flying nurses, on the other hand, shared almost none of this detailed knowledge and so could only locate Robillard as "a generic person." These differences seem to be critical in the initial phases of initiating a new acquaintance into using the communication board. Robillard reports that the very first conversations between him and individual nurses (both local and flying) invariably started in the same general way (questions about where he came from and what he did). However, flying nurses could not pick up on his answers in the same way as local nurses. Where local nurses could quickly begin to chase common threads and affirm a strong social and cultural bond, the flying nurses were left searching for further things to say. The flying nurses had no stake in continuing a conversation; their patients were individuals with whom they would have no future contact and with whom they shared no significant acquaintances. As a result, they had no motivation to continue using the alphabet board. In fact, some flying nurses never even tried, and Robillard (1994) notes that the most memorable flying nurse addressed him on their first meeting by stating "I am the nurse from hell and do not try any of that communication shit with me" (p. 388).

The differences between the two groups of nurses not only meant that each would have a different evaluation of the fruits to be gained from the time and effort spent in interaction with Robillard, it also meant that the pragmatic resources they could draw on were different. The wealth of shared knowledge (and shared interactional strategies) that Robillard and the local nurses possessed meant that they were better able to anticipate each other's moves than Robillard and the flying nurses were. The problem for Robillard was that the vast majority (90%) of nurses with whom he had to interact on a daily basis in the ICU were flying nurses. Since communication with these nurses was impaired by the fact that they wouldn't use his communication board, real problems ensued. Robillard (1994) describes the situation as follows:

> My insistence in talking and being heard, expecting what I said to influence behavior, led to a spiral of mutual antagonism between myself and the flying nurses. Communication with flying nurses was a lost cause. I quickly came to think of them as nearly anonymous parts, universally interchangeable, mirroring what I thought they thought of patients. (p. 389)

As noted above, not all local nurses entered into consistent communication board use with Robillard. Thus, this shared background was not sufficient to guarantee positive interactional outcomes. In particular, Robillard (1994) noted a difference between males and females; it is his experience, not just in the hospital setting, that "males, in general, appear not to have the patience or the multiple communication rhythms to be able to use alternative means of communication" (pp. 389–390). Such observations deserve a wider investigation. Still, it is significant that certain individuals can step out of the normative grip of the time order of socially consensual real-time conversation and enter into the different time order of alphabet board use with Robillard. He ends his paper with the apt observation: "Yet, as I learned from the local nurses, there are a few people who demonstrated the normal time order is but one among many time orders and structures for communication" (p. 394).

Still, it should not be forgotten that Robillard was unable to negotiate an alternative time order and structure for communication with the vast majority of his care providers. The result was that "not having a real time voice was the equivalent to not having any defense to what was done to" his body (Robillard, 1994, p. 386). The inability to intersubjectively coordinate his communication patterns with the rhythms of those responsible for his care challenged the very fabric of his sense of self.

CASE STUDY

To expand on the first-person commentaries sketched above, this section presents an observational case study of the time and timing issues that arise in one augmented speaker's selective deployment of both a communication board and a computerized device. These observations are further contextualized by her own commentary on specific instances of communication and on her augmented communications more generally.

The primary participant in the research presented below is Jane Denton.[5] On completing her undergraduate degree in chemistry in 1967, she contracted encephalitis. As a result of this disease, Jane is incapable of producing sustained vocal speech and must use a wheelchair to locomote. Approximately 15 years after the onset of her illness, Jane returned to school to complete a master's degree in chemistry. Currently, she resides at a nursing home for persons with disabilities in Erie County, New York. Jane has known and worked with the first author since 1989.

This study focuses on Jane's use of two different augmentative devices (a communication board and a Dynavox) to communicate "verbally" with her interactants. As described in detail in another study (Higginbotham & Wilkins, 1997), Jane also uses a wide variety of face, head, and limb gestures during interaction. Depending on the particular communication setting, she may either interact entirely with her gestures, or rely on her communication devices for linguistic support.

Her communication board consists of the alphabet, several punctuation marks, numbers 0 through 10, the days of the week, 281 words arranged (and color coded) in alphabetical order, and several regulatory phrases (e.g., "end of word," "by the way") (Appendix A). Jane's Dynavox is a computerized communication device equipped with a dynamic, touch-sensitive display screen and synthesized speech output. Although Jane has a number of different communication displays at her disposal she was only observed using her word prediction display. The word prediction display consists of an output window, the letters of the alphabet, the numbers 0–10, several device control buttons ("backspace," "clear display," "speak") and 5 "prediction" buttons (Appendix A). To operate the device, Jane keys in the letters of the intended word. After each letter is selected, the Dynavox searches its database for the five most likely words to be used and displays those words on the prediction buttons. If the desired word is shown, Jane can select it, otherwise she must keep typing out the word. After constructing her utterance, Jane can speak the message through the speech synthesizer by pressing the speak button. She uses a standard desktop computer to correspond with friends and colleagues via E-mail. She also writes with a pen and pencil, although, because of her physical condition, handwritten communications are usually limited to her signature.

The primary data used for this study includes one audio and two videotape recordings taken during February and March 1997. These materials were supplemented by additional recordings of a shopping trip, a class lecture and two debriefings about prior observations made between January 1990 and June 1997. Table 3.1 details the data sources.

---

[5]In order to provide a direct way of discussing Jane Denton's performance in the transcriptions, as well as her commentaries on communication, we use her first name.

TABLE 3.1
Data Sources Used in Study

Data Source	Setting	Devices Used
1. Audiotape. 1 hour 48 minutes, recorded February 1997.	Conversed with Jeff (1st author) during equipment preparation, and Jake (friend) in the library.	Wordboard and Dynavox with Jeff; Dynavox with Jake
2. Videotape. 2 hours, recorded March 1997.	Conversation with Jeff during equipment setup and participation at a residence council meeting.	Wordboard and Dynavox with Jeff; Dynavox during meeting
3. Videotape. 2 hours, recorded March 1997.	Conversation with Jeff in living quarters.	Wordboard and Dynavox
4. Videotapes (2), recorded in June 1997.	Performance testing of devices, conversations, and interview.	Wordboard and Dynavox
5. Audiotape. 1 hour, recorded August 1994.	Shopping trip with two research assistants of the first author.	Dynavox
6. Videotape, 1 hour, recorded January 1990.	Lecture to graduate class in augmentative communication (UB).* One camera focused on Jane, the other on her communication board.	Communication board

*State University of New York at Buffalo.

Time and Communication Rate

As with most augmented communicators, rates of Jane's communications are approximately an order of magnitude or more slower than that of mouth-speech communicators.[6] Jane is fastest at using her communication board, achieving communication rates averaging 19 words per minute (table 3.2) during solitary or dyadic communication situations. In contrast, her productions on her Dynavox communication aid are over two-thirds slower, averaging 6.5 words per minute.

Interaction with Jane via her communication board is usually a collaborative affair between Jane and her interlocutor, involving a rapid interplay between Jane's board indications and her interlocutor's response to her pointing. When Jane employs a communication board, her communication rate is determined by a functional interaction between her word choices (spelled out or selected), the latency and duration of her interactant's response to her points, and her interlocutor's deployment of various interaction strategies such as guessing. The differences in communication board communication rates in Table 3.2 may evidence a collaborative attempt by Jane and her interlocutor to adhere to the temporal imperative

---

[6]The average rate of mouth-speech for English speakers is around 150 words per minute.

TABLE 3.2
Average Communication Rates for Jane D.[1]

Device/Context	Communication Rate
Communication Board	
1. June 1997—question answering/no facilitator (80 words over 3 utterances)	16 wpm[2]
2. March 1997—conversations with Jeff (2 sessions: 42 words over 4 utterances)	22 wpm
3. February 1990—lecture to class/with facilitator (46 words over 3 utterances)	17 wpm
4. February 1990—lecture to class/no facilitator (30 words over 3 sentences)	20 wpm
Average communication board rate	19 wpm
Dynavox	
5. June 1997—answers question w/ word prediction (59 words over 3 utterances)	5 wpm
6. June 1997—answers question w/ no prediction (55 words over 2 utterances)	6 wpm
7. March 1997—conversation with Jeff w/ prediction (50 words over 5 utterances)	7.5 wpm
8. March 1997—group meeting w/ prediction (12 words over 2 utterances)	7 wpm
Average dynavox rate	6.5 wpm

[1]Average communication rate was obtained by taking the median utterance level communication rate for a given session. Utterances of 3 words or less were omitted from this analysis.
[2]Words per minute.

through the selective use of these strategies. For example, utterance length is shorter and communication rate is faster in the fully interactive sessions, compared to Jane's performance on the non-co-constructed question-answering task.

Below is a typical example of collaborative board use:

[16:34][7]
1. Jane: W-O-U-L-D[8]
2. Jeff: would
3. Jane: YOU

---

[7][minutes:seconds].
[8]Augmented utterances are displayed in capital letters. Spelled out words are indicated by dashes between letters. Spoken works are in lowercase. Terminal punctuation indicates rising (?) and falling (.) speech intonation. Neutral intonation is not marked. Conversational overlap is marked by a caret (^). Unintelligible speech is marked by (. . .).

4. Jeff: I
5. Jane: LIKE
6. Jeff: like
7. Jane: T-O H-E-A-R
8. Jeff: hear
9. Jane: w-h-a-t
10. Jeff: what
11. Jane: I A-M
12. Jeff: You're going to say?
13. Jane: YES
14. Jeff: Yes. It is three to two, is that an issue?

[16:54] (total elapsed time 20 seconds for an utterance-level communication rate of 33 wpm.)

In this example, Jeff can be observed (#12) to increase the communication rate by interactively recasting Jane's utterance and by guessing the last 3 words. These tactics, although unconsciously deployed, may have saved time by alleviating Jeff's need to reiterate the utterance and reducing Jane's utterance production by 3 words, thus reducing the total utterance production time by about 7 seconds, or 25%. To interact successfully, Jane's interlocutor must attend to the ongoing message production and co-construct an utterance-in-progress after each letter or word is indicated. The interlocutor's spoken account provides a public record of the utterance, offering an overt means for establishing and developing common ground and verifying for Jane that her productions have been successfully received.

The openly collaborative effort observed in communication board utterance formulations is largely absent when Jane uses her Dynavox. Instead, she composes most of her message in silence, without her interactant's co-construction efforts—"uttering" them on their completion. For example:

1. Jake: Ohh yeah the rose I gave ya. Still alive?
2. Jane: [shakes head]
3. Jake: Dead already. I never did get to see it in full bloom anyway. Of course (. . .) that's all that counts. Did it have a peaceful death?
4. (55)[9]   (Jane formulates sentence, Jake intermittently looks at Jane, looks around library, stares into space)
5. Jane: IT NEVER REALLY BLOOMED.
6. (4)
7. Jake: Oh it didn't? Somebody's head will roll for that one.

In the above example, it took Jane 55 seconds to respond to her friend's query, with the vast majority of that time spent in silence while Jane con-

---

[9]Silent interval, in seconds.

structed her response. Although it allows her to construct utterances independently from her interlocutor, the Dynavox imposes other temporal costs on Jane's message productions, which interfere with her and her interlocutor's ability to communicate. An analysis of the videotape taken of Jane and her device when obtaining rate data (Table 3.2, #5), showed that there was a noticeable delay from the time Jane selected the letters or words to the time the computer registered the choice by highlighting the selection. This delay ranged from about a quarter of a second to 4 seconds in length. Jane was also observed to pause for several seconds each time she visually scanned her prediction list. Such device-related delays can impose significant limits on utterance production rates—in this case contributing to the more than 65% percent decrease in speed compared with her communication board use.

Jane's strategy of constructing an entire utterance in silence on the Dynavox before speaking it, makes adherence to the canonical temporal imperative impossible (i.e., speaking turn must be initiated within a few seconds after the previous turn has ended). Jane and her interlocutors are required to arrive at an alternative temporal order in which to sustain interactive communication. During her Dynavox productions, it is common practice for Jane's interlocutors to disattend to her while she formulates her message, then to reattend to her when they hear the utterance being produced by the communication device. This particular attentional organization allows Jane to construct and issue utterances with her Dynavox while minimizing the communication effort of her partner. It is not a cost-free solution to the problem of the temporal imperative, as is seen in following sections.

Timing

According to Clark (1996), successful temporal coordination of actions is necessary to successfully transact face-to-face interactions. When using an augmentative device, Jane's coordination problem is one of utilizing particular pieces of communication technology, given her physical abilities, within the joint time constraints she shares with her interlocutors.

Having engaged her interactant in conversation, Jane deftly moves her stylus from item to item with only a fraction of a second separating some of the points, as can be seen below:

1. Jane: [22:90 - 23:00][10]   ALL
2. Sue: [24:60 - 25:23]   about
3. Jane: [25:47 - 25:57]   NO
4. Jane: [26:50 - 26:57]   ALL

---

[10][seconds:milliseconds].

5.	Sue:	[26:50 - 27:30]	all?			
6.	Jane:	[28:27 - 28:40]	MOST			
7.	Sue:	[29:47 - 29:90]	almost^.			
8.	Jane:	[29:73 - 31:53]		I-M-M^		
9.	Sue:	[32:23 - 32:93]			immediately?	
10.	Jane:	[33:20 - 33:27]	YES			
11.	Jane:	[34:27 - 37:30]	T-H-I-N-G^S			
12.	Sue:	[37:03 - 37:33]		things		
13.	Jane:	[38:97 - 41:10]	B-E-G^A			
14.	Sue:	[40:43 - 41:00]		began		
15.	Jane:	[42:30 - 42:33]	TO			
16.	Sue:	[43:30 - 43:83]	to			
17.	Jane:	[43:57 - 44:40]	H^A			
18.	Sue:	[43:90 - 44:27]		happen		
19.	Jane:	[44:70 - 44:80]	YES			

The interaction depicted above exemplifies how Jane and her interlocutor are able to achieve a close temporal coordination with one another. Note for example how Jane's turns occur within a second or less of Sue's, and in fact occasionally overlap Sue's utterances, as at #7 when Jane begins to spell out "immediately." Note that Jane quickly adjusts to Sue's guesses either by providing feedback ("YES," "NO") as to the success of Sue's reading and guessing, or by moving on to the next word.

Thus, with her communication board, Jane could participate in the joint interaction activity well within the temporal limits of face-to-face turn taking and maintain her interlocutor's attention throughout the process. Here the coordination of the process of utterance production is temporally synchronous with the production of content. In order to accomplish this, Jane's interlocutor must pay close visual attention to each finger point as it occurs. When misreadings do occur, the point-response routine observed here also allows the interactants to locate and resolve their communication problems, as they are recognized, within the just produced discourse (Buzolich & Wiemann, 1988; Higginbotham, 1989; Higginbotham, Mathy-Laikko, & Yoder, 1988). This looks to be an important manner in which the interactants can resolve local difficulties immediately and ensure a progressive establishment of common ground: letter-by-letter or word-by-word.

Jane's abilities to engage in temporally synchronous actions with her interlocutor are dampened by the performance characteristics of her Dynavox. Because of the time it takes to produce a message with her electronic device, it is difficult for Jane to temporally coordinate her utterance with the expectations of her interactant. For example, when beginning to converse with her friend Jake, Jane takes more than a minute to construct her utterance. Commenting on the long period of silence, Jake urges Jane to speak by saying, "Your turn, Jane." Later in the interaction (see example below), she responds to a statement made by Jake about his family, and a problem arises due to the 98-second interval (#8, #10) between Jake's last topic-relevant utterance ("But I never heard of them") and Jane's response ("They may be related from way back"). During the intervening time Jake spoke several utterances (#7). What followed was a repair extending across several turns in which Jane kept reiterating (i.e., replaying) her utterance until it was correctly understood by Jake:

1. Jake: Ever see those Rococco commercials on TV before?
2. Jane: (head shake)
3.   (4)[11]
4. Jake: Is that yes or no?
5.   (4)
6. Jane: NO.
7. Jake: Oh, those people aren't related (. . .) to my family. But I keep lookin at them tryin to see (. . .) They're two brothers. With a car dealership, and I looked at them and try to see if there was some resemblance. But I never heard of them. (. . .)
          There are a lot of people in the phone book, there are a lot of people in the phone book have that name.
8.   (42)
9.   There used to be a priest named Monsignor Rococco.
10.   (56)
11. Jane: THEY MAY BE RELATED FROM WAY BACK.
12.   (2)
13. Jake: What?
14.   (2)
15. Jane: THEY MAY BE RELATED FROM WAY BACK.
16.   (2)
17. Jake: See there, they made you . . .
18.   (4)
19. Jane: THEY MAY BE RELATED FROM WAY BACK.
20.   (5)
21. Jake: Maybe. Sound like you said, they may . . . I heard a word, "lady," in there didn't I?
22.   (7)
23. Jane: THEY MAY BE RELATED FROM WAY BACK.
24.   (4)
25. Jake: Oh, they may be related, could be, could be, but there are a lot of people with that name.

Fortunately, the Dynavox allowed Jane to repeat her utterance promptly until it was understood by Jake. If she had to reconstruct the utterance word-by-word or letter-by-letter, even more time might have been expended in the repair. Part of Jake's problem was his inability to understand the

---

[11]Silent interval, in seconds.

words in the utterance. This may have been due both to his difficulty recalling the topic and to the intelligibility of the communication device. This problem was exacerbated by the inability of the device to isolate and modify selected portions of the message text. For example, Jane could not repeat just the word "related" or have it spelled out unless she rekeyed the entire word again. And altering down the speed with which the utterance is produced is impossible for single utterances. In combination, these constraints can exact a significant temporal toll, by impeding interactional synchrony, interrupting the construction of common ground, and contributing to comprehension failure.

Not all of Jane's Dynavox-mediated utterances were so slow and delayed. When the utterance could be spoken in just a few selections, she could often produce it within a few seconds. Saying "NO" in the example above took Jane only four seconds to speak,[12] and it only took between 2 and 7 seconds to generate each repetition of her utterance later in the conversation. Jane would also strategically use short, nonspecific utterances to minimize the amount of interaction delay involved in the utterance construction process.

Another timing strategy Jane used was to pre-store anticipated utterances prior to the conversational encounter. At a meeting of her local Residence Council, Jane uses this strategy to enter into the group discussion at the proper moment:

1. [37:22-37:38][13]
2. Ken: Rita has drafted a letter, concerning vending prices to see if they could lower em. Because this is a nursing facility we don't have the money to pay the high prices that factories pay.
3. [37:39-37:42]
4. Jane: HAVE YOU CONSIDERED OTHER VENDORS AND THEIR PRICES?
5. [37:45-37:53]
6. Ken: That, I believe Jane, is up to uhm contract. That's a contract number. We have a contract with uh (. . .)[14]
7. [37:53-39:03]
8. Jane: (*starts message preparation*)
9. [38:23-39:04]
10. Rita: Does everybody understand Jane's original response?
11. .
12. .   (Talk about the contract)
13. .

---

[12]Even though Jake could not make it out, her head shake was even more immediate (and was at least recognized as an interactive attempt to answer his question).

[13][minutes:seconds].

[14](. . .)—unintelligible utterance.

14.   . . . but I think Jane is having a suggestion here for us.
15.   39:05 39:07
16.   Jane: WHO DO WE GO SEE ABOUT CHANGING IT?
17.   [39:37-39:42]
18.   Ken: Dennis Gorski
19.   Rita: Probably not, or do we . . .
20.   Ken: its (. . .) with the county—they serve all the buildings, the Rath
                building, I believe they get the CFC, I think there're machines
                there, . . . I imagine you have to go through the county then, to
                change machines, to change vendors.
21.   [40:12-40:12]
22.   Ken: (whispered) Jane is busy.
23.   [40:13-40:14]
24.   Jane: THAT DOESN'T SEEM FAIR
25.   [40:19-41:56]
26.   Rita: Ahm, do you have um . . . Well contracts run out. You know con-
                tracts aren't for life. I mean they do eventually run out. uhm.
27.   Ken: But that is the lowest bid. Whoever bids the lowest for the con-
                tract gets the contract.

        .
        .
        .

28.   Rita: Can we stick with the topic in terms of the canteen.
29.   [41:59-42:02]
30.   Ken: Do you guys want to wait until we hear back from this vendor?
31.   [42:02-42:27]
32.   Jane: (*starts message preparation*)
33.   [42:02-42:27]
34.   Rita: We've asked ^ them if they'd lower the prices. Then maybe we
                can think of a strategy or think of some steps to find out, if there
                is another vendor that could bring the stuff in cheaper? Wanna
                just wait until, I'm getting nods from everybody on that.
35.   Ken: I don't think we can do anything until we get it, ahm, something
                back from that vendor, to find out if they're going to lower their
                prices ^
36.   [42:27-42:28]
37.   Jane: ^   ^HOW LONG.
38.   [42:31-42:48]
39.   Rita: I would say if we haven't heard from 'em by the next meeting.
                that we should probably take some reaction, but we just got that
                letter out last week. So, I guess by the next executive council
                meeting we should know, something. That, suffice or [. . .]
40.   [42:53-42:53]
41.   Jane: OK
42.   [42:53-42:54]
43.   Rita: All right, So we'll wait until we hear from the ah, present vendor.
                . . .

At #3, Jane was able to begin speaking within a second of Ken's utterance termination. She indicated, in a follow-up interview, that she was able to produce the utterance in a timely manner because she had constructed the utterance prior to the meeting. When asked why, she stated: "BECAUSE I KNEW IT WOULD BE DISCUSSED. I HAD ALREADY DONE THAT. . . . BECAUSE I WOULD NOT BE ABLE TO PREPARE IT WHILE IT WAS BEING DISCUSSED." Inspection of the videotape also revealed that she physically prepared herself to produce the utterance at its appropriate projected point by placing her stylus (a pencil) on the selection 7 seconds prior to utterance production. She then waited until the turn-relevant point and lifted her pencil, which initiated the utterance. At #8, Jane begins to construct a response to Ken's talk at #6. She delivers her response over a minute later, after Rita has reiterated the vendor situation to the rest of the group. Similar to her preceding utterance, Jane pre-positions her pencil to lift off at an appropriate occasion. Her physical readiness to communicate, like posture and gaze behavior in typical communicators, may have served as a coordination device, cueing Rita at #9 to relinquish the floor and allocate her turn to Jane (". . . but I think Jane is having a suggestion here for us").

Jane's utterance productions are not always so overtly collaborative. At #32, she begins to construct a response to Ken's prior utterance. But during the intervening seconds, Ken responds to Rita, taking the conversation in a different direction. Instead of giving up, Jane interrupts Ken 25 seconds later (#37) by asking the question "HOW LONG?"

After viewing the videotape, Jane commented (with her communication board) on her motivations for interrupting Ken:

Jane: I DID NOT HAVE TO LOSE THE OPPORTUNITY TO ASK MY
          QUESTION, AND I INTERRUPTED BECAUSE I DID NOT
          KNOW HOW MUCH MORE HE WAS GOING TO SAY AND I
          HAD TO HURRY TO GET IT IN.
Jeff: And what is the risk of not getting it in quickly?
Jane: HE WOULDN'T HAVE UNDERSTOOD THE TIME OF MY
          QUESTION IN THAT I WOULDN'T HAVE BEEN ABLE TO
          ASK IT AT ALL BECAUSE HE WOULD HAVE MOVED ON [IN
          HIS HEAD].[15] . . . THAT WAS RUDE, (BUT) I DON'T THINK
          HE REALLY MINDED.

If she had let it go further, her utterance wouldn't have made sense. Jane made the right timing choice. Her utterance was delayed, but its impact wasn't lost as it sometimes was in her earlier interactions with Jake. Through interruption, she was able to maintain her footing in the conversation and avoided Robillard's (1994) out-of-context problem.

---

[15]Interviewer's words, agreed to by Jane.

Minimizing Communication Costs Through Device Choice

Jane makes clear choices as to which device to use with particular individuals, based on their ability to understand her communications, her
particular physical situation, and her time budget. In the following E-mail,
Jane gives us a typical morning schedule of who she communicates with
and what device she typically uses:

```
8; aide comes in . . . discuss when i will get up 10-10:30 aide
comes in . . . discuss what i will wear, washes me, puts me in
w/ch nrs 2 does treatments to skin areas affected . . . as i have
requested

     btw,¹⁶ KEY . . . INDICATES COMMUNICATION WITH
COMMUNICATION BOARD
            ////     "          "         "
DYNAVOX

10:45 am in w/ch with dynavox . . . or //// depending on aide
discuss what
       else  i   need     e.g.  Bible. papers, reading material,
etc.

11 or 11:30 -12 in chapel doing daily devotions sometimes ////
singing-limited
```

Jane uses different devices for different nursing aides. The communication board allows rapid communication with those staff members she
can relate to and who see and read well enough to use it. Similarly to
Robillard, Jane also finds that not all staff are willing to spend the time
using it with her. If the staff person was uncooperative, Jane was unable
to use any device to convey her thoughts. The Dynavox posed its own set
of advantages and disadvantages. Although "bulky and slow" it does provide
Jane the means to speak, regardless of her interlocutor's willingness to
participate actively in the message construction process. As she noted in
her E-mails to us, the Dynavox was well suited for communication with
persons with visual, reading, or memory problems—people who have difficulty communicating with her via her communication board:

```
. . . ptL¹⁷ & thank U, Jesus for my dvx! without it I wudnt be abl
to com w/ my 3 best frends her at th hom. al 3 r mal, in mid 50s
& sufr frm m s, whch hs lft thm unabl to red my com brd. it has
brot me untold hrs of joy to be abl to com w/them.
   . . . ablty t sav selectd wrds & letrs [to mk up wrds] on scren -
```

---

¹⁶"by the way."
¹⁷"praise the Lord."

```
so it cn b sen by thos wh hv difclty rembrng begng o wrd or msge.
ths is partclrly tru fr thos les eductd, whm del w/ on daly basz,
& esp fr thos wh hav ben tught in modrn schl ciriculms
. . . ablty t convrs w/kids - tis surprisngly ezy fr thm t
undrstnd cuz thy hv bn brot up w/ cmptrs & cn hr synthtc voc
clrer
```

However, as Jane points out in an E-mail message, she couldn't use her Dynavox to communicate with everyone:

```
. . . also, for my setng, i e , nrsng hm, mst othr resdnts r
eldrly & hrd o hrng, nt to mntn thir inablty to undrstnd syn-
theszd voic. it seems tht w/ag comz ls of desr to chnge, evn hrng
ptrns. . . . and, evn fr ths usd to hrng syntheszd voic, is
difclt to stp & rept buz wrd or imp phraz & cant be slod dwn.
```

Unlike Robillard's means of communication, Jane's Dynavox at least produces an audible voice that must be dealt with by staff—especially when utterances are strategically prepared. In follow-up interviews, Jane stated that she selectively used her Dynavox with fellow residents (like Jake) whose vision was poor and who couldn't read her communication board. When confronted with varying communication situations, Jane would choose the technology best suited for the particular circumstance. For example, once when Jeff was kneeling in front of her chair to attach a remote microphone on her communication device, Jane switched to her Dynavox to talk, then switched to her board when Jeff became available for face-to-face interactions. She employed this strategy on a number of other occasions, depending on Jeff's proximity and focus of attention. Through the coherent pattern of her device selection, Jane aptly demonstrates that there are particular times and particular persons for which a given device will be best suited.

CONCLUSION

As McDermott and Verenne (1995) have noted, questions about the nature of disability "go beyond etiology to function and circumstance" (p. 328) and lead one to ask "When does a physical difference count, under what conditions, and for what reasons?" To answer such a question requires us to situate individuals in their cultural matrix, and to recognize that different cultural matrices (and the individuals that constitute them) are the agents by which certain members of a social group become either enabled or disabled. In this chapter we have attempted to examine how the functions of interactive communication in the circumstances of augmented communication use are constrained by a socially constructed time matrix for the patterning of American English face-to-face interactions. Augmented interactions often require the participants to negotiate an alternative time order for communication. When such a time order is successfully negotiated by its interactants, it has the positive effect of socially constructing a dynamic, intelligent, communicatively competent individual. However, failure to negotiate an alternate time order means that the very same person may, in another context, be construed as a difficult, suspect, and communicatively incompetent individual. In the preceding discussion, we hope to have demonstrated how the situation, the social matrix, and the nature of the jointly constructed communicative actions conspire to reveal or mask competence, not the individual.

Even from their own perspective, augmented communicators operate under considerable temporal constraints making it difficult, or even impossible, to maintain socially consensual real-time interactions. Such constraints involve body movement, the communication device, and the information-processing abilities of both the augmented speakers and their interlocutor(s). Joint interaction emerges from this set of constraints to operate within a synergistic whole.

As we have shown, the temporal imperative is a dominant feature of face-to-face interaction, influencing and shaping the attention, processing, and communication styles of the participants. The commentaries by Creech, Robillard, and Denton, along with our actual observations of Denton's face-to-face interactions, provide ample evidence that the temporal imperative plays a dominant constraining force throughout the interactive communications of these individuals.

In face-to-face interaction, unlike written communication, the temporal imperative cannot be suspended, and any significant breach or modification of the temporal imperative has significant ramifications on the communication event. The three individuals discussed in this investigation are all highly educated, intelligent, and articulate, as evidenced through their comments and behavior, yet, because of the temporal differences in their augmented interactional abilities as compared to the socially constructed norm, they display difficulty accomplishing otherwise mundane communication goals—such as allocating addressee attention, turn taking, getting one's message out, interrupting, etc. That is, their departures from the temporal norms of mouth-speech communication result in delays, misunderstandings, and other social sanctions. The onus for these is often placed on the shoulders of the augmented speaker.

Although the issue of time and timing in interaction is a joint problem, it is still fruitful to examine possible points in the interactional system that could be improved to ameliorate any difficulties. One aspect that must be tackled concerns the augmentative communication technologies used by augmented speakers. The input and message display characteristics of these technologies place limits on the speed of message output, the manner and ease of message processing by one's interlocutor, the interactive style that participants must engage in order to converse, and ultimately who one can interact with. These communication technologies impose a significant set of temporal constraints on any interaction and challenge the participants to find ways around those limits.

Slowness in message production leads to frustration, misunderstanding, and reluctance on the part of the addressee to communicate. Delays in message output result in disattention, forgetting, and mishearings on the part of the addressee, and the inability of the communicator to enter into the conversation when temporally mandated. Problems with message revision lead to even longer stretches of frustrating communication repair. The commentaries by Creech, Robillard, and Jane Denton, and our observations of Jane's interactions, evidence both the impact of these constraints and the conscious effort taken by these individuals to develop interactional strategies that compensate for those temporal barriers fostered by their augmented technologies.

The moment-by-moment problems with time and timing experienced by augmented communicators become problems in the presentation of self in at least two senses. First, there is an impact on self-expression. Can you take enough time to say what you want to say without losing or aggravating your addressee? Second, there is an impact on the individual's sense of self. Do your interactions function to alienate you or integrate you within other communities of speakers?

Evidence from all three of the augmented communicators we have discussed in this chapter reveals that disattention by one's interlocutor is very common, as is the reluctance of certain potential interlocutors to enter into conversations. While "[t]he problem of time affects both the person with the speech disability and the communication partner" (Sweidel 1991/1992, p. 203), the social consequences have a greater impact on the former rather than the latter. Even though many of the problems with interaction can be seen to reside in the nature of the communication technologies and/or the inability of addressees to attend to and process augmented speakers' communications, it is augmented speakers who are commonly blamed for failed or "inefficient" communications, and they are the ones who suffer social stigmatization.

Group membership also enters into time and timing issues. In their observations concerning the perspectives taken by "non-disabled people who do not stigmatize, stereotype, and reject those with obvious disabilities," Bogdan and Taylor note the importance of "seeing individuality in the other" and of "defining a social place for the other" (1989, p. 138). As we have seen from Robillard's and Denton's commentaries, the people who most readily enter into the alternative time order that their augmented interactions require are individuals who already share a considerable amount of cultural common ground with them. It should be obvious that the ability to "define a social place for the other" will be much easier when that individual already has a locus within the local social matrix that one inhabits. There are huge savings in joint time in interactions when both speaker and addressee can presume large amounts of shared background knowledge (communal common ground).

We conclude by returning to one other aspect of group membership that is often taken for granted, but which must be considered more carefully when investigating the cultural matrix of augmented communications. In the introduction we noted that, by being members of the same culture, we are all (both the them and the us) subject to the same institutional reference points, and in our communicative interactions we rely on the same set of unquestioned sociocultural givens. Not surprisingly, it is a fact that with respect to their face-to-face augmented interactions, Creech, Robillard, and Denton also share many of the same beliefs as to what constitutes the nature of effective communication held by other speakers of American English. For instance, Robillard (personal communication, April 1997) states that his choice of device and his temporal problems with regulating interlocutor attention are based, in part, on his own affiliation with the broader community of English speakers and the prominent use of gaze in that community. He writes:

> I think it is a question of membership. I belong to the gaze membership and I equally belong to the notion that others belong to gaze as a method of regulating conversation. There is nothing sacred about gaze. It is only a membership qualification. Of course, this is played out in experience.

The identification and elucidation of such "membership qualifications" and the examination of how they are "played out in experience" must be seen as crucial components in any future investigation of augmented interactions, and in the broader discourse on how communicative competence and incompetence are both socially constructed and deconstructed.

REFERENCES

Bogdan, R., & Taylor, S. T. (1989). Social construction of humanness: Relationships with severely disabled people. *Social Problems, 39*(2), 135–148.

Buzolich, M. J., & Wiemann, J. M. (1988). Turn taking in atypical conversations: The case of the speaker/augmented-communicator dyad. *Journal of Speech and Hearing Research, 31*, 3–18.

Clark, H. (1996). *Using language*. New York: Cambridge University Press.

Creech, R. (1992). *Working toward a master's degree in speech pathology as an augmented communicator.* Paper presented at the Minspeak Conference, Wooster, OH. (Available HTTP://kaddath.mt.cs.cmu.edu/scs/procs.html)

Creech, R. (1996a). *Extemporaneous speaking: Pragmatic principles.* Paper presented at the 4th Annual Pittsburgh Employment Conference, Pittsburgh, PA.

Creech, R. (1996b). *Speaker's bureau: System operators.* Paper presented at the Minspeak Conference, Wooster, OH. Available HTTP://kaddath.mt.cs.cmu.scs.procs.html

Higginbotham, D. J. (1989). The interplay of communication device output mode and conversational style between nonspeaking persons and their speaking partners. *Journal of Speech and Hearing Disorders, 54,* 320–333.

Higginbotham, D. J., Mathy-Laikko, P., & Yoder, D. E. (1988). Studying conversations of augmentative systems users. In L. Bernstein (Ed.), *The vocally impaired: Clinical practice and research* (pp. 265–294). New York: Grune & Stratton.

Higginbotham, D. J., & Wilkins, D. P. (1997). *Factors governing the contextual selection of different communication media in the interactions of a person who cannot produce mouth speech.* Manuscript in preparation.

Hoag, L. A., Bedrosian, J. L., Johnson, D. E., & Molineux, B. (1994). Variables affecting perceptions of social aspects of the communicative competence of an adult AAC user. *Augmentative and Alterative Communication, 10*(3), 129.

McDermott, R., & Varenne, H. (1995). Culture as disability. *Anthropology & Education Quarterly, 26*(3), 324–348.

Robillard, A. B. (1994). Communication problems in the intensive care unit. *Qualitative Sociology, 17*(4), 383–395.

Sacks, H., Schegloff, E. A., & Jefferson, G. N. (1974). A simplest systematics for the organization of turn-taking for conversation. *Language, 50,* 696–735.

Sweidel, G. B. (1991/1992). Management strategies in the communication of speaking persons and persons with a speech disability. *Research on Language and Social Interactions, 25,* 195–214.

APPENDIX: JANE DENTON'S COMMUNICATION DEVICES

yes	A	B	C	D	E	F	G	H	I	J	K	L	M	no
PTL	N	O	P	Q	R	S	T	U	V	W	X	Y	Z	Denton
0	1	2	3	4	5	6	7	8	9	10	+	's	$	
	Sun	Mon	Tues	Wed	Thur	Fri	Sat		!	?	+…	-	BT.W.	Jane
A	about	add	Dad	Day	did	is	I	its	other	our	out	them	then	there
after	again	aide	diff-	do	does	joy	Jesus	just	outside	over	own	these	they	thing
all	also	always	don't	down	Dr.	keep	knew	know	pants	part	peace	think	this	these
am	Amen	an	each	eat	-ed	left	leg	let	people	phone	place	thought	time	to
and	answer	any	enough	-er	-es	like	little	long	please	praise	pray	today	told	tomorrow
anything	anyway	are	even	ever	every	look	Lord	lot	prayer	pretty	Psalms	too	top	try
around	am	as	for	faith	first	love	loving	-ly	put	quiet	quite	Ugh!	um-	under
ask	at	ate	get	friend	from	make	man	many	really	right	room	until	up	us
back	be	before	go	give	glory	may	me	mean	S	said	saint	use	verse	very
because	been	between	good	God	going	mine	Mom	more	same	saw	say	want	was	way
behind	better	bless	hair	got	had	morning	most	M.	see	seen	self	we	week	well
Bible	big	brother	have	hallelujah	has	Mrs.	much	my	she	should	side	went	what	what
book	bottom	by	here	he	her	name	never	new	sister	sit	so	wheelchair	when	where
build	but	can	him	hi	high	next	no	not	socks	some	something	which	white	who
call	can	Christ	home	his	Holy	now	-n't	nurse	speak	start	study	why	will	with
chapter	change	class	i	how	I	of	off	old	take	talk	teeth	won't	word	work
Christian	church	course	in	I'll	I'm	on	one	only	than		that	would	year	yesterday
come	could			-ing	into	open	or	order	that's	the	their	you	your	Denton

FIG. A.1. Graphic reconstruction of Jane's word and letter board. The original board is color coded.

81

FIG. A.2. Dynavox communicaiton device. Note that the top row presents a new set of "predicted" words after each keystroke.

Chapter 4

How Opposing Perceptions of Communication Competence Were Constructed by Taiwanese Graduate Students

Carol Jorgensen Winkler
University of Texas at Austin

For a year and a half, I have followed six Taiwanese women who were new to the United States and new to a graduate program in a large university. As a part of that study I asked the question, "How has a sense of communication competence (or incompetence) been constructed in these individuals' interactions with friends, fellow students, teachers, and others?"

This chapter discusses how two opposing perceptions of communication competence were created, how they evolved over time, and ultimately, what impact these perceptions had on the participants' views of themselves. Rather than recount the stories of all six participants, I report on the two that represent the extremes of the competence continuum. In essence, these stories reveal how one individual constructed a belief in her communication competence, while the other created a strong sense of communication incompetence. Though differing in outcome, each of the two accounts reflects the power of seminal or watershed events in altering perceptions of competence and ultimately beliefs about the self.

A BRIEF LITERATURE REVIEW

The term *communication competence* was first coined by Dell Hymes (1972), who wanted to account for the social and functional rules of language. The second language learning literature established its own version of communication competence as the ability to convey meaning and to successfully combine a knowledge of linguistic and sociolinguistic rules in communicative interactions (Savignon, 1971). In the 1990s, communication competence has come to be defined as "that aspect of our competence that enables us to convey and interpret messages and to negotiate meanings interpersonally within specific contexts" (Brown, 1994, p. 227).

In the field of speech communication, effectiveness and appropriateness are viewed as the primary features in defining competence (Rubin, 1991; Spitzberg & Cupach, 1984). More specifically, communication competence is defined as "knowledge about appropriate and effective communication behaviors, development of a repertoire of skills that encompass both appropriate and effective means of communicating, and motivation to behave in ways that are viewed as both appropriate and effective by interactants" (Rubin, 1991, p. 289).

Although the ostensible focus of this chapter is communication competence, there is a wider lens that not only frames the discussion of competence but that also explains or accounts for the changes in identity which the participants experienced in themselves. The wider lens is social construction—the creation of self in the context of social interaction using language as the interactive medium (Gergen, 1994).

Gergen traced constructionist views to recent explorations in ideological critique, literary and rhetorical processes, and the social basis of scientific knowledge, all of which form the foundation for the "postmodern turn" in the academic world. This "postmodern turn" has paved the way to the scientific practice known as social constructionism. There are five major suppositions that according to Gergen (1994, pp. 49–51) are central to a social constructionist account of knowledge. Two of them have particular relevance for this chapter:

- The terms by which we account for the world and ourselves are not dictated by the stipulated objects of such accounts.
- The degree to which a given account of world or self is sustained across time is not dependent on the objective validity of the account but on the vicissitudes of social process.

Below, I elaborate on each supposition and look at the implications not only for interpretation, but for the individual participants involved.

The first supposition states that *the terms by which we account for the world and ourselves are not dictated by the stipulated objects of such accounts.* Expressed in another way, there is no direct one-to-one correspondence between what is "out there" in the physical world and the language used to describe it, explain it, and account for it. According to Gergen (1994), "in its most radical form, [this supposition] proposes that there are no *principled* constraints over our characterization of states of affairs" (p. 49).

The implication for this research is that the particular rendering or interpretation of the participants' words and stories expressed within these pages represents only one of many possible depictions. Another researcher could look at the multiple pages of transcripts and render a completely different account. Similarly, the words that the participants used to describe and share their experiences represent only one possibility of many. Given a different interviewer, a different day, a different mood, they might have told a different story—yet the events about which they speak would not have altered. The ephemeral, dynamic, even idiosyncratic nature of representation through language is made apparent with this first supposition of social constructionism.

The second supposition states that *the degree to which a given account of world or self is sustained across time is not dependent on the objective validity of the account but on the vicissitudes of social process.* Any individual's account or interpretation of the world or of him- or herself may remain stable in spite of actual variations in that world and/or the self; similarly, that account may alter even when the world or the person undergoes no change. The "objective truth" is not the key to the accounts (or their alteration), rather it is the social relationships that play the determining role.

Such a supposition sounds a cautionary note for research interpretation. It must be kept in mind that what the participants shared about themselves across the course of the year may or may not have corresponded to the actual objective experience. The participants may have altered their perceptions of themselves without any corroborating real-life events or happenings, or likewise, maintained as stable a self-perspective in the face of counter evidence. The determining factor in their accounts is the social relationships of which they were a part.

To summarize, then, within the frame of social constructionism, a particular interpretive point of view is required—that of seeing both the participants' words and the author's words as *interpretations* or *stories* of actual events that arose out of a variety of social relationships.

Social constructionism as explanation requires that we look to Gergen (1991, 1994) and Bruner (1986, 1990). As stated earlier, in the constructionist view, self is created or constructed in social interaction using language as the interactive medium (Gergen, 1991, 1994). By participating in a variety of social interactions using English as the medium of exchange, the two participants altered their sense of themselves, and in effect constructed new identities for themselves.

Bruner (1986, 1990) asserted that we construct ourselves and our worlds using language in the context of social interactions: "Just as I believe that we construct or constitute the world, I believe too that Self is a construction, a result of action and symbolism" (1986, p. 130). Bruner saw the self as a narrative text about "how one is situated with respect to others and toward the world—a canonical text about powers and skills and dispositions that change as one's situation changes from young to old, from one kind of setting to another" (1986, p. 130). To Bruner, the interpretation of this text by an individual "*is* his sense of self in that situation" (p. 130)—made up of expectations, feelings of esteem and power and inextricably linked in relationship. "Self becomes enmeshed in a net of others" (Bruner, 1990, p. 114). The implication is that self is not stable or permanent, but changes over time and circumstance.

Gergen (1994), like Bruner, saw the power of narrative and relationship in creating the self. "I replace the traditional concern with conceptual categories (self-concepts, schemas, self-esteem) with the self as a narration rendered intelligible within ongoing relationships" (p. 185).

> In the postmodern world there is no individual essence to which one remains true or committed. One's identity is continuously emergent, re-formed, and redirected as one moves through the sea of ever-changing relations. In the case of "Who am I?" it is a teeming world of provisional possibilities. . . . For good or ill, it is the individual as socially constructed that finally informs people's patterns of action. (Gergen, 1991, pp. 139, 146)

As frame and explanation, social constructionism provides the basis for interpreting the stories shared within this chapter.

THE PARTICIPANTS

A total of six Taiwanese females participated in the study. They ranged in age from 22 to 26 years, were new to the graduate program, and also newly arrived to the United States as of the summer of 1995. Their chosen majors included journalism, second language teaching, curriculum and instruction, adult education, and nursing. All participants displayed sufficient English conversational proficiency to converse about themselves and their feelings as demonstrated through verbal interviews conducted at the study's outset. They were recruited through the Taiwanese Student Association, the university's international student programs, and through social network leaders within the Taiwanese community. The focus of this chapter is a more detailed history of the two individuals, "Valerie" and "Mary."[1]

Valerie was a 24-year-old journalism major who grew up in Taipei with her parents and an older brother and sister. Her father was retired from a career in agricultural products, her mother was a housewife, her brother

---

[1]Although these are not their real names, both participants adopted American names on their arrival in the United States—Valerie at the suggestion of an English teacher in Taiwan; Mary at the suggestion of an aunt who lived in Canada.

a graduate student in law, and her sister a host for a children's TV program. When asked what values her parents conveyed to her, Valerie replied, "My parents just want me to live happy. . . . They just want me to have professional knowledge and I can get a job and then live happy."

Valerie described her life growing up in Taiwan as happy, carefree, and very comfortable. As the youngest child, she was sheltered by her parents and older siblings; she considered herself outgoing, always smiling, and having many friends. When she talked about the year she spent before coming to the United States (and just after college graduation), she said, "I could go anywhere I wanted, buy anything I wanted. . . . I just play and don't have any troubles."

Valerie's English training began, as it does for all Taiwanese students, in junior high and continued through high school. All of Valerie's junior high and senior high teachers were native Taiwanese who focused more on the reading aspect of English than on either speaking or listening. In fact, Valerie indicated that the students did not speak English in their classes and that, "the teachers [even] taught English in Chinese." At the university, Valerie majored in English literature, and it was in this environment that she experienced her first native English teachers. Even here, however, she had only a few courses where she spoke English. This formal education provided Valerie's only experiences with English.

When Valerie graduated from the university, she didn't want to work, so she decided to come to America to study. For her, it was an easier way to accomplish higher educational goals. "Because in Taiwan, if you want to study in graduate school, you have to take a test and you have to read a lot of books . . . but chance you can get to graduate school is very small, so I don't want to take it." According to Valerie, it was much easier to get into a graduate school in the United States than in Taiwan and so that's what she decided to do.

Mary was a 25-year-old adult education major who grew up in Taipei with her parents and a younger brother and older sister. Mary's father was a manager of personnel at Johnson and Johnson, her mother an elementary school teacher, and her brother a stockbroker. Mary's sister died in her senior year at the university after an 8-year battle with leukemia. Two days prior to her sister's death, her parents divorced.

When asked to describe herself, Mary replied, "I'm shy. I think I hate to speak. . . . it's hard for me to care somebody else, my feelings inside, I always hide." According to Mary, she grew up as "the stupid child." As if she were providing a textbook example, Mary shared that she learned to think about herself as others thought of her.

> I think I still don't think about myself with my opinions. It's because someone else opinion about me influence me a lot. I think I'm good, not because I'm good but because they tell me I'm good. Yeah, so, my parents have

three children and they always told me I'm the stupid one. . . . And I agree
with that because my elder sister very smart and my younger brother, too.
But, so I always think I'm not good enough. Since my childhood.[2]

Mary was the only one of the six participants who grew up in a Christian
family. She stated, however, that the beliefs that come from Christianity are
really no different from traditional Chinese thinking: ". . . if you are
Christian, the Bible influence you. But I think in the Bible, we must be kind
person and to be nice to others, and it's . . . almost like traditional Chinese."

Mary's junior and senior high English classes were also taught by native
Taiwanese teachers. In Mary's case, the emphasis was distributed evenly
among reading, writing, and speaking English. Mary acknowledged, however, that English was spoken in class but not in any part of daily life. Mary
majored in history at the college, where all of her classes were taught in
Chinese. The extent of Mary's English learning, therefore, was the 6 years
spent in junior and senior high school.

For Mary, the decision to come to the United States was not hers, but
her parents': "my parents give me a idea that I have to go abroad to study."
Although Mary's graduate major at the university is adult education, her
first preference would have been music. The expense of a music career
prohibited her pursuit of that field.

Summary

The two women present very different portraits of their lives in Taiwan.
Valerie had been pampered and looked after, and had lived a carefree
life of leisure with virtually no problems. Mary, on the other hand, grew
up feeling stupid and not good enough. She lost an older sister to leukemia
when she was in college and experienced her parents' divorcing two days
prior to her sister's death. Valerie described herself as outgoing and happy,
Mary as quiet, shy, and hating to talk. Valerie chose to come to the United
States to study; for Mary, the choice was her parents' and not her own.
Valerie's major in English literature provided her with numerous courses
in college English. Mary received no English training beyond high school.
After 1 year in the United States, one of these individuals constructed a
strong perception of herself as communicatively competent, the other
communicatively incompetent.

DATA COLLECTION

Data were collected almost entirely via individual interviews. Each participant was interviewed in her home four to five times between August of

---

[2]These are Mary's *perceptions* and *memories* from her past, and may be remembered
differently by others in her family.

1995 and June of 1996. Interviews lasted 1½ to 2 hours and were both audio and video recorded and later transcribed. This researcher also communicated with the participants via E-mail messages. The level of participation varied for each participant, with the total number of messages ranging from 5 to 28 throughout the study.

The initial interview was conducted to gain background information on the participants, including family and cultural backgrounds, English-learning experiences, expectations about living in America, stories heard regarding Americans, motivations for coming to the United States, cultural perceptions of self and identity, existing support structure, and career plans. Additional interviews were open-ended, but guided by general requests to share their communication experiences, their perceptions of those experiences, and the impact these experiences had on their views of themselves and others.

In the E-mail interactions, participants were asked to share various experiences and encounters and to pay specific attention to how these experiences affected the ways they viewed themselves and others. In addition, the participants frequently initiated interactions via E-mail with topics of their own choosing.

In an effort to uncover the evolving nature of the participants' perceptions of their communication competence, a naturalistic or qualitative research methodology was utilized. Data were analyzed via a cyclical process of sampling, inductive analysis, grounded theory building, and emergent design until a coherent story on these views emerged.[3]

Valerie's Story: The Construction
of Communicative Incompetence

Although journalism is a particularly taxing field for foreign students because of its heavy requirements for both writing and speaking, Valerie felt confident in her English ability and fully capable of tackling her graduate work in the United States. However, out of one critical interaction, Valerie related in the following story that she was no longer a competent communicator in English and should stop communicating in her classes and with her American acquaintances for fear of revealing her poor communication skills.

As part of the standard routine for international students newly arrived in the United States, each student is interviewed by the university's international director to determine any needs the student might have, particularly regarding his or her English. During Valerie's interview, the director told her that it might be necessary for her to take an oral communication course. She asked Valerie to return to her office for another interview in

---

[3]It should be noted that the issue of interest in this study is the not the participants' written work, but rather the changes in their sense of competence that came about from their oral interactions.

about six weeks. In Valerie's own words (as shared with me in our first interview on September 25, 1995):

> V: After the international director, Karen Keen,[4] asked me to take oral communication, because I think my English okay, not as bad as that, I should take the oral communication course. So after she talk to me that I have to take a course, I just feel so frustrated and I just feel that my English so bad. And at this time, I don't want speak English and I just don't dare to speak English, I just feel, just right now I just that my English so bad because Karen Keen ask me to take the course. And I just OH! my English so bad and right now I little bit afraid to talk English and I sometimes don't want to talk English. If my friend here, I just let him talk, I just don't talk English because at first in the beginning I don't afraid to talk, but just because say that my English is so poor, from that time I just think I am so poor and I am afraid to talk.
>
> C: So, so in other words ... just her saying that made you have a different view of yourself as an English-speaker.
>
> V: Yeah. Yeah. A lot, a lot, she change me a lot in my view to my English communication.

This was clearly a seminal event in Valerie's life. After just one interchange with the international director, Valerie's view of herself was significantly altered. Confidence in her English ability was replaced by doubt. A willingness and eagerness to communicate was replaced by resistance and fearfulness. In reality, nothing about Valerie's "actual" English ability changed during the interview—that ability was virtually the same at the end of the interview as it was when the interview began. What *did* alter, however, was Valerie's view of herself as an English communicator; her perception was *reconstructed* from one of competence to one of incompetence.

During this first interview together, Valerie talked more about what happened to her sense of confidence after speaking with the international director.

> V: But maybe I lose my confidence. . . . . It's hard to get your confidence back you know. For someone to check you. It's hard.
>
> C: How would you think the best way to get your confidence back would be?
>
> V: I don't know. . . . . Karen Keen word said that my English is poor. It's really, how to say in English. It's really a big change, I don't how to express English. . . . . It's really a big shock. . . . . I just totally lose my confidence.

The fallout from that one interaction kept occurring for Valerie. Not only had she lost her confidence as a competent English-speaker, she

---

[4]A false name has been substituted for the director's real name.

didn't have a sense of how to regain it. To make matters worse, other incidents eroded her confidence. Setting up phone service with Southwestern Bell was particularly challenging and frustrating for her:

> Because in the beginning, you have to apply for a telephone, so I call Southwestern Bell, but I cannot understand what she is talking about. Yeah. I just say yes, yes, yes, yes, yes. And then my friend telephone for me to say, no, no she doesn't want these item, she doesn't yeah.

As we ended our first interview, Valerie shared how frustrating these first months in the United States had been for her. Not only had the situation with the international director and her problems with English upset her, she was lonely and desperately wanted the happy and carefree life she had left in Taiwan:

> [At home] I don't have any trouble, anything that I should think about. Every day I was so happy. But after I come here, just myself alone. . . . I just feel, so I cry. I feel so uncertain. And I become very sad. . . . I tell myself the Valerie in Taiwan disappear. . . . All of the things I have to deal with, just by myself. I have to decide everything.

Valerie's whole sense of herself—as competent communicator and as happy, carefree girl—was slipping away from her. Here in the United States she not only had to do things she had never done before, she had to do them on her own, without the support she had always known.

Valerie and I had a number of conversations via E-mail following our first interview. Many of those conversations revolved around the upcoming interview with the international director and Valerie's continuing and overwhelming feelings of incompetence. In late October, we exchanged the following E-mail messages:

From Valerie on October 17th.

I haven't talk to Karen Keen yet. I plan to talk to her next week. But I think she will absolutely ask me to take the oral communication course. Take care!

My reply on October 17th.

Tell me why you say that Karen Keen will "absolutely" ask you to take the oral communication course. What makes you think that?

By the way, you were going to be calling me to get some practice with your English. Don't you want to do that anymore? I would be more than willing to do that with you. As a matter of fact, I would like it. Let me know.

From Valerie on October 18th.

Hello, Carol: Why I think Karen Keen will absolutely ask me to take the course is because that her requirement is very high. And people tell me that international office always wants students to take their courses, and then they can have students and earn money. Besides, I don't think my English can improve a lot in such a short period of time.

I really would like to practice my English with you, but I think it's just waste you time. I am afraid that it is inconvenient to you. So that's why I am not calling you to practice my English. Thank you for your kind attention.

You can see from these exchanges that Valerie was becoming resigned and fatalistic. She was sure she would have to take the oral communication course and just as sure that practicing her English would make no difference in her performance.

Valerie was scheduled to meet with the international director for her follow-up interview on October 22. She called me that morning, extremely nervous and apprehensive. I wished her luck and asked her to call or E-mail me once the interview was completed. I received an E-mail that afternoon.

Hi, Carol: Thank you for your help and encouragement. I finally passed "the exam." Karen Keen just talked to me about 7–8 minutes, and then she said I really improve a lot and she thought that I didn't have to take the oral communication course. It really a great relief to me. Anyway I feel very happy today. Hope you have a nice weekend.

I responded with the following:

Congratulations!! That is wonderful that you don't have to take the course. Now, here are my questions related to that:
1. What do you think about your English speaking ability now?
2. Do you feel like you have improved (in other words, do you agree with Karen Keen's assessment of you?)
3. What is your predominant feeling about yourself right now?

Valerie sent an E-mail a few days later.

Hi, Carol: What list below is my answer.
1. I just think it was the same. But at least I can use my English to communicate with others.
2. I don't think that my English has improved. I don't know why Karen Keen thought that I really improved a lot.
3. The same as I used to be.

While Valerie was happy she didn't have to take the course, she was not willing to accept the idea that she might have improved. She did admit she could communicate with others, but overall, Valerie was forming an identity of herself as an incompetent English-speaker.

My second interview with Valerie occurred on November 1, 1995, not quite two weeks after her "passing" interview with the international director. I was interested in how she'd been feeling about herself since Karen Keen had commented on her improved English and released her from the oral communication course.

C: Since you've had your meeting with Karen Keen have you felt better about your English?

V: No, because I don't think . . . I don't think that my English have been good. So I just . . . I think I have used it while I have wanted to how I speak to her just like in the first time I talked to her. I don't think I have improved, so I just feel strange why she say I have improved a lot.

To get a sense of how others might be reacting to her, I asked about any feedback she was receiving.

C: Has anybody said anything to you about your speech?

V: . . . I think most Americans . . . always say, "Oh, your English is very good or something else," they won't say, "Your English is very bad." They always encouraging you, I think. So as of right now I don't hear people say that your English is very bad. I always hear people say, "Oh, your English is quite good."

C: And do you believe that?

V: I don't believe that.

Notice again how Valerie was not willing to believe (or not willing to acknowledge that she believed) feedback that ran counter to the way she was thinking about herself in terms of her English incompetence. Rather than accept what others offered her, she had found a way to explain it: they don't want to hurt her feelings, they're being nice, that's what Americans do. In addition, these people did not hold the prestige or power that the international director held—they weren't in any kind of gate-keeping role. Nevertheless, the sense of self that she had created as an incompetent English-speaker was becoming ingrained and she seemed unwilling to give it up.

In that same interview, I asked Valerie if there was anything that would change her mind about her competence in English.

C: Is there anything that would make you think you were good in English?

V: I don't think so.

C: But you came thinking you were good in English.

V: . . . actually because in class or social settings right now, I don't think that I can communicate very well because some times we talk to our classmates . . . for example we met my classmates in . . . in library or we went to a barbecue last time. Sometimes I want to talk about some-

thing but I don't know how to . . . I can express but I don't think I
express very well.

Valerie admitted that there was nothing that anybody could say or do to
have an impact on her perceptions of herself in relation to her English
ability. And she supplied evidence to support her perception of herself as
incompetent to show that she experienced trouble communicating with
friends and classmates.

Valerie also stated that her incompetence in English might be the reason
that she couldn't become good friends with Americans: "I just think that's
why we can't make good friends with Americans because it's a barrier
there, you can't communicate very well." So the belief that she was not a
good communicator had given rise to a reason why she could not be good
friends with Americans. Out of her *perception* came claims and beliefs about
what she couldn't do.

When I saw Valerie for our third interview, it was February of 1996, and
she had just begun the second semester of her graduate program. I discovered in this interview that she had almost quit school on her return from her
month-long Christmas break in Taiwan, and had even begun the tuition
refund process before a friend (an older Taiwanese Ph.D. student) persuaded her to stay. On the positive side, she had also gotten a Korean roommate, and by the time I saw her Valerie seemed fairly happy with the roommate arrangement and with her choice to stay and complete her degree.

She talked about the communication problems she was encountering
with her new roommate and also spoke about an incident that happened
in the airport in California on her way back from Taiwan over Christmas
break. In both incidents Valerie saw that her English skills actually changed
depending on the skills of the conversational partners with whom she was
interacting. I've italicized the phrases that reflect Valerie's awareness of
that influence. In each case, Valerie found that her skills either improved
or deteriorated, but they always altered to match the skills of her partner.

C: And so the two of you [you and your new roommate] converse in English
then?
V: Yeah, we have to converse in English.
C: That is so cool!
V: I know, but you know *because his[5] English not very good, my English not
very good* [italics added]. He's even worse than me. . . . So, I just, I think
my English is become worse and worse and worse. Yeah, because when
I came back to Taiwan, I stop by San Francisco. And I have no, I have

---

[5]Valerie tends to misuse masculine and feminine pronouns. Her roommate is actually a
female. You will notice that the mix-up continues throughout this exchange.

know a lot of guy there. And they have very good at English, so I just keep talking and talking and talking, after feel, oh, "my English is very good, cuz I can speak fluently." I, *so I think because they speak English very good, so that's why I speak very good too* [italics added]. But I talk to her sometime, I will feel problem. I think, so I think my English sound worse and worse. When I talk to her.

C: When you talk to her.

V: Yeah, *because he has problem communication. I will influence by her* [italics added].

Valerie continued this discussion. Notice that for the first time she was willing to acknowledge (at least occasionally), that she *could* speak English fluently and that she *could* express what she wanted to say. An important question to ask is, does this mark the beginning of a departure from the identity of incompetence that Valerie had constructed or did she view it as a fleeting, temporary aberration?

C: So when you, when you said you came back through San Francisco and you had a bunch of friends there?

V: I just met them in the airport. . . . They are Malaysia and some Asian country but they stay the States for many years, so their English is very good. . . . Yeah, and they just say, "oh, your English is very good. Just got United for about four months." They say it's incredible, I think, I say no, my English. *But I can feel, when I talk to them, I can talk very fluently.*

C: Yeah. Why do you think you could talk so fluently with them?

V: I don't know but I don't have any problem communication with them. I just feel very strange. . . . *because I can express what I want to say.* I just keep talking to them in English I feel, at that time I feel it's very good because I. . . . Yeah, I don't know why, *that's the first time I feel I can speak English very fluently.*

C: Yeah.

V: Yeah. But, never again. [Mutual laughter]

The last line of this interchange, "But, never again," seemed to answer the question posed. Valerie was not constructing herself anew as a competent English-speaker. The sense of fluency and competency she felt was simply a short-lived, momentary experience.

There was more evidence that Valerie's view of herself as an incompetent English-speaker was not changing. I asked her how much of the time she'd been talking in English and she responded, "I think most of the time I talk in English right now. . . . But it's a bad English." Even though she was speaking English the majority of the time, she was not improving (i.e., she was still incompetent). She also provided two reasons why she wasn't improving. First, "The people I met is not good at English. They will make my English be more bad." And second, "I think maybe cuz it's not American if I talk to American 80%, I think will make difference. . . . Yeah. I think that's why can't improve my English, even though I spend lot of time speak English. . . ."

By saying that her English would be improving *if* that English-speaking time were with Americans, by admitting to how poor *her* English was when she interacted with poor English-speakers, she was also acknowledging how important conversational partners were to her own competence.

Just as Valerie's view of herself as incompetent was not changing over time, neither was her mistrust and disbelief in the positive feedback she received. It was February, and Valerie's comments regarding feedback were virtually the same as the comments she made in her second interview in November.

> V: Feedback. . . . I have a presentation, but I just tell you I think the teacher's classmates is really kind, so when I finish my presentation, the teacher just say, "Wow, you are good." I can't believe that.
>
> C: You don't believe it.
>
> V: My teacher say, "I believe you have done such a good job," and my rest of my class claps his hand. I just say thank you thank you so much, but I don't think I have, I have done my job so good, but they just keep press me, say, "oh, you are very good." but they are so kind, you know. Yeah.

Even though she shared specifics about the kind of feedback she was getting (the teacher saying "Wow, you are good") and about what people were actually doing (the classmates applauded her), she seemed unwilling to deviate from describing herself as an incompetent English communicator.

I interviewed Valerie for the fourth and final time in April of 1996, a few weeks before the second semester was over. She seemed happier and more peaceful than I'd ever seen her. I asked her how she was feeling about her English and she said that it was the same or possibly just a bit worse. Since she'd just returned from a trip to Taiwan for spring break, she was finding it more difficult to express herself and to organize her thoughts in English.

I asked her where she thought she was most competent now as an English-speaker.

> C: Where do you feel that you're, you're best as an English-speaker? Where do you feel like you do the best job? You're most competent?
>
> V: I still feel if I talk to a stranger, we don't know each other . . . if I go back to Taiwan, have to transfer the plane. . . . If I meet someone there, I don't know him or her, and they don't know me, and we just talk, I think at that time I can do good job, I can talk fluently and they will say, "Wow, your English is good." and I say, "no, no, no" but I can tell

that time I can speak very well, I don't know why. I can talk and talk and talk and they can understand me, I can understand them. We just talk, but I don't know why.

Valerie also shared where she felt least competent.

V: But when I talk in class I feel I can't express my opinion or something very well.

C: Yeah. It's hard for you to do that.

V: Yeah, but I think. I don't know, I get tongue-tied or something. . . . I don't know, I just—I just—try to explain my feeling and—suddenly, I just get tongue-tied, I don't know. How do you say that? Hard to—hard to explain what I want to say to the teacher. I don't know.

But at this point, Valerie described a shift in her attitude about her "incompetent" English or about the mistakes she made.

But I won't feel sad about that. Because I'm pretty—kind of get used to that this semester. "Oh, it's okay" I just—talk. I think—they can understand me even if I don't talk in a correct way, but I just keep talk. [Laughs] Yeah. If the teacher don't understand you, he will ask you again, so, I don't mind.

Two things seem to have altered for Valerie. First, the overwhelming sadness she had been experiencing was not present for her as it was in the past; second, she was not letting her mistakes or her concern about being inadequate stop her. In other words, her "incompetent" English was no longer holding her back or incapacitating her. She admitted that she still might feel a little sad when people couldn't understand her, but the amount of time she spent dwelling on that sadness was short.

C: And it doesn't bother you if somebody has a little bit of trouble or if you don't feel you do a great job.

V: Actually, if I—actually I will feel "oh, if I can't say" I still feel, I still feel so low, but people still can't understand me, actually sometime I will feel a little bit sad, but not too sad. After a while, one or two minutes? It's okay. . . .

C: So you get over it fast.

V: Yeah. Well actually I will feel sad at the beginning of one or two minutes, yeah, but, later, nothing. Not a big deal.

Valerie shared in this final interview that she'd actually started to feel happy about living in the United States. She felt she'd finally adjusted and was enjoying her life here. It had taken her almost two full semesters, but she now was doing what she wanted—in spite of her constructed identity of incompetent speaker. She had managed to see English speech as only one part of her self in the United States.

Mary's Story: The Construction
of Communicative Competence

In this section we will explore Mary's evolution from the shy, quiet, un-communicative individual who arrived in the United States in the summer of 1995, to the confident and self-expressive English-communicator that she became after a year of living here. Mary's story is a counterpoint to Valerie's story. In a phenomenal re-creation of herself into a competent, confident speaker of English, Mary overcame a past in which she knew herself (and was known as) the shy, quiet one who didn't share herself and who listened more than she talked. Out of her experiences here in the United States—with her church, her university classes, and her room-mates—Mary confessed to feeling more confident as a speaker of English than she was as a speaker of Chinese.

My first interview with Mary took place on September 21, 1995. You may recall that Mary was the participant who had no English experience or practice beyond high school. At the time of the interview, Mary had been in the United States for only 1 month. I was curious about what had been most difficult for her in using English to communicate.

> M: Hardest thing? Everybody wants me to talk about my country, my family. It's hard for me to speak. But I can listen, but it's hard for me to speak. I think . . . it's a big problem. But the other is, even in my country, when I in my country, I speak less. It's I think a personality.
> C: So you're shy in general.
> M: Yeah. Yeah.

She shared that speaking in class was also hard for her. She was not sure she comprehended the reading assignments, and to then be asked to share her opinions about them was terrifying for her. Though volun-teering and speaking in class made her nervous in Taiwan, the language component here made it worse for her.

When I asked Mary what she thought about herself in light of these difficulties, she said: "I think I'm not good enough and I have to prepare and learn more." This perspective was consistent with her identity in Tai-wan: "not good enough" and "stupid."

However, in spite of her fears and self-judgments, Mary had already created a number of opportunities for speaking English. She was attending a Christian church where "on the Lord's day, we honor him in English." Of her two roommates, one was American with whom she had to speak English. And, as part of the adult education graduate program at the university, Mary belonged to a cohort of graduate students who would remain together throughout their graduate program. Because there were no other Chinese or Taiwanese individuals in this cohort, Mary was forced to speak English with them. Mary noticed an inability to communicate deep thoughts and feelings in English; as of this first interview she had only spoken such thoughts and feelings to her Chinese roommate. This ability was important to Mary and she was anxious to see how this aspect of her English communication would unfold over time, particularly since one of her goals was to remain in this country. To be successful, however, she knew that she would have to present herself differently—as someone who shared herself, was more social, and who was willing to converse with people she didn't know.

> M: Um, because if I want to survive here and live happily I must to change my, the way I live.
> C: In what way?
> M: I need to get along and do things that I don't like to, talk to someone else so much and I think . . . I'm not used to say "Hi" on the bus. . . .

Between our first and second interviews, Mary and I communicated with each other via E-mail. In a series of exchanges in early October, Mary wrote about a frustrating incident that happened at the university computer center with the computer aide:

> I told him I want to send a letter by E-mail. I wanted him to show me how. And that man just started talking and told me how to do. But he used a lot of professional vocabularies that I never heard before. I was so shocked and afraid that I did not know what to do. His manner and face showed me that I am the most stupid person he had ever met. Finally, I called my Chinese roommate and asked her to come here and help me. The solution is I told her what I want to do and she translated it for me to the student and again translated what the man said in Chinese to me. After we sent my letter, it is after 12 a.m. It is terrible.

Clearly, an incompetence in communication was created in this interaction. Mary's inability to comprehend what the aide was saying and his resultant frustration with her ("His manner and face showed me that I am the most stupid person he had ever met") confirmed her long-held belief of herself as stupid. Instead of solving the dilemma through English communication, Mary called in her roommate to translate into Chinese.

In the same E-mail message, Mary told me that two different teachers had praised her use of English—one time for being class moderator and the other for a paper she had written. Mary's reactions indicated that the positive exchanges boosted her self-image, whereas the negative feedback (as with the computer helper) diminished that image.

> At first, I will be very emotional about the situations. I will be very high or very down and be controlled by the feelings. Two or three days past, I will cool down and start to think about how I should do to maintain my good performance and avoid doing wrong again. I appreciated every situation I went through and I told myself I must learn something from it. I am not afraid of making mistakes. I am afraid that I do not get something from the enjoyment or sufferings. I think the experiences could help me grow up.

According to Mary, this reaction represented a shift from who she had been in the past. She was actually looking at how she could benefit from each experience, including the negative ones, and how she could use them to grow and mature.

> Yeah, at—yeah, in Taiwan, I think I am bad and I don't have some kind of ability. I cannot speak in front of my classmates . . . and so someone gave me negative feedback . . . some people will point it out and say, "Mary you . . . made a mistake. You have to improve something." And I just very upset, I cannot do anything, and I will feel in that feeling a long time.

On October 29, Mary sent me an E-mail message telling me she'd been able to express her deeply felt emotions in English. She'd gained a new friend from her classes at school. Since this friend was from Indonesia and did not share the same native language as Mary, the two of them could only communicate using English.

> I have a classmate who came from Indonesia. . . . We are the only foreigners in our classes. . . . We spent a lot of time together since we are alone here. . . . One night, we ate out together tried to treat ourselves. We were talking about our feelings and loneliness. . . . We laughed, felt sad, made fun, and supported each other. We had a wonderful time. We have to communicate in English and we don't speak well. But we still can realize each other and be realized well. I felt happy because having a friend who understands me is exciting for me. And knowing that someone needs me, I can be helpful to my friend is also made me feel worthy. *I am not nobody. I am somebody.* [italics added]

This represents one of the pivotal events for Mary in altering her sense of competence and her sense of self. From this experience, Mary described herself as being a "somebody" instead of a "nobody"—all out of a successful communication in which she could share intimate emotions with a friend and be of service to that person. And Mary stated that even though "we don't speak well," each of them was able to express herself to and be understood by the other. She ended her E-mail to me with a powerful insight: "Actually, language is a problem in communication, but it's not a big deal. Once you want to, you can make it. People can feel if we also open our hearts."

Mary seemed to be saying that with intentionality ("once you want to") and the sharing of one's self ("if we also open our hearts"), communication can take place even if language is a problem. In other words, competence has more to do with a desire and willingness to communicate than it does with grammar and sentence structure.

I interviewed Mary for the second time on November 13, 1995. She'd been living in the United States about three months and although she hadn't perceived improvement in her English, she stated she was much more comfortable speaking English and that almost 60% of the time she spoke in English. What's remarkable is that she estimated that a majority of that English-talking time was spent sharing her feelings. She'd become best friends with the Indonesian woman she spoke about earlier and she was also learning to share her feelings with her cohort of classmates.

Another pivotal set of events occurred for Mary out of her classmates' support of her. When the semester began, Mary wasn't able to say "Hi" to her classmates. Over time she ventured an occasional "Hi" and finally advanced to hugs. Here's how Mary described the progression:

C: What have you noticed that you *have* done, that's different from the way you were when you came?
M: I have done, I mean in the beginning of the semester, when I came to class and I saw my classmates, I did not say anything, I look at them and it means that I say hello to them, but I didn't *say* hello or give them a hug. Now I can "Hi." (Mutual laughter)
C: And are you comfortable doing that?
M: Yeah, I comfortable—and I love to—they teach me. Because at first I hug my classmate I hug her and she tell me, "It's not a hug, Mary," and I say "It *is* a hug." She say "No, I show you how is an American hug." [Sounds of a big hug and laughter]
C: That's amazing.
M: Yeah, at first I'm very uncomfortable because you see, I'm not used to except my boyfriend, so close to the other person. . . .

At this point in her story, I asked Mary how learning to hug made her feel about herself.

M: OK. I know that I change, because it's a big change for me and I notice the change. But sometimes maybe my English improve, maybe, but I don't know. I didn't notice that. But this kind of change I can notice it and I love the change because I know it's there, I know myself. And other ways, I want to, because I want to change too. I want to stay here I must adjust to some of the situations.
C: That's really great.

M: And it seems to me that I can do this, but I can't do the other part.
C: And what's the other part?
M: Speak in front of a lot of people. . . . Yeah, I want to confront the problem.

Through positive experiences with her classmates (as revealed in learning to hug) and the development of a close friendship with an individual, Mary had gained a new confidence for making future communicative adaptations. She seemed ready, for example, to now "confront" her "problem" of speaking in front of groups.

Mary and I met for our third interview on February 3, 1996. She had just begun her second semester at the university and shared that this semester was harder for her because she had not been as excited as she was starting her first semester. However, she did tell me how much more confident she was in her ability to speak English—in fact she confided feeling more confident as an English-speaker than as a Taiwanese-speaker—a phenomenal statement!

C: So you have more confidence when you speak English than when you speak Chinese? Is that what you're saying?
M: Yeah.
C: Wow! How come, do you think?
M: I don't know. I think maybe it's because the people around me they give me feedback. Sometimes I think I cannot describe something and I try, they they have patience, a lot of patient on me.
C: Patience with you, yes.
M: Patience with me, so I say some, I try to describe something and after that they say, "I can totally understand what I feel or what I describe" so I think that make me have more confidence to speak and when, even though I am with a stranger I don't feel that I'm afraid of or I'm shy. . . . You know, when I speak English I'm more confident than when I speak in Chinese.

Relationships with friends have also been pivotal in Mary's increasingly positive view of herself. From their patience and understanding, their support and validation of her, Mary reported increased confidence and less fear and shyness, even with strangers.

The newly confident Mary continued to benefit from both positive and negative feedback. When Mary received negative feedback in Taiwan, she would be immobilized and not able to speak. Here, in the United States, she was disappointed for a while, but worked to improve and ultimately saw the feedback as a contribution to her. Because she was committed to speaking well and doing a good job here, negative feedback occurred more as an opportunity, rather than a self-deflating event. "But here, I am upset too, but after maybe one or two days, I will practice more, I think I must confront the problem . . . if I have to do the presentation next time I will be, I must be better. Yeah."

When I asked what caused this change in her, she wasn't sure, but thought it was the American culture: people, here, were confident and she wanted to gain and possess that confidence.

The newly confident Mary also saw possibility for herself in living in the United States permanently. In the first interview, she saw that if she was to do that successfully, she must become proficient and capable with the English language. In that early interview, however, she had doubts about her ability to do that. In this third interview, she acknowledged that she still had a long way to go, but added, "Now I think it will be possible [if] I keep practice and I learn; it will be possible."

In this third interview, Mary shared that she spoke her best English when she was with her American roommate; next best was in class with the cohort; and third was with salesclerks (as Mary put it, "when I'm go shopping with the sales girls"). Mary spoke a little more about her American roommate and the closeness and sharing they had developed:

> One thing that does surprise me is I have two roommates, one is Chinese and I usually speak with her in Chinese and the other one is American. But after the one semester, I found out that I am more close to the American roommate than the Chinese one because at first I think I'm . . . closer to the Chinese roommate, because we all speak Chinese. Of course . . . I share my feelings to both of them, but it's different kind of feelings. And I'm surprised that my American roommate, she shares some thing I think she might not want to share with foreigner, but she does share with me.

Mary believed she did her worst speaking with people who were acquaintances but not close friends—people who ask questions that seem to her to require that she go below the surface for her answers, but who may not want to hear those deep answers. As she described it:

> . . . it's more like with, not friends, acquaintance. You know we know each other. But not so bad, not so well. And they will ask you this, that, and at that time I cannot express or speak English very well. . . . They always ask a lot of different kind of things. They may ask, "How's your school?" and I think that means they didn't want to spend a lot of time to hear what my school goes, they only *ask*, but I don't think they really want to listen. So I if my roommate, she ask me, "How's your school?" I can, I know what she expect me to say.

Mary had a sense that people didn't want long answers, but she was not quite sure how to respond in those situations. Through her unfamiliarity with these circumstances, a certain sense of interactional incompetence surfaced.

Another place where incompetence may have emerged was when Mary was in stores and had to speak slowly in order for the salespeople to understand her. Yet she noticed that Americans speak very quickly and she found herself wanting to match their rapid rate so they wouldn't be impatient with her. But when she did, she made more mistakes and people had difficulty understanding her. For example, when Mary attempted to match the rate of American speakers (to please them and avoid their impatience) her speech deteriorated and the salesclerks couldn't understand her.

C: Where [else do] you feel like you're least able to communicate?
M: When I speak with someone, they, he or she speak very quickly.
C: Okay, so with rapid speakers.
M: Yeah. Because I know they speak quickly so I have to speak quickly too. I don't know if this is right or wrong, but I think that kind, they don't have so many, so much patience with someone speak very slowly, so I will try to speak quickly too, but that I will make a lot of mistakes.

We ended our third interview with Mary expressing how happy she was and how much she loved school and living in the United States.

I saw Mary for our fourth interview on April 24, 1996, just a few weeks before the end of the second semester. Another watershed event had occurred. She related that she had experienced a very rough time since I last saw her and had almost dropped out of school and returned to Taiwan. She had an English class that was particularly challenging for her, and because she had not completed a paper she had stopped attending school for 2 weeks. Her advisor finally persuaded her to return, arguing that since Mary considered herself a failure whether she quit or didn't quit, she might as well go back and finish. Mary followed that advice and in the process discovered a number of things about herself and the extent of her classmates' support. At the beginning of each week, Mary's teacher asks them to share their feelings and experiences with the class. On the day that Mary returned from her 2-week hiatus, she chose to share with the group. Here are parts of her story:

C: How did you feel [about sharing with the group]?
M: At the beginning I'm very nervous and I don't want to share. But after I share and they gave me feedback. I feel, I feel I came home . . . that kind of feeling. But because our cohort is, the teacher, she wanted our cohort is a group, a team, we do things together. So . . . then we know them, then they know me.

I asked Mary how sharing with her classmates made her feel about herself.

Uh, I feel, I have more blending, or I have more . . . mutual freedom with my classmates. Before I didn't ask for help, I didn't ask my problem, I will think, that's maybe my only problem. And I don't understand that's because I'm a foreigner, I don't understand. But sometimes now, after the class I ask, "What is she saying? I didn't understand at all." And they will tell me, they too didn't understand either. And I think, oh, it's not only my problem. And that's the *teacher's* problem!

By sharing and getting feedback from her classmates, Mary got a chance to see that her self-portrayal as incompetent because of not understanding the teacher was also experienced by native English-speaking classmates; it was not the result of being a foreigner. She also saw the extent to which she was an integral part of her group.

During this fourth interview, we also talked about how she was doing with her English. She told me that she'd increased her English-speaking time to almost 80%—half of that time with native English-speakers and half with non-native English-speakers. Her best friends now included an American and her friend from Indonesia. Both were in her school cohort.

Mary shared further how the sense of competence she now possessed had come from the interactions she had with her cohort.

C: Where do you feel like you're the most competent, the most effective?
M: In my class. . . .
C: How come? What makes you say that?
M: I think [pause] because I feel I'm safe in that group. And they can understand and they *want* to understand me, so I feel more comfortable in speaking in that group. And I know why I speak I not influence but have some reaction to the people I'm talking with, talking to.

Mary's competence emerged from her interactions with and feedback from that group. She saw that her communication had value (her classmates not only understood her, they wanted to understand her) and power (her speaking actually caused reactions in her classmates).

Recall that in the third interview Mary shared that she felt more comfortable as an English-speaker than as a Chinese-speaker. In this interview, she shared how that sense of confidence was continuing and increasing the more she lived here.

I don't know how to say that, but, as a Chinese-speaker, it's easy for me to, to act like before, so I say, so if now I'm with a Chinese-speaking group, then I won't speak. I just stay the way I were. But as English-speaker, if people don't understand me, so I have to speak, try to explain my feelings, describe what I'm thinking. And after I speak I have I have, they give me reaction, feedback, and I feel confidence. But in Chinese, I don't know why. Every time even though some, during last semester I went home, except share my feelings with my boyfriend. With the other friends, I'm just the way I were. And they and they are used to what I want. I just stay what I were. . . . So I think that's why I feel more confident as an English-speaker. And especially people . . . don't know what I was before so . . . for me it's a new start. New beginning that I can talk and they urge me to talk.

Mary was more confident as a speaker of English than of Chinese. Why? Because in Taiwan people thought of Mary in a particular way: Mary doesn't talk, Mary is quiet, Mary doesn't express her opinions. Here in the United States, Mary could create herself anew, without those preconceived notions in place. When she spoke here, people asked her to clarify or explain or to say more, and she did. She worked at making herself understood. And out of that she received positive feedback for her talking, for taking the time and effort for her listeners. And out of that she felt good about herself, and gained confidence that she was a person with valuable things to say and one who could influence her friends. Out of that myriad of interactions, Mary created a confidence that did not exist for her as a Chinese-speaker.

DISCUSSION

At the beginning of this study, I asked the question, "How has a sense of communication competence (or incompetence) been constructed in these individuals' interactions with friends, fellow students, teachers, and others?" I began the chapter with brief definitions of communication competence from the perspective of second language learning and speech communication, but pointed out that the theoretical lens of social constructionism not only frames the discussion in this chapter, but also explains or accounts for the changes in self that the participants experienced. I then recounted the stories of two of the participants who represented the extremes on the communication competence continuum. One individual, Valerie, constructed a belief in herself as an incompetent communicator and the other, Mary, constructed herself as a competent communicator. Both stories (briefly summarized below) demonstrate social constructionism in the real world and confirm the importance of watershed or seminal events in altering perceptions of communication competence and self.

Valerie came to the United States confident and self-assured. She'd lived a happy and carefree life in Taiwan and had successfully completed an undergraduate degree in English literature in Taiwan. She came ready to tackle the journalism program at the university. Just days after her arrival, however, Valerie met with the university's international director and was told she might have to take an oral communication course to improve her skills. From this seminal event, Valerie actually reversed her view of her competence and constructed an identity of *in*competent English communicator. She decided to stop communicating in English and became hesitant and fearful in class and with American acquaintances.

Although Valerie continued to speak of herself as incompetent, she acknowledged certain times and places where she believed she did have good skills—for example, with people she didn't know who had excellent English. Her acknowledgment pointed to the contextual and interdependent nature of her sense of her own competence. Over the course of a year, Valerie grew to accept this identity of incompetent speaker (she became less upset about it and even ceased having it stop her from doing things she wanted to do), but she never relinquished it.

Mary, on the other hand, arrived in this country shy, introverted, and hating to talk. She'd grown up in Taiwan as the one in her family who was "stupid" and "not good enough." Her older sister died of leukemia when Mary was in her last year at the university and her parents divorced that same year. Here in the United States, Mary was enrolled in the adult education program at the university and became part of a cohort of students who functioned as a group throughout her first year of schooling. Out of a series of pivotal events, Mary reconstructed her identity into one of confident, competent English communicator. As with Valerie, there were certain places that brought out increased competence in Mary (in class, with close friends, with roommates), while others fostered a certain incompetence (with salesclerks, casual acquaintances), thus also corroborating the contextual nature of Mary's construction of her own competence. Mary's reconstruction into competent speaker evolved more gradually and slowly, but over the course of two semesters and a number of pivotal experiences, she became more confident as an English-communicator than she was as a Taiwanese-speaker.

Let's now add the frame of social constructionism, with its particular interpretative point of view. What Valerie and Mary shared about their past was not an objective truth, but a construction, an interpretation of what they'd perceived and remembered. Did Valerie have the idyllic, happy-go-lucky past she claimed? I don't know, but it's what she presented to me in the interview. Was Mary really the stupid one in her family? It's her perception that she was; she constructed it that way, but we don't actually know. Additionally, what Valerie and Mary recounted about each interaction here in the United States—with the international director, friends, and teachers—was also a construction, a story created out of the actual event. Did the international director tell Valerie she had poor English skills? Valerie certainly heard it that way; it became the pivotal event in her construction of herself as incompetent speaker. From a constructionist perspective, every aspect of each woman's story is a derived construction from her particular perceptions, points of view, and past experience.

Just as the participants constructed themselves in their social interactions, I, in turn, constructed the participants through my own interpretations and renderings. All accounts, all constructions are interpretations derived from relationships. This, then, is the frame provided by social constructionism.

With social constructionism as explanation, we look to Bruner (1986, 1990) and Gergen (1991, 1994) who assert that we construct ourselves and our worlds using language in the context of social interactions. As stated earlier, Bruner (1986) saw the self as a narrative text about "how one is situated with respect to others and toward the world—a canonical text about powers and skills and dispositions that change as one's situation changes from young to old, from one kind of setting to another" (p. 130).

Using Bruner as our guide, both Mary and Valerie have a story, a "narrative text," about their lives. Certain chapters in that text are devoted to their lives in Taiwan (as children, as adolescents, as college students, and so on). At least one chapter will include the story of their lives at the university and what they constructed themselves to be there. As Bruner asserted, each chapter will represent how they "situated" themselves with respect to others and the world. In the "university chapter," Valerie situated herself as an incompetent English-communicator, Mary as someone more confident speaking English than Chinese. These situated selves had their source in the social relationships of which Valerie and Mary were a part, more specifically in those crucially important relationships and events that were key in causing a reversal in their perceptions of competence.

In the view of the constructionist, one's identity or self is linked so closely to others it becomes fluid and dynamic and interdependent on the particular relationship of the moment. "One's identity is continuously emergent, re-formed, and redirected as one moves through the sea of ever-changing relations. In the case of 'Who am I?' it is a teeming world of provisional possibilities" (Gergen, 1991, p. 146).

Gergen (1991) argues that as we interact in these ever-changing relations, we become a "plurality of voices" that are "products of perspective" vying to be accepted as legitimate expressions:

> As we absorb multiple voices, we find that each "truth" is relativized by our simultaneous consciousness of compelling alternatives. We come to be aware that each truth about ourselves is a *construction of the moment, true only for a given time and with certain relationships.* [italics added] (p. 16)

Gergen's words address the process of identity construction. As Valerie and Mary moved through that "sea of ever-changing relations," as they participated in social interactions, they constructed themselves in the moment, moment by moment.

While we could argue that Valerie's and Mary's sense of self and competence fit perfectly into Gergen's framework, that they are "constructions of the moment," capable of altering with interactional partners and contexts, it is important to note that Valerie and Mary may not view themselves that way. Rather, Valerie may believe she has lost her true self and become someone she doesn't recognize. Mary, on the other hand, may believe that she has found her true self and that who she was in Taiwan was simply her true self waiting to be released. Regardless, Valerie and Mary know that their perceptions of themselves and their communication competence have altered—they view themselves as different from the two women who arrived in the United States in 1995. In Gergen's words, their identity has been "reformed" in that "sea of ever-changing relations."

In their first year in the United States, each participant constructed an identity for herself within and inseparable from the various social relations of which she was a part, using language as the means of construction. In both cases, alterations in perceptions of self came from watershed events. Keep in mind, however, that these identity constructions, according to social constructionism, do not represent an essential or objective truth out there in the real world. Rather, they are constructions, interpretations, created initially by the participants during their social interactions, created again as they shared themselves with me in our interviews, and created lastly by me in my telling of their stories—all via language in social interchange, all in narrative form. In this sense, then, social construction can explain and account for the participants' identity constructions.

Bruner and Gergen have provided the theoretical framework for Mary's and Valerie's construction of themselves (not only in the United States, but throughout their lives). Likewise, the stories Mary and Valerie told of their experiences have demonstrated social constructionist theory in the real world. From them, we find confirming evidence that perceptions of self do not remain stable, but are dynamic and alter over time depending on conversational partners, particular contexts, and language spoken. By following the social constructionist viewpoint to its logical conclusion, we must acknowledge that the stories by Valerie and Mary are only representative of them in the moment they shared them. As their lives move forward, their stories will continue to evolve and change. In fact, the world and the identities that they construct for themselves are changing even as I write these words and as you read them.

REFERENCES

Brown, H. D. (1994). *Principles of language learning and teaching.* Englewood Cliffs, NJ: Prentice Hall Regents.

Bruner, J. (1986). *Actual minds, possible worlds.* Cambridge, MA: Harvard University Press.

Bruner, J. (1990). *Acts of meaning.* Cambridge, MA: Harvard University Press.

Gergen, K. (1991). *The saturated self: Dilemmas of identity in contemporary life.* New York: Basic Books.

Gergen, K. (1994). *Realities and relationships: Soundings in social construction.* Cambridge, MA: Harvard University Press.

Hymes, D. (1972). On communicative competence. In J. B. Pride and J. Holmes (Eds.), *Sociolinguistics: Selected readings* (pp. 269–293). Baltimore: Penguin.

Rubin, R. (1991). Perspectives on communication competence. In B. Phillips (Ed.), *Communication incompetencies: A theory of training oral performance behavior* (pp. 289–305). Carbondale: Southern Illinois University Press.

Savignon, S. (1971). *Communicative competence: An experiment in foreign language teaching.* Philadelphia: The Center for Curriculum Development, Inc.

Spitzberg, B., & Cupach, W. (1984). *Interpersonal communication competence.* Beverly Hills, CA: Sage.

Chapter 5

The Social Competence of Children Diagnosed With Specific Language Impairment

Terry Irvine Saenz
California State University, Fullerton

Kelly Gilligan Black
Anaheim City School District

Laura Pellegrini
Placetinia Yorba Linda Unified School District

Traditional approaches to the study of social competence of children have not considered the full range of factors involved in judging a child's social competence. The approaches have typically designed abstract measures of children's social competence and used the measures to classify the children as socially competent or socially incompetent. Some researchers, for example, have used teachers' and children's judgments of a student's likability as a sole indicator of that child's social competence (e.g., Black & Hazen, 1990; Denham & Holt, 1993; Masters & Furman, 1981; Terry & Coie, 1991). Other researchers, with the aim of assessing the social abilities of children with communication problems, have asked the children to perform tasks that require social knowledge, such as solving problems requiring social information (e.g., Stevens & Bliss, 1995; Tur-Kaspa & Bryan, 1994). These approaches to determining children's social competence fail to consider the multidimensional and socially situated nature of social understanding and performance.

This chapter reviews and critiques research using abstract, dimensionalized views of social competence. Data are then presented from interactions among children with specific language impairments. Detailed analysis of a particular interaction is used to illustrate how social competence can be revealed in situated contexts and how a child's competence might be judged differently depending on what is going on at the time.

TRADITIONAL APPROACHES TO STUDIES
OF SOCIAL COMPETENCE

Much of the research on social competence has focused on social acceptance of children by teachers and other children. The studies have mostly been of nondisabled, middle class, European-American children. The degree of social acceptance by peers has been measured through nomination procedures and rating scales (e.g., Terry & Coie, 1991). The nomination-based method requires children to name or point to pictures of children they like best or like least. In a peer-rating method, children use a Likert-type rating scale to indicate how much they like or would like to play with each classmate. Researchers using these approaches compile the responses of a group of children, and use the results to determine which children are accepted, ignored, or disliked by their peers. Popular children are defined as those who receive more positive nominations or ratings and fewer negative nominations or ratings from peers.

Certain communication behaviors have been found to be consistently associated with popularity. Children who are perceived as more popular are more likely to alternate turns, produce explanations for playmates, and participate in extended discourse with a conversational partner (Black & Logan, 1995). Well-liked preschoolers have been found to demonstrate less aggressive and difficult behavior than peers (Denham & Holt, 1993).

Popular children have been deemed effective in dealing with problematic situations: boys adopt other boys' frames of reference, make comments relevant to a group's purpose, and exhibit greater accuracy in perceiving peers' behavior (Black & Hazen, 1990). In contrast, unpopular children generate fewer effective solutions to problematic social situations (Stevens & Bliss, 1995; Richard & Dodge, 1982). They are also less effective in entering play groups than their popular counterparts, providing significantly more informational questions ("What is that for?"), and disagreements, during entry attempts.

In addition to nomination and rating scales, experimental approaches have been used to evaluate children's social competence. Experimental studies designed to measure children's social knowledge have indicated, for example, that children with learning or language problems had trouble performing tasks designed to measure social competence. Tur-Kaspa and Bryan (1994) found that children with learning disabilities had more difficulties with some aspects of a social information processing task than average and low-achieving peers, particularly in attending to environmental cues and storing social information. Stevens and Bliss (1995) discovered that children with severe language impairments offer fewer and less cooperative strategies when proposing hypothetical solutions to peer conflicts.

The above studies of children's social competence have assumed that children who are not accepted socially by their peers or those who perform below average on tasks measuring social competence are lacking in social competence. These traditional approaches to studying social competence in normal children have also been used to study the social competence of children with language/learning difficulties. For example, Haager and Vaughn (1995) and Merrell (1991) found that teachers rated children with learning disabilities as less socially competent than their typical peers; and Fujiki, Brinton, and Todd (1996) obtained similar results when studying children with specific language impairment (SLI). Peer ratings have also revealed that children with learning disabilities, SLI, or low achievement are less popular than their schoolmates (Gertner, Rice, & Hadley, 1994; Haager & Vaughn, 1995; Priel & Leshem, 1990).

There are two approaches that offer a departure from traditional ways of studying children's social competence. The first is to treat a particular type of behavior as a cultural construct and study how commonly occurring behaviors are interpreted by members of different groups. Using this interpretive approach, researchers have compared interpretations of social behaviors made by children from different cultural groups and with different temperaments. For example, comparisons have been made of how aggressive and unaggressive male adolescents interpret hostility in their peers. Unaggressive males from both European-American and African-American communities were found to be less likely to attribute hostile intentions to peers than their more aggressive classmates (Hudley & Graham, 1993; Graham & Hudley, 1994). Other studies have interpreted how children interpret verbal assertiveness and witty verbal play in others. Low-income children from both African-American and European-American backgrounds were found to value such behavior (Miller & Sperry, 1987; Mitchell-Kernan & Kernan, 1977). Lastly, Canadian and Chinese children were found to differ in their interpretations of shyness and sensitivity in others. The traits of shyness and sensitivity were negatively correlated with peer acceptance among Canadian children, but were positively related to peer acceptance by Chinese children (Chen, Rubin, & Sun, 1992).

These cross-cultural comparisons imply that a child who is judged to have social problems as the result of acting in a particular manner in one context, may be seen as socially adept in another, based on the same behaviors. The evaluation would depend on the framework within which the child's behaviors are evaluated.

Another departure from the nomination, rating, and experimental approaches to studying children's social competence is one in which specific social interactions of children are studied in detail. Researchers, for example, have compared the way children with language/learning problems and typical children negotiate entry into play groups. Using such an approach, Craig and Washington (1993) found that young typical children gained entry into play groups within 20 minutes by approaching the groups, producing an action to advance group play, and describing the action as they performed it. Two of the five children with SLI in the study gained entry. These two children performed actions that advanced the group's play, but did so without speaking. The other three children with SLI, who did not perform actions advancing play, failed to gain access to play groups. These findings reveal the complexity of social interaction as it is enacted during a specific activity. Of particular relevance in the Craig and Washington study is that the language deficit may or may not impact on a child's success in entering play. The child's successful entry into group play in these cases depended on whether the child used nonverbal behaviors compatible with the ongoing play activity.

In summary, the literature on children's social interaction has tended to dichotomize children into those who are socially competent or popular, using teacher or peer evaluation approaches or designing tasks as quantitative measures of children's social competence. Children who are diagnosed as having language or learning problems are more likely than their typical classmates to be classified by their teachers or peers as socially incompetent. These dichotomous characterizations and single-dimension measures of social competence have not considered what may be contributing to the ratings of children, and have failed to appreciate the complexity and contextually based nature of communicative interaction. They have treated social behaviors as value free and amenable to standardized measuring instruments.

The following study, like that of Craig and Washington (1993), examined children's interactions as they unfolded. The children in the interactions have been diagnosed as having specific language impairment. Data reveal that teachers' judgments of who is more socially competent on a particular occasion depend on the frame of reference used to interpret the children's behavior. Furthermore, data suggest that traditional measures of social competence are insufficient to account for the complexity of the social negotiations that take place in everyday interactions. The children in this study, whether rated as competent or incompetent by their teachers, demonstrated highly sophisticated interactional competencies as they went about achieving their social goals.

SOCIAL COMPETENCE OF CHILDREN WITH SLI AS DISPLAYED IN THEIR EVERYDAY PLAY

This study involves detailed analysis of interactions between preschool children, all of whom have been diagnosed as having specific language impairment. The data to be presented were part of a larger study of two classrooms of children, a kindergarten and a preschool (see Saenz, 1992, for details about the larger study). The children in the larger study were from two classes for the communicatively handicapped in a school in the metropolitan Los Angeles area (see Table 5.1). All of the children but two, Cathy and Charles, had been placed in these classrooms because of a diagnosed language disorder, and the majority had other medical or learning problems (see Table 5.2). One class included 8 preschoolers ranging in age from 3 years, 1 month to 5 years, 3 months; the other class was made up of 7 kindergartners aged 4 years, 11 months to 6 years, 11 months. One of the children in the preschool class was female and there were two female children in the kindergarten class. The preschool class was comprised of four Mexican-American children and four European-American children, and the kindergarten class included four Mexican-American children and three European-American children. All bilingual students demonstrated limited English proficiency, as well as limited proficiency in their primary language of Spanish. In addition, an older child with language and medical problems from another classroom occasionally joined the younger children in play.

Procedures

Students were observed during 19 free-play sessions of 25 minutes each from January to June of 1994. For the first 15 minutes, the two classes played together, then the older class left. Thirty sessions of free play were videotaped, totaling 749 minutes. The videotaped data reported on here focus on the preschoolers and their efforts to obtain objects from other

TABLE 5.1
Preschool Subjects and Kindergarten Playmates

Subject	Gender	Grade	Age	Ethnicity	Primary Language
Ana	F	Preschool	5-3	Latino	Eng/Span
Bob	M	Preschool	4-4	Euro-American	English
Bobby	M	Preschool	4-7	Latino	English
Cathy	F	Preschool	4-1	Euro-American	English
Dean	M	Preschool	4-5	Euro-American	English
Gabriel	M	Preschool	4-10	Latino	Eng/Span
Jeannette	F	Preschool	4-6	Euro-American	English
Juan	M	Preschool	3-1	Latino	Spanish
Amy	F	Kinder	6-6	Latino	English
Charlie	M	Kinder	4-11	Euro-American	English
Emma	F	Kinder	5-10	Euro-American	English
James	M	Kinder	6-4	Latino	English
Morris	M	Kinder	6-11	Latino	Nonverbal
Rob	M	Kinder	10	Latino	English
Todd	M	Kinder	6-8	Euro-American	English

TABLE 5.2
Preschool Subjects and Medican and Other Disabilities

Subject	Birthdate	Disabilities
		Preschool Class
Ana	1-11-89	Language disorder, visual and motor problems
Bob	12-14-89	Prader-Willi syndrome, self-help, motor problems
Bobby	9-3-89	Language and motor problems
Cathy	3-30-89	Other health impaired with visual problems, shunt
Dean	11-18-89	Language disorder
Gabriel	6-1-89	Language disorder, other health impaired, kidney failure
Jeannette	10-6-89	Language disorder, seizures
Juan	3-19-91	Language disorder, other health impaired, seizures
		Kindergarten Class
Amy	10-1-87	Language disorder
Charlie	5-1-89	Other health impaired, visual impairment, suspected prenatal drug exposure
Emma	5-28-88	Language disorder
James	12-12-87	Language disorder, visual impairment, prenatal drug exposure
Morris	5-7-87	Language disorder, autism
Rob	6-11-88	Language disorder
Todd	8-31-87	Language disorder

children. Instances in which the words and actions of the participants were not clearly audible or visible were omitted from analysis.

All instances involving efforts to obtain objects were transcribed orthographically by the first author. For reliability, a research assistant independently transcribed 23 segments, each 1 minute long, of the videotaped interactions. Comparisons of the same segments between both transcribers revealed 82.9% coder agreement for the transcription of words and nonverbal actions.

The second and third authors were trained by the first author to identify incidents in which one child tried to obtain an object from another and to code incidents by requesters' strategies, requestees' initial responses, and requesters' success in obtaining objects. To be described as an object attainment incident, the requestee had to be touching the object at the time the requester attempted to touch it or take it away.

Success in obtaining an object was defined from the requester's point of view and occurred whenever the requester was able to physically touch an object and play with it. In most cases, the requester gained exclusive possession of the object, but in some instances the requestee continued to play with the object as well.

The second and third authors independently reviewed transcripts of the videotaped free-play sessions and identified all incidents in which a preschooler attempted to obtain an object from a peer. The percentage of agreement between the two authors was 75%. The two authors then met and resolved all discrepancies.

Five strategies for obtaining objects were selected for coding. They were adapted from Saenz's (1992) study of typical preschoolers' strategies for obtaining objects from peers. The strategies were:

1. Movement toward an object
2. Verbal intentions with movement toward an object
3. Verbal intentions
4. Claiming with movement toward an object
5. Claiming

The strategy of movement toward an object was defined as any physical attempt to obtain an object held by another child, including reaching, touching, or grasping. Verbal intentions included verbal requests, demands, or statements used to obtain an object held by another child, such as "gimme." *Claiming* was an assertion of the right to obtain an object from another child, and involved such utterances as "mine" and "it's mine." The percentage of agreement between the second and third authors for coding these strategies was 86%.

Results

Three of the five strategies were displayed by children in this study: movement toward an object, verbal intentions with movement toward an object, and claiming with movement toward an object. As Table 5.3 illustrates, movement toward an object constituted 15 (50%) of the 30 incidents and was successful on 6 (40%) of those 15 occasions. Verbal intentions with movement toward an object occurred in 12 (40%) of the instances and was successful 7 times (58%) when attempted. Claiming with movement toward an object occurred three times (10%) and was successful only once.

The frequency of occurrences and their relative success provide one index of social competence. However, these data, like that in the experimental studies, do not describe how these successful and unsuccessful attempts were carried out. For this purpose, an interaction of two of the children, Gabriel and Bobby, will be analyzed as it unfolded.

Gabriel was a sociable Latino child with limited verbal communication skills in Spanish and English. He was soft-spoken and often relied on gestures and actions, as opposed to words, to communicate. Gabriel con-

TABLE 5.3
Effectiveness of Strategies Used to Obtain Objects

Strategy	Frequency of Strategy Use	% of Total	# Times Requester Got Object	% Times Requester Got Object
Movement toward object	15	50	6	40
Verbal intentions with movement toward object	12	40	7	58
Verbal intentions	0	0	0	0
Claiming with movement toward object	3	10	1	33
Claiming	0	0	0	0
Total Sample	30	100	14	47

sistently demonstrated close attention to the actions and words of other children and adults, turning these observations to his advantage during his efforts to secure objects from peers. He joined students in the class and they played together with their toys, or he allowed other children to join him in his play. His two most frequent playmates, Ana and Juan, did not display resistance to his incursions into their play space and often shared their toys cooperatively with Gabriel. Although he said far less than Bobby, he was judged by classroom teachers to exhibit more appropriate social skills in the classroom. Gabriel's high level of nonverbal communication was perceived by his teachers to compensate for his lack of verbal skills. In addition, he was often successful in obtaining objects from peers or resolving conflicts with peers. In sum, Gabriel was not only well liked by his teachers, he was regarded by them as more interactionally competent.

Bobby, also Latino, differed from Gabriel in that he was often unwilling to share toys. On one occasion, Bobby picked up a Fisher-Price clubhouse to remove it from other children who were also playing with it. Unlike other children in the class, Bobby frequently protested to teachers when other children's behavior did not meet with his approval. As a result, teachers often observed a play group more closely after Bobby entered it, in the expectation that conflict might occur.

The transcribed excerpt reveals that although Gabriel is viewed as a more sociable child than Bobby in terms of his ability to interact with others, his means for obtaining objects did not necessarily display a concern for negative reaction from his peers, particularly Bobby. In this segment, Gabriel succeeded in playing with Bobby's train track in spite of Bobby's attempts to make him leave. During their disagreement over the train track, Bobby communicated his distress through speech and gesture while Gabriel responded nonverbally.

TRANSCRIPTION (APRIL 26, 1996)

			Bobby constructs a circle of track, then Gabriel sits down and joins him.
01	*Bobby:*	Gabriel, no.	Gabriel runs the car around the tracks (referred to hereafter as Bobby's track).
02	*Bobby:*	Mrs. Watt, Gabriel.	Bobby looks off camera.
03	*Mrs. Watt*	(off camera): There's more track.	
04	*Watt:*	Why don't you build your own?	
05	*Watt:*	Your own, Gabriel.	
06	*Watt:*	Can you build some more track?	
07	*Bobby:*	Gabriel, move.	Bobby slightly pushes Gabriel back with a car.
08	*Watt:*	Try building your own.	
09	*Bobby:*	Gabriel, move.	Bobby slightly pushes Gabriel back with a car.
10	*Bobby:*	That my train.	Bobby pulls the track slightly back toward himself.
11	*Bobby:*	No!	Gabriel continues to run his car on the track.
12	*Bobby:*	Gimme.	Bobby fans his hand back and forth in front of Gabriel.
13	*Bobby:*	Make circle.	Gabriel places a piece of track next to Bobby's track.
14			Bobby pushes a car along the circle of his track.
15	*Bobby:*	Gabriel.	Bobby pushes Gabriel's track away from the side.
16	*Bobby:*	(unintelligible).	
17			Bobby pushes his car once, then pushes it so hard that it runs Gabriel's car off the end.
18	*Bobby:*	I got your back.	Bobby runs his car on his own track, and Gabriel picks up his car and puts it back on Bobby's track.
19	*Bobby:*	No.	Bobby sweeps Gabriel's car off the track using his car.
20			Gabriel puts two pieces of track close to Bobby's track.
21	*Bobby:*	Woo!	Bobby sweeps around his own track with his car, knocking Gabriel's track away.

22	*Bobby*:	(unintelligible).	Bobby puts his hand on Bobby's track and reattaches track pieces.
23			Gabriel takes his car and taps it on Bobby's track, then picks it up again.
24	*Bobby*:	Mrs. Watt.	Bobby reaches for Gabriel's car and looks briefly off camera.
25			Gabriel runs his car on the carpet.
26	*Bobby*:	Stop?	Bobby points at Gabriel's car.
27	*Bobby*:	No, stop.	Gabriel puts his car on the circle of track again.
28			Bobby bats it away.
29			Bobby puts his left hand on his track to protect it and to block Gabriel's car from moving on the track.
30			Gabriel puts the car on the track again, but Bobby pushes it off.
31			Bobby now has both hands sheilding the track and Gabriel puts his right hand on the side of the track to shield his own car from Bobby.
32	*Bobby*:	No.	Bobby pushes Gabriel's hand off with his right hand holding his car and loosens two pieces of track from his circle of track.
33	*Bobby*:	Out of the way, boy.	
34			Bobby reattaches the loosened pieces of track.
35	*Bobby*:	Gabriel.	
36	*Bobby*:	Gabriel, get out.	Gabriel shields his car with his right hand on the outer edge of the track.
37			Bobby pushes Gabriel's car away from him.
38	*Sharon*:	(off camera): Hands to self.	
39	*Bobby*:	Gann	
40	*Gann*	(off camera): Hands to self.	
41	*Bobby*:	Gann.	Gabriel runs his car on his own track next to Bobby's track.
42			Bobby reaches for Gabriel's track.
43	*Bobby*:	Gabriel, move.	Bobby points at Gabriel.
44	*Mrs. Gann*	(off camera): We need to share the toys.	Gabriel plays with his car on a piece of track far from Bobby's track.
45	*Bobby*:	No on my train track.	
46	*Gann*:	Is that your circle?	
47	*Bobby*:	No.	
48	*Gann*:	Can you make one for Gabriel?	

49 *Bobby:*	No.	
50 *Gann:*	Get some circle tracks.	Mrs. Gann bends down and moves pieces of track next to Gabriel.
51 *Gann:*	Make one for Gabriel, help him.	
52		Bobby pushes loose pieces of track in Gabriel's direction.

Gabriel's nonverbal persistence in obtaining toys eventually overcame Bobby's verbal and nonverbal protests. Even though Mrs. Watt instructed Gabriel to build his own railroad track (turns 4–6), he proceeded to build a track immediately adjoining Bobby's, potentially interfering with Bobby's solitary play. Then Bobby tried to block Gabriel's action with his hand (12). Undaunted by this action, Gabriel laid down an adjacent piece of track (13). Bobby responded by moving Gabriel's track away (15), and later by pushing Gabriel's track apart (21). From 22 through 48, Gabriel continued to place his own car on Bobby's tracks while Bobby attempted to push or sweep the car off. Finally, in 49–52, Mrs. Gann, another teacher, urged Bobby to help Gabriel make a circle for himself. Bobby relented and pushed some of the train track in Gabriel's direction (53).

In order to interpret and evaluate the online social competence of Bobby and Gabriel as it took place in this interaction, one must assume a particular point of view. Two views that can be applied to Bobby and Gabriel are often framed as explicit or implicit social rules for children to follow: (a) children should share their toys, and (b) if someone is already playing with a toy, that child should have first rights to that toy. Mrs. Gann, in line 45, explicitly tries to resolve the conflict between Bobby and Gabriel in light of the first rule by saying "we need to share the toys." This view, when used to evaluate the interaction, would place Bobby at fault for not sharing his track with Gabriel. Bobby is thus cast as the one who is creating the social problem.

Mrs. Watt, interestingly, responds to the same interaction (but earlier) in accord with the second view. She tells Gabriel early on in the interaction that there is plenty of track to go around. This implies that Gabriel is the one causing the problem, encroaching on Bobby's territory. Bobby, when appealing to each of his teachers, might be doing so in anticipation that the teachers will intervene on his behalf. That is, they would stop Gabriel's intrusions. If his appeal were, indeed, acted on by a teacher, it would be under the aegis of the territorial rights rule, not the sharing rule.

Both children display complex social competencies when making their goals explicit to one another. Bobby was clear, both verbally and nonverbally, in expressing his desire to retain sole control over the toys. In defending his play territory, he showed social versatility in telling Gabriel to

move (7), by suggesting that Gabriel build his own track (13), and by
making a variety of different physical and verbal attempts to block Gabriel's
intrusions (e.g., 19, 21, 26, 33, 34).

Gabriel communicated his intents and negotiated with Bobby nonverbally. He alternated direct intrusions on Bobby's track with lesser intrusions, as if to test the territoriality rule held by Bobby. His most direct
intrusions were to put his car on Bobby's already formed track and, if it
remained there, to run it around Bobby's track. He did this several times
(1, 11, 18, 27, 30). When Bobby reacted, Gabriel retreated from this direct
approach to assume a less confrontational one. He began making and
running his cars on his own track next to Bobby's track (13, 20), then
retreated to a weaker position of running his car on the carpet (25), and
later to building a new track (45).

When viewed from the framework of "children should share," the conflict is seen as originating with Bobby's reluctance to share his toys with
Gabriel. When viewed as an instance of children's need to assert their
territorial rights, Gabriel becomes the culprit and problem person, lacking
in social knowledge or skills.

CONCLUSION

This detailed analysis of a single interaction is presented to illustrate how
an individual's judged social competency can depend on what goes on in
highly complex social interactions and how they are interpreted by participants and onlookers. Assessment approaches designed to determine
whether or not individual children or a group of children are socially
competent fail to capture the nature of the everyday experiences that lead
teachers and children to their nomination and rating decisions. Assessment
approaches that employ tasks for measuring children's social knowledge,
such as problems-solving tasks involving social situations, also fail to provide
insights into how children are able to use their social knowledge to achieve
their personal goals.

The analysis of the single excerpt between preschoolers Gabriel and
Bobby, both diagnosed as having specific language impairment, revealed
significant skills from both as they worked to achieve their desired goals.
Perhaps one of the most striking features of the excerpt was Gabriel's
ability to obtain objects that were in the possession of other children,
irrespective of their reactions and without verbal language. Gabriel was
more favored socially by his teachers than Bobby, and yet from a certain
vantage point it is hard to claim that his actions were more socially acceptable. He was confiscating toys from his peer in spite of the peer's protest.

The excerpt also reveals that Bobby employed verbal as well as nonverbal
means to achieve his goal. Bobby was quite clear in communicating his

protests to both Gabriel and the teachers. Bobby's verbal efforts to solicit help from the teachers, coupled with his verbal and nonverbal attempts to fend off Gabriel's actions, were quite consistent with other data on how typically developing children in a mainstream day-care center sought to resolve their conflicts over objects (Kovarsky, 1993).

Judgments of Bobby's social competence by his teachers seemed to be closely tied to his lack of willingness to cooperate with his peers. His frequent protestations of other children's actions and reluctance to share toys with peers seemed to be the basis on which his teachers judged him as having social difficulties.

These data would suggest that incompetence is not the sole possession of the individual and that children should not be evaluated as having "social problems" that are intrinsic to their nature. Rather, portraits of competence and incompetence should be regarded as complex constructions, which can differ with the situation and are likely to be based on values and interpretations of those making the competency judgments, and not just on the performance or abilities of those who are being evaluated.

AUTHOR'S NOTE

This chapter was completed with the support of an Affirmative Action grant from California State University, Fullerton. Data were adapted from the graduate project completed by Kelly Gilligan Black and Laura Pellegrini as a requirement for their masters' degrees.

REFERENCES

Black, B., & Hazen, N. (1990). Social status and patterns of communication in acquainted and unacquainted preschool children. *Developmental Psychology, 26,* 379–387.

Black, B., & Logan, A. (1995). Links between communication patterns in mother-child, father-child, and child-peer interactions and children's social status. *Child Development, 66,* 255–271.

Denham, S., & Holt, R. (1993). Preschoolers' likability as cause or consequence of their social behavior. *Developmental Psychology, 29,* 271–275.

Fujiki, M., Brinton, B., & Todd, C. (1996). Social skills of children with specific language impairment. *Language, Speech, and Hearing Services in Schools, 27,* 195–202.

Gertner, B., Rice, M., & Hadley, P. (1994). Influence of communicative competence on peer preferences in a preschool classroom. *Journal of Speech and Hearing Research, 37,* 913–923.

Graham, S., & Hudley, C. (1994). Attributions of aggressive and nonaggressive African-American male adolescents: A study of construct accessibility. *Developmental Psychology, 20,* 365–373.

Haager, D., & Vaughn, S. (1995). Parent, teacher, peer and self-reports of the social competence of students with learning disabilities. *Journal of Learning Disabilities, 28,* 205–215, 231.

Hudley, C., & Graham, S. (1993). An attributional intervention to reduce peer-directed aggression among African-American boys. *Child Development, 64,* 124–138.

Kovarsky, D. (1993). Understanding language variation: Conflict talk in two day cares. *ASHA Monographs, 30,* 32–40.

Merrell, K. (1991). Teacher ratings of social competence and behavioral adjustment: Differences between learning-disabled, low-achieving, and typical students. *Journal of School Psychology, 29,* 207–217.

Miller, P., & Sperry, L. (1987). The socialization of anger and aggression. *Merrill-Palmer Quarterly, 33,* 1–31.

Mitchell-Kernan, C., & Kernan, K. (1977). Pragmatics of directive choice among children. In S. Ervin-Tripp & C. Mitchell-Kernan (Eds.). *Child discourse* (pp. 189–208). New York: Academic Press.

Priel, B., & Leshem, T. (1990). Self-perceptions of first-and second-grade children with learning disabilities. *Journal of Learning Disabilities, 23,* 637–642.

Richard, B., & Dodge, K. (1982). Social maladjustment and problem solving in school-aged children. *Journal of Counseling and Clinical Psychology, 50,* 226–233.

Saenz, T. I. (1992). *Strategies for obtaining toys at Head Start.* Unpublished doctoral dissertation, Temple University, Philadelphia, PA.

Stevens, L., & Bliss, L. (1995). Conflict resolution abilities of children with normal language. *Journal of Speech and Hearing Research, 38,* 599–611.

Swisher, L., & Plante, E. (1993). Nonverbal IQ tests reflect different relations among skills for specifically language-impaired and normal children: Brief report. *Journal of Communication Disorders, 26,* 65–71.

Swisher, L., Plante, E., & Lowell, S. (1994). Nonlinguistic deficits of children with language disorders complicate the interpretation of their nonverbal IQ scores. *Language, Speech, and Hearing Services in Schools, 25,* 235–240.

Tantam, D., Holmes, D., & Cordess, C. (1993). Nonverbal expression in autism of Asperger type. *Journal of Autism and Developmental Disorders, 23,* 111–133.

Terry, R. & Coie, J. (1991). A comparison of methods for defining sociometric status among children. *Developmental Psychology, 27,* 867–880.

Tur-Kaspa, H., & Bryan, T. (1994). Social information-processing skills of students with learning disabilities. *Learning Disabilities Research and Practice, 9,* 12–23.

Chapter 6

Deaf Members and Nonmembers: The Creation of Culture Through Communication Practices

Madeline Maxwell
University of Texas at Austin

Diana Poeppelmeyer
Texas School for the Deaf

Laura Polich
University of Redlands

PRESENT AT, BUT . . .

Uncomprehending, a young boy wanders through a Civil War battlefield in an 1891 short story by Ambrose Bierce (1891/1971). The boy witnesses, but does not understand, the blood and injuries of the men scattered on the ground. He hears neither the guns nor the shouts exploding around him. He does not know he is an orphan. He watches, but does not know he is in the midst of a war. Thus, Bierce, one of the United States' most bitter writers, captured the devastating sense of being present at, but not a part of a scene.

The story is fictional, but we hear many autobiographical narratives that converge at the same point. Following are descriptions by deaf people of being present at their families and jobs, but not a part of the interaction taking place.

- A 13-year-old deaf girl wakes up to wander her empty house, wondering first if anyone is home and then, with mounting anxiety, where they all have gone. Later she learns that she was copresent at, but did not understand, a dinner table conversation in which plans had been made for the other family members to go shopping the next morning.
- An 11-year-old girl and her 15-year-old brother surreptitiously ask a teacher dropping by for a home visit what it is their mother is saying.
- A deaf man resolutely shares that he is hiring an interpreter to accompany him to an upcoming family reunion. At previous reunions,

once everyone had greeted him, he always spent the ensuing 2 days standing around with no idea of what was going on.

- A deaf college teacher who gets along well with his colleagues turns down invitations to departmental parties. He explains that after everyone has said hello, there is only one person who will have a conversation with him. Because he talks regularly with her he feels guilty taking her away from the party.

This chapter focuses on the importance of full participation in everyday communication to an individual's identity. Participation is basic to an individual's sense of well-being, but is also crucial in the development of the individual's social identity.

The conclusions in this chapter are based on a wide range of materials about the experiences, life stories, and anecdotes of individuals who have experienced life with severe-to-profound hearing loss from an early age,[1] and on field observations, ethnographic interviews, unpublished theses and dissertations, and published materials (such as poetry, articles from magazines and newsletters, stories, and autobiographies written by deaf individuals).[2] The topic of communication is one that deaf individuals always seem eager to talk about, sometimes for hours at a time.

---

[1]The senior author has conducted field research in deaf communities for 25 years. The other two authors also have many years of professional experience and field research with deaf individuals. All have participated in the deaf community and have conducted in-depth interviews with deaf individuals and those associated with, and related to, deaf adults and children. Two authors have worked as sign language interpreters and teachers in schools for the deaf and in the community; the other author is an audiologist.

[2]Observations and interviews include both prominent and politically active deaf individuals, and those more obscure and/or unemployed. They include deaf friends as well as deaf strangers. The majority of individuals involved are active to some extent in the deaf community in different regions of the United States. They were located through informal contacts in the deaf community and through social, religious, and professional activities. Twenty individuals were approached because they had significant hearing loss but did not identify themselves as part of a deaf community. In some cases, these individuals were encountered during attendance at social or educational functions with the deaf community members, or through their college or graduate studies in deaf education. In other cases, they were identified through informal contacts, through a support group for hearing-impaired individuals, or through audiological services.

Most of the identity narratives in this chapter were collected by the second author as part of her dissertation study of what it means to be deaf (Poeppelmeyer, 1995). Poeppelmeyer interviewed 16 deaf individuals who considered themselves members of the deaf community, and 11 who did not. Twenty interviews were conducted by Jennifer Bryce (1996) from deaf adults involved in deaf education.

The interviews (from 1 to 3 hours) were audio- or videotaped and transcribed. Other materials came from field observations, interviews, unpublished theses and dissertations, and published materials (i.e., poetry, magazine articles, newsletters, stories, and autobiographies written by deaf individuals).

THE PARADOX OF DEAFNESS

One might assume that deaf persons who can speak and lipread would naturally be integrated into the hearing society, whereas those who cannot, would be forced to find a community among the signing deaf. We have not found it to be that simple. Although signing is often seen as a last resort by educators and parents who prefer that deaf children rely on speech, it is rare for deaf individuals to communicate orally with ease. Even those who can communicate orally find it difficult and unpleasant to communicate with more than one other person at a time. Integration with hearing children may isolate a deaf child in a crowd. A study of the interaction of 20 high school students who were included as the only deaf students in their respective schools found that none of their fellow students ever had a conversation with them, and they never tried to initiate a conversation with another student. The only communication they experienced all day at school was with the teacher (Raimondo & Maxwell, 1987). Just as the deaf child who lives at home may be isolated with no one with whom to communicate, the deaf child integrated in regular schools may be stranded. A number of deaf adults say they have quit jobs or changed careers in order to work in an environment with at least some deaf co-workers. Although some say they could communicate with hearing co-workers for essentials, and some of these appear to us to have clear speech and lipreading abilities, they were unable to establish relationships with co-workers because, they say, they could not communicate freely.

Of those we studied, more nonmembers of the deaf community than members do seem to have intelligible speech. Not all nonmembers, however, have intelligible speech, and many members of the deaf community do have intelligible speech. Jan is a woman with excellent speech and lip-reading skills. For all practical purposes, she seems to manage very effectively in oral conversations. She was raised among the hearing and did not encounter the deaf community until she decided to go to Gallaudet University.[3] After graduating, she moved back to her home state and began working on another degree at a hearing university. During this time she wondered if she should return to her home town, where there was a small deaf population, or move to an area where a large number of deaf people

---

The material in this study includes English and American Sign Language (ASL). The portions used here are presented as English narratives, with no attempt to represent the qualities of the consultants' speech, which varies greatly in intelligibility, or original ASL. Because this study is not about the language but about meaning, an attempt was made to present stories as seamlessly as possible. Except where otherwise indicated, the long narratives are taken from Poeppelmeyer (1995).

[3]Gallaudet University, located in Washington, DC, was established in 1864 to provide postsecondary education for the deaf.

lived. Eventually, she made the decision to live primarily among the deaf. She moved to a city with a large deaf population, married a fourth-generation deaf man, got a job at a deaf school, and became deeply immersed in the local deaf community. Indeed, the designations of "hard-of-hearing," "oral deaf," "deaf," or "real deaf" have more to do with speaking and interaction with hearing people on the one end, and the use of ASL and visual modalities on the other, than they have to do with hearing level.[4]

Why would a person who could handle life so well among the hearing choose a life among the deaf? Her answer was she wanted more from life than just "to handle it": she wanted to live it. Getting by "for all practical purposes" was a far cry from a life of fulfillment. This kind of life was unknown to her until age 18, when she encountered members of the deaf community. For the first time she experienced complete, unencumbered, and unfettered conversations. Although it took her a while to learn to communicate with the deaf, the result was a feeling that the world was open to her. No longer did she have to expend so much energy on the surface of communication, trying so hard simply to read lips and follow conversations. As she became adept at signing, she could lose herself in the deeper aspects of communication. Finally she knew what it was to be fully engaged in real conversation, and as a result, went from "living in part, to living in whole." Although Jan's oral abilities were functional for many purposes, they had not given her access to the deeper aspects of communication and significant relationships.

We suggest that although hearing loss can be rated along an audiological continuum, the cultural identities available to individuals with hearing loss cannot. Indeed, cultural identities must be understood as fundamentally different, even dichotomous. Nor do the identities link, in any simple way, to an individual's oral ability.

THE PRESENT, BUT NOT FULLY
PARTICIPATING, DEAF

The most striking contrast between the narratives of members of the deaf community and individuals with hearing loss who are not members is the *solitariness* of the latter: The solitary effect that arises from the stories and lives of nonmembers is, in part, created by the experience of feeling isolated from others like themselves. One woman, Vicki,[5] shared:

---

[4] Padden and Humphries (1988) pointed out that, from the deaf perspective, a person a little bit hard-of-hearing is one who can interact with hearing people a little bit, and one who is very hard-of-hearing can interact with hearing people easily. This is the opposite of how hearing people use these terms. The issue is interaction with hearing people rather than audiological abilities.

[5] All names are pseudonyms.

I was never with hearing-impaired people when I was growing up. And it would have been helpful just to know that I had somebody to share with, like the frustrations, for example. There was another girl, Sandra. She was born deaf and I lost my hearing at 2½. We had the same speech teacher from second through sixth grade. But it wasn't until years later, even after we both went to the same college, that we had a talk and both of us realized that we were so alienated. We were not allowed to mix with other . . . we couldn't mix with each other when we were growing up. You follow me? It was kinda like you have to be with the hearing world. So she and I never had each other growing up or never had each other even in the same classroom. We knew each other, but we were never allowed to mix together, to be friends. We didn't even have parties together. I think we were deliberately kept apart. After her phone call, we became friends. We became the friends that we never were.

Often the separation from others like one's self leaves the nonmembers with a feeling of being unique and singled out. Carly put it:

I guess what bothers me most is that I don't know other people like me. And it's not that I want to have this little group session with these other people. I just want to know that there are other people out there that exist, because most hard-of- hearing people, well most hard-of-hearing that I know or see, are old. And I don't relate as well to old people as I do to someone that's my own age. And Bradyn is the first person that I've ever known that has the same, well really not the same, feelings, but at least the same general sense of feelings about things or the same experiences. Like he sails and he uses saran wrap for his hearing aids and I used to do that when I was on a rowing crew and I thought "Wow, someone else does that, too." And it was just kind of a neat thing. So I don't want this whole group thing, I just want to know other people. I just don't feel like there's anybody else around my age and that makes me feel like I'm the only one.

Later Carly elaborated on feeling set apart:

I'm considered more oral deaf than hard-of-hearing because my hearing is so borderline. Without my hearing aid, I'm deaf. With it, I can hear you. With my hearing aids on, I'm a hearing person, and I can fit into the hearing world except . . . I don't know . . . there are little things that separate me. I'm in a sorority and they have this thing called Spring Carnival where you can buy pies to throw at your friends. If you get pies in the face, it means you're well-liked but no one has ever done that to me and I know that people would love to buy me one. I found out the reason why they don't get me is that they are trying to protect me. Someone spread it around that I shouldn't get hit with the pies because it could ruin my hearing aids. That really made me mad. It may sound dumb to somebody else, but I wanted the pies, because not getting them is one of those little things that separates me and makes me feel like I am not part of things.

For these deaf individuals, the self is situated on the outside or, the margin, of the scene. Although they have access to the large sense of culture, as evidenced from their knowledge about shopping and education, they lack involvement in the everyday give and take of communicative life. They are left out not because someone has rejected them deliberately, but because they are not aware of what is happening, who is talking, or what is being said. While taking a college course in communication and culture, a deaf man who is a very competent speaker and lipreader commented he had never understood why people behaved the way they did around him, or had the reactions to him that they did, because he had "never known how to communicate." He said this in very clear English. He had acquired native-level competency in English and had the ability to speak, yet had no sense of belonging, and little understanding of the relational dimension of communication. A nonmember self is situated outside the communication, periodically interjecting something but excluded from the center. Such a self is continually mystified about other people and about his or her identity. As Carly said, they are often not part of things and they seldom know why not.

As isolated as such individuals may feel among the hearing, they may be just as isolated among the deaf. The nonmember tends to be viewed as deaf by the hearing, and as "not really deaf" by the deaf community. When someone with a nonmember background begins to attend a school for the deaf, or appear at deaf community social events, deaf community members may reject her or him, or shake their heads and say that the person will never fit in. The person who speaks may be ridiculed for doing so. With young people, especially, the teenage demand for conformity or rejection can be quite harsh. Good English skills may also be ridiculed. The individual may be considered to be a hearie, someone who is deaf on the outside but hearing on the inside. This response to the nonmember can be heartbreaking and very disconcerting. Nonmembers often grow up with the idea that they can always seek refuge in the deaf community and can always learn to sign if they have trouble in the hearing world. Finding that to be false sometimes causes enormous pain.

THE PROBLEM OF GROUPS

Due to the common experience of discomfort in communicating in groups, many nonmembers are disinclined to participate in gatherings. Numerous stories of being "the only one" weave a thread of solitariness through the texture of the lives of the nonmembers that is elaborated by common tales of difficulty in contending with groups. Several shared the sentiments expressed by Jinny:

> *I hate really large groups—any group larger than 7 or 8 or so. If the group is larger than 10, just forget it, because it's just too much conversation, because everyone talks*

at the same time. In a perfect world, only one person would talk at a time, but usually everyone has something to say, and I'm trying to lipread right and left. Especially if we're sitting at a square table, I can't do it. But if we're sitting at a round table, I have a better opportunity. Like last night I went to the library and we were sitting around a table playing a card game and it was only a few of us so it was okay, and they all knew that I just need to lipread, and so they were willing to do that and that's fine. But in a larger group, it's not as easy to accommodate, and so I don't like large groups, and I haven't been going to parties. I haven't gone to parties in a long time, because it's just too much. It's too draining to keep up with everything. Most parties are dark, so I can't really see, and half the people have been drinking or something, so they are slurring their words. Anyway, with the noise and the confusion, I mean, ugh . . . it's just too much tension. I could never be a waitress just because of the fact that there's too much noise. But I get along great with people. I love people. I love talking. I love to talk, but I prefer to talk to people in small little conversational groups or just one on one.

Eric said of his social life:

Well, I'm working on it. I go to A. G. Bell.[6] I mean, I can't have a perfect life. Nobody has a perfect life. But I feel that . . . I'm very thankful that I'm able to stand on my own two feet. I've been overseas three times. I think once you can talk to most people one on one, you can do a lot. So I may not have a great social life in terms of a group situation, I think that's one of the main differences between deaf culture and mainstreamed people. Deaf culture, they can do a lot of things on a group basis. In my case, I tend to do things one on one. I can have dinner with a very intelligent person. I can talk to the President of the United States. I can do a lot of things one on one. So I tend to avoid group situations unless I go to a basketball game, or a sporting event, or maybe a funny movie.

Vicki complained:

I'm single, so it's easy for me to get out and meet people, but I find myself staying at home more because . . . I don't know if it's just because I like being home a lot or if I just feel like there isn't any place to go without feeling I have to put that much more effort into communicating. I want to sign. I want to be able to communicate, but I want to be able to catch up with everybody so I have to find one person who will tell me what they [the deaf] are talking about in ASL, because I'm not able to sign with them and I lipread really well. I'm in the SHHH[7] group, but I'm not really active as far as doing things with them. I just attend the meetings out of courtesy. The oral deaf[8] adult group doesn't really get together socially. We tried to get a group

---

[6]The Alexander Graham Bell Association promotes the reliance on speech and hearing by those with hearing loss. It has a subsection for "Oral Deaf Adults."

[7]Self Help for the Hard of Hearing, a self-help group.

[8]"Oral deaf" refers to deaf individuals who do not use sign language. It does not necessarily connote highly intelligible speaking and skilled lipreading.

of people together last summer, but nobody really responded to where they wanted to meet.

When SHHH does meet, every member works to gain full access to the interaction, and the group accommodates this goal. This can result in sign language interpreters, auditory loops, various microphones and receivers, and much repeating. Such meetings do not have the quality of social interaction; they are more like business meetings in which turns are formally regulated. One of the ironies of attempts by oral deaf individuals and hard-of-hearing individuals to socialize is precisely that they find it so difficult to understand each other. It may be worth the effort, but it is a huge effort.

The preference for the individual over the group is evident in Cory's explanation of why he occasionally seeks out the deaf:

I don't need deaf culture. I just want to make new friends, meet new people. The deaf culture just doesn't fit any of the requirements I have other than socializing. But in some sense, I'm pretty much of a loner. I have friends . . . but I'm not like some people I know who say, "Oh, I'm friends with everybody." I'm never lonely. I'm not the type of person who needs people, who needs to be active. It makes no difference to me. I could bury myself in a book easily. And I don't use the phone, so I don't have any phone friends, and I have trouble with group conversation so that really cuts it down.

In addition to the image he paints of being a loner, Cory's description of his social needs as "just" one of many requirements plays a part in the perception of the individual orientation of the nonmembers. Although he says he wants to make new friends and meet new people, he diminishes them and his need of them. He reduces both to an aspect of his life that he relegates, through his use of the qualifying "just," to a relatively low priority. Later, when he says, "It's not a support group I'm looking for, just a close group of friends and family," he again uses "just" to downplay his social needs. Rather than thinking of these groups in social terms, Cory, like many other nonmembers, tends to think of these groups in instrumental terms, as sources of support.

Mary also frames deaf community groups instrumentally: "It's not like [I want] a support group, it's not a rally, it's not like a coalition for me, I don't align myself up with those people." Mary describes her distance from the deaf using terms that better describe her own participation among groups of nonmembers. To her they are primarily practical groups, either for support or political purposes, and her membership is based on these instrumental concerns. Because the practical purposes of the group are more salient than the relationships within them, groups of nonmembers tend to be aggregations of individuals temporarily united for a specific cause. They tend to be limited to task forces and advice and information sharing, and not to forming extended social communities. Any affiliation tends to be for the usefulness of the meetings; not for the social membership.

Nowhere to Belong

Some nonmembers do find a sense of place (although limited) in these functional groups, but others report feeling that they have nowhere to belong. Carly said:

> [If you're deaf] you can go to the Deaf Action Center or a Deaf Community Center and there's all these deaf people, but there's no hard-of-hearing community. How do you find hard-of-hearing people? I feel like I'm caught between two different worlds and I don't fit into either one of them completely because I'm not deaf. With my hearing aids I know what it's like to be hearing. Without them, I know what it's like to be deaf. So I can be sympathetic. I know what the problems are, facing deaf people, but at the same time, I'm a hearing person with my hearing aid, and so I know all the benefits or whatever that go with that, and it's just . . . I just don't fit in with either one.

Whereas Carly describes her feeling of belonging nowhere as being caught between worlds, another deaf individual says the experience of adults who become deaf after language development (sometimes called ALDAs[9]) is like having no country: They lack both expertise in ASL and the experiences of growing up deaf. Many feel like outsiders in both hearing and deaf communities. Another ALDA says:

> Actually, I have never felt completely comfortable with either hearing or deaf; I always seem to be somewhere in the middle, sort of like the man without a country.

Casey makes a different distinction: "I am deaf but not Deaf, Hearing but not hearing," reflecting a common practice of using capital letters to designate culture and lowercase letters to designate audiological status. Mary wishes for "more categories, not just deaf and hearing. What happens when you fall in between?" A magazine article explained:

> Becoming late-deafened means living in a paradoxical . . . situation. Late-deafened adults are culturally hearing, but audiologically deaf. They grew up in the hearing world, have hearing spouses and friends, and functioned as hearing people but now they are deaf. The hearing world views them as

---

[9]ALDA is the Association for Late-Deafened Adults and its members are referred to as ALDAs.

deaf; the Deaf world views them as hearing. Their formerly secure identities have dissolved. Where do they belong? (Lavation & Holmes, 1991, pp. 11–12).

Sometimes the uneasiness of having no place to belong or no group identity to share results in a sense that life is not worth living. The authors have been involved as interpreters in four cases in which deaf students were placed in psychiatric hospitals after threatening suicide when their sense of belonging was jeopardized. In each of these cases students were at a crossroads in their education and were told they would need to go to special schools or colleges for the deaf only. None of these teens felt they belonged among the deaf. Their place, they insisted, was with the hearing, even though they were unable to communicate effectively. The prospect of being cast with the deaf was devastating enough that all four had to be placed under psychiatric supervision to protect them from hurting themselves. For these teens, isolation among the hearing was preferable to the isolation they anticipated among the deaf. They had the larger sense of belonging with the hearing world, but no sense of belonging in social communication with anyone. When assigned to an environment that would actually support their need to connect with other people, they lost all hope. They saw this move as condemnatory. Their selves were situated in the abstract in a place they could not truly enter—the hearing world. Thus, they had no place.

The emphasis placed on just getting communication access can rob the individual of the opportunity to communicate other aspects of social identity. The individual's deafness, or inability to speak and hear clearly, becomes the social identity of the individual. A deaf person among the hearing experiences *exceptionality* and avoids groups. For some, this avoidance is acceptable and even maybe a source of pride, but more commonly it denotes isolation. In our studies, the deaf individuals most competent in oral language are ironically most isolated. Most avoid group activities, most are involved in functional rather than organic groups, and most feel between worlds. Most selves are precariously situated: present at but never in the center of communication.

THE COMMUNITY OF THE DEAF

The isolation of the non-signing deaf is in sharp contrast to the celebration of community by members of the deaf community. The group identity of deaf community members stands out as a major characteristic. For members, *deaf* is fundamentally and constitutionally a group identity. Nonmembers tend to focus on their isolation, whereas members tend to focus on the importance of communication to their communal experience. Non-members tend to tell their own personal feelings; deaf community members tend to tell illustrative stories, some about themselves and some about others. Nonmembers tend to describe how things are—"the way it is." Deaf community members often tell historical stories, and of radical changes between the past and the present. Members select a Miss Deaf America, are entertained by Deaf Comedy Club performers, bowl in Deaf Leagues, party together, and occasionally establish church congregations. Members share information through gossip networks and help each other out with advice and information about every aspect of living. Although there are newsletters and organization magazines aimed at both nonmembers and members, members have a glossy national magazine called *Deaf Life*. The only web pages found for nonmembers were institutional, yet there are more than 30 web pages maintained by individuals aimed at members. Members of the deaf community are very aware of the importance of communication in mundane interaction. They tend to celebrate it—many are willing to talk about communication endlessly. A deaf community leader gave this illustration of the importance of community:

> *The deaf have a craving to be together. I want to tell you a story that I think will help you understand clearly this very situation. I heard this story while I was in college and that was some time ago. In those days, the deaf boys and girls drove or took the train to Washington, DC.[10] There were no planes then. Students returning to Gallaudet from California passed through Arizona. There were a few deaf people who lived in Arizona who always knew when that train was passing through from California. One of them would drive a great distance . . . 150 miles to that train station just to talk [sign] through the windows with the people on the train. Some people got off, but it was a real hurry. They were rushed, they had maybe 30 minutes at the most and then they would get back on the train and leave. So to go there would, for a while, fill that guy's need or craving. Now we have a smaller world and things are different, but regardless, I think all deaf people still have that craving to be together.*

This same story was also told to the first author by deaf Arizonans 20 years ago. To further emphasize his point that the deaf love to get together with one another, the same man explained that "deaf senior citizens flock to conventions *not* primarily for the information they can gain from workshops but more importantly for what happens in the halls between sessions

---

[10]Gallaudet College (now University) is a liberal arts college for the deaf, funded by the federal government, and located in Washington, DC. Until the 1970s, there were no other special programs for deaf students in higher education. Gallaudet, for many, symbolizes a deaf world, where the hearing are few. For many, it symbolizes independence and growing up. For many, and perhaps most importantly, it is where they learn that a deaf life could be a good life.

where people stand around and gab.[11] At one such meeting of senior citizens, people were exchanging hugs, catching up, reminiscing, making plans, swapping jokes, and getting acquainted. There was the feeling of a reunion, more than the feeling of a conference, with much celebration of being together—the communion of a community. When describing gatherings, deaf members tend to talk about all the communication going on. Reunions of deaf school classes are typically described as "more like family reunions than class reunions." We have seen this level of emotion in gatherings such as a reunion of the class of 1938 of a school for the deaf, regular supper clubs that have been meeting for 20 years, monthly women's card groups, weekly bowling leagues, and summer softball leagues. Such closeness is also exhibited at weddings, funerals, baby showers, other special occasions, and routine get-togethers. Deaf community members take cruises and bus trips together, attend deaf conventions, establish deaf churches, and so on. In all these what is striking is the sense of celebration at getting together with other deaf people for communication.

An older member of the deaf community was asked why, at deaf events, did deaf people meeting her insist not only on paying attention to the finger-spelling of her first name, but demand to know her last name as well. "It's an unusual last name. Nobody will ever remember it. My first name is usually enough. Hearing people never care about my last name." His reply illustrates the value communication has for the deaf:

> Yes, I think it is different. You hearing people have so many possible contacts that you don't value them all very much. But the deaf world is much smaller. Deaf people assume that they will meet again, so it is important to pay attention when being introduced in order to remember that person the next time. Deaf people assume there will be a next time. I don't think hearing people think that way.

This celebration of communication persists even during major community splits over politics or personalities. There are factions, rivalries, and animosities. In public forums such as political meetings and in private conversations and incidents, there is as much mudslinging, fighting, and general stretching and straining of the ties that bind as one could find in any group of people. Members will say of someone else, so-and-so "is not "real deaf""; nevertheless, they tend to welcome the spectrum into the celebration and to make sure that all are accommodated. During one period of political agitation, the decision was made to stop hiring interpreters for meetings of a task force; the message was intended to be directed

---

[11]The sign used here is usually glossed CHAT. It conveys a sense of talking with ease, abandon, and familiarity, and thus evokes a sense of communion that, for some, implies that the conversation is taking place in ASL, without barriers to communication.

at hearing people that they should communicate in ASL or "butt out." After one such meeting the plan was abandoned because many deaf individuals could not follow the ASL discussion without interpreters. Grumbling about the need for interpreters disappeared without a trace.

Deaf community members are situated within their community, and revel in the freedom to communicate with other participants in that community, and attend to communication needs of other members. They are present at and part of the scene, and tend to see being part of the scene as central to their identity. They urge others to make this identity possible for all deaf children.

Deafness as Territory

Many of the community members talk about their community as a tangible entity. For example, Chris said of another "He is not from ASL"—as if ASL were a physical location. Patricia, in talking about her feelings about Gallaudet, said, "It's deaf to its deepest core and deaf is in the air." Louise said she was going back to Gallaudet for a master's degree, even though she thought the program in her city was better and she and her husband were happy there. At Gallaudet, she said, "They teach *me*" (rather than the interpreter).

For many hearing people who enjoy associating with the deaf, attending a deaf community function is like traveling to another country, where everything is the same, yet different. It is more than being outnumbered by the deaf. The hearing are often outnumbered by the deaf in schools for the deaf, but even when administrators are deaf, the structure of the schools and practices is based on the hearing world. Accommodations are made for the deaf, but schools for the deaf are not deaf worlds.

A sense of the deaf world prevails sometimes when the event is designed and carried out by the deaf, possibly with special accommodations for the hearing. A deaf event is organized around eye contact, sound, language, pace, rhythm, agenda, physical setup, jokes, and atmosphere, all contributing to the sense of a different world, a deaf world. People sometimes use the phrase "the deaf way" to capture this sense. The first international conference to celebrate deaf cultures the world over was called Deaf Way. Interestingly, in cities with large deaf populations, deaf individuals report that they tend to live in the same areas of town (although not concentrated in the same neighborhood).

Deaf members situate themselves within communication, within a mass of deaf individuals. They take on identities as native communicators. They take control and reach out in all directions. It is not too strong to say many deaf members experience the language of signs and the community of the deaf as a homeland.

Deafness as History

The deaf sense of community is strengthened and enlarged by the connection to past and future generations of the deaf. This is significant
because almost all deaf individuals are born to normally hearing parents.
This connection to past and future generations is cultural, not genetic.
Deaf poet Ella Lentz addressed hearing parents, "He may be your son, but
he is my child." The diachronic connection is caught by a stand-up
comic/poet, Ken Glickman:

> Deaf or Something?
> Someday, someplace, somebody
> Will, to my face, scream
> You deaf or something?
> And, I will pause momentarily—
> With profound thanks
> To all the Deafies[12] that came before me . . .
> And with great camaraderie
> For all the Deafies that will come after me . . .
>
> —and I will then say nothing . . .
> Except to say . . .
>
> Something.

In *Habits of the Heart*, a book about the discourses and values in modern
U.S. life, the authors say a geographic community "almost always has a
history and so is also a community of memory, defined in part by its past
and its memory of the past" (Bellah, Madsen, Sullivan, Swidler, & Tipton
1985, p. 333). The deaf have a collective history that provides current and
future generations a sense of grounding and place so that each new generation feels part of an extended community. There are books that chronicle the history of the deaf (e.g., Gannon, 1981) and stories passed down
from one generation to the next, creating folklore (Rutherford, 1993).
    There is also a sense of living history born of younger generations that
are in touch with older generations. At a high school reunion we videotaped, a class of deaf alumni shared their school memories with younger
students and added these taped memories to the official school archives.
They talked about old rules such as when boys and girls were not allowed
to play outside at the same time. They talked about educational methodology that has waxed and waned, and their experiences with these changing
trends. They talked about specific individuals and how those people shaped
their lives. Thus, older deaf people become ancestors who pass on their

---

[12]Defined by Glickman (1993) as "a deaf person who acts and looks like one."

stories, and this sharing between generations becomes a part of the ties that bind the deaf into a community.

Patricia's story illustrates the role history plays in sustaining a sense of connection to an extended community:

> *I moved around a lot to different communities and I would see people and say hello and try to get to know them and I'd see them signing in ASL, and we were able to join because we had the important key. We had good communication and all this other stuff. We could converse in ASL and we had deaf history inside of us.*

At another high school, a student heard stories about the old days from a groundsman and proposed a story for the school journal. The whole school buzzed about the days when the boys and girls in the high school used different stairways and the students farmed the grounds to produce some of their own food.

Recently, there has been a movement to reclaim the history of deaf education to show the prominent leadership roles of deaf individuals. In schools for the deaf around the United States, "Gallaudet Day," in early December, has been a day of assembly programs and other celebrations of the story of Alice Cogswell, a deaf child whose parents commissioned Thomas Gallaudet to teach her. In recent years, most schools have celebrated the day as Gallaudet *and* Clerc Day. Laurent Clerc was an experienced deaf teacher who came from France to work with and teach Gallaudet. There is currently an attempt to raise funds for a monument to him at the original school in Connecticut. This sense of history is important for local communities, and national and international history.

The sense of history among the deaf community is matched by a sense of the future. In 1912, John W. Jones went on record saying "There is no danger of sign language disappearing. It will live long after you and I are dead. If we were all to die tonight, a hundred years from now it would still be alive and serving the deaf" (reprinted in Garretson, 1991). In 1913, another visionary deaf leader made a film of sign language to preserve its beauty for future generations of the deaf. The entire 1993 issue of *A Deaf American Monograph* (Garretson, 1993) is devoted to hopes for the deaf community of the 21st century.

At a conference to determine legislative priorities for an upcoming session of a state government, one deaf leader announced, "the issues decided today are for the future of our deaf children" while another advised the delegates, "to predict the future is to invent it. That's what you are doing now, you are controlling your destiny."

In these public arenas, as well as in more private exchanges, the deaf community is extended into the future. A deaf woman quits her clerical job so she can work as a houseparent at a school for the deaf and make a difference in the next generation. Another volunteers her time to raise money for a retirement village for the deaf; deaf couples adopt deaf children partly because it is a way to provide for the future of the deaf community. It is not uncommon to hope that one's children are deaf, partly as a way to affect the future of deaf people. Young deaf college graduates who work at a school for the deaf are conscious of the possibility of making life better for deaf children because of what they have learned from their own experiences.

The point is not whether these motivations are indeed this simple but that people express this consciousness of the future as a factor in explaining their own lives. Such connections to the past and to the future nourish in the deaf a sense of having roots in a broad and expansive community. Thus deaf members situate themselves in time to create a sense of continuity and connection with those who preceded them and those who will come after. Although there is little familial continuity, the deaf create an historical continuity with deaf forbears and deaf descendants. They create a place for themselves between the past and the future. They are not only present at the scene; they create the scene.

Deafness as Ethos

The sense of belonging to a community larger than the immediate is also seen in the international bonds of the deaf. Patricia shared her feelings of connection to the deaf around the world in her thoughts about what she learned at the first international conference to celebrate deaf cultures the world over, called Deaf Way:

> At Deaf Way, I found that things are the same all over the world. There is a tendency to cherish deafness and their sign language, ASL, or whatever it may be. There's a lot of deaf people all over the world worrying that the hearing people are changing our language. And we all cherish our different deaf cultures. It's interesting that it's the same issues all around the world.

Thus many deaf members feel part of a larger world and take an interest in the deaf in other parts of the world. From the global to the local sphere, there exists generally in the deaf community a feeling of belonging. Many members project a belief that certain attitudes and ways of being are quintessentially deaf and are shared by other deaf people around the world. In sharp contrast to the isolated identity of nonmembers; for members, a deaf identity is a communal identity.

Deafness as Communication

When asked to talk about the central thing about the deaf community, members over and over again respond, "communication, clear communication" or "real communication." In clear communication lies the possibility of relationship. The longing for relationship draws the deaf to each other to form the basis for a community. Through "real" communication they are able to achieve deep relationships that create a rich vitality within this community. Members tell many stories of the contrast between the isolation of deaf individuals in the hearing world, even their own families, and the fabric of relationships within the deaf community. Recalling the tragic scene at his mother's deathbed, LaVesque (1994) wrote:

> *It was obvious that we had very little time left, so we tried to say all the things we had in our hearts. I talked and lipread her. Toward the end, she wanted to tell me something. I didn't understand and asked her to repeat it. Twice more I asked her to repeat, then finally I gave her a piece of paper. She was only able to write the letter O or maybe C, before her eyes closed and the deep sleep of coma overtook her.*
>
> *In the weeks and months before my mother's death, we spent many hours going over issues and preparing for her death. It was done verbally, not comfortably, but adequately.*
>
> *My mother made sure I had the finest oral education around. She was proud of my speaking ability, and impressed by my less-than-perfect lipreading. But we never had a real conversation. Oh, I knew she loved me. I knew she was proud of me. But I'll never know her last words to me . . . the frustration of our final moments together will haunt me. If she had learned sign language, she would have been able to tell me clearly whatever it was that was so important to her.*
>
> *That moment was a painful one. It made me think of all the other things she might have told me over the years, but she didn't.*

This longing to know and be known by a parent, the regret that such a relationship was never possible, is expressed by many members of the deaf community. Many talk about feeling closer to people at their school for the deaf than to their families, because at school they could communicate. The alienation from families may be related to the need for many children to board at central schools far from their homes. We frequently encounter day students whose communication with parents is also severely restricted.

COMMUNICATION AND RELATIONSHIPS

Many members claim that life in its fullest sense did not begin for them until they were able to partake of real communication. Many believe that communication is the basis of close relationships among the deaf. Whether it happens at 6, 12, or 25, people often tell essentially the same story: a story of finding oneself in the middle of other deaf people for the first time—deaf people who are signing—and suddenly realizing that they are home. Seventeen-year-old Melanie was taken to board at her residential school for the deaf when she was 6:

> *One day my parents drove me here and then they got in the car to leave without me. I cried and cried, but they went away. I didn't know. . . . Then I looked around and I saw other kids—like me—for the first time! My eyes drank it in, and I started to experience communication. I saw a girl—she was Black—and I didn't know what to think. I'd never seen anyone with Black skin before, and I was a little bit scared. But I looked at the other kids, the ones with skin like mine, and they seemed perfectly comfortable, so I was, too. We could all communicate.*
>
> *Then one day I got on the school bus for a long ride, and as I was staring out the window, who do I see but my parents! I cried and cried and they were so happy to see me. I spoke some words for them and they were so happy because that made it worth it to have me so far away from home. But no, they never learned to sign or communicate. Clear communication was something I found at school.*

The Language of Signs: Freedom or Limitation?

Nonmembers who are not members of a deaf community, like most hearing people, see the language of signs as a burden and a limitation. They often are proud of never signing. Or they are embarrassed to sign in front of hearing people. They may be grateful to parents and therapists who helped them to "go the oral route." One 19-year-old said she was so grateful that her mother had fought to keep her in public school, because if she had been sent to the deaf school, she would have learned to sign and become "handicapped." But others talk about finding signs in themselves the way a sculptor might talk of finding a statue in marble. Signs were forbidden in most schools—even in dormitories after school hours until the 1970s. Many feel that the new policies of tolerance are like the end of slavery. In the words of a man in his 60s:

> *[Today] the deaf are free. The shackles are unleashed and we can step into the fresh air and breathe again. We are like withered people who have come back to life.*

To members, the biggest difference between the deaf and the hearing is signs. Many members feel they can be themselves only by using ASL. Many say this is the only way they can express their true selves. Others are comfortable and feel "like themselves" using oral English, but they still say they cherish ASL as their true language. Contrast this view with that of nonmembers and hearing people: For them the biggest difference between the hearing and the deaf is hearing loss. For Cheryl Heppner (1992), life for a deaf person among the hearing is "*Life as a Spectator Sport*" while life among the deaf allows one to be "a participant in all possible parts" of life (p. 189). She tells about driving home after only a week at Gallaudet College. In the supermarket at home, she experienced an epiphany about her life before Gallaudet:

> *I walked inside the store, as I had twice a week for the past year, and suddenly, for the first time, I felt frightened. The din was unbelievable. And everywhere I looked I was surrounded by people saying things I couldn't understand. It was such a complete change from the past week that I could barely handle it. This was the world I'd grown up in, but suddenly I felt like a foreigner coming to it for the first time. I was so shocked by the depth of my feeling that I clung to my cart for several minutes before my hands stopped shaking (Heppner, 1992, p. 137).*

The language of signs is the key to clear communication and the key to the deaf individual's ability to enter into the center of a scene. Without clear communication, the scene is busy and confusing. The deaf individual must watch and guess what is going on and must manage the scene through conscious effort. With clear communication, the deaf individual has the luxury that all cultural members have—the luxury of taking communication for granted. Only then can one lose oneself in communication; that is, only when communication is transparent can one focus on meanings, feelings, relationships, and free interaction. The sublime irony is that the visibility associated with sign that so many people fear is actually the mechanism that makes it possible for communication to be transparent. Only when communication is transparent can one participate in "all possible parts" of life. Only then can one move from a spectator role to a central role in a scene. Members believe this transparency is possible only with signs.

Emotional Release or Repression?

Stories like the ones presented here are common. People tell such stories passionately, ruefully, or angrily. Many of the life experiences that elicited weeping surprised the tellers and the listeners, because they seemed so trivial—routine encounters with clerks at store counters, for example. But it is exactly the ordinary aspects of such routine encounters that make it extraordinary for deaf individuals. The emotional relief of discovering that there are places where one can enter freely into relationships often makes way for joy. Niemenen (1990, pp. 218–219) said, "I've never been able to laugh anywhere except in the deaf world."

In sharing these findings with hearing audiences, we have found it difficult to convey and explain this emotionality. One man responded,

"That's nothing new. Lots of people have trouble communicating with their parents." Other hearing people tell us the same thing. It is as if these hearing people are picturing an *Oprah* show about the problem of having one's motives and needs misunderstood (Carbaugh, 1996). These deaf individuals are light years short of worrying about misunderstanding of motives or emotional needs. They are not even at the first level of exchanging mundane information in their own homes.

Picture again the girl wandering from room to room to see if anyone is home and wondering where everyone has gone. Picture the 6-year-old left in a strange place because no one has the ability to communicate what is happening to her. She has no way of knowing if she will ever see her family again or why she is being abandoned. Picture another girl—14 this time—looking for the half-eaten lemon she left on the table. She says to her father, "Where's my lemon?" She speaks and she signs several times, but her father cannot understand even this rudimentary message. The mother is sought. After 10 minutes, they all understand that the lemon was mistakenly discarded. A little later they sit down to dinner. Mother, father, and younger brother chat a bit. Daughter eats. The two kids exchange a gaze to laugh at the amount of food on father's plate. This is the only message exchanged with daughter.

In contrast, the next day the daughter sits in the library at her school for the deaf, discussing her crushes on movie stars, gossiping about friends, and engaging in word play with a friend. The second scene involves sign language. The second scene fully and freely involves the girl. In the second scene she is immersed in the communication, and it can be transparent.

For members, life among the hearing is restricted to surfaces, to watching as spectators, whereas life among the deaf is a full participatory experience, with the full range of social identities available. What makes the difference is access to real communication, that is, conversation. Nonmembers, like hearing people, tend to look at life among the deaf as restricted and constricted. But for members, the converse is true: Life among the deaf is wide open, bursting, full of possibilities. A tremendous emotional release is associated with the ability to have normal, full, and real conversations, and members have had that experience only among the deaf. Created is a deep sense of community in the deaf who find in their togetherness what they cannot find alone. Perhaps most important, life among the deaf, by offering access to communication, offers access to the self. As Jan said:

> It wasn't until I went to Gallaudet that I met signing deaf people. To me, it was like coming home. For the first time in my life, I felt like I really belonged. When I found the deaf, I found me.

CULTURAL PRAGMATICS

This chapter focuses on the importance that being able to participate fully in everyday interaction has on one's sense of well-being. The focus has been on people who are deaf, and the impact on their social and cultural identity of participating (or not) in everyday communication. Underlying our discussion has been the theory that communication practices create culture and cultural identity, and we demonstrate this process through the experiences of deaf individuals.

Culture can be seen as a constructed reality that is inherited and built from symbols that shape our actions, identities, thoughts, and sentiments. Symbolic forms are independent of, but gain their meaningfulness through, social sharing. Communication is a creative process of building and reaffirming relationship through symbols. Culture essentially becomes our communicative activities and refers primarily to the products of the arts and language. Our constitutive relations as human beings are linguistic. Vygotsky, Mead, and Cassirer all stress the reciprocity of learning from social interaction and constituting social identity through communication.

Much of our folk knowledge about culture stresses the notion of inheritance. We expect culture to be handed down from adults to their children as a legacy. But, if this were all that actually happened, culture would be static or degraded over time, and an individual's role would be minimal. Inheritance is only part of the story, however, because individuals continuously engage in interaction that builds their own identities and reconstitutes the overall culture. Agar (1996) highlighted the necessary duality of language and culture by coining the blended term, *languaculture*. Each single practice is part of the larger expressive system in which one lives. Thus there is a "large, 'super-sense' of the cultural community" (Carbaugh, 1996, p. 15) that is presumed to extend across time and person and is not tied to particular moments. This is a set of thoughts, images, and expectations carried in the mind. The symbols of identity then cycle to identify human agents in particular communicative practices.

Because identity is interactively constituted, interactants' ascription of an identity to an individual is significant. If one ascribes an identity to an individual, one is making interpretations according to one's understanding of the ascribed identity. Such ascribed identities may, in fact, not fit and thus problematize identity for such individuals. There are many individuals whom others would place as part of an ethnic system, for example, but who are not part of that system, because they were raised outside it and are not part of an ethnic community of practice (Hanks, 1996). They may not share at all in the larger sense of the ethnic community or in specific communication practices of the community; they may even be excluded by those who do.

Nevertheless, because of others' expectations they are forced, in some ways, to define themselves through or in contrast to this ethnic community. *Cultural pragmatics* is the study of "particular communicative practices-in-use" and the interpretation of "the symbols, forms, and meanings that comprise them" (Carbaugh, 1996, p. 14). One key concept in the study of particular communicative practices-in-use is that they are always situated in particular contexts. Thus the method of study is a form of thick description (Geertz, 1977). Although there may be a larger sense of the extended culture and a larger sense of the abstracted self, the self never actually acts except in particular situations with particular others. Social identity is, in Carbaugh's (1996) term *immanent* in individual, situated communication practices.

Social identities are immanent; they are taken for granted because they implicate other identities and social structures. Most communication is not strategic or deliberative but automatic, and the social implications of the communication are also automatic. These implications are on two levels. On one level they enact the notion of cultural agent that obtains in a society. For U.S. citizens, cultural agency is related to individuality, equality, rights, and so on. The deaf are cultural agents within their societies. The issues of identity for deaf individuals are at the level of social identities, especially the aspect of social identity made operational through conversation. The study of deaf individuals, whose participation in conversation cannot be taken for granted, casts light on the importance of conversation to this process of social identification.

SUMMARY

Full participation in everyday, routine, "taken-for-granted" communication is not always an option for non-signing deaf persons who function within a hearing world, but it is for signing deaf persons who function within the deaf community. This real communication and participation is made possible through the language of signs. The emotional release and belonging that comes with discovery of the deaf community is a sharp contrast to the loneliness that many deaf people feel among the hearing. The key feature of the deaf community membership identity is immersion in communication within relationships.

The observing, but not participating, deaf do not create or experience a cultural community. They even have trouble getting together in functional, limited groups. Although they have much in common with one another, their affiliation is practical and occasional. In contrast, the signing deaf create a cultural community. It is a community with a perceived territory, history, global ethos, and language. Most significant for the theory of cultural pragmatics, it is a community that is perceived by its members and created through communication (Philipsen, 1989). Members have a *sense* of the practices and symbols of identity in the community. They have a *sense* of belonging and recognition. Unlike self-help groups, hobbyists, or other kinds of partial affiliations, the *sense* shared by deaf community members "create[s] a large, 'super-sense' of the cultural community" (Carbaugh 1996, p. 15). This supersense comes from the fullness of free communication through sign language. Each single practice is part of the larger expressive system in which one lives.

The different experiences presented in this chapter demonstrate that a deaf identity can lie in a larger community that is only partially accessible to the deaf individual and where communication is never transparent. Thus deaf nonmembers certainly have the cultural identity of Americans. In social interaction, their enactment of identity is often limited to their disability. Identity can also be located in a larger community that is fully accessible to the deaf individual, where communication is transparent, and where a full range of social identities is available to the deaf individual. They also illustrate the importance of the freedom to mix aspects of identity rather than forcing individuals into only two profiles.

What is striking about the identification of the deaf community is that there is a shared identity of deafness—and especially of a signing, "real deaf" identity. Within that identity, there are different social identities enacted. The members can accentuate different identities and affiliations. Future research in the deaf community can identify scenes in which actors identify agents-in-scenes as different and differentially important. That is, we can focus on when the communal identity is accentuated and when other social identities are emphasized. Our research has focused on explication of the communal identity. We are beginning to understand how blind we have been to what deaf people have been telling us all these years. They long for the freedom to be themselves and to be able to enact different social identities. Life without full access to communicative interaction can result in life lived as an observer, while unimpeded access can result in life lived as a participant. For all of us, as humans, this is an important difference.

REFERENCES

Agar, M. (1996). *Language shock.* New York: Quill.

Bellah, R., Madsen, R., Sullivan, W., Swidler, A., & Tipton, S. (1985). *Habits of the heart.* New York: Harper & Row.

Bierce, A. (1971). *Tales of soldiers and civilians* (J. H. Jackson, Ed.). Norwalk, CT: Heritage Press. (Original work published 1891)

Bryce, J. (1996). *Retrospective accounts of deaf adults and their implications for current education of the deaf.* Unpublished master's thesis, University of Texas, Austin.

Carbaugh, D. (1996). Situating selves. Albany: State University of New York Press.

Garretson, M. (Ed.). (1991). *Deafness: 1993–2013* (A Deaf American monograph, Vol. 41). Silver Spring, MD: National Association of the Deaf.

Garretson, M. (Ed.). (1993). *Deafness: 1993–2013* (A Deaf American monograph, Vol. 43). Silver Spring, MD: National Association of the Deaf.

Gannon, J. (1981). *Deaf heritage: A narrative history of deaf America.* Silver Spring, MD: National Association of the Deaf.

Geertz, C. (1977). *Interpretation of cultures.* New York: Basic Books.

Glickman, K. (1993). Deaf or something? In M. Garretson (Ed.), *Deafness: 1993–2013* (p. 119). Silver Spring, MD: National Association of the Deaf.

Hanks, W. (1996). *Language as communicative practices.* Boulder, CO: Westview.

Heppner, C. (1992). *Seeds of disquiet.* Washington, DC: Gallaudet.

Lavation, L., & Holmes, V. (1991). ALDAN: Out from in between. *Deaf Life, (3),* 10–17.

LeVesque, J. (1994). My mother's last words. *The Endeavor,* 2ff.

Niemenen, R. (1990). *Voyage to the island.* Washington, DC: Gallaudet University.

Padden, C., & Humphries, T. (1988). *Deaf in America: Voices from a culture.* Cambridge, MA: Harvard University Press.

Philipsen, G. (1989). Speech and the communal function in four cultures. *International and Intercultural Communication Annual, 13,* 79–92.

Poeppelmeyer, D. (1995). *The meaning of being deaf.* Unpublished doctoral dissertation, The University of Texas, Austin.

Raimondo, D., & Maxwell, M. (1987). The modes of communication used in junior and senior high school classrooms by hearing-impaired students and their teachers and peers. *Volta Review, 89,* 263–275.

Rutherford, S. (1993). *Study of deaf American folklore.* Silver Spring, MD: Linstok.

Chapter 7

Spiraling Connections:
The Practice of Repair in
Bektashi Muslim Discourse

Frances Trix
Wayne State University

Linguistic anthropologists have long recognized the great variety of speech communities and the perspective that research in different speech communities offers on discourse generalizations and findings (Brody, 1991; Duranti, 1988; Goodwin, 1981; Gumperz, 1982; Hill, 1995; Hymes, 1981; Ochs, 1988). They have also recognized the perspective that research in different speech communities offers on the social construction of cultural categories, for example, the social construction of incompetence as a Foucaultian sort of "dividing-practice," often expressed in asymmetrical relationships of dependency in certain institutions of Western cultures. In this paper, however, I present a non-Western speech community wherein the central relationship promotes asymmetrical dependency but at the same time profoundly nurtures competence through language.

The purpose of the paper is thus to present cultural perspective on Western social construction of incompetence through language by analyzing interaction in a very different speech community. The speech community is that of a minority Muslim group dating from the 13th century, the Bektashis,[1] whose devotion to their spiritual masters, and community-based mystic practices invite parallels with Hasidic communities.[2] The central

---

[1] The best source on the Bektashis in English is still Birge (1937).

[2] There are many sources on Hasidism and on particular Hasidic masters. Fewer, however, focus on the student-master relationship. Of these, an interesting one, albeit based on the secondary source of Martin Buber, is Feinberg (1972).

relationship is the age-old one of spiritual master and student, studied
here in the religious center of an Albanian Bektashi immigrant community
in America. The discourse data is taped weekly dialogues in Turkish with
the spiritual master. Such dialogues have long been understood as a main
medium of learning of the student with the master. The focus of analysis
is the discourse feature of repair as described in Schegloff, Jefferson, and
Sacks' (1977) classic article as well as in Jefferson's (1987) article on exposed and embedded repair, and how such repair figures in discourse data
from 10 years of taped weekly dialogues with the spiritual master.

Repair is often an interactional strategy used to construct incompetence
through replicating power asymmetries. The conceptual strength of the
category of repair over simple correction is that repair includes self-correction and modification, as well as correction by another. And while the
dialogues of master and student are framed by Bektashi tradition as non-
confrontational in any direct sense, they are also understood to promote
the self-confrontation that is deemed necessary for spiritual growth of the
student. What then are the forms and implications of self-correction, other-
correction, and repair-opportunity space in such ongoing interaction?

Besides the unusual cultural setting, the 10-year data set of interaction
with the same master and student contrasts sharply with the multiple
sources and contexts of interaction often cited in studies of repair (excep-
tions to this are Goodwin, 1990; Philips, 1992; Tannen, 1984). In contrast,
the data of this study allows the possibility of studying repair within an
evolving relationship over what is for linguists, albeit not historians, the
longue durée. In one sense it poses the question to what extent our understanding of repair has been a reflection of data and analysis wherein relationships among participants are deemed irrelevant. In another ethnographic sense this study uses findings from Conversational Analysis on
repair and their legalistic forms to contrast and foreground the Bektashi
practice of repair.[3]

In presenting Bektashi practices of repair, I first relate dicta from Conversational Analysis on repair to Bektashi conventions and discourse formulations of interaction. Then I contextualize the immigrant Balkan Muslim community in the larger world of Islamic and Bektashi discourse, and
the vulnerability of a student in a particular classic instance of repair by
a Bektashi master. After that I present select examples of embedded repair

---

[3]Other possible ways of analyzing Bektashi nonconstruction of language incompetence
could be with reference to positive and negative politeness, deference and demeanor à la
Goffman (1967), or even the concept of "face" in different cultures. However, I prefer the
contrast with repair in Conversational Analysis for two main reasons. First, Conversational
Analysis is firmly grounded in data that readily compares with my discourse data. Secondly,
the unabashedly Western scientific form in which findings of Conversational Analysis are
expressed provides a most telling contrast with how Bektashi ways are expressed.

and exposed repair of the master, student, and community. Finally, I summarize findings and speculate on the social construction of incompetence through language and what in Bektashi cultural practice mediates against its construction.

But first, to orient the reader to the Islamic Ottoman cultural world that Bektashi tradition draws from, and to give insight into attitudes toward public construction of incompetence there, I offer a cultural "translation" of a popular American game show by a culture that also draws from a common Islamic Ottoman past. The American game show is "Name That Tune." Its translation, by the same name, which I witnessed on Turkish television in 1985, draws on the tradition of Turkish classical music that has been passed down from master to student in a fashion similar to the way religious knowledge is passed down among the Bektashis (who have long been Turkish-based). In the American form of "Name That Tune," incompetence is socially constructed in that the multiple contestants, who are played selections of popular music to identify, are given a limited period of time in which to respond. Sometimes they do not know the tune, the buzzer sounds, and so their relative "incompetence" is made public. As for those who successfully identify the tunes, their performances are compared and they are given prizes whose cash value can also be compared across the program and across different programs.

In contrast, in the Turkish version the music is not popular music but rather modes from the classical musical tradition. Contestants are treated more like guests, they appear one at a time, and are not timed in their responses. There is no buzzer and no one is ever wrong. That is, no one ever makes an error of identification of a mode. Viewers may test themselves in the process, and thus may be privately incorrect, but there is no public display of incompetence. Finally, instead of prizes that can be accorded dollar values and compared, the participants receive the opportunity to perform, that is, to sing from a classical mode, on television.

The conclusion that I would draw from this contrast is not simply that no category of incompetence was constructed in the Turkish version. Rather I would suggest that aspects of the American format were rejected precisely because such categories of incompetence do exist in the Ottoman cultural world but are deemed more serious business. For an owner of a television station to invite people to participate in a way in which they could be publicly shown wrong would be a grave insult. Rather, what is missing is the ambiguous category from Western society of the value of "not winning but playing the game." Indeed, in Ottoman culture historically there were contests of poets in which the loser lost not just the contest but also his head.[4]

---

[4]For a 20th-century view of these contexts, one in which the winner took the lute of the loser rather than his head, see Kurban Said (1970).

CONTRASTING FORMULATIONS OF REPAIR: CONVERSATIONAL ANALYSIS AND BEKTASHI WAYS

As mentioned, repair is a common strategy for construction of incompetence through language. Consider, for example, a doctor's correction of a patient's reference to "low blood," or an attorney's correction of a client's notion of slander, or for that matter, a judge's correction of an attorney's behavior—or even, for a more appropriate comparison, certain interactions of therapist and client (see Ferarra in this volume). Repair, however, includes not just correction by another, but also modification and most significantly self-correction.

The classic article on repair in Conversational Analysis by sociologists Schegloff, Jefferson, Sacks (1977) notes the important place of self-correction in "ordinary conversation" in the first two of its three dicta. (This preference for self-correction has been supported by Moerman, 1977, in Thai conversational data.) Notice also the third dictum for its reference to incompetence:

1. There is an organizational preference for self-correction.
2. Other-initiations overwhelmingly yield self-corrections.
3. Occurrence of other-correction is highly constrained, except in transitional situations of "not yet competent."

As Bektashi discourse is centrally concerned with relationships—of master and student and human and God—it too has formulations relevant to discourse repair. But based on a much older and more oral culture, and one that does not suffer the weight of authority invested in Western scientific laws, Bektashi rhetoric is quite different from the above dicta. One of these relevant Bektashi formulations is the following aphorism told to me by Bektashi leader Baba Rexheb: "We would never pull the veil from anyone's face." Notice that whereas the Conversational Analysis dicta are phrased in the positive, the Bektashi aphorism is phrased in the negative, thereby leaving the larger field of what happens, either self-correction or no correction, unspecified. The implications of this Bektashi saying relate to questions of dignity, that one should never put another human in a position of indignity. In the highly oral culture of Bektashi societies, direct correction by another would often be seen as bringing indignity. Notice also the third dictum under Conversational Analysis. In cultural terms, the constraint on other-correction except in transitional situations of "not yet competent" is grounded in assumptions of progress and development. In contrast, the Bektashi student is understood to be always in transition in spiritual matters; nevertheless there is no public construction of incompetence.

Building on the category of other-correction, there have been further formulations from Conversational Analysis. In particular, Jefferson (1987) developed the distinction in other-correction between exposed and embedded correction, as follows:

exposed correction (whatever has been going on prior to correction is discontinued; correcting becomes the interactional business).

embedded correction (the correction is incorporated into ongoing talk).

In terms of Bektashi formulations relevant to repair, most refer to potential other-initiated correction, but more in terms of warning against drawing any public attention to perpetrators than in measures that differentially dilute this attention. For example, another type of Bektashi commentary relevant to questions of repair is associated with the most important piece of clerical garb, namely the *hirka*. The *hirka* is a long sleeveless vest that is traditionally worn by Bektashi dervishes (monks) and Babas (abbots). The outside of the vest is understood to symbolize the vow of poverty of dervishes, while the inside of the vest symbolizes the duty of Bektashi dervishes to "cover the sins of others." Note that "covering the sins of others" is a positive formulation, stronger than the negatively formulated interdiction "not to pull the veil from anyone's face."

A short Bektashi tale serves to make clearer the meaning of the *hirka* commentary to "cover the sins of others." The main personage of this tale is Imam Ali, who was both the son-in-law of the Prophet Muhammad as well as the bringer of mystic understanding of the Qur'an, and was highly revered by Shi'a-oriented Bektashis.

One day Imam Ali was walking down a narrow road. On either side were dry brick walls that surrounded the courtyards of the houses. One wall was slowly falling down, however, and where a brick had fallen out, Imam Ali could see a man and woman in the courtyard of the home engaged in something they shouldn't have been doing. Immediately the Imam picked up a brick from the road and put it in the hole so no one could see in, and then walked on.

Unlike other traditions wherein a similar situation led to the stoning of the woman, or at best the shaming of those about to carry out a stoning and then an admonition to the woman, here the Bektashi way is to literally cover the visual access to others' behavior, to cover their sins without comment.

Yet another dictum of Conversational Analysis on repair (Schegloff, Jefferson, Sachs, 1977, p. 375) relates to the range, in terms of turns at talk, within which repair occurs: "The repair opportunity space is continuous and discretely bounded—three turns long starting from the trouble source turn." In Bektashi discourse the closest parallel to turns at talk would be couplets, in their rich tradition of spiritual poetry and chants. But the notion behind the Conversational Analysis dictum, that repair occurs relatively close to the trouble source, is of little significance to Bektashi ways. Rather, what is more important is that at some time those who have been corrected recognize this.

For example, in the following Bektashi tale two villagers were on their way to give false testimony for payment in a large town. They stopped at a Bektashi *Tekke*, a sort of Muslim monastery, on their way and the Bektashi Baba immediately recognized the purpose of their journey. As they sat drinking coffee with the Baba, and no doubt after an appropriate amount of polite small talk, the Baba told them this story:

> Far to the north in a Bektashi *tekke* there took place an initiation ritual of a new member. At the initiation, another member of the *tekke* recognized that the new initiate was a man who years earlier had stolen a horse from him. After the ritual and the time of *muhabbet*, or sharing of spiritual chants, the other member started hinting that there was a man among them who didn't belong, one who had done ill in the past and never paid or come clean. The Baba interrupted this talk with other talk. But again the member hinted more broadly. Again the Baba tried to steer the conversation to other topics, yet the man persisted in stating that there was one there who had done something wrong in the past and who didn't belong. The Baba then looked directly at the older member and said, "Here we do not mention such things. Here is not the place for such talk."

The villagers recognized that the Baba knew of their plans. They left the *Tekke* and journeyed back to their village, abandoning their earlier intentions of giving false testimony.

This is a most discretely negotiated instance of repair. And while there could be seen to be a time constraint in terms of the proposed court testimony, in terms of repair what is important is the eventual recognition of the repair and its discreteness. In terms of Conversational Analysis, however, this then is an example of other-initiated self-correction. That is, the Baba initiated the repair, but the villagers were the ones who followed up on self-correction, all without public mention, that is, without having the veil pulled from their faces.

The Bektashi forms of commentary on repair are here expressed on the canvas of activities including but not restricted to spoken communication. In the following sections, the examples of master-initiated and student-initiated repair show how specific verbal interactions with the Baba are continuous with such commentary.

CONTEXT AND CLASSIC BEKTASHI PRACTICE
MEDIATING FOREIGNER INCOMPETENCE

In the last section I reviewed formulations of repair in Conversational Analysis and contrasted these with related Bektashi discourse to familiarize the reader with the very different cultural world of the Bektashis, one that is vitally concerned with relationships and is orally sophisticated. The very fact of the existence of these Bektashi tales and commentary shows that Bektashi tradition has deemed such teachings worthy of attention. In this section I contextualize the particular community in the larger Muslim and Sufi traditions. I also give a classic example of repair by the Bektashi Baba in the context of my study with him.

The immediate setting of research for this paper is an immigrant community of first and second generation Albanians in southeast Michigan. Albanians are a Balkan people with strong oral traditions. Thanks to the technology of the telephone and to the cultural tradition of visiting as the primary social recreation, Albanians are able to live in different parts of the Detroit metropolitan area, but still interact as if they were in a much smaller town. There is a rich variety of discourse forms: from public rhetoric and eulogies by men to laments by women; from songs whose manner of singing represents the earliest polyphony in Europe to spiritual chants individually performed; from gossip and verbal jousting by both men and women to metalanguage about the many Albanian dialects of the mountainous lands where Albanians have long lived on the Western side of the Balkan peninsula.

The community is also Muslim, which adds to an already rich discourse world the special importance accorded the Arabic language by Islam and the Islamic discourse forms of commentary and prayer. Recall that the Qur'an is understood as the Word of God, and that the first pillar of Islam is the *shehadah*, or creed, whose reciting, with faith that "there is no God but God and Muhammad is His prophet," is the essence of Islam as well as the oath of conversion. But even more important, the community is Bektashi Muslim, a minority Muslim Order from 13th-century Anatolia, renowned for its spiritual poetry.

Bektashism, like other Muslim Sufi or mystic Orders, affords its members a more personal expression of affiliation and love of God through community rituals and gatherings than is generally available to the Sunni or orthodox Muslim community. Indeed Sufi Orders, like Hasidic communities in Judaism, often stand as a sort of critique of a legalism that has developed in both Islam and Judaism at different times in their histories. Thus the Bektashis have great faith in their spiritual masters, whom they see as intercessors; they place less emphasis on only fulfilling external practices of the letter of the law. This antilegalism mediates against simplistic categorizations of incompetence. The Bektashis also have the distinction of having accepted women as initiated members since their beginning in the 13th century, as well as having a muted belief in reincarnation.

The anchor of the Bektashis is formed by their spiritual masters, who trace their authority through chains of previous spiritual masters; their sense of time is cyclical, as great spiritual masters are embodied again and again. Learning is through being with such a master. In line with this, the data set is taped dialogues with the Bektashi master Baba Rexheb (1901–1995), who lived the last half of his life in America. The language of the dialogues is Turkish, long the main language of this Anatolian Order and of its spiritual chants, but a first language to neither Baba nor myself. Indeed, Baba and I speak different dialects of Turkish, his being a West Rumelian dialect, mine an Istanbul dialect, although we both move into each other's dialects on occasion. There is even a sense, after study together since 1968, that we have developed a common dialect, affected partly by our common Indo-European first-language backgrounds (Albanian and English), but more by the length of time spent together. The actual taping, however, was from the last 10 years of study, from 1984 to 1994. Thus the earliest taped dialogue represents some newness in getting used to the tape recorder, but not in terms of interacting with each other.

Across the tapes, certain conventions of master-student interaction stand out. First, it is up to the student to ask questions, to initiate inquiry. Secondly, the preponderance of talk is by the master; that is, the master talks, the student listens, but there is also give-and-take. Thirdly, it is the master who initiates closure, thereby eventually giving the floor back to the student should other questions arise. (For a fuller discussion of these conventions, see Trix, 1993.)

Considering the greater knowledge and authority of the master, the expectation would be that repair would tend to originate with the master. Indeed, this is a common occurrence, either when the master initiates repair and the student then self-corrects, or when the master initiates repair and then gradually builds on this repair. Of the first sort, where the master initiates repair and the student self-corrects, a memorable example took place early in my study with Baba.

We were reading together the poetry of Omar Khayyám, a Persian poet whose works are best known in the West through the broadly construed 19th-century English translations of Edward Fitzgerald ("a jug of wine, a loaf of bread—and Thou"). Although Baba knew Persian, I did not, and so we were reading these 11th-century poems in Turkish translation. Only, the Turkish translator had left many words in Persian. My reading aloud took on all the features of foreigner incompetence, worsened by my resentment of the translator for not translating more thoroughly. As I stumbled along, it seemed that most often the Persian words I didn't know referred to "wine glass" or "wine cup" or "wine container." I reached another Persian word I didn't know, looked at Baba, and said in Turkish "wine vessel?" Baba looked at me and then said in Albanian, "Fes të kuqë Libohovit?" That is, "Are all who wear red fezzes from Libohova?" Then he sat back, took his prayer beads, or *tesbih*, from the pocket of his *hirka*, and told me the following story:

> Once there was a shepherd from near Libohova [a town in southern Albania]. Now, you know that in the Ottoman Empire at this time men wore red fezzes, except that on the Western edge of Empire, the Albanians had long worn white felt caps. Only in one town in Albania, in Libohova, the men wore red fezzes, for they had men from their town who had served in the imperial judiciary and were proud of their connection to the center of power.
>
> Well, this shepherd, who had never been beyond the next mountain, was drafted into the Ottoman army and sent to, of all places, the capital city of Istanbul—"Dar es-Saadet" [an old Ottoman name for Istanbul, roughly, "the Abode of Happiness"]. After several years in the army, the shepherd returned and people asked him what Istanbul was like. The shepherd responded, "I never knew there were so many people from Libohova."

In making every unknown Persian word a wineglass, I had been like the Albanian shepherd who saw every man in a red fez from his provincial frame of reference. But in explaining the parallel, I have left out the pleasure, for both Baba and I laughed. And from that day on we shared a way of referring to other situations where frames of reference were too constricted, and always it was with merriment, building on our earlier shared experience. In terms of Conversational Analysis, this represented an exposed form—we had left off the earlier topic of the poem by Omar Khayyam to focus on the "correction"—and an other-initiated repair at that. But like the villagers who had changed their plans from giving false testimony, mine too was a self-correction. Baba initiated it, but I recognized myself in the shepherd. Of course this "exposed other-initiated self-correction" is known in older parlance as the time-honored genre of parable. Thus, far from constructing incompetence through a direct correction of my error, the Bektashi repair strategy instead allowed me to recognize my situation in the parable. That I was able to do this was a positive experience, and through this, Baba's and my relationship was strengthened and another memorable connection of shared experience created.

RANGE OF FORMS OF REPAIR:
EMBEDDED, EXPOSED, OVEREXPOSED

The preceding example of Bektashi repair through telling the parable of the shepherd was described in Conversational Analysis terms as an exposed form of other-initiated self-correction. In Figure 7.1, which summarizes

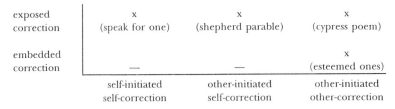

	x (speak for one)	x (shepherd parable)	x (cypress poem)
exposed correction			
embedded correction	—	—	x (esteemed ones)
	self-initiated self-correction	other-initiated self-correction	other-initiated other-correction

FIG. 7.1. Potential repair forms and distinctions from Conversational Analysis (marked to show major examples of this study).

the range of potential repair forms described by Conversational Analysis (CA), the shepherd parable is marked. Notice that this figure is organized is such a fashion that the further to the right and the higher up the gradients, the greater the potential indignity or marking of incompetence. That is, exposed other-initiated other-correction poses much greater indignity potential than embedded self-initiated self-correction.

Notice also that I do not focus on embedded self-initiated self-correction, or embedded other-initiated self-correction—forms of repair that are often the bedrock of repair studies and certainly have important ramifications for syntax studies (Fox et al., 1996). This is not to say that these do not occur in the 10 years of taped interactions with Baba. Indeed, they are most frequent. However, I choose to focus on the other forms of repair because they are more relevant to questions of creating categories of language incompetence.

What is missing from the Conversational Analysis repertoire is notice of relative levels of authority of the self and other. This is consistent with Conversational Analysis' lack of interest in backgrounds of interactants. The default assumption is that they are peers, of equal status and authority. That is not at all the case with Bektashi master and student, nor is it the case in many other situations. For example, it matters greatly whether it is the attorney who corrects the judge or the judge the attorney. To compensate for this missing parameter, I always note whether the corrector is master or student, and include a section on the delicate matter of correction of the master by the student. But I begin with more common forms of repair that potentially lead to the creation of incompetence, namely embedded other-initiated other-correction.

Baba's embedded other-initiated, other-corrected repairs of my comments only emerged when I transcribed[5] tapes of the dialogues; I had not been aware of them during their occurrences. One example of such an embedded repair, which I have translated from Turkish, took place in November 1985. My error was a confusion of the phrase, "esteemed ones"

---

[5]Transcription is according to modified conventions of Discourse Analysis transcription, similar to those of Tannen's book on conversational style (1984).

(13th-century spiritual teachers from the time of the organizing of the Sufi Orders) with a separate phrase denoting "friends of the Prophet," that is, friends of the 7th-century Prophet Muhammad. (Numbers to the left of the transcriptions refer to turns at talk. Here they show that this section was relatively early in the discussion.)

Transcription 1: Embedded Master-Initiated Master-Correction

9.	*Baba*:	So that even in "the words of the great ones"
		the *murshid* [spiritual master] is to his student
		as the prophet to his community
		that is the re- tie
		between the *murshid* and the student
		resembles the tie a—
		of the prophet and his community
10.	*FT*:	hmmm
11.	*Baba*:	like
		that between the prophet and his community\
12.	*FT*:	where does this saying come from Baba?
13.	*Baba*:	ha "the words of the great ones"
		the esteemed ones said this\
14.	*FT*:	ha\ **that means from the prophet**
		the time of the Noble prophet
		from *his* friends/
15.	*Baba*:	**from friends**
		from the esteemed ones
		they said this
16.	*FT*:	yes
17.	*Baba*:	yes\

Notice how Baba does not bring to my attention that I am only off by 600 years. Rather, he repeats a general word of mine, "friends," without the incorrect "of the Prophet," and then restates the correct term, "the esteemed ones." Then 36 turns later, Baba again cites the aphorism, "the murshid is to the student like the prophet to his community," only here he directly ascribes this to early Bektashi spiritual leaders. Since the Bektashi Order was founded in the 13th century, this clearly places the source of the quotation. According to strictures of Conversational Analysis this cannot be a repair because it is farther than three turns from the trouble source. A counter argument would be that dialogue of master and student is not ordinary talk, and yet it is very frequent and not at all stilted. Rather, I would say that to be able to identify repair at greater distances, the context of talk and interactants must be taken into consideration. In terms of questions of construction of incompetence, however, what this form of repair shows is a preference for subtle correction that may or may not be picked up, and an avoidance of direct correction.

Another somewhat less common form of repair in dialogues with Baba is exposed self-initiated self-correction by the student. A particular example I have of this on tape took place over a 2-year period and centered around the meaning of the phrase "to speak for someone." In the first instance of this on tape, in the context of Baba telling me the life story of Ali Baba, the Head Baba was encouraging a young Ali Baba to go back to Albania to a city known for its cantankerous people. The Baba promised "to speak for" the young Ali Baba, and always to be with him. I assumed the phrase meant that the Baba would "supply him with words" whatever the situation. However, when there indeed arose a difficult situation for Ali Baba in Albania, he didn't make any speeches or use any special words.

Two years later, Baba again told me the story of the life of Ali Baba of Elbasan. In turn 83, Baba noted the Head Baba saying that he would "speak for Ali Baba" should the occasion arise. In turn 114, there is a plot hatched against Ali Baba in the town in Albania, and the Head Baba back in Turkey pauses with his coffee cup in hand, doesn't drink, just stands there, then announces to the others present that Ali Baba was in a dangerous situation but that now he is safe. A dervish who is present writes down on a piece of paper that on such and such a day the Head Baba said this, and then he puts the piece of paper in his headpiece. Years later Ali Baba goes back to the Bektashi headquarters in Turkey, where he encounters the dervish who much earlier had noted the Head Baba's strange behavior and comment.

Transcription 2: Exposed Student-Initiated Self-Correction

129. *Baba:* he [the dervish] took it out of his headpiece
and read the paper
thus it was such and so\such and so\such and so\
ahhh he [Ali Baba] said
he kept his word my Dede [Head Baba]
for when he said that
YOU WHAT ever happens to you~
I will speak with you\
and WHAT happened if~
ya- as for separation if that's what you wish
I will not be away from you
we are together
thus it is true what he said
it came to be his words

130. *FT:*   excuse me Baba~
I will speak for you
that means that he spoke to the Majesty of Truth for him

131: *Baba:* eyyy of course\

Baba's words in Transcription 2 are the third reference to "speaking for someone" in the taped session. Only here, Baba used a different preposition, "with." Already there was some question in my mind of what the phrase meant, for in the difficult situation in Albania, Ali Baba didn't make any speeches. Here though I had a hypothesis, unlike my earlier notion in 1984 and 46 turns earlier in this session where I still assumed that "speaking for someone" meant "giving someone the necessary words." Here I asked if "speaking for someone" meant speaking to God (the "Majesty of Truth" is the Bektashi mystic term for God) for that person, that is, "praying for them." Baba confirmed that this was the meaning he intended.

What does this example represent for repair opportunity space? Recall that in Conversational Analysis the repair opportunity space is given as up to three turns from the trouble source. Here the immediate trigger for my self-correction in Transcription 2 was Baba's previous turn, but this was only part of the picture. The tendency is not to interrupt Baba with questions, but along with this, the tendency is for discussions to recycle, so that stories told are told again, often from different perspectives and with added episodes. This spiraling of story and reference over time encourages rethinking of understanding, such that the repair opportunity space, which in Conversational Analysis is deemed as at most three turns from the trouble space, warrants extension.

In the above example of Transcription 2, the trigger for my repair is indeed Baba's previous turn, but what is corrected was my assumption of what it meant to "speak for someone," an assumption probably first held when Baba first told me the story of Ali Baba's life years earlier. On tape there is a reference two years earlier, and in this tape, a reference 46 turns earlier and 15 turns earlier. It would be a diminished human whose reflections only lasted up to three turns.

The situation of learning in Bektashi practice is a stretching in the other direction, where a goal is to become *insan-i kamil*, that is, "the perfect human"—all that the image of the Majesty of Truth within us makes us long for. Only, as Bektashi discourse also notes, we are "like an ant going on pilgrimage." How far can we go? As far as we are given strength. But even this ant goes beyond three turns.

Besides student-initiated self-correction, there is also the more problematic student-initiated repair of the master. The power asymmetry of master over student would predict that this would be the least likely sort of repair strategy. From examination of the tapes, such instances do occur, but invariably with some form of modulation, like "excuse me" in the formal second person, along with reference to Baba's title. Another stricture of these forms of repair is that they occur at places of transition, most notably after Baba has signaled initial closure of a discussion. If these two strictures were omitted there could potentially be another form of incompetence constructed—not the usual one where power asymmetries are replicated but one where they are overthrown. As parents of teenagers may experience, this too can lead to forms of incompetence.

The following example of exposed student-initiated student-correction of the master took place late in 1994, at a transition place near the end of the taped interaction. The correction referred back to an unsuccessful double name search Baba had voiced 64 turns earlier, when he sought the name of a congress and name of its organizer. Again, this counters the Conversational Analysis dictum that repair be conducted within three turns of the trouble source. But unlike the earlier example of correction of the notion of what it meant for a Bektashi Baba to "speak for someone," here there is no apparent trigger.

Transcription 3: Exposed Student-Initiated Repair of Master

110. *Baba*: we even made them dervishes\
            thus that way\ this way\ that way\   [discourse marker of closure]
111. *FT*:   **excuse me Baba**
            you mentioned a congress   [64 turns earlier]
            what sort of congress/
                                      politi—political/
112. *Baba*: no—no\
            of course- . . ehh—
113. *FT*:   *lidhje*   [league]
114. *Baba*:   *lidhje e Prizrenit!* [the League of Prizren]
115. *FT*:   haa\
116. *Baba*: you know of the League of Prizren\
117. *FT*:   I know it\
118. *Baba*: ehh\
            . say/
            . . eh—the father of Midhat Bey/
            how did they call him/
119. *FT*:   oooo\ **of the Frashëri's/**
120. *Baba*:   Frashëri\
121. *FT*:   **was it Abdyl/**

Here, after Baba had summarized the point of the main narrative of our previous talk, I was able to call up Baba's first unsuccessful name search from 64 turns earlier and give half of its formal designation, *lidhje* ("league"), in Albanian. Baba immediately picked up on this. He then recalled his second, much earlier unsuccessful name search, which he had had regarding the organizer of the congress. He even remembered the name of the organizer's son, to which I was able to provide both the family name, "Frashëri," and the first name of the father, "Abdyl."

The placement of the exposed student-initiated correction, after the main body of the interaction and Baba's reiteration of the main point, followed by his discourse marker of closure ("thus that way\ this way\ that way\"), is significant. As mentioned earlier, one of the conventions of interaction, attested to throughout the 10 years of dialogues and presumably earlier, is that it is the master who draws dialogues to a close through various discourse markers and strategies. After the master's signal for closure, the student often affirms the closure and then the master confirms this affirmation. Other forms of affirmation are most often connections of earlier associations that I have with the topic of discussion, often from earlier dialogues. Thus, the above correction of the student can be categorized by its location as part of the larger category of connection, only here what was connected was an earlier question of the Baba within the same discussion.

There remains the category of repair of greatest potential indignity, of exposed other-initiated other-corrected repair. This is the form of repair most likely to lead to construction of incompetence. In the following example of this sort, I go beyond Jefferson's (1987) notion of "exposed," as having the correction become the focus of attention, to a community notion of "exposed," meaning "made public fun of." The interaction leads to the reiteration of the social category of foreigner, a common model of incompetence constructed through language.

The incident occurred in the early 1980s before I had learned much Albanian. I was at the Michigan Bektashi *Tekke* in the basement, helping the women prepare ritual food for many hundreds of people for the major Bektashi holiday the next day. There were large cauldrons for cooking this food, only they were stored up high in the basement cupboards. As I reached up for one I noted, in my faulty Albanian, that I was "longer" than any of the women there. Immediately I was greeted with cackles by the older Albanian women. All repeated my words of my amazing length. Of course, I was trying to say that I was "taller." For the rest of the day my words got repeated to much amusement. By the evening, the joke had worn thin. Then at the dinner table, before the meal—a special time of sharing and of poetry and *meze*, or hors d'oeuvres—again my words were repeated to Baba.

He sat back, closed his eyes, and chanted to me in Turkish the third stanza from the famous 16th-century poet, Pir Sultan Abdal:

Transcription 4: Exposed Master-Initiated Repair of Other-Initiated Other-Correction

Benim uzun boylu servi cinarım,
Yüreğime bir od düştü yanarım,

Kiblim sensin yüzüm sana dönerim,
Mihrabımdır iki kaşın arası. *hu*

* * *

My tall and graceful cypress, my plain tree,
A fire strikes my heart, I blaze,
Toward you I pray, I turn always facing you
My prayer niche is between your two brows. *hu*

The connection was the Turkish phrase in the first line meaning "tall."
But the connection was more than that, for what Baba had done was take
my uncomfortable situation and tie it to a poem he loved, a poem that
ever after would be mine as well. It was a repair of a repair; that is, Baba
was repairing the correction the whole community had been making all
day of my Albanian, and the incompetence I had come to feel as outsider.
Baba's repair transformed my embarrassment to pleasure and drew me
into the world of Bektashi discourse, long famous for its spiritual poetry.

In so doing he strengthened our relationship and broadened my world
of reference. For such connections would I gladly fall on my face again
and again.

CONCLUSION

What does this study of the Bektashi practice of repair contribute to
understandings of repair and of the social construction of incompetence
through language? The last example is the most memorable. In it Baba
transformed community attention to my early incompetence in Albanian—
a construction of foreignness through language—to connection with him
and the Bektashi tradition of mystic poetry. In all fairness though, the
immigrant community whose members effected this public construction
of incompetence live on a daily basis, in work and bureaucratic situations,
with constant construction by English speakers of their incompetence. Yet
Baba, their community leader, corrected their initiation and correction of
my error with reference to a tradition that recognizes no ethnic boundaries.
A strength of Bektashi tradition, one that has made it especially effective
in missionary work, is precisely this sort of overarching practice.

It is at the level of practice that Bektashi tradition can be related to
findings of Conversational Analysis on repair. Here there is significant
overlap. Where Conversational Analysis asserts the preference for self-correction; Bektashi practice abounds in instances of self-correction, not just
at the morphological and phrasal level, but also at higher conceptual levels.
Where Conversational Analysis distinguishes embedded and exposed repair

strategies; Bektashi practice too shows examples of embedded other-initiated correction of the graduated form, as well as exposed other-initiated correction of parable form.

The main disparity between the Conversational Analysis findings on repair and those exemplified in the data of Bektashi master and student, apart from rhetoric, lies in repair opportunity space. Where Conversational Analysis asserts that correction takes place within three turns of the trouble-source turn, Bektashi practice includes correction at distances of 36 turns (Transcription 1), 46 turns (Transcription 2), or 64 turns (Transcription 3). Some faulty assumptions can even be traced back several years. This longer distance of repair opportunity space in Bektashi practice relates only partly to the convention of reticence in interrupting the master's discourse and to the convention of the student's formalized place of participation after the master's initiation of closure. These conventions serve to heighten attention in the student, as ideas tend to be held longer before they can be referred to or queried.

The spiraling of stories and interlocking narratives across years of study and across single periods of interaction further facilitate such attention and the possibility for later corrections. This spiraling provides the student with appropriate material for affirming the closure of the interaction. This spiraling of stories also allows for reframing of understanding, often times self-corrections, where later narratives make clearer the point of narratives told much earlier. The wealth of shared experiences of previous interactions and the relatively long duration of Bektashi master and student relationships further contribute to the stockpile of potential connecting and redefining references. These can provide scaffolding for more complex ideas and the refining repair of the student's spiritual understanding.

These Bektashi conventions—specific discourse features of master and student talk, the spiraling of stories over time, and the relatively long relationship of master and student—although they are from somewhat specialized interactions, still shed light on assumptions of interaction of "everyday talk" in Conversational Analysis research. In particular, it appears that the data of Conversational Analysis is from interactions where, unlike the Bektashi master and student, the participants have generally equal claim to the floor. It also appears that the interactions from which Conversational Analysis draws its data do not have broader pedagogic purpose and could involve virtual strangers. Indeed, the question arises to what extent the emphases on morphosyntactic and phrasal repair across a short number of turn sequences reflect the disjointed nature of many data sets in Conversational Analysis. It is intriguing to speculate whether researchers' lack of concern with ongoing relationships among participants in data of Conversational Analysis is the crucial constraint that bars recognition of repair at greater distance than three turns. But then, the focus on adjacency pairs and close sequences that has characterized Conversational Analysis's pursuit of an organizational architecture of talk,[6] may also blind it to the possibility of longer-distance repair.

With reference to the social construction of language incompetence, recall that at the outset of this chapter I characterized the Bektashi speech community as a sort of contrasting example, one wherein power asymmetries led not to the construction of language incompetence but rather to the nurturing of language competence in a profound manner. This is the Bektashi community at its best, with particular attention to master-student relations. The example of the community derision of my early Albanian provides a valuable counterexample, a context to which Bektashi practice by the leader offers critical commentary. Regarding this context, recall again the example of the culturally linked Turkish game show through which I tried to demonstrate that the cultural context is not one unaware of possibilities of construction of incompetence, but one most wary of such possibilities. One way to guard against such constructions is with clear delineation of role, as with uniforms and ornaments in the military, or vestments among the clergy. These markers serve to narrow appropriate behavior of those confronting the wearers of the garments as well as the behavior of those wearing them. Of course language is the greatest garment of them all.

In American society, however, our concern is more often with construction of incompetence in those not allotted special higher-status clothing, people whose incompetence is often generated through evidence of marked forms of their language. These are the people most subject to "footing" shifts, as Goffman put it (1982)—that is, abrupt changes of alignment in interaction that involve loss of individual identity and merging with a class of, say, "the young," or "female," or "minority," or "teenager," or "foreigner," or "incapacitated," or "old," or any combination of these. Mediating against such downward shifts of categorization in our society is long-term interaction with an individual wherein novel dialects and communication patterns may develop, or personal development in an individual's ability to pull himself or herself into another, better-regarded category through schooling, work, and financial resources—these last again expressed through expansion of language repertoires.

In contrast, in the Bektashi tradition of master-student relations, which serves as a model for the larger Bektashi speech community, long-term interaction is the norm, whereas personal development apart from this interaction is irrelevant. The student studies with and serves the master until

---

[6]For an interesting discussion of a sociologist's perspective on the sociological framework of Conversational Analysis as contrasted with the linguistic framework of Discourse Analysis, see Sharrock and Anderson (1987).

the master dies. The language of any import is their language of communication. The master continues to intercede for the student after death—there is teaching beyond the grave. Western notions of agency and personal development as grounds for construction of competence are clouded by the understanding of outcomes as based on intercession of earlier spiritual masters, not achievement of individuals in the here and now.

In such a speech community and particularly in the discourse of master and student, repair and correction fall within the larger category of connecting—of connecting the student with the master, as exemplified in the parable of the red fez, and connecting the student with the larger world of Bektashi discourse, as exemplified in Baba's matching a 16th-century Bektashi spiritual poem with the community's correction of my error in Albanian adjective choice. In the larger spiritual frame, the repair that the master works to effect is a connecting not with a discourse trouble source but with the source of our being, a sort of "darning of the universe," since in this life we have all been separated from our true source. In Hasidic terms, there is the notion of repair as "*tikkun*," the mending and transforming of this imperfect world.[7] In linguistic terms, what matters is communication most personally entered into and yet expressed through the sharing of Bektashi spiritual poetry (Trix, 1993).

Recall yet again the Turkish cultural translation of the American game show, "Name That Tune," whose focus involved classical Turkish music. In the Turkish form this game demonstrates, as in the Bektashi tradition of learning, a spiraling of listening and performing, of passing on tradition with careful avoidance of creating categories of incompetence. Like the student in the Bektashi tradition, the direction is to replicating the tradition, the emphasis on connecting with that tradition, not defining its boundaries by those publicly constructed as incompetent.

REFERENCES

Birge, J. (1965). *The Bektashi order of dervishes*. London: Luzac & Co.

Brody, J. (1991). Indirection in the negotiation of self in everyday Tojolab'al women's conversation. *Journal of Linguistic Anthropology*, *1*(1), 78–96.

Duranti, A. (1988). Intentions, language, and social action in a Samoan context. *Journal of Pragmatics*, *12*, 13–33.

Feinberg, H. (1972). *Teacher and student in Buber's Hasidic tales*. Unpublished doctoral dissertation, Department of Education, Harvard University, Cambridge, MA.

---

[7]See Steinsalt (1993, pp. xxii, 1993) for Rabbi Nachman of Bratslav's (1772–1810) understanding of the use of folktales as a form of *tikkun*, or "repair of the world," as a way of raising up divine sparks for the redemption of the world.

Fox, B., Hayashi, M., & Jasperson, R. (1996). Resources and repair: A cross-linguistic study of the syntactic organization of repair. In E. Ochs, E. Schegloff, & S. Thompson (Eds.), *Interaction and grammar*. New York: Cambridge University Press.

Goffman, E. (1982). Footing. In *Forms of Talk* (pp. 124–159). Philadelphia: University of Pennsylvania Press.

Goffman, E. (1967). *Interaction ritual*. New York: Pantheon Books.

Good, D. (1990). Repair and cooperation in conversation. In P. Luff, N. Gilbert, & D. Frohlich (Eds.), *Computers & conversation* (pp. 133–150). London: Academic Press.

Goodwin, C. (1981). *Conversational organization: Interaction between speakers and hearers*. New York: Academic Press.

Goodwin, M. H. (1990). *He said she said: Talk as social organization among black children*. Bloomington: Indiana University Press.

Gumperz, J. (1982). *Discourse strategies*. New York: Cambridge University Press.

Hill, J. (1995). The voices of Don Gabriel: Responsibility and self in a modern Mexicano narrative. In D. Tedlock & B. Mannheim (Eds.), *The dialogic emergence of culture* (pp. 97–147). Urbana and Chicago: University of Illinois Press.

Hymes, D. (1981). *In vain I tried to tell you: Essays in Native American ethnopoetics*. Philadelphia: University of Pennsylvania Press.

Jefferson, G.. (1974). Error correction as an interactional resource. *Language in Society, 2*, 188–199.

Jefferson, G. (1987). On exposed and embedded correction in conversation. In G. Button & J. R. E. Lee (Eds.), *Talk and social organization* (pp. 86–100). Clevedon, England: Multilingual Matters Ltd.

Moerman, M. (1977). The preference of self-correction in Tai conversational corpus. *Language, 53*, 872–882.

Ochs, E. (1988). *Culture and language development*. New York: Cambridge University Press.

Philips, S. (1992). The routinization of repair in courtroom discourse. In A. Duranti & C. Goodwin (Eds.), *Rethinking context* (pp. 311–322). New York: Cambridge University Press.

Said, K. (1970). *Ali and Nino*. New York: Random House.

Schegloff, E. (1987). Recycled turn beginnings: A precise repair mechanism in conversation's turn-taking organization. In G. Button & J. R. E. Lee (Eds.), *Talk and social organization* (pp. 70–85). Clevedon, England: Multilingual Matters Ltd.

Schegloff, E. A., Jefferson, G., & Sacks, H. (1977). The preference for self-correction in the organization of repair in conversation. *Language, 53*(2), 361–383.

Sharrock, W., & Anderson, R. (1987). The definition of alternatives: Some sources of confusion in interdisciplinary discussion. In G. Button & J. R. E. Lee (Eds.), *Talk and social organization* (pp. 290–321). Clevedon, England: Multilingual Matters Ltd.

Steinsalt, A. (1993). *The tales of the Rabbi Nachman of Braslav* [retold with commentary]. London: Jason Aronson.

Tannen, D. (1984). *Conversational style: Analyzing talk among friends*. Norwood, NJ: Ablex.

Trix, F. (1993). *Spiritual discourse: Learning with an Islamic master*. Philadelphia: University of Pennsylvania Press.

DIAGNOSIS AS
SITUATED PRACTICE

Good Reasons for Bad Testing Performance: The Interactional Substrate of Educational Testing*

Douglas W. Maynard
Indiana University

Courtney L. Marlaire
Marquette University

Children who experience difficulties in school or at home may be referred to a diagnostic clinic and there take a battery of examinations, including some that test their educational level and learning abilities. In analyzing the administration of a variety of test instruments, we argued that the results of these examinations are collaborative productions (Marlaire & Maynard, 1990).[1] This is contrary to the stimulus–response model of the testing relationship, which presumes that examiners are neutral conduits of prespecified items to which examinees respond with correct or incorrect answers reflecting individual levels of ability. Videotapes and transcripts of actual exam episodes show that each part of a "testing sequence" is assembled in the socially organized interaction between examiner and examinee.

Whereas the previous analysis utilized excerpts from a variety of testing instruments,[2] in this chapter we concentrate on a single subtest, called *blending*, of the Woodcock–Johnson Psychoeducational Battery, which is designed to measure both aptitude and ability in a variety of learning-

---

*Originally published in *Qualitative Sociology*, *15*, 177–202, 1992. Reprinted with permission.

[1]See also Cicourel et al. (1974); Heap (1980); Holstein (1983); Mehan (1973); Mehan (1978); Mehan, Hertweck, and Meihls (1986).

[2]Included here were the Woodcock–Johnson Psychoeducational Battery, the Brigance Diagnostic Inventory of Early Development, the Ongoing Developmental Assessment Tool, and the Psychoeducational Profile. For descriptions of these, see Marlaire and Maynard (1990, p. 85). Special Education assessments rely, by legal mandate, on the use of more than one testing instrument in order to minimize test bias in the reported results. In addition, clinicians choose specific tests on the basis of what they judge to be the target "problem" and/or characteristics (such as the age, emotional or physical disability) of the subject.

related functions. The blending subtest involves the clinician breaking up words into components and speaking them to the child, whereupon the child must reconstitute the sounds as the appropriate word. According to the test manual, the purpose is to measure a child's ability to verbalize whole words after hearing syllabic and phonemic components that the examiner presents sequentially. The subtest by itself does not determine how clinicians will assess the child's ability; rather, the blending score, along with those from other subtests, becomes part of a cluster that indicates "broad cognitive ability" and "reading aptitude."

By investigating this one subtest intensively, our purpose is to deepen our understanding of the test process as a collaborative accomplishment. It seems that participants interactively assemble the individual parts of a "testing sequence"—that is, that each question or answer *as a performance* is routinely embellished with the minutiae of actions exhibiting the participants' efforts to work together to produce the utterance. More than that, this sequence itself is an embedded detail of an organized substrate of nonvocal as well as vocal activities. We refer to the *interactional substrate* of educational testing as consisting of those skills of the clinician and child that allow them to arrive at an "accountable" test score. By "accountable" test score, we mean one that is taken as objective, verifiable, valid, properly achieved, and so on, where that achievement depends on an organization of concerted practical actions that constitutes the participants' interaction. Actual testing, then, is nothing other than the interactional achievement of which it consists, and from which test scores can be extracted. Although the capacity to engage in these practical actions is not itself being tested, the possibility of displaying those abilities which are subject to examination utterly depends upon them.[3]

Our title is meant to suggest that the interactional substrate of educational testing may be a factor that interferes with the proper standardization and, hence, validity of testing scores. However, we do not mean to describe the testing process in an ironic manner—that is, to somehow debunk the exams[4] and show the ineptitude of administrators and consequent unfairness to children. If anything, our adult subjects were impressive for the amount of professional expertise they deployed in questioning and probing

---

[3]See also Lynch's (1984) discussion of how the questions in a mental status exam work to "turn up signs" of neurological disease: "An interactional context first had to be created before any signs were available for interpretation" (p. 67).

[4]There is a critical literature concerning these tests, which casts doubt on whether questions and answers do, in fact, offer an indication of subjects' generalized cognitive abilities. Critics (e.g., Adelman, 1979; Coles, 1978; Ysseldyke, 1986) maintained that these exams are unable to discriminate accurately among identified "learning problems," primarily for reasons of construct validity. That is, it is claimed that research fails to show that the tests accurately tap the attributes they are said to measure. This concern, however, is not ours, except as what we identify as the "interactional substrate" interferes with the possibility for standardizing the administration of the test, and hence its facility for unbiased measurement.

children. Rather, our title obviously adverts to Garfinkel's (1967) classic study, "Good Organizational Reasons for Bad Clinic Records," where it is demonstrated that apparently incompetent recordkeeping has an organizational basis in the reflexivity of documents to the courses of action that clinicians engage in their everyday routines. In our investigations, we "came upon" a seemingly vast amount of behavior that might threaten the ideal of standardized test-giving practice.[5] However, detailed analysis reveals just the opposite of unprofessional, sloppy, or uncontrolled conduct, for the giving and receiving of test items depends on *interactional* systematicity and already orderly modes of collaborative behavior.

PRELIMINARY

We videotaped three clinicians who were individually paired (according to a system of rotation) with 10 children ranging in age from 3 to 8 years. We chose to study the Woodcock–Johnson Blending Subtest for two reasons: It is short enough to analyze intensively from beginning to end, and we have two episodes involving different clinicians and children. We have transcribed Episode 1 (with Clinician 1 and Child 1) and Episode 2 (with Clinician 2 and Child 2) in detail, using conventions adapted from the work of both Gail Jefferson (1974) and Charles Goodwin (1981) (see Appendix). In excerpts from these episodes and in the text, we refer to the children and clinicians with abbreviations (CL1 = Clinician 1, CH1 = Child 1, CL2 = Clinician 2, CH2 = Child 2).

Initially, three aspects of the interactional substrate stand out. They are exhibited in the first excerpt:[6]

(1) Episode 1:1

1. *CL1:* This is kind of a game, and this game (0.2) means you
2. have to figure out what I'm sa̲ying. I'm gonna say a
3. word. One part at a time. And you have to tell me what
4. word I'm saying. Okay? Listen to this one.
5. *CH1:* Kay
6. *CL1:* Fing? ger.
7. *CH1:* Finger.
8. *CL1:* Goo::d. You know this game, don't you.
9. (0.4)
10. *CL1:* Okay. Listen to this word. Win dow.

First, there is *co-orientational* work on the part of clinician and child; both posture themselves in characteristic ways while engaging in the examination

---

[5]For a discussion of the idealization of the testing and assessment process as a feature of the academic/scientific literature, see Marlaire (1992).

[6]Until discussing nonvocal activities in more detail, we use transcripts in simplified form.

FIG. 8.1.   Displays of co-orientation.

(see Fig. 8.1). While we will eventually discuss this matter in some detail, we can note here that the clinician manages several tasks through what may be called displays of "administrativeness": paying attention both to the child and to reading and scoring tasks. Co-orientation by the child involves displays of "recipiency" (Heath, 1984) or shows of readiness to receive a testing item. When such displays are absent, the clinician regularly issues a co-orientational summons, such as "listen to this one" (line 4) or "listen to this word" (line 10). A second aspect of the interactional substrate consists of *instructional sequences* that prepare the child for an upcoming series of tasks. At lines 1–2, the clinician formulates what the subtest task is; at lines 2–4, assigns jobs to specific parties; and at lines 6–8, rehearses a testing sequence. The transition from instruction to actual testing is regularly marked with some proposal about the child's understanding (line 8, "You know this game, don't you").[7] In the context of neurobehavioral

---

[7]Although the clinician's comment, "You know this game, don't you," might propose that the child is familiar with the subtest (indeed, there were several instances in the larger corpus of videotaped examinations where children displayed prior knowledge of a specific subtest), clinicians use the "game" metaphor consistently enough across the corpus to suggest more general functions. First, they use the metaphor to engage the child in an activity (such as testing) that otherwise might not be inviting. Second, clinicians thereby indicate that the test idiom has certain game-like qualities. In the blending subtest, for instance, the clinician presents it as a puzzle (". . . you have to figure out what I'm saying"). It may be, then, that the consequentiality of the activities is thereby obscured.

examination, Lynch (1984, pp. 71–72) also notes the importance of "prefatory" instructional components and notes that the transition to testing involves a "stripping away" of these components.[8]

Finally, then, are the *testing sequences* to which we have already referred. Both rehearsal and actual testing appear to incorporate a three-part sequence:[9]

Part 1; testing prompt:	Fing? ger.	(Line 6)
Part 2; reply:	Finger.	(Line 7)
Part 3; acknowledgment:	Goo::d.	(Line 8)

---

[8]One of the effects of stripping away prefatory components during actual testing, Lynch (1984) argued, is to "trivialize," or press into the background, the interactional accomplishment on which successful adherence to the structure of testing sequences depends. In our terms, "testing" as an observable/reportable activity is truncated from its reflexivity to the interactional substrate, including the instruction and coaching which precede the use of testing sequences proper. It is by way of such truncation that it is possible to analyze correct and incorrect answering as the child's success or failure at the skill being measured.

[9]In characterizing testing sequences as three-part units, we are following a literature in which a variety of researchers (McHoul, 1978, 1990; Shuy & Griffin, 1978; and Sinclair & Coulthard, 1975) identified and described what Mehan (1979) called an "instructional sequence" (pp. 52–53):

1. Initiation.	*Teacher:*	(Holding up card) This is the long word. Who knows what it says?
2. Reply.	*Student:*	Cafeteria.
3. Evaluation.	*Teacher:*	Cafeteria, Audrey. good for you!

In these terms, "testing sequences" are similar to the instructional sequence, except that the third turn is officially to be neutral rather than evaluative. However, we wish to note that there is debate over whether the minimal units of interaction, including instructional sequences, are two or three parts. Schegloff and Sacks (1973) argued that the base unit of sequence construction is an adjacency pair. This adjacency pair can be expanded through the use of pre-sequences (see, e.g., the discussion in Maynard, 1984, pp. 86–87), or through insertion sequences such as those occupied with repair (Schegloff, Jefferson, & Sacks, 1977). If instructional or testing sequences followed the two-part format (question and answer), then the evaluative component is an add-on of some kind. In contrast, Jefferson and Schenkein (1977) proposed that a three-turn sequence (such as appeal, acceptance/rejection, and acknowledgment) may be a base conversational unit or "action sequence," which also can be "expanded," and the third turn is an integral part of that unit. (Participants' orientation to its use for controlling the interactional "so what" of the prior two parts may engender considerable jockeying to be in position to produce the third turn.) We cannot settle here whether instructional and testing sequences are two or three parts. Our strategy, in following the literature on classroom interactions and referring to a three-part testing sequence, is heuristic. Our analysis is meant to be consistent with the *phenomena* of interaction (such as pacing, as will be discussed), however, they are ultimately parsed in and as the achievements of organized practices such as sequence parts. Although, in the body of our text, we discuss the three-part testing sequence, at relevant points we footnote how these phenomena are to be understood in relation to a hypothetical two-part sequence.

This sequence can be either *elaborated* or *collapsed* according to the contingencies of actual interaction.

An elaborated test sequence results when a clinician initiates "repair" or correction[10] with respect to the child's answer:

(2) Episode 2:18

1. *CL1:* Can dee
2. *CH1:* Can dee
3.   (0.1)
4. *CL1:* Can you sayitfast?
5. *CH1:* CANdee
6. *CL1:* Good.

The basic sequence here consists of the prompt (line 1), the correct answer (line 5), and the acknowledgment (line 6). However, the correct answer is arrived at by way of the child first offering a reply (line 2) whose cadence closely mimics the prompt. Thus, at line 4, the clinician asks for a speeding up of the reply, which she models through very swiftly speaking the latter part of the request, "say it fast." McHoul (1990, pp. 365, 372) suggests that repair initiations of this sort deal with "procedural" rather than substantive or informational aspects of answering, although it is clearly the case here that the procedural issue relates to the substance of the answer. That is, the child's answer may be regarded as incorrect if the "parts" are there but not spoken in the correct modality. In any case, repairs like this exhibit how instructions provided at the outset of the subtest are inherently incomplete. That is, it may be impossible to anticipate all the ways in which the child might have to be cued to provide appropriate answers when the test is actually in progress; accordingly, clinicians introduce instructive activities according to contingencies that are local to the *in vivo* performance of particular test items.[11] Resulting largely from clinicians' initiations of repair and correction, then, elaborated testing sequences show further aspects of the interactional substrate. It is through such sequences that, when children do not at first provide what a question intends, clinicians, in various ways, can seek a better, more appropriate, and ultimately correct answer.

A collapsed test sequence is visible in the clinician's elimination of the third-turn acknowledgment. When a clinician first elides the third turn,

---

[10]On repair and repair sequences, see Schegloff, Jefferson, and Sacks (1977). For lengthy and technical studies on the operation of repair in classroom lessons, see Mazeland (1986) and McHoul (1990).

[11]See Drew's (1981) illuminating discussion of the instructive features of adults' corrections of children's mistakes in ordinary conversation. On how the organization of repair relates to giving instruction in classroom talk, see McHoul (1990).

this may launch a *chained series* of collapsed sequences.[12] This happens with our second clinician–child pair (see lines 7–16):

(3) Episode 2:9

1.	*CL2:*	I want you to tell me what the word is. I'm gonna say
2.		f:in:: ger: What word did I say.
3.		(0.4)
4.	*CH2:*	Finger?
5.	*CL2:*	Okay. Good. You've got these. Win: dow.
6.	*CH2:*	(0.2) Window?
7.	*CL2:*	Good. (1.0) Muh: ther:
8.	*CH2:*	Mother?
9.	*CL2:*	(1.4) Ta: bl::.
10.	*CH2:*	Table?
11.	*CL2:*	(1.0) .hhh Can: dee
12.	*CH2:*	Candy?
13.	*CL2:*	(1.2) Rho: dah:.
14.	*CH2:*	Road.
15.	*CL2:*	(1.4) Soh: puh:.
16.	*CH2:*	Soap.

The clinician's last use of an acknowledgment (line 7) occurs after the child correctly provides the answer "window" (line 6). Subsequent to "mother" (line 8) and for the next 10 items, the clinician provides only a prompt. Thus, it seems that rather than using an acknowledgment to indicate the completion of a sequence, the clinician does so by pausing and then producing a new prompt. There is a simultaneity here (the closing of one sequence and the opening of another) that is similar to what Schegloff (1986, pp. 130–131) describes as the "interlocking" of sequences. It is only when the child gives an incorrect answer that this chaining or interlocking stops, and the clinician once again uses an acknowledgment.

FURTHER ASPECTS OF THE INTERACTIONAL SUBSTRATE

So far, we have described the interactional substrate in terms of sequences—co-orientational, instructional, and testing. It is through such sequences that participants engage in much of the work of actual examination. However,

---

[12]If the testing sequence is only two parts—question and reply—then the chained series would be simply a number of contiguous and complete sequences rather than a collection of "collapsed" units.

these sequences only scratch the surface of the interactional substrate. We wish to deepen our analysis in two ways. First, we consider another expanded test sequence and, among other things, show that it is important to situate that sequence within the local history of the coordinated activity comprising the test so far. Second, and at greater length, we will examine nonvocal, embodied activity of the exam's participants.

Local History of Testing Sequences

The episode we wish to examine occurs just after excerpt (2) just mentioned. In this next episode, the child is ultimately scored as answering incorrectly. We will consider how the interactional substrate may contribute to such an outcome.

(4) Episode 1:23

1. *CL1:* Roh::duh.
2.   (1.2)
3. *CH1:* Rohduh.
4. *CL1:* Inkay. Roh::°duh
5.   (3.8)
6. *CH1:* Roh::
7.   (0.2)
8. *CL1:* Can you say it fast?
9. *CH1:* Rohduh
10. *CL1:* Oka::y.

Several things are of note here. For one, after CH1's first try at an answer (line 3), CL1 initiates repair with regard to that answer (line 4), but also modifies her own prompt by softening her pronunciation of the last sound ("duh"; the degree sign indicates this softening), which may exhibit her awareness that the source of the incorrect answer may be her original prompt whose sound bursts are distinct and forceful. Thus, it is not only the child who may have to do some *in situ* learning (as we just noted). In the course of giving an exam, the clinician may modify her own behavior in relation to responses of the child, acquiring expertise as she goes.

More to our concern is the possibility that the child's first answer reflects her just-acquired sense of speed. Having been successful at the speeding-up strategy on the previous word ("candy"), CH1 appears to employ the same strategy here, saying "rohduh" (line 3) very quickly. Her focus on the speed of pronunciation may deflect attention from something crucial that differentiates this word from the previous ones, its syllabic structure. Moreover, if CH1 is preoccupied with the rapidity issue, CL1 reinforces this. After the repair initiation (at line 4), CH1 looks away from the clinician and slows down her pronunciation of the word by lingering on the initial sound (line 6), whereupon CL1 requests repair (line 8) in a way that again signals the need for a faster tempo. This time, CH1's answer (line 9) is much like her first try (line 3); CL1 subsequently produces an acknowl-edgment (line 10) and scores the reply as incorrect.

The syllabic difference between the prompting word here and earlier ones is important. The subtest, we noted, starts with the rehearsal item "finger." Next, in order, are "window," "mother," "table," "candy," and then the prompt for "road." Thus, while all of the previous items are two syllables, this is just one. The significance of this is that, as Sacks (Lecture 12, Fall 1967, pp. 8–9) has argued, the "position of an item on a list is relevant to hearing what that item is."[13] Hence, in at least two ways—that is, with regard to the signaled concern for speed and the indicated syllabic structure of words, the local history of preceding talk and action provide a context for the child to mishear and even err in this particular segment. Just as in the courtroom Pollner (1979) studied, ". . . the developing session may act as its own socialization agent . . . every transaction in the ongoing activity may become fraught with instructional possibilities" (p. 235). Here, to the extent that the child is learning what this exam is from within the interactive practices of which it consists, she arguably has been socialized to produce a wrong answer. It is not the clinician's incompetence nor the child's inabilities that allow this, however, but rather the structures of interaction.

A final matter of note here is, in the acknowledgment turn, a significant change from what has gone before. Previously, when the child provided correct answers, the clinician produced the term *good*. Here, when the child seems to err, the clinician uses *okay* (line 10). This is a subtle shift but can occur regularly in accordance with whether the child is right or wrong, despite the fact that clinicians are not to provide evaluative feedback to children (Marlaire & Maynard, 1990, p. 96).[14] Thus, it is not only that any

---

[13]Thus, there can be a sequential basis for the sort of thing Grimshaw (1980) identified as "partial" understandings and "mishearings." As one example, Sacks (1967, p. 8) provided the following:

> *A:* I went out a lot then. One weekend I went to hear Pete Seeger, the next weekend I went to hear Joan Baez, and the next weekend I went to hear Wayne Morse.
> *B:* Who's Wayne Morse.
> *A:* Wayne Morse. The Senator.
> *B:* Oh. Wayne Morse.

B, displaying recognition of Wayne Morse in the last utterance, evidently "knew" who he was all along. However, hearing the first two persons (Seeger and Baez) in the list to be singers, B may have been listening for another singer, and therefore did not originally identify the politician.

[14]Note that during the "rehearsal" in excerpt (6), which involves CL2 and CH2, the clinician (at line 6) produces "okay" and "good" in tandem (followed by "you've got these"). Evaluations, then, sometimes involve more than just one component.

given testing sequence *has* a history, it may also be *historicized* in certain ways. In a manner similar to how astronomers discover a pulsar (Garfinkel, Lynch, & Livingston, 1981), clinicians must extract from the "foliage" of their and their subjects' embodied interactional practices, (a) an object that can be heard as an assessable answer and as achievedly produced according to proper methodic procedure, and (b) an assessment (correct or incorrect) that would stand as any competent clinician's determination in the circumstances of the answer's production. Accordingly, we have noted that when the clinician responds to the child's candidate answers, she may modify her own behavior, and thereby show an awareness that an improperly given prompt may have misled the child. We have also shown how the design of the exam itself, which the clinician incorporates as a particular sequential pattern in the giving of testing prompts, may provide the occasion for a subject's mishearing. Nevertheless, clinicians' initiations of repair and correction work to obtain further utterances from the child that are the official exhibits for professional inspection.[15] Thus, no matter what the cues to the child from the foliage of embodied practices that comprise the exam's historicity, an extracted incorrect answer ultimately devolves to the child's inability as its source (Drew, 1981, pp. 259–260; Marlaire, 1990).[16] As Lynch (1984) has remarked about neurobehavioral examinations, "Failures during the collaborative activity of testing were transformed into failure *of* the patient's performance of the test" (p. 80).[17]

Nonvocal and Embodied Behavior: The Clinician

So far, we have concentrated on vocal aspects of these testing encounters, but the interaction is considerably more complex in the ways that clinician and child comport themselves bodily and do so collaboratively. We will

---

[15]Lynch (1984, p. 78) notes that the use of repair during a mental status exam is also a method for "objectifying" the patient's response and providing a clinician with an opportunity to closely scrutinize it.

[16]This works both ways, of course. That is, an extracted "correct" answer is seen to reflect the child's ability, no matter what the contribution of the clinician in coaching it from the child. On how a correct answer can be coached, see Marlaire and Maynard (1990, p. 88). For a treatment of the way that teachers can "clue" children into producing a correct answer during classroom lessons, see McHoul (1990, pp. 355–362).

[17]Lynch (1984) discussed how, in administering "mental status exams," clinicians came to see patients' expressions of hostility, unresponsiveness, or disinterest as symptoms of clinical syndromes, whereas we are pointing to the manner in which a variety of accommodative behaviors of both clinician and child, contingently produced according to the exigencies of asking and answering exam questions, dissipate as clinicians render a judgment of correct or incorrect in regard to a child's response. For a phenomenon similar to Lynch's (1984), see Lloyd's (1991) discussion of how therapists, during examinations designed to determine if sexual abuse has occurred, treat children's lack of responsiveness to questions as evidence of that abuse.

demonstrate how the two participants finely tune their embodied behaviors in a concerted way, by discussing the separate tasks to which the parties attend, and then analyzing how their complementary management of these tasks is part of an overall activity structure of which, as we indicated earlier, the three-part testing sequence is only a part.

The clinician has to manage at least four jobs, and does so through co-orientational practices that we have glossed as displays of "administrativeness." She must read the test items, give them to the child, listen to the child's answers, and score correct and incorrect answers. Thus, a clinician sits with the examination instrument between herself and the child, has a score sheet on the table in front of her, and holds a pencil or pen, which she uses for scoring. In patterned ways, the clinician moves her head and gaze in such a way as to be noticeably attending to the child, the instrument, and the writing that she does on the sheet. How the testing sequence is coordinated with this nonvocal behavior is mapped in detail on the next transcript segment. Understanding the excerpt may necessitate consulting the transcription conventions for gaze behavior in the Appendix. In the segment, notice in particular the "X's," which mark where the clinician brings her gaze to the child:

(5) Episode 1:5

```
 1. CL1:  And you have to tell me what word I'm saying okay?

         VVVVVVVV......X--------------
 2. CL1:  Listen ta this one.  F::in?ger.
         ----------------------------

         ----------,,
 3. CH1:  (0.2) Finger.                          ((CH1 smile))
         -----------

         VVVVVVVVVVVVVVVVVVVVVVVVVVVVVVVVVVVV
 4. CL1:  Ghoo::d.  You know this game, don't you.   ((CL1 smile))
         -------------------,,VVVVVVVVVVVVVVV

         VVVVV
 5.      (0.4)
         VVVVV

         VV,,,,WWWWWWWWWWW.....^^^^^^X--------
 6. CL1:  Okay.   Listen to THIS word.  Win::dow.
         VVVVVVVVVVVVVVVVV,,,,,X--------------

         -----
 7.      (0.2)
         -----
```

```
        ----,,
 8. CH1: Window.                                    ((CH1 smile))
        ------


        VVVVVVVVVVVVVVVV...X-----
 9. CL1: Goo:::d.  (0.4)  muh: ther.         ((CL1 smile, head
        -------------------------                nod on "good"))


        --,,VV
10. CH1: Mother
        ------


        VVVVVV......X-------
11. CL1: Good.  (0.4) Ta: bull.          ((CL1 head nod on "good"))
        --------------------


        ----,
12. CH1: Table.              ((CH1 moves head down and to the right))
        --,,,


        ,,,,,,VVVVVV..X--
13. CL1: (0.1) tch can dee.             ((CL1 head nod on "tch"))
                    ..X----


        -,,VVVV
14. CH1: Can dee.                       ((CH1 head nod on "can"))
        -------


        ..... X----------------
15. CL1: (0.1) can you sayitfast?     ((CH1 tilt head on "fast"))
        ----------------------


        ----------,,
16. CH1: (0.2) CANdee.   ((CH1 duck head, tilt torso back, smile))
        -----------


        VVVVVVVV
17. CL1: Goo:::::d.                                 ((CL1 smile))
        ---------


        VVVVV
18.      (--)                          ((CH1 rolls head to right))


        .....X---
19. CL1: Roh:: duh.
          ...X---


        -----------
20. CH1: (1.2)  Rohduh.                             ((CH1 smile))
        -----------
```

The points at which the clinician's gaze arrives on the child are various, but still show a clear pattern: at line 2, the point is one word before the testing prompt; at line 6, it is just before the prompt itself; at line 9, it is during the prompt but before its second component: and at line 11, it is at the initial sound of the prompt. Invariably, in both of our blending subtests, the clinician's gaze will have reached the child at least by the end of the testing prompt.

This shows a readiness to receive the child's answer, and once the clinician's gaze is directed to the child, it stays there for at least the beginning of the child's response. Regularly, the clinician withdraws her gaze before a candidate answer is finished, whereupon she looks at the testing instrument (observe the commas, which mark withdrawal of gaze, at lines 3, 8, 10, and 12). This enables the clinician to be reading the next item from the instrument and sometimes scoring the answers while producing a third-turn acknowledgment or assessment.[18] Thus, while one version of the third turn in a testing sequence is that it completes the sequence and aids with the transition between test items, we would suggest that the clinician's gaze (and head movements), in anticipating or expecting that a complete answer is underway, indicate and help achieve the completion and transition process before an assessment appears. Moreover, because at least two tasks—the child answering and the clinician beginning to read the next item—are done in partial simultaneity, the glancing away of the clinician figures in the pacing of the exam.

Nonvocal and Embodied Behavior: The Child

Complementary to the clinician's displays of administrativeness are the child's displays of "recipiency." As Heath (1984) described them, displays of recipiency are ways of showing a readiness for talk; in the context of examination, they exhibit a readiness for receiving the testing prompt.[19] Displays of recipiency on the part of the child are required at each moment when the clinician is ready to deliver a prompt. The child provides them

---

[18]If instructional sequences are two parts, it may be that the addition of an acknowledgment is "holding" the connection between contiguous sequences while the clinician completes her scoring and reading in preparation for vocalizing the next test item.

[19]The complementarity between clinician and child is more complicated than our discussion here might indicate. We have already noted that part of the clinician's work is listening to and thus being in a position of recipiency with regard to the child's answering. This is a momentary aspect of the clinician administering the exam, which is why we generally refer to her shows of co-orientation as "administrativeness." Correspondingly, because the children's answering is done from a basic position of waiting for the test prompts, we gloss their co-orientational displays as "recipiency."

as seemingly natural accompaniments to the activity underway. That they are required, effortful acts becomes evident when a clinician takes notice of the child's comportment and produces a *co-orientational* request, which we illustrated in episode (1) at lines 4 and 10.

Children display recipiency through at least three types of behavior: keeping the torso in an upright position, facing the clinician with the head, and directing gaze toward the clinician, at least by the time that a prompt is given (see Fig. 8.1). The interactional substrate is very finely tuned with respect to co-orientation. In the aforementioned excerpt, for instance, the clinician appears very sensitive to the slightest alteration in the child's recipiency. Thus, in excerpt (5), during the rehearsal prompt (line 3), its answer (line 3), and the clinician's evaluation (line 4), CH1 keeps her gaze fully on CL1. As CL1 says, "You know this game don't you," however, CH1 looks down at the test booklet. Then, before going on to the initial testing prompt, CL1 issues the co-orientational summons ("Listen to THIS word," line 6) to which we earlier referred. During this summons, CH1 brings her gaze back to the clinician so that she is looking fully at CL1 before the latter produces the prompt (line 6). Furthermore, CH1 continues to keep her gaze and head fully directed toward CL1 during the subsequent three testing sequences (from lines 6 through 11). This expression of attentiveness, in fact, seems to solicit the evaluation or acknowledgment that the clinician provides (e.g., at lines 9 and 11). However, when answering the prompt for "table" (line 12), CH1 begins to withdraw her gaze, also moving her head down and to the right. Immediately, two things happen. CL1 eliminates the evaluation or acknowledgment, and she pauses (also clicking her tongue, line 13) for a shorter duration than she did with preceding prompts (compare silences at line 9, 11, and 13). It appears, then, that CL1 regards the child's movements as an attentional lapse to be remedied with a faster pace, which is achieved in part through moving more quickly to the next test item.[20]

Further evidence that clinicians may deal with problems in co-orientation by eliminating the third turn of the testing sequence derives from a similar happening in Example 2.[21]

---

[20]Immediately after this, CL1 returns to using the third turn of the testing sequence. This seems to occur because of the repair sequence that is inserted after CH1's reply (line 14 in excerpt 5) to the prompt for "candy" (line 13). CH1 had mimicked the deliberateness with which CL1 gave that prompt. After CH1, responding to the repair initiation (line 15), "says it fast" (line 16), CL1 once more gives an evaluation (line 17).

[21]Note that if the instructional sequence is two parts, it is not that the third turn is being eliminated, but that an extraneous component, which can be employed to manage the transition from one testing sequence to another, or to provide evaluative feedback when a child seems solicitous of it, can be dispensed with.

(6) Episode 2:9

```
           ----------,,WWWWWWWWWWWWWWWWWWWWWWWWWW
 1. CL2:    . . . And I want you to tell me what
           VVVVVVVVVVVVVVVVVVVVVVVVVVVVVVVVVVVVVV

                      ((leans in))
           WWWWWWWWWWWW......----------X-------------
 2.        the word is.  I'm gonna say (.2) f:in::ger:
           VVVVVVVVVVVVVVVVVVVVVVV......X-------------
                                     ((slightly closer))

           ------------------
 3.        What word did I say.
           ------------------

              ---
 4.        (---)
           ,,VV

           ------
 5. CH2:   Finger
           VVVVV

                 ((flips page))
           ,,VVVVVVVVVVVVVVVVVVVVVVVV,,,,
 6.        O:KAY.  Good.  You've got these.
           VVVVVVVVVVVVVVVVVVVVVVVVVVVVVV

           WWW...X---
 7.        Win: dough
           VVVV..X---

           -----
 8.        (0.2)
           -----

           --------X--,,,
 9. CH2:   (0.2) Window.
           ------VVX--VV

           WWWW
10. CL2:   Good
           VVVV

           .VVV..
11.        (-----)
           VVVVV
```

```
                ---------
12.             Muh: ther:
                VVVVVVVV


                ,,WWWWW
13. CH2:        Mother?
                VVVVVVV


                WW..V.X
14.             (------)
                VVVV..X


                -------,
15. CL2:        Ta: bl::
                --/---,,


                VV,,WW
16. CH2:        Table?
                VVV...


                WWWW.
17.             (-----)
                ..(--)


                .VV..X--
18. CL2:        Can: dee
                (----X--)


                ,,WWWW
19. CH2:        Candy?
                (---,,)


                WWW..-
20.             (------)
                VVVVVV


                ----X-----
21.             Rho: dah::
                VVV^^VVVVV


                ---,,
22. CH2:        Road.
                VVVVV


                WWWWWW..
23.             (-------)
                VVVVVV..
```

Initially, CH2's gaze behavior here is similar to that of CH1. She brings her eyes to rest on the clinician just before the prompt is given, as during the rehearsal sequence involving "finger" (line 2), or she brings her gaze to the clinician on the second and last component of the prompt for "window," line 9). After CH2 answers each of these prompts, CL2 provides the third part of the testing sequence, an acknowledgment. Next, however, during the prompt for "mother" (line 12), CH2, rather than looking at CL2, gazes downward at the test booklet, and continues doing so even as she answers (line 13). Then, while scoring and reading, CL2 simply pauses (line 14) and then produces the next prompt at line 15 ("table").

At this distinct moment and in this precise way is the series of collapsed sequences, which we examined previously, begun. This is different from Episode 1, where, after the third-turn acknowledgment was eliminated, CH1 answered the next item incorrectly, the clinician asks her to repair the candidate answer and (when the child does so), says "good."[22] CH2, in similar circumstances, answers correctly and continues doing so until the prompt for "about" (later in Episode 2). In dealing with CH2's incorrect answer to "ah: bow: t:," CL2 reintroduces a third-term acknowledgment, "Okay." It seems, then, that continuing to engage the collapsed form of a testing sequence depends on the child obtaining correct answers. Also noticeable in Episode 2 is that throughout the series of collapsed testing sequences, CH2 mostly gazes away from CL2, only momentarily looking at her during the prompts for "table" (excerpt (6), line 15), "candy" (line 18), and "soap" (not in excerpt (6)). Mostly, CH2 is gazing at the test booklet, the table, and even the floor. As compared with CH1, she appears much more listless and less solicitous of the third-turn acknowledgment.

Recipiency and Alignment Toward the Testing Activity

Both interviews suggest that the components of recipiency are ways of enacting an alignment toward the proposedly central activity of testing. On the one hand, clinicians respond to gross head and bodily movements with co-orientational summonses. For example, in Test 1, after the child's try at "road," CL1 next gives the prompt for "soap":

(7) Episode 1:38

```
       vvvvvvvvvvvv,,----
1. CL1:  .hhhhhhh  ss::oapuh
       ------------------


       -----
2.      (0.4)
       -----
```

---

[22]See footnote 19 and excerpt (5), lines 13–17.

```
            ---------
 3. CH1:  ss::uppoh                                    ((CH1 smile))
          --,,


          -------------------------------------
 4. CL1:  okay listen to this and you say it fast
              ,,,---------------------------


          -----
 5.       (0.2)
          -----


          ---------
 6. CL1:  ss:oa°puh
          ---------


          -------------
 7. CH1:  ss::°poh °puh                                ((CH1 smile))
              ((CH1 leans back and puts hands on hips))


          -----
 8.       (0.6)
          ,,,,


          ,,,,,,VVVVVVVWWWWWWWWWWWW
 9. CL1:  pretty good, pretty close.                   ((CL1 smile))
          ------------------------


              ,,,
10.       (0.1)
              ---


          ----------------------
11. CL1:  That one's .h (0.2) soap!
          ----------------------


          -----
12.       (0.6)
          -----


          ----------------------
13. CL1:  ss::oa°puh  (0.2)   soap
          ----------------------


          --,,VV
14. CH1:  S:oap                                        ((CH1 smile))
          ,,
```

```
              vvvv
    15.       (0.2)


              vvvvvvvvvvvvvvvvvvvvvvvvv
    16. CL1:  mkay listen to this, one                    ((CL1 smile))
              ((CH1 moves head in semicircle))


              , , , ,---
    17. CH1:  hhhhhhh                        ((brings head to gaze at CL1))
              , , , , ,--


              --------
    18. CL1:  Pihl low.                      ((CH1 has hands on hips))
              --------
```

As CH1 answers (line 3), she withdraws her gaze and then also moves her head down and to the right. At that moment, CL1 issues a co-orientational summons (line 4). Then, during the latter part of that utterance, CH1 returns her gaze to the clinician. She keeps it there, except for a brief moment during the silence at line 8, until the end of a rehearsal sequence (lines 11–14). When CH1 repeats the word "soap" (at line 14), she again withdraws her gaze. CL1 almost immediately produces a co-orientational summons (line 16), whereupon CH1 moves her head in a semicircle and ends up redirecting her head and gaze at CL1 (lines 16–17) in time to receive the prompt for "pillow" (line 18).

In both of our episodes, every time the child either moves her head or body out of the base recipiency position, such summoning activity occurs. Figure 8.2 shows a prototypical example of the child looking away; it is just that turn of the head to which the clinicians responds with "listen to this one." Thus, asking a child to "listen" is not an indiscriminate action whereby clinicians offhandedly remind children to pay attention; rather, it squarely corresponds with a child's change in alignment toward what the clinician regards as the focal activity. It seems, therefore, that such gross movements enact an unacceptable alignment that threatens the interactional substrate. Clinicians, from within the midst of that substrate, work to preserve it through explicit vocal and nonvocal summoning behavior.

On the other hand, children can distance themselves from the central activity in less extreme forms, withdrawing gaze while maintaining proper displays of bodily and head recipiency. Rather than using an orientational request and explicitly asking for the child's return to attentiveness, clinicians may "speed up" or even "rush through" (Schegloff, 1982) the evaluation parts of testing sequences and in that way manipulate components to command the child's orientation. As the child continues to answer correctly, the two parties concertedly achieve "rapid pacing" as an orderly feature of their interaction.

FIG. 8.2.   Child's head and gaze averted; Clinican: "Okay. Listen to THIS word."

DISCUSSION

The interactional substrate of educational testing underlies the accountable production of test results. While both participants contribute to and collaboratively organize the substrate, the involved skills are not themselves subject to measurement, except indirectly. The substrate consists of such practical activities as prompting with test items, answering, initiating repair and correction of prompts and answers, doing the repair and correction, acknowledging, evaluating, and engaging other vocal and nonvocal, embodied practices so as to effect the test as an official and valid enterprise.

One way of approaching the interactional substrate is through the issue of standardization. Examinations are to be administered in a uniform manner, and environmental factors are to be controlled so that the test truly measures the child's ability. Metaphorically speaking, the interactional substrate is like an environmental factor that has not been adequately investigated, much less controlled. We explore this metaphor with two main points, the *learning* that clinician and child experience during the test, and the *feedback* that clinicians may be giving their subjects.

Learning in the Midst of the Test

Even though children are given instructions and participate in a rehearsal of the subtest, excerpt (1), in which CL1 asked CH1 to say her answer "fast" shows that instructions can never be complete. In other words, for the child, there is in-process instructing and learning, even though she is supposed to know the "rules of the game" beforehand. This is true for the clinician as well. CL1's self-repair on the prompt for "road" in excerpt (2) is evidence that she may notice her own performance as a source of trouble. In short, the participants to a test are like "Agnes," the transsexual whom Garfinkel (1967) studied and who, from within the interior of the process of passing as a "natural, normal" female, simultaneously was learning what that passing entailed as a practical accomplishment. Or, the participants are like the judges and defendants in traffic court, who "live within" the very order of courtroom affairs and features that they simultaneously manage as a practical task (Pollner, 1979). From within the interior of the exam experience, children and clinicians learn what they should do to give, receive, and answer test items properly and correctly.

An implication of participants being attuned to what the *in situ* experience can teach them is that the child can acquire presumptions about a subtest and how to perform. When a clinician says to "say it fast" on one item, the child may use that strategy like an algorithm to be applied to any next answer. If a series of items show a pattern or characteristic (such as prompting words being one or two syllables), the child may use her knowledge of that pattern to fashion subsequent responses. Our point here is not that this is uniformly dysfunctional for the child. Indeed, what is perhaps being tested is the child's ability to adjust to the nuances of different testing prompts. However, if errors introduced in a child's answer reflect orderly processes that are not adequately controlled or held constant in the design of the test, it may bias the results (cf. Schaeffer, 1991). Following our metaphor, the interactional substrate, as an *organization* of practical activities, may be a systematic source of such influence on testing outcomes.

Feedback

Although permitted to provide comments of a generalized nature ("you're doing fine," for example), clinicians' feedback is very circumscribed because of the possibility that it might influence the child's performance. For instance, the Woodcock–Johnson (of which the Blending exercise is a subtest) specifically admonishes the clinician, "Be careful that your pattern of comments does not indicate whether answers are correct or incorrect" (cf. Mehan, Hertweck, & Meihls, 1986, pp. 96–97). Yet we see that clinicians, perhaps inadvertently, regularly do give such feedback, in at least two major ways.

First, clinicians and children, in being sensitive to one another's activities and especially displays of recipiency, produce and alter their behaviors moment-to-moment in a contingent fashion. Thus, differences occur with respect to pacing and rhythm both within and across particular dyads engaged in the examination.

Indeed, the interactive structure of the testing sequence seems to be a product of collaborative pacing practices, although such pacing and structure are also responsive to the perceived accuracy of a child's replies. Collapsed sequences only seem to occur in the context of correct answers, and the full three-part sequence is re-invoked in an environment of errant answering and/or difficult testing prompts. Thus, the type of sequence employed can provide feedback to children on their performance or the difficulty of prompting items.

A second way that feedback occurs is in clinicians' altering their third-turn acknowledgments between "good" (when an answer is correct) and "okay" (when incorrect). Recall that in episode 1, the clinician pronounced the term "good" after correct answers to "finger," "window," "mother," "table," and "candy." When the child errs on "road," however, CL1 says "okay." Also, clinicians may give encouraging nonvocal signals when a child answers correctly, while remaining more taciturn when she errs. In Episode 1, CL1 smiles and/or nods at lines 3, 9, 11, 13, and 17, whereas no such gestures are present subsequent to the "rohduh" episode. The pattern is operative throughout the episode.

Smiling is not just a matter of the clinician's style or independent method of encouraging a child. It seems that the child, when giving her answers, smiles expectantly at the clinician. That is, there may be something of a smiling *sequence* in operation, where the clinician's smile is a response to the child's initiation, and the absence of the clinician's smile may be a *noticeable absence* (Schegloff & Sacks, 1974), or one from which it is possible for the child to draw inferences about her own performance.

That nonvocal nodding and smiling behavior is a crucial aspect of the interactional substrate that can have consequences for the child's performance is lent credibility from Goodwin and Goodwin's (1987) consideration of the interactive structure of assessments in ordinary conversation. When speakers reference an "assessable" object, they may provide a characterization that proposes how their recipients are to understand and appreciate that object. Recipients, who are highly attuned to what Goodwin and Goodwin (1987) call the "participation possibilities" that assessments invoke, may reciprocate by producing an evaluation complementary to the initial characterization. Therefore, assessments are a conversational nexus of organized, collaborative actions. In the testing situation, a child's answers are assessable objects. Clinicians, in vocal and nonvocal ways, regularly evaluate these answers in third-turn acknowledgments. If these assessments work at all like they do in conversation, children can inspect them to decide what they might implicate for their own concurrent and subsequent activities. On the part of clinicians, then, even slight alterations between "good" and "okay," smiling and not smiling, or going relatively slow or fast, may provide children with the opportunity to infer how well they are doing.

If children are making such inferences, we do not know exactly what they are, nor how they might influence subsequent behavior. However, it is possible that the famous "Pygmalion effect" (Rosenthal & Jacobson, 1968; Rubovits & Maehr, 1973) or transmission of what becomes a self-fulfilling expectation, is, to the extent that it is real, brought about through the organization of activities in the interactional substrate of educational exams. More generally, our point is that until we know more about this substrate, there may be unknown and uncontrolled influences on testing behavior that are sources of distortion in the scores that children receive.

CONCLUSION

By discussing issues of standardization, we do not mean to engage in an ironic impugning of educational testing. We cannot claim that these examinations are *un*standardized, and by no means were our clinician–subjects incompetent or unprofessional. Rather, our aim was to simply describe and analyze an infrastructure of collaborative actions that make generating accountable test scores possible. The interactional substrate is like a scaffolding on which clinicians depend in order to obtain access to measurable, quantifiable abilities. It is something that underlies other information-generating interviews, such as the survey (Schaeffer, 1991; Suchman & Jordan, 1990). After all is said and done, the reportable score that is the child for the purposes of educational placement, or the attitude that is registered in some poll, depends on this infrastructure, or substrate, or scaffolding of organized, practical skills. Ultimately, interviews as real-world accomplishments are inseparable from the substrate or scaffolding of skills through which participants make both the process and its products observable in their specificity. The clinical signs of deficit, just as the codable manifestations of subjective regard on social issues, emanate from what Lynch (1984, p. 81) has referred to as a "primordial grounding in the life world" (cf. Cicourel, 1982).

Despite our initial lack of interest in the effectiveness of test administration, problematic aspects of the testing immediately stood out as we reviewed our tapes. That is, we saw "mistakes" on the part of the clinician as well as the child, many of which appear not to stem from the inabilities or incompetencies of the clinician, or of the child, but precisely from the interactional competence they both exhibit. That competence resides in a set of skills through which they bring off official testing activities, such as providing a "stimulus" and a "response." Thus does it appear, in our paraphrase of Garfinkel (1967), that there can be good interactional reasons for bad testing performance.

APPENDIX

Transcription Conventions

For the audio portion of transcripts, conventions are adapted from Gail Jefferson's (1984) system (for example, see published version in J. Maxwell Atkinson & John Heritage, 1984, *Structure of Social Action*, pp. ix–xvi). Following is a transcription key for gaze behavior; these conventions adapted from Charles Goodwin (1981), *Conversational Organization: Interaction Between Speakers and Hearers* (New York: Academic Press).

Gaze Transcription

1. Clinician gaze is above each utterance. Child gaze is below each utterance.

2. VVVVVVV = gaze directed at test booklet between participants
3. WWWWWWW = gaze directed down on table (especially at score sheet while writing)

4. ------- = gaze is directly on co-participant

5. .... = gaze is coming toward co-participant

6. ,,,,,,, = gaze is dropping

7. ^   = quick movement of gaze upward

8. /   = quick movement of gaze downward

9. X   = marks where gaze reaches co-participant

```
          --,,
10. (----)
```
= if gaze changes during a silence, the silence is shown with a dash for each two-tenths of a second, and gaze is marked above or below the silence with the regular notation

```
          ---
11. (0.4)
          ---
```
= if gaze does not change during a silence, the silence is recorded with the standard numeric system, and notation is marked above or below with the regular notation.

REFERENCES

Adelman, H. S. (1979). Diagnostic classification of LD: A practical necessity and a procedural problem. *Learning Disability Quarterly, 2,* 56–62.

Atkinson, J. M., & Heritage, J. (Eds.). (1984). *Structures of social action: Studies in conversation analysis.* Cambridge, MA: Cambridge University Press.

Cicourel, A. V. (1982). Interviews, surveys, and the problem of ecological validity. *American Sociologist, 17,* 11–20.

Cicourel, A. V., Jennings, K. H., Jennings, S. H. M., Leiter, K. C. W., MacKay, R., Mehan, H., & Roth, D. R. (Eds.). (1974). *Language use and school performance.* New York: Academic Press.

Coles, G. S. (1978). The learning-disabilities test battery: Empirical and social issues. *Harvard Educational Review, 48,* 131–340.

Drew, P. (1981). Adults' corrections of children's mistakes. In P. French & M. MacLure (Eds.), *Adult-child conversation* (pp. 244–267). London: Croom Helm.

Garfinkel, H. (1967). *Studies in ethnomethodology.* Englewood Cliffs, NJ: Prentice-Hall.

Garfinkel, H., Lynch, M., & Livingston, E. (1981). The work of discovering science construed with materials from the optically discovered pulsar. *Philosophy of the Social Sciences, 11,* 131–158.

Goodwin, C. (1981). *Conversational organization: Interaction between speakers and hearers.* New York: Academic Press.

Goodwin, C., & Goodwin, M. H. (1987). Concurrent operations on talk: Notes on the interactive organization of assessments. *IPRA Papers in Pragmatics, 1,* 1–54.

Grimshaw, A. (1980). Mishearings, misunderstandings, and other nonsuccesses in talk: A plea for redress of speaker-oriented bias. *Sociological Inquiry, 50,* 31–74.

Heap, J. L. (1980). What counts as reading: Limits to certainty in assessment. *Curriculum Inquiry, 10,* 265–291.

Heath, C. (1984). Talk and recipiency: Sequential organization in speech and body movement. In J. M. Atkinson & J. Heritage (Eds.), *Structures of social action* (pp. 247–265). Cambridge, MA: Cambridge University Press.

Holstein, J. A. (1983). Grading practices: The construction and use of background knowledge in evaluative decision-making. *Human Studies, 6,* 377–392.

Jefferson, G. (1974). Error correction as an interactional resource. *Language in Society, 2,* 181–199.

Jefferson, G., & Schenkein, J. (1977). Some sequential negotiations in conversation: Unexpanded and expanded versions of projected action sequences. *Sociology, 11,* 87–103.

Lloyd, R. (1991, August). *Initiating interrogative talk.* Paper presented at the annual meeting of the American Sociological Association, Cincinnati, OH.

Lynch, M. (1984). Turning up signs in neurobehavioral diagnosis. *Symbolic Interaction, 17,* 67–86.

Marlaire, C. L. (1990). On questions, communication, and bias: Educational testing as "invisible" collaboration. In J. A. Holstein & G. Miller (Eds.), *Perspectives on social problems* (Vol. 2, pp. 233–260). Greenwich, CT: JAI Press.

Marlaire, C. L. (1992). Professional idealizations and clinical realities. *Current Research on Occupations and Professions, 7,* 59–77.

Marlaire, C. L., & Maynard, D. W. (1990). Standardized testing as an interactional phenomenon. *Sociology of Education, 63,* 83–101.

Maynard, D. W. (1984). *Inside plea bargaining: The language of negotiation.* New York: Plenum.

Mazeland, H. (1986). *Some aspects of the organization of repair in lessons.* Paper presented at the International Conference on Discourse in Institutions, Dourtmund University, Germany.

McHoul, A. (1978). The organization of turns at formal talk in the classroom. *Language in Society, 7,* 183–213.

McHoul, A. (1990). The organization of repair in classroom talk. *Language in Society, 19,* 349–377.

Mehan, H. (1973). Assessing children's language using abilities: Methodological and cross-cultural implication. In M. Armer & A. D. Grimshaw (Eds.), *Comparative social research: Methodological problems and strategies* (pp. 309–343). New York: Wiley.

Mehan, H. (1978). Structuring school structure. *Harvard Educational Review, 48,* 32–64.

Mehan, H. (1979). *Learning lessons.* Cambridge, MA: Harvard University Press.

Mehan, H., Hertweck, A., & Meihls, J. L. (1986). *Handicapping the handicapped: Decision-making in students' ethical careers.* Stanford, CA: Stanford University Press.

Pollner, M. (1979). Explicative transactions: Making and managing meaning in traffic court. In G. Psathas (Ed.), *Everyday language: Studies in ethnomethodology* (pp. 227–255). New York: Irvington Publishers.

Rosenthal, R., & Jacobson, L. (1968). *Pygmalion in the classroom.* New York: Holt, Rinehart, & Winston.

Rubovits, P. C., & Maehr, M. L. (1973). Pygmalion black and white. *Journal of Personality and Social Psychology, 25,* 210–218.

Sacks, H. (1967). Unpublished lectures. Irvine, CA: University of California.

Schaeffer, N. C. (1991). Conversation with a purpose—or conversation? Interaction in the standardized interview. In P. P. Biemer, R. M. Groves, L. E. Lyberg, N. A. Mathiowetz, & S. Sudman (Eds.), *Measurement errors in surveys* (pp. 367–391). New York: Wiley.

Schegloff, E. A. (1982). Discourse as an interactional achievement: Some uses of "uh-huh" and other things that come between sentences. In D. Tannen (Ed.), *Analyzing discourse: Text and talk* (pp. 71–93). Washington, DC: Georgetown University Press.

Schegloff, E. A. (1986). The routine as achievement. *Human Studies, 9,* 111–151.

Schegloff, E. A., & Sacks, H. (1973). Opening up the closings. *Semiotica, 8,* 298–327.

Schegloff, E. A., Jefferson, G., & Sacks, H. (1977). The preference for self-correction in the organization of repair in conversation. *Language, 53,* 361–382.

Suchman, L., & Jordan, B. (1990). Interactional troubles in face-to-face survey interviews. *Journal of the American Statistical Association, 85,* 232–241.

Shuy, R. W., & Griffin, P. (Eds.). (1978). *The study of children's functional language and education in the early years.* Final report to the Carnegie Corporation of New York. Arlington, VA: Center for Applied Linguistics.

Sinclair, J. M., & Coulthard, R. M. (1975). *Toward an analysis of discourse: English used by teachers and pupils.* New York: Oxford University Press.

Ysseldyke, J. E. (1986). The use of assessment information to make decisions about students. In R. J. Morris & B. Blatt (Eds.), *Special education: Research and trends* (pp. 8–27). Elmsford, NY: Pergamon.

Chapter 9

An Afro-Centered View of Communicative Competence

Toya Wyatt
California State University, Fullerton

INTRODUCTION

For years, clinicians and researchers on children's language have faced the problem of distinguishing difference from disorder in children who speak African-American English (AAE; also referred to as Ebonics, African-American vernacular English, Black English, Black English vernacular, and African-American language). The difficulty in making this distinction is largely attributed to the fact that many of the linguistic features commonly associated with AAE (e.g., variable absence of auxiliary and copula *be,* past tense *-ed,* plural *-s,* and possessive *-s*) serve as indicators of language disorder in children acquiring Standard American English (SAE) as their primary language code (Wyatt, 1996). This problem is compounded by the fact that the majority of language analysis frameworks and assessment tools used by speech and language clinicians for evaluating the communication skills of children are based on SAE. This often results in the misdiagnosis and inappropriate placement of child speakers of AAE in speech therapy programs.

Over the years, language analysis frameworks and notions of children's communicative competence have expanded beyond the level of the sentence to include larger units of communicative behavior, such as the speech event, narratives, and conversation. One primary difference between these types of analysis and sentence level analyses is the greater emphasis on social context—how language is used within various speaking situations

197

and contexts dependent on variables such as setting, activity, background of the speaker, addressee, and audience. These types of analyses have also been used in the past to highlight the role that culture plays in the construction of discourse (Ervin-Tripp & Mitchell-Kernan, 1977). For example, there have been a number of studies that have revealed differences in the ways that children from diverse cultural backgrounds engage in various speech events and acts (Heath, 1986; Jordan, Au, & Joesting, 1983; Michaels & Collins, 1984; Watson-Gegeo & Boggs, 1977).

In spite of research concerning the latter (cross-cultural differences in how children construct speech events), clinicians have typically analyzed the conversational abilities of African-American children using normative frameworks derived from studies of other child populations. This creates additional problems when testing some African-American children. For example, Labov, in his article "The Logic of Nonstandard English" (1975), notes that some African-American children tend to be less verbal during structured testing and other language elicitation situations as compared to their White mainstream American peers; he provides an example of this in his book when he describes a typical interaction between an adult examiner and an African-American child respondent during a structured testing situation (see Appendix A).

The limited verbal responsiveness of African-American children in these types of communication situations has led many educators in the past to label African-American children as "language-deprived" (Bereiter & Englemann, 1966). This is because this style of interaction contrasts with that considered normal according to mainstream American cultural views of communicative competence. In mainstream American communities, homes, and classroom settings, children are generally viewed as co-conversationalists in adult-child exchanges. As such, they are expected and encouraged to initiate conversation with adults. Heath (1982), Schieffelin and Eisenberg (1984), van Kleeck (1994b), Ward (1971), and others have noted, however, that there are many more traditional African-American cultural communities where adults do not treat children as conversational equals. In these communities, children learn early that they are to only speak when spoken to. They also learn that when they respond to the questions or comments of adults, they are to respond by saying the absolute minimum.

Heath (1982, 1983, 1986) also observed that it was rare for adults in some Southern working-class African-American communities to ask children known-information questions (questions where the information requested is known to both the speaker and listener). In her study of one such community in the Piedmont Carolinas (Trackton), Heath (1982, 1983, 1986) also noted that African-American adults were less likely than White adults from a neighboring middle-class community to use label requests (e.g., asking children to label pictured objects that are already within the view of the adult making the request). The less-frequent use of these language genres in their home communities may explain why African-American children tend to respond more slowly than their White mainstream peers, at least initially, to known-information questions and picture labeling requests during formal testing situations (Wyatt, 1995b). Such differences are generally misinterpreted as signs of disorder rather than difference.

There are a number of different solutions that have been proposed for addressing the problems of evaluating the communicative abilities of African-American children. Solutions range from focusing on the non-dialect-specific aspects of English grammar (Craig & Washington, 1995) to the more universally shared aspects of language development and use (semantics and pragmatics) as advocated by Stockman (1986a, 1986b, 1996). Child language scholars have also recommended the use of naturalistic language sampling procedures conducted within communicative contexts that are more familiar and representative of children's encounters within their own home speech environments. According to Lund and Duchan (1993), children are more likely to participate in familiar social and communicative events because the rules for behavior are nonambiguous, clear, and easily understood; they also state that "children comprehend best when language is embedded within a familiar event" (p. 57). The latter can greatly impact on how children respond in varied language situations. The use of more naturalistic language sampling procedures would also provide clinicians with the flexibility to use culturally appropriate norms and standards (e.g., information from existing language studies of African-American children) for interpreting the language performance of a given child (Stockman, 1986b, 1996).

All of these modifications would lead to a more ecologically valid assessment process. Ecological approaches to assessment are based on the assumption that every individual is "an inseparable part of a social system" and that one's "behavior cannot be understood without considering its context" (McCormick, 1997, p. 227). As such, ecological approaches stress the importance of:

sampling communication in a variety of differing contexts and environments, including classroom, community, and home environments,

obtaining information concerning the communication expectations of adults who are part of a child's natural environment, and

considering the contexts in which a child's learning occurs before drawing conclusions about his or her communicative abilities.

All of these considerations can be extremely important when evaluating the communicative skills of African-American children who have grown up in homes that have communicative expectations different from those valued in mainstream American classrooms. Ecological assessment approaches also help with the development of culturally relevant intervention programs and goals.

SPEECH EVENTS IN THE AFRICAN-AMERICAN SPEECH COMMUNITY

One of the naturalistic communicative contexts that would perhaps be most useful for examining the language skills of African-American children is one in which some of the speech events (e.g., "playing the dozens," "signifying," and "rapping") typically associated with the African-American cultural discourse tradition are elicited. Such events are frequently described in ethnographic accounts of African-American speech communities.

One of the best-known descriptive accounts can be found in Thomas Kochman's (1972b) book *Rappin' and Stylin' Out.* Here, Kochman describes several language performance events that he observed during communication exchanges among African-American adolescents and/or adults (primarily males). His observations were taken from studies of discourse patterns used in Northern urban African-American speech communities. A description of some of these speech events can be found in Appendix B.

According to Abrahams (1968, as cited in Kochman, 1972a) and Dalby (1991), there are a number of speech events in the West Indies and Africa that seem to resemble in function and structure those reported by Kochman (1972a, 1972b) and others. The similarity between African-American speech events and those found in other African-based communities provides some support for theories suggesting African-based origins for these language uses. Comparative ethnographic studies of community discourse patterns have also revealed similarities between African-American and African communities in the degree of value and emphasis placed on verbal expression. The strong emphasis on verbal ability is perhaps best exemplified by the word *nommo,* an African term that refers to the power of the word (Baber, 1987; Dandy, 1991; Smitherman, 1994).

Linguistic analyses of Afro-centered communicative events have also focused on the highly sophisticated level of metalinguistic awareness and skill required to perform each. The term *metalinguistics* refers to the ability to separate form from content, to reflect on language as an object or entity separate from meaning (Owens, 1996), or to view language as an object of play (van Kleeck, 1994a). The notion of "language as an object of play" is particularly relevant when discussing Afro-centered discourse patterns, since much of Black communication, according to Baber (1987), is performance (p. 105). There is a great deal of emphasis, therefore, on "style" or "the way in which something is said rather than . . . components such as . . . topic" (Mitchell-Kernan, 1972a, p. 164). "Rhythm and rhyme," which "add poetic cadence, aesthetic force, and magic to Black speech" are also key elements in many of these acts (Baber, 1987, p. 103).

As with any speech event in any speech community, there is a pre-established set of culturally defined rules that prescribe the organizational structure of the various African-American speech events. These rules enable native speakers to distinguish one event from others. Any changes in the type of features employed can lead to misinterpretation or inappropriate execution of an act (Mitchell-Kernan, 1972b); skillful execution of each, therefore, requires strict adherence to community-based rules and "shared cultural knowledge" (p. 327). A discussion of some of the rules associated with three traditional African-American events follows.

The Dozens

"Playing the dozens" is a verbal game that involves the exchange of insults, generally directed at members of participants' families. According to Harris, Levitt, Furman, and Smith (1974), the name of this game originated from the common practice, during slavery, of selling slaves who were determined to have some sort of physical, mental, or other flaw, by the dozen. Being sold in this fashion was perceived, by many slaves as humiliating—thus the connection to a speech game that also has at its roots humiliation. Other theories about the origins and history of this game are reported by Percelay, Ivey, and Dweck (1994).

One of the best examples of the dozens occurs in a fairly recently released movie called *Bebe's Kids* (Hudlin & Hudlin, 1992). The movie is based on the fictional exploits of a "brother" named Robin who is interested in establishing a relationship with Jamika, a young woman whom he has just met. In an attempt to gain her affection, Robin invites Jamika and her son to an amusement park, Fun World. At Fun World, however, Robin runs into his ex-wife, who decides that she is going to cause a little trouble for him and his new girlfriend. So when Jamika goes into the bathroom at one point in the movie, Robin's ex-wife and her girlfriend follow her. The ex-wife and girlfriend then proceed to have a very loud conversation, which they hope Jamika will overhear, about Robin's supposed visit to the ex-wife's apartment the previous night. Jamika obviously becomes upset and leaves the bathroom to confront Robin about his whereabouts the previous night. When Robin finally figures out what has happened, he storms back into the bathroom with Jamika on his arm to confront his ex-wife. They become involved in a heated exchange, which eventually evolves into the dozens. An excerpt from this exchange can be found in Appendix C.

One key element that is clearly emphasized in this exchange is the ongoing references to each other's mother. Each verbal contribution is linked to preceding ones in terms of topic as well. The ongoing reference to a shared topic is a key part of the dozens and can even be seen in the early one-liners produced by fifth- and sixth-grade boys in Chicago who are just learning to play the game (Kochman, 1972b): "Your family is so poor the rats and *roaches* eat lunch out." "Your house is so small the *roaches* walk single file." In this example, the targets of the insults change from family to home; however, some form of topical reference is still maintained through the continued reference to roaches.

The emphasis on this form of linguistic contingency can even be seen in the organization of some recent books that provide examples of the dozens. For example, in the book *Mo' Yo' Mama!* (Pop & Rank, 1996), the authors organize a variety of different "snaps" (teasing one-liners that criticize some aspects of a listener's family, home, body, etc.) according to headings such as "Yo' mama's so dumb," "Yo' mama's so fat," "Yo' mama's so ugly," and "body parts." Examples of snaps categorized under body parts include one-liners that criticize some aspect of the anatomy (i.e., teeth, feet, nose, hair, etc.). For example, under the heading of "Yo' mama's teeth," there are snaps such as "Yo' mama's missing so many teeth, when she opens her mouth it looks like a graveyard" and "Yo' mama's teeth are so bad, she's the original model for the jack-o'-lantern." The same can be seen in two other related books, *Snaps* (Percelay, Ivey, & Dweck, 1994) and *Triple Snaps* (Percelay, Ivey, & Dweck, 1996), which are organized according to headings such as "Fat snaps," "Ugly snaps," "House snaps," "Old snaps," "Hair snaps," and so forth.

Signifying

Signifying is another African-American speech event that also has as its ultimate goal the undermining of another. Like the dozens, signifying, therefore, involves some element of verbal insult and is used to indirectly "make fun of" or "put down" a person or situation (Abrahams, 1964). The primary difference between the two speech acts is that while the dozens involves insults hurled at some member of an individual's family, signifying involves insults aimed at the individual to whom the remarks are being made (Kochman, 1972a, 1972b). Another important difference is that the insults are delivered in a more indirect or subtle manner than in the dozens. Signifying therefore involves "an element of indirection" (Mitchell-Kernan, 1972b, p. 315); as such, the underlying content and function of a remark "is potentially obscured by the surface content or function" (p. 317). This obscurity is designed to make interpretation of any of the following difficult: "(1) the meaning or message the speaker is adjudged as intending to convey; (2) the addressees—the person or persons to whom the message is directed; (3) the goal orientation or intent of the speaker" (Mitchell-Kernan, 1972b, pp. 317–318).

Mitchell-Kernan (1972b) goes on further to state that:

> The black concept of signifying incorporates essentially a folk notion that dictionary entries for words are not always sufficient for interpreting meanings or messages, or that meaning goes beyond such interpretations. . . . A particular utterance may be an insult in one context and not another. What pretends to be informative may intend to be persuasive. The hearer is thus constrained to attend to all potential meaning-carrying symbolic systems in speech events—the total universe of discourse. (p. 317)

Situational, nonverbal, and verbal context are, therefore, crucial for interpretation. The ability to manipulate form and content in a creative way is equally important. One other important dimension is the obligation for listener response. According to Kochman (1972a), if the target of a signifying remark fails to respond immediately and aggressively, his or her social status is likely to be compromised.

The role of situational context, verbal indirection, and listener response can be seen in an incident that occurred several years ago between my sister Mona, a singer-dancer-actress, and a young man whom she encountered on the streets of New York one day. Mona, who has always been chided in our family for her "distinctive" dressing, happened to be wearing a silver outfit that had a shiny aluminum/metallic appearance to it. A young "brother" who happened to be passing by commented on her outfit by saying: "Ooooooh, baby!! Lookin' like 'ET' today." Mona, who immediately recognized the signifying tone of the brother's comment, quickly responded in a warning tone: "That's right, my brother! *ET . . . Evil Today!!!!*" Her quick-witted response was immediately acknowledged by the young man, who in turn responded, "Oooh, I'm scared of you!" which could be translated as "That was a good one! You got me!"

Rapping

Although the term *rapping* has been used for a long time within the African-American community, its meaning has changed somewhat over the years. Traditionally in the past, rapping has been used to refer to a way of talking in which one "tells it like it is" or attempts to persuade another through smooth talking. The best example of the latter would be a male who raps to a female with the hopes of persuading her to become intimately involved. Today, however, the term is used most widely to refer to a relatively new verbal/musical art form used in the music world. It generally refers to the rhythmical, lyrical style of talking that is imposed on a strong musical base or beat. According to Baber (1987), rap is music created through words. It is also a verbal and musical art form that has found its way into mainstream American culture, because of the crossover appeal of rap music to non-African-American teenage audiences.

Like the dozens and signifying, rapping involves the creative manipulation of language form (in this case, rhyming). Rhythm and rhyme are essential. An example of this (cited in Sexton, 1995, pp. 11–12) can be found in Kool Moe Dee and Big Daddy Kane's verbal introduction (Dee & Kane, 1989) to the song "Birdland" in Quincy Jones' *Back on the Block* album:

A tribute to the Birdman,
The father of Birdland,
A masterpiece of release:
The home's words and
The musical greats
Salute the late
Mentor, inventor
Of a sound that dates
Back from bebop to pop
And pop to hip-hop
We fused the times
Of jazz and rhymes and got
Kool Moe Dee and Big Daddy Kane
To bring on the legends.
Kane, hit the names!

The manipulation of other prosodic features, such as intonation, inflection, tone, pitch, and the rate of delivery, are also important (Baber, 1987). Dandy (1991) notes that one has to marvel at the skill of young people who can "recite detailed rhymes that carry a message with no apparent preparation and deliver them at speeds up to 200 to 250 words per minute, not missing a beat" (p. 80).

Repetition and redundancy are two other key elements. Evidence of this can be found in many of the current raps, which use the new *sampling* technology. This technology involves introducing edited segments from other musical pieces into an ongoing rap sequence. Rhythmic elements are repeated and reconfigured in such a way that there is heightened attention to the patterns and movements of the song (Rose, 1995, p. 48).

One last characteristic of verbal rap is the emphasis on collaboration and group involvement. The raps are collaboratively constructed by several different individuals who are able to play off of each other's verbal contributions.

THE AFRICAN-AMERICAN SPEECH EVENTS
OF PRESCHOOLERS

Until recently, African-American speech events such as rapping, signifying, and playing the dozens have been studied in preadolescent, adolescent, and adult populations. However, in a study of AAE copula production patterns in preschool speech (Wyatt, 1991), I found that as early as 4 years of age, some African-American preschoolers are already beginning to become proficient in the use of these sophisticated verbal acts.

For example, during one language sampling session, three 4-year-old boys became involved in a verbal dispute over the placement of a puzzle piece. The dispute escalated into a preschool version of the dozens. It began when one of the three boys, DN, began to complain about where another boy (JW) was placing the puzzle piece. At one point in the debate, one of the two boys said to the other, "Your mother!!!!" This immediately led to an ensuing string of verbal insults about each other's mothers. My initial reaction to the ongoing debate was shock, since I had never heard children this young playing the dozens. However, after I got over my initial reaction of shock, I immediately ran over to turn on the tape recorder to capture the ongoing debate. Unfortunately, the boys had discontinued their verbal interchange before I could get to the tape recorder. I was successfully able to elicit continuation of the dozens exchange by asking one of the boys, "What did you say about his mother?!" The exchange went as follows:

??*:	Your mother don't have no /mʌdə /[mother]/
??:	(Laugh)/
DN:	Your mother don't have no mo-tor and your mother. . . ./
??:	(All three children overlapping in unison) . . . don't have no ???**/
DD:	Your daddy don't have no car/
DN:	Your mother have a car but she don't have no keys/
TW:	Oh! (Laughing)/ Excuse me!/
DN:	No/ No. . . ./
JW:	My mother do drive/ She drive it with her hands/
TW:	She drives with her hands?/
DD:	(In background, softly singing) Mo-tor . . . mo-tor . . . motor/
DN:	And that's why your mother don't have no mo-tor/
TW:	OK, fine. . . . And what do you have to say to that, John/
DN:	Wait . . . wait . . . wait . . . wait . . . wait. . . . Ease up . . . ease up . . . ease up man . . . ease up . . . ease up . . . ease up . . ./
JW:	(Overlapping DN) Your mother don't have no car/
DN:	Ease up . . . ease up . . . ease up/

*?? refers to unknown speaker
**??? refers to unintelligible utterance

On another occasion, I also had the opportunity to watch two of the same boys (DN and DD) initiate a spontaneous rapping sequence. The rap occurred in response to a conversation about the absence of my female student assistant, Monica. The children, who were used to seeing Monica with me on each of my previous visits, wanted to know why she was absent one day. After explaining that she had to stay home to prepare for a test, I began to ask the two boys, in a teasing way, why they were so interested in Monica. Was it because they liked her? After admitting to the fact that they had a slight crush on her, one of the two boys (DD) began to construct a spontaneous rap about what he would do if Monica were his "girl." DN picked up on DD's lead and immediately began to chime in with his own verbal contributions. JM, a third child, provided additional background support:

DN: (Rap tempo) An' I LOVE her!/
DD: An' tell her I LOVE her/ I LOVE her!/
JM: (Overlapping DD, in background) I LOVE her!/
DN: I LOVE her/ I'ma LOVE her everyTIME/
JM: (In background) I'ma LOVE her EVERYtime/
DD: An' she can call me EVERYtime
DD: An' I answer the PHONE, I say GET off the PHONE, mom!/
DN: She's MY GIRL and I'ma SEE HER/
DD: EVERYtime, she call me, I say MOMS, get off the dag-gone PHONE/I wanna TALK to the girl/
DN: (Laughs)/ EVERYtime, I see HER, I'm GOnna kiss HER/I'm GOnna love HER and I'm GOnna kiss HER/
DD: EveryTIME she call me, I'ma KISS the phone/ I'ma say "HELlo, WHO is it?"/ AH, babes/Shut the HECK up / I'ma tell my brother, "get the heck off the phone"/ "It's my GIRLFRIEND, man!"/ "I'm not joking around with you, MAN"/
[Intervening dialogue]
DD: (Singing) An' I'ma say, "I GOT to GET the woman"/ I GOT to SING the woman/
DN: (Singing) I GOTta KISS the WOman/
DD: (Singing) (Unintelligible) the WOman look nice and COOLin'/ I like the WOman/
DN: I LIKE, HOW, SHE, LOOKS!/I like her LOOKS on her FACE cause she looks so PRETty/ Cause I love her WHOLE BODY though she doesn't KNOW ME!/

IMPLICATIONS FOR ASSESSMENT

Assessing Pragmatic and Metalinguistic Skills

An examination of the two preceding preschooler dialogues reveals evidence of developing skills, as defined by van Kleeck (1994a): *metalinguistic*, the ability to focus on and manipulate language form; *metapragmatic*, awareness of the social rules for language use; *pragmatic*, the skillful use of language in social contexts; and *metacommunicative*, knowing how to use nonlinguistic devices, such as body gesture, facial expression, intonation, pitch, and loudness, to convey meaning and interpretation. It is clear that the children understand the cultural community rules for constructing each discourse event and that they possess some of the skills necessary for performing each.

When rapping, the children seem to understand the obligation for listener participation and response, even when no question is posed. As soon as DD completes one rapping turn, DN immediately adds his contribution, which is then followed by DD. Active audience response is a salient feature of communication in the African-American community (Dandy, 1991) and contributes to the ongoing flow of collaborative discourse events like the dozens. This type of response pattern could be characterized as a form of *call and response*, which is a "basic idiom of Black communication" (Baber, 1987, p. 95).

The children also seem to realize that their verbal contributions must be linked in form, content, or topic to the preceding speaker's utterances. This element of linguistic contingency is evident in the dozens exchange that takes place between DD and DN where there is an ongoing reference to things associated with automobiles: *motor, car, keys.*

DN: Your mother don't have no *mo-tor* and your mother. . . .
DD: Your daddy don't have no *car.*
DN: Your mother have a *car* but she don't have no [car] *keys.*

The children also understand the most primary requirement of this verbal game: the need to produce utterances that criticize or insult a member of the other's family (in this case, daddies and mothers). In some instances, the insults are indirect, giving them a signifying tone, as evidenced by DN's last utterance ("Your mother have a car but she don't have no keys"). DN indirectly implies that it wouldn't even matter if DD's mother had a car; she wouldn't be able to use it because, according to DN's assertion, she doesn't have keys.

Evidence of emerging metalinguistic abilities can also be seen in the children's attempts to manipulate the cadence, stress, rhythm, and rhyme of their rapping sequences. In at least one instance, one boy does a pretty decent job of selecting words ("girl" and "her") that bear some phonetic similarity to each other:

DN: She's MY *GIRL* . . . and I'ma SEE *HER.* . . .

In another instance, DN uses repetition of the same word ("her") and word stress patterns to give the appearance of phonetic rhyme:

DN: EVERYtime I see *HER* . . . I'm GOnna kiss *HER* . . . I'm GOnna love
        HER . . . and I'm GOnna kiss *HER.*

This playful manipulation of language requires some level of phonological
awareness, a skill that begins to emerge during preschool years (van Kleeck,
1994a).

In sum, the children seem to be aware of the importance of verbal
spontaneity and creativity in African-American speech performance. According to Baber (1987), "The artifice of Black communicative behavior
is found in its ingenuity, originality, spontaneity, and resourcefulness" (p.
76). The latter point is demonstrated best by DD's response to the examiner's question about the origin of his rap. When the author asked DD at
the end of his rap, "How do you know all of these songs?" DD replied,
"Cuz, I just got it from my body, man!" (Wyatt, 1991, p. 131).

The Elicitation of Language Sample Data

There can be an advantage to using verbal routines such as rapping and
playing the dozens as a method for eliciting language from some African-
American children. The primary benefit is that these conversational routines are likely to be more familiar than those traditionally used during
the speech and language assessment process. Those who are successful in
eliciting or observing these spontaneous verbal routines are, therefore,
likely to obtain more reliable, valid, and culturally appropriate language
sample data.

For example, when one compares the type of language responses that
were elicited from DD during more traditional speech screening procedures (picture description and labeling tasks, and conversation about topics
and characters portrayed in the pictures) to those elicited during the
rapping and dozens sequences, it becomes clear that the latter are likely
to evoke longer and more complex language productions. A sample of
the utterances produced by DD in more structured language elicitation
contexts can be found in Appendix D. As one can see, there is a drastic
difference when this sample is compared to the type of language elicited
during speech event performances elicited in spontaneous language elicitation situations.

Distinguishing Difference and Disorder: A Case Study

The use of these familiar verbal routines can also assist with the differential
diagnosis of language disorder in those situations where it is difficult to
distinguish between dialect difference and disorder. During the subject
selection stage of my AAE copula study (Wyatt, 1991), I encountered a
3-year-old boy, JM, who during informal speech and language screening

procedures displayed several phonological and grammatical differences that could have been attributed to developmental or dialect influences as well as other speech sound and grammatical productions that could not be explained solely by either development or dialect. For example, he produced a number of speech sound errors that are generally considered normal for 3-year-old English-speaking children, such as substituting /s/ for /ʃ/ in a word like "brush," /w/ for /r/ in a word like "rabbit," /j/ for /l/ in a word like "leaf," and reducing /s/ consonant clusters in a word like "screw." Normal developmental difficulties with irregular verbs in the past tense, such as "caught" (e.g., "He *catched* the ball"), were also noted (see Appendix E).

However, JM also produced a number of speech sounds that could potentially have been dialect based, given the fact that he was being raised in a community where AAE was frequently spoken. JM also attended a day-care program where he was exposed to AAE during interactions with other African-American children on a daily basis. Examples of possible dialect-based productions included the devoicing of final voiced sounds in a word like "five," absence of the plural -*s* marker in a word like "scissors," and absence of auxiliary "is" in sentences like "He walkin'." These are all commonly cited features of AAE. (The reader is directed to Wolfram, 1986, Fasold & Wolfram, 1975, and Wyatt, 1995a, for examples of common AAE features.)

On the other hand, there were also a number of phonological and grammatical productions that could not be as easily attributed to dialect-based influences. Examples included the substitution of /s/ for /θ/ in a word like "three" and the substitution of /s/ for /z/ in a word like "zipper." Although /z/ and /θ/ are later-developing English sounds and /θ/ is a sound commonly produced as /f/ in adult AAE, the type of sound substitutions made by JM would be considered somewhat atypical for most AAE speakers. Other examples included the absence of the articles "a" and "the" in sentences like "I wanna get [a] sticker" and "He goes in [the] water [to] sleep"; the absence of the preposition "on" in a sentence like "He's puttin' [on] his hat"; and the use of the phrase "both hims" for "both of them" in a sentence like "*Both hims* in the water."

This left some question about the normalcy of JM's speech and language skills even when dialect and developmental influences were taken into account. In addition, speech intelligibility and pragmatic and semantic difficulties were noticeable during conversational interactions with peers. For example, during one such interaction with two of JM's peers, DD and DN, JM's expressive language difficulties became evident:

01 DD: (Slamming puzzle piece down on table) Come on you daggone
           puzzle, man/
02 JM: /dækən pʌkl mæn?/ [daggone puzzle man?]/

03 DD: I got it/
04 JM: I got it! (Reaching for another puzzle piece) /kʌpɪsɪn/
            [???]/ (Quietly) I got it /kɑpɪsɪn/ [???*]/
05 DN: (To JM) What are you talking?/
06 JM: /pɪsm/ [???]
07 DN: /pɪsm/? Ah, that's a funny thing (Laughs)/
08 JM: (Looking down) A bread/
09 DN: (Pointing in direction of puzzle box cover) Move that truck cuz
            we can't see/
10 JM: (Jumps up, holding a puzzle piece in the air) This is the coco-
            bread/This is coco and bread/
11 DN: (Looking at JM) Cocobread?/
12 JM: Hm-mm/ Coco and bread/
13 DN: Coco and bread?/
14 JM: Un-hm/Look at this bread too/
15 DN: Ahhhh (Smiling to himself)/
16 JM: (Quietly to himself) This good/Look at this one. . . ./
17 JM: (Holding up a puzzle piece and looking at it) This good. . . . look
            at this, look at this peanut butter/
18 DN: What are you talking?/

*[???] refers to unintelligible productions

JM's communication difficulties with peers are evident from DD's and
DN's queries regarding the intended meaning of intelligible as well as JM's
unintelligible (e.g., "/kɑpɪsɪn/") word productions (utterances 05, 11, 13,
and 18). The comment made by DN in line 07, which ridicules JM's communicative attempts, also provides some support for the view that his peers
considered his productions to be inappropriate.
    Similar problems were also noted during a second communicative situ-
ation when JM attempted to initiate a spontaneous rap similar to the one
produced by DD and DN (discussed earlier in this chapter):

19 JM: (Singing, tapping his foot on the floor) Oh girl . . . you got what
                I need/ It's take me for the tape/
20 DD: (Chimes in, tapping a puzzle piece on the table) Say he's just a
                friend/
21 DN: (Singing and looking up) Oh girl . . . you got. . . ./
22 DN, JM, DD: (Singing in chorus) . . . what I need/
23 DN: Eeeee—You say he's just a friend/
24 JM: (Overlapping DN and singing) Is take me for the tape/
25 DN: (Singing) Oh girl . . . you . . ./
26 JM: (Coughing while DN is singing)/
27 (Singing dies out while DN reaches for a new puzzle piece)/
28 DN: This goes right here/
29 DD: (To DD) No, you messin' that one up/

30 JM: (Overlapping DD, singing) Oh girl, you got what I need/
31 DN: (Chimes in) Girl. . . . (stops abruptly and looks at JM)/
32 JM: (Overlapping DN, singing) It's take me for the take/
33 (DN stares for a moment at JM, glances toward the camera, and then back at JM)/
34 JM: It's take me for the take/
35 DD: (looking down with his eyebrows raised, frowning) Take me for the tape?/
36 JM: Uh-hm. . . . It's take me for the tape/ It's take me for the tape/
37 (DN and DD glance at each other)/
38 DN: What the heck is he saying?/
39 (JM looks at DN)
40 DD: (Looking up, smiling) Take me from the tape?/
41 JM: (Looking at DN) Take me from the take/
42 DN: What song is that?/
43 JM: /mæsəz/ song/ Your song/
44 DN: That ain't my song/
45 JM: That my song then/
46 DN: Shut up, man/ I don't know what you're talkin' about/

Observations of JM's peer interactions provide crucial information about his communication skills in naturally occurring, culturally familiar contexts. According to Mattes and Omark (1991), there are several different signs of communicative difficulty that provide evidence of possible communication handicap during interactions between peers from similar cultural and language backgrounds. Examples include:

gestures versus speech being utilized as the primary form of communication by the child in question,

utterances that appear to have little or no effect on the actions of peers, and

facial expressions and/or actions of peers that indicate they may be having difficulty understanding a child's communicative attempts.

An examination of JM's interactions with peers reveals a number of these difficulties. For example, he seemed to have difficulty maintaining an ongoing conversational interaction with his peers during the rap that he initiated. The rapping sequence dies out shortly after it is initiated at line 27 when DN and DD return their focus to the puzzle task. JM seems to recognize the communication breakdown and attempts to repair this by re-initiating the rap in line 30. This time, however, he encounters a second communication breakdown when both DN and DD (lines 31, 33, and 35) question JM about the meaning of his utterance "Take me from the tape." Each of his attempts to repair this second communication breakdown, in lines 36, 41, 43, and 45, are largely unsuccessful as DN and DD continue to question his responses to their queries. The sequence concludes with DN's final directive to "Shut up, man, I don't know what you're talkin' about" (line 46).

The preceding discussion demonstrates the value and cultural validity of using culturally familiar and natural communication events (e.g., conversational exchanges with peers from similar cultural and language situations) for helping to resolve questions regarding a child's communicative competence. This type of communication-event analysis also provides a good profile of communicative strengths and weaknesses. For example, from one perspective, JM seems to be an ineffective communicator when one examines the type of communication breakdowns encountered with peers from similar cultural and language backgrounds. On the other hand, one also finds evidence of JM's communicative strengths when one considers his demonstrated awareness of the need for conversational repair and his subsequent attempts to do so. The identification of JM as an effective or ineffective communicator, as with most children, depends to some extent on the social communicative context in which behaviors are elicited and analyzed and what the evaluator chooses to focus on.

CONCLUSIONS

By using a wider range of culturally relevant discourse contexts for evaluating the communicative competence of African-American children, clinicians can avoid many of the pitfalls associated with the use of standardized tests and language sampling/analysis procedures developed for other child populations. The continued reliance on tests and normative frameworks originally developed for SAE populations can result in a "distorted and incomplete view" (Seymour, 1986, p. 53) of African-American children's language skills, and can lead to erroneous assumptions about their communicative competence. In contrast, information obtained from language samples collected within naturalistic, Afro-centered discourse contexts and interpreted in terms of existing normative language profiles, based on studies of African-American child populations, provides more culturally valid and accurate analyses of communicative ability.

One additional advantage of using the culturally relevant discourse contexts presented in this chapter is that they provide clinicians with the ability to evaluate several aspects of communication: phonology, morphology, syntax, pragmatics, semantics, and metalinguistic awareness simultaneously. Language can also be viewed from a more holistic perspective. According to Lund and Duchan (1993), it is not enough to consider the individual function of communicative speech acts but one must also consider how various acts relate to the overall organization of any speech event (p. 18).

Analyzing communication within organized speech event contexts also helps clinicians identify those points of communication breakdown because of language weaknesses (Lund & Duchan, 1993). The significance of such breakdowns become even more significant when they occur in contexts that should be more familiar to a child. As Lund and Duchan (1993) point out, when children communicate in familiar contexts, there is less "fine-tuning" that they need to accomplish because they have a good sense of their conversational partner's role and communicative needs. When communicative breakdowns occur in less familiar contexts, one should therefore question whether such breakdowns can be attributed to true communicative disorder. The evaluation of African-American children's communicative skills in more culturally familiar contexts helps to clarify whether such breakdowns and perceived communicative weaknesses are the result of a true underlying disorder or of differing communicative expectations.

APPENDIX A:
TESTING SESSION WITH AN AFRICAN-AMERICAN CHILD

The following is a sample of dialogue that takes place between an African-American child and a White interviewer who has put a block and a fire engine on the table in front of the child:

> Interviewer: Tell me everything you can about this. . . .
> [12 seconds of silence]
> Interviewer: What would you say it looks like?
> [8 seconds of silence]
> Child: A space ship.
> Interviewer: Hmmmm.
> [13 seconds of silence]
> Child: Like a je-et.
> [12 seconds of silence]
> Child: Like a plane.
> [20 seconds of silence]
> Interviewer: What color is it?
> Child: Orange. [2 seconds of silence] An' whi-ite. [2 seconds of silence] An' green.
> [6 seconds of silence]
> Interviewer: An' what could you use it for?
> [8 seconds of silence]
> Child: A je-et
> [6 seconds of silence]
> Interviewer: If you had two of them, what would you do with them?

[6 seconds of silence]
Child: Give one to some-body

Note.   From "The Logic of Nonstandard English," by W. Labov, in P. Stoller (Ed.), *Black American English*, p. 74. Copyright 1975 by Dell Publishing Co., Inc. Reprinted with permission.

APPENDIX B:
DESCRIPTIONS OF SELECTED AFRICAN-AMERICAN
SPEECH EVENTS

Tomming

Tomming involves the adoption of a certain nonverbal and verbal posture whenever one encounters situations of potential difficulty or danger. Such situations include social encounters with authority figures like "the Man" (e.g., police officers, bosses, etc.). Tomming is used as a verbal strategy for talking oneself out of the difficult situation. It involves doing whatever it takes to appease the involved authority figure. In many cases, this includes feigning an image that is likely to be acceptable to that authority figure (i.e., the stereotypical slave image: "Yessir, Mr. Charlie"; "Anything you say, Mr. Charlie"). The term "tomming" partly derives from the first name of the main slave character in Harriet Beecher Stowe's *Uncle Tom's Cabin*, who did whatever was necessary to appease his White slave owner.

Copping a Plea/Gripping

This includes forms of begging or pleading that are used in situations where deference to an authority (e.g., teachers or judges) is perceived as necessary for obtaining their pity or mercy. It involves either partial (gripping) or total (copping a plea) "giving up of face."

Signifying

Signifying is an indirect verbal strategy used for "making fun of" or putting another person down through the use of teasing, taunting language.

Playing the Dozens

This verbal game consists of a series of topic-related verbal insults generally aimed at a member of a person's family (usually one's mother). It usually occurs within group settings. Playing the Dozens begins with an initial insult from one member of the group that is responded to by a round of return insults from those who are targets of the original insult.

Rapping

Rapping is a "colorful," persuasive style of talking that can be used to: (a) disclose the true nature of some past event (often described in narrative form), (b) flirt with a member of the opposite sex, or (c) talk an individual into giving up desired goods or services. A more contemporary use of the term refers to the rhythmical, lyrical style of delivery used in much of today's African-American hip-hop music.

Note. The above descriptions are partly derived from Kochman, T. (1972). Toward an ethnography of Black American speech behavior. In T. Kochman (Ed.). *Rappin' and Stylin' Out.* Urbana, IL: University of Illinois Press. The last definition (rapping) is updated to reflect newer uses of this term.

APPENDIX C:
"PLAYING THE DOZENS"

The following segment was taken from the movie *Bebe's Kids* during a confrontation between the main character in the movie, Robin, and his ex-wife:

Robin (Storms into the bathroom, almost knocking down an old woman in the way. He turns toward her): Ain't nobody lookin' at you. (Robin then turns to Jamika, takes her hand) Come on! (He and Jamika begin looking under the bathroom stalls for his ex-wife and her friend).

Jamika (Points to a set of feet under one stall): That's them! I can tell by them Lee™ press-on toenails.

Robin's ex-wife (Comes out of bathroom stall, crosses her arms, and looks at Jamika, angrily): Hmmph! I see some women can't do anything without a man!

Robin (Points his finger in his ex-wife's face): Why you lie on me?!! (Pulls Jamika toward him in an embracing hug) Don't you know this kind of game only brings me and Jamika closer and guarantees that you and I will NEVER get together again! NEVER!!

Robin's ex-wife: Well, for me to lie on you, I would have to care about you. (Places her hands on her hips and rolls her head in a circular fashion) . . . and believe me, I don't give a damn about neither one of y'all (Snaps her fingers and walks away from the stall).

Robin: Ain't that a . . . (Approaches his ex-wife pointing to his ring finger) That's why I wear my ring on the WRONG finger because I married the WRONG woman.

Wife: Hmmmm!

Robin (Points at his ex-wife's head): Hair look like the back of a toaster.

Wife (Squeals—then jumps in Robin's face): Your momma!

Robin: My momma?!!!

Wife (Points her finger at Robin): Yeah, your whole family!

Robin: Ain't that a. . . . Look at you! Yo' momma so old, she was there the first day of slavery.

Wife (Moves her head in a circular motion, and crosses her arms): Yo' momma so old, she older than yo' grandmama.

Robin: Yo' momma so fat, she on both sides of the family (Mimics with gestures and facial expressions the dimensions of a fat person).

Wife: That's OK, your momma's so dumb, she thought a quarterback was a refund! (Places her hands on her hips and moves her head in a circle).

Robin: Oh, ain't that. . . . Look, (points his finger at his ex-wife) your momma's so dumb, they told her it was chilly outside an' she went and got a bowl (Holds his hands in a bowl shape while adopting a begging posture).

Wife (Gives an angry look while her girlfriend begins to laugh hysterically in the background).

Note. Segment transcribed from Hudlin, R., & Hudlin, W. (1992). *Bebe's kids* [Film]. Hollywood, CA: Paramount Pictures.

APPENDIX D:
SPEECH AND LANGUAGE SCREENING SESSION
WITH AN AFRICAN-AMERICAN PRESCHOOLER

(DD)

Segment 1

Stimulus materials: Smurfs Colorforms set.

TW: Right/What's that Smurf doing?/
DD: Playin with a kite/
TW: That's right/He's also flyin' pretty high/OK, put another Smurf on/We're gonna make a really nice picture/What's that one doing?/
DD: Swimmin' in a pool/
TW: That's right, swimmin' in a pool/Do you know how to swim in a pool/
DD: (Nods yes))
TW: You do?!/Are you afraid of water?/
DD: (Nods no)

TW: Get out of here/I'm afraid of water but you're strong, huh?/That's good/
OK, what else do we wanna put on the picture?/
TW: You know what that guy is called?/
DD: Father/
TW: That's right/Papa Smurf, too/I can tell you've been watching your TV/OK, what's this?/
DD: (no response)
TW: Do you know what that thing is?/
DD: Uh-uh/
TW: That's a snail/A yucky, yucky snail/OK, pick some other things to put on your picture/
(Long silence)
TW: Wow!/What's this thing?/
DD: A hook thing/
TW: That's right/A hook thing/ What's he doing?/
DD: Skatin'/

Segment 2

Stimulus materials: 3 Sesame Street pictures. In the first, the Sesame Street gang is in the classroom where a number of things are occurring (i.e., a teacher writing on the chalkboard, a little girl playing a violin, Ernie painting, a nurse doing an X ray of Cookie Monster's stomach, etc.). The second picture shows the Sesame Street gang at Thanksgiving dinner.

TW: Tell me about Ernie/
DD: Ernie's writing/
TW: That's good/Tell me about the little girl/
DD: The little girl's playing a thing/
TW: Uh-hm/What about Cookie Monster?/
DD: Cookie Monster's eatin' the cookies/
TW: Yeah, see, the nurse is checking his stomach 'cuz it looked like he ate too many cookies/ Think he has a stomachache/What about the teacher?/
DD: Writin'/
TW: Uh-hm/What is she writing on the board?/You know what she's writing?/Writing her ABCs/You know how to do your ABCs yet?/
DD: (Nods no)
TW: What's Ernie doing this time?/
DD: Makin' a woman/
TW: Yeah/(Shows another picture)
DD: Big Bird/
TW: Yeah, what about Big Bird?/
DD: He's talkin' to them/
TW: Yup/(Show another picture)

DD: Cookie Monster eatin' a fat turkey/
TW: Yeah, he sure is/It's almost that time of year for turkey too/
DD: They cuttin' some meat/
TW: Yeah, sure nuff!/

APPENDIX E:
JM'S SPEECH AND LANGUAGE SCREENING PRODUCTIONS

Articulation Screening Errors

fɪsi/fish
faɪv̥/five
wæbɪt/rabbit
ʃɪsɚ/scissors
teɪɚ/chair
was/watch
jif/leaf
bʌs/brush
besʧəbəlz/vegetables
swi/three
ɛlfænt/elephant
sku/screw
sɪpə/zipper

Language Screening Errors

"He walkin' "
"I wanna get sticker"
"Him licked his teeth"
"He's puttin' his hat"
"Both hims in the water"
"He goes in water sleep"

REFERENCES

Abrahams, R. (1964). *Deep down in the jungle.* Hatboro, PA: Aldine.
Abrahams, R. (1968). Public drama and common values in two Caribbean Islands. *Trans-action,* 5, July–August, 62.
Baber, C. R. (1987). The artistry and artifice of Black communication. In W. L. Baber & G. Gay (Eds.), *Expressively Black: The cultural basis of ethnic identity* (pp. 75–108). New York: Praeger.

Baugh, J. (1983). A survey of Afro-American English. *Annual Review of Anthropology, 12,* 335–354.

Bereiter, C., & Englemann, S. (1966). *Teaching disadvantaged children in the preschool.* Englewood Cliffs, NJ: Prentice-Hall.

Craig, H., & Washington, H. (1995). African-American English and linguistic complexity in preschool discourse: A second look. *Language, Speech, and Hearing Services in Schools, 26(1),* 87–92.

Dalby, D. (1972). The African element in American English. In T. Kochman (Ed.), *Rappin' and stylin' out.* Urbana, IL: University of Illinois Press.

Dandy, E. B. (1991). *Black communications: Breaking down the barriers.* Chicago, IL: African-American Images.

Dee, K. M., & Kane, B. D. (Speakers). (1989). Jazz corner of the world (Introduction to Birdland). On Q. Jones (Producer). *Back on the block* (cassette recording). Burbank, CA: Qwest Records.

Ervin-Tripp, S., & Mitchell-Kernan, C. (Eds.). (1977). *Child discourse.* New York: Academic Press.

Fasold, R., & Wolfram, W. (1975). Some linguistic features of Negro dialect. In P. Stoller (Ed.), *Black American English* (pp. 49–83). New York: Delta.

Harris, M. A., Levitt, M., Furman, R., & Smith, E. (1974). *The Black book.* New York: Random House.

Heath, S. B. (1982). Questioning at home and school: A comparative study. In G. Spindler (Ed.), *Doing the ethnography of schooling: Educational anthropology in action.* New York: Holt, Rinehart & Winston.

Heath, S. B. (1983). *Ways with words: Language, life and work in communities and classrooms.* London: Cambridge University Press.

Heath, S. B. (1986). Sociocultural contexts of language development. In California State Department of Education (Ed.), *Beyond language: Social and cultural factors in schooling language minority students.* Los Angeles, CA: Evaluation, Dissemination and Assessment Center, California State University at Los Angeles.

Hoover, M. (1978). Community attitudes toward Black English. *Language in Society, 7,* 65–87.

Hudlin, R., & Hudlin, W. (1992). *Bebe's kids* [Film]. Hollywood, CA: Paramount Pictures.

Jordan, C., Au, K. H., & Joesting, A. K. (1983). Patterns of classroom interaction with Pacific Islands children: The importance of cultural differences. In. M. Chu-Chang (Ed.), *Asian and Pacific-American perspectives in bilingual education.* New York: Teachers College, Columbia University.

Kamhi, A. B., Pollock, K. E., & Harris, J. L. (Eds.). (1996). *Communication development and disorders in African American children: Research, assessment, and intervention.* Baltimore: Brookes.

Kochman, T. (1972a). Black American speech events and a language program for the classroom. In C. B. Cazden, V. P. John, & D. Hymes (Eds.), *Functions of language in the classroom* (pp. 211–261). New York: Teachers College Press.

Kochman, T. (Ed.). (1972b). *Rappin' and stylin' out.* Urbana: University of Illinois Press.

Labov, W. (1969). Contraction, deletion, and inherent variability of the English copula. *Language, 45(4),* 715–762.

Labov, W. (1975). The logic of nonstandard English. In P. Stoller (Ed.), *Black American English* (pp. 89–131). New York: Dell.

Lund, N., & Duchan, J. (1993). *Assessing children's language in naturalistic contexts* (3rd ed.). Englewood Cliffs, NJ: Prentice-Hall.

Mattes, L., & Omark, D. (1991). *Speech and language assessment for the bilingual handicapped.* Oceanside, CA: Academic Communication Associates.

McCormick, L. (1997). Ecological assessment and planning. In L. McCormick, D. F. Loeb, & R. L. Schiefelbusch (Eds.), *Supporting children with communication difficulties in inclusive settings: School-based language intervention* (pp. 223–256). Boston: Allyn & Bacon.

Michaels, S., & Collins, J. (1984). Oral discourse styles: Classroom interaction and the acquisition of literacy. In D. Tannen (Ed.), *Coherence in spoken and written discourse.* Norwood, NJ: Ablex Pub. Co.

Mitchell-Kernan, C. (1972a). Signifying and marking: Two Afro-American speech acts. In J. Gumperz & D. Hymes (Eds.), *Directions in sociolinguistics: The ethnography of communication.* New York: Holt, Rinehart & Winston.

Mitchell-Kernan, C. (1972b). Signifying, loud-talking and marking. In T. Kochman (Ed.), *Rappin' and stylin' out.* Urbana: University of Illinois Press.

Owens, R. (1996). *Language Development: An introduction* (4th ed.). Boston: Allyn & Bacon.

Percelay, J., Ivey, M., & Dweck, S. (1994). *Snaps.* New York: Quill.

Percelay, J., Ivey, M., & Dweck, S. (1996). *Triple Snaps.* New York: Quill.

Pop, S. C., & Rank, K. (1996). *Mo' Yo' Mama!* New York: Berkley.

Rose, T. (1995). Rhythmic repetition, industrial forces, and Black practice. In A. Sexton (Ed.), *Rap on rap* (pp. 45–55). New York: Dell.

Schieffelin, B. B., & Eisenberg, A. R. (1984). Cultural variation in children's conversations. In R. Schiefelbusch & J. Pickar (Eds.), *The acquisition of communicative competence* (pp. 377–420). Baltimore: University Park Press.

Sexton, A. (1995). Don't believe the hype: Why isn't hip-hop criticism better? In A. Sexton (Ed.). *Rap on rap* (pp. 1–13). New York: Dell.

Seymour, H. N. (1986). Alternative strategies for the teaching of language to minority individuals. In F. Bess, B. Clark, & H. Mitchell (Eds.), *ASHA Reports No. 16: Concerns for minority groups in communication disorders* (pp. 52–57). Rockville, MD: American Speech-Language-Hearing Association.

Smitherman, G. (1994). *Black talk: Words and phrases from the hood to the amen corner.* Boston: Houghton Mifflin.

Stockman, I. J. (1986a). The development of linguistic norms for nonmainstream populations. In F. Bess, B. Clark, & H. Mitchell (Eds.), *ASHA Reports No. 16: Concerns for minority groups in communication disorders* (pp. 101–110). Rockville, MD: American Speech-Language-Hearing Association.

Stockman, I. J. (1986b). Language acquisition in culturally diverse populations: The Black child as a case study. In O. Taylor (Ed.), *Nature of communication disorders in culturally and linguistically diverse populations.* San Diego, CA: College Hill.

Stockman, I. J. (1996). The promises and pitfalls of language sample analysis as an assessment tool for linguistic minority children. *Language, Speech, and Hearing Services in Schools, 27*(4), 355–366.

van Kleeck, A. (1994a). Metalinguistic development. In G. P. Wallach & K. G. Butler (Eds.), *Language learning disabilities in school-age children and adolescents* (pp. 53–98). New York: Merrill/Macmillan College Publishing Co.

van Kleeck, A. (1994b). Potential cultural bias in training parents as conversational partners with their children who have delays in language development. *American Journal of Speech, Language Pathology, 3*(1), 67–78.

Ward, M. (1971). *Them children: A study in language learning.* New York: Holt, Rinehart & Winston.

Washington, J., & Craig, H. (1994). Dialectal forms during discourse of poor, urban, African-American preschoolers. *Journal of Speech and Hearing Research, 37*(4), 816–823.

Watson-Gegeo, K. A., & Boggs, S. T. (1977). From verbal play to talk story: The role of routines in speech events among Hawaiian children. In S. Ervin-Tripp & C. Mitchell-Kernan (Eds.), *Child discourse.* New York: Academic Press.

Wolfram, W. (1986). Language variation in the United States. In O. L. Taylor (Ed.), *Nature of communicative disorders in culturally and linguistically diverse populations* (pp. 73–115). San Diego, CA: College Hill.

Wyatt, T. A. (1991). Linguistic constraints on copula production in Black English child speech *Dissertation Abstracts International, 52*(2), 781B. (University Microfilms No. DA9120958).

Wyatt, T. A. (1995a). Language development in African American English child speech. *Linguistics and Education, 7*(1), 7–22.

Wyatt, T. A. (1995b). *Non-biased assessment of the African-American child* [Videotape]. (Available from Info-Link Video Bulletin, Box 852, Layton, UT 84041)

Wyatt, T. A. (1996). Acquisition of the African-American English copula. In A. G. Kamhi, K. E. Pollock, & J. L. Harris (Eds.), *Communication development and disorders in African-American children: Research, assessment and intervention* (pp. 95–115). Baltimore: Brookes.

Chapter 10

Reports Written by Speech-Language Pathologists: The Role of Agenda in Constructing Client Competence

Judith Felson Duchan
State University of New York at Buffalo

Speech-language pathologists (SLPs) use a variety of discourse genres for their various activities. They engage in different types of oral discourse depending on who they are talking to and what they need to accomplish. When obtaining referrals, for example, they may converse with their professional peers about a client's communication; when obtaining background history, they conduct interviews with their client or members of that person's family; and when engaging in assessment and therapy activities they are likely to follow a preestablished oral script dictated by the test protocol or by an activity plan.

There are also behind-the-scenes discourses that involve SLPs in what they sometimes disparagingly refer to as "paperwork." These are written reports or notes designed to document assessment findings, to lay out therapy goals, to aid in recalling aspects of client performance during therapy, and to report on progress a client makes resulting from a treatment regimen. Clinicians use different descriptive terms to label these various reports. Their descriptions, in many cases, coincide with what they hope to accomplish by the report. In evaluation reports, for example, they aim to report what they did when evaluating a client's communication, what they found out, and what to do about their findings. They use progress reports somewhat differently from evaluation reports. Progress reports are designed to convey what was done during an intervention program and what progress a client made as a result of the program. Table 10.1 outlines several types of reports written by SLPs and the different purposes of these reports.

TABLE 10.1
Types of Reports Written by Speech-Language Pathologists

Type of Report	Purpose of the Report
Evaluation reports	To report evaluation procedures and results and to suggest a course of action for remedying a problem if a problem was found
Progress notes	To make note of particular information from a particular session
Individualized educational plans Individualized family service plans Individualized habilitation plans	To document short- and long-term intervention plans agreed upon by professionals, family members, and clients
Progress reports Discharge summaries Annual reports	To report on progress made during intervention and suggest remedies for any remaining problems

The few authors and researchers who have discussed different types of clinical report writing have described their formats (outlines) and commented on the purposes or agendas fulfilled by the different report types. (For a recent example, see Middleton, Pannbacker, Vekovius, Sanders, & Puett, 1992.) However, there has been no direct discussion in the clinical literature of how the discourse formats are related to the reports' purposes and how those purposes may be affecting the ways the clients are portrayed (Haynes, Pindzola, & Emerick, 1992; Hegde, 1994; Meitus, 1983; Middleton et al., 1992; Neidecker, 1987; Sanders, 1972).

One possible way to examine how agendas impact on report writing is to compare the formats and wording of two types of reports that are designed to accomplish different agendas. Evaluation and progress reports provide an interesting contrast in this respect. Evaluation reports describe the existence (or absence) of a communication problem and offer a remedy. Progress reports, on the other hand, presuppose the existence of a communication problem and describe, instead, the progress a client has made as the result of a therapy regimen (Neidecker, 1987, p. 154). In order for evaluation reports to successfully argue for services to remedy a problem, they must contain an argument for client incompetence. Progress reports, on the other hand, if they are to achieve their purpose, must contain an argument that clients are improving.

Prescriptive formats for evaluation and progress reports have focused on a listing of major headings that correspond to the major discourse subsections of the report. Examples of subsections listed for evaluation reports are ones containing: identifying information, background information, assessment procedures, results, summary of findings, and recommendations (Emerick & Haynes, 1986; Lund & Duchan, 1993; Middleton et al., 1992; Sanders, 1972). Progress reports have been described as containing subsections similar to those in evaluation reports, such as identifying information and background information, and as having an additional section entitled progress, not present in the evaluation report. Authors describing formats for evaluation and progress reports have not discussed the logical relations between the subsections nor have they described the way the information is organized within each of the sections. Finally, there have been no studies of how such prescriptive formats compare with those used in actual reports written by practicing speech-language pathologists.

To investigate the influence of agendas on client portrayal and to fill some of the gaps in the literature, a discourse analysis was done of evaluation and progress reports written by practicing speech-language pathologists. The two types of reports were compared for how they formatted the information and how they described the clients. These reports were also compared with those described in the literature and with a report of a personal futures plan.

The personal futures plan is a report that has recently been developed by a small group of professionals and advocates of those with disabilities. The aim of a personal futures plan is to describe a set of procedures designed to support a person with disabilities to achieve future goals (Beukelman & Mirenda, 1992; Mount & Zwernik, 1988). Such plans contain a listing of goals and a set of procedures for achieving them. The emphasis of a personal futures plan is not to recommend ways of remediating a focus person's disability, but to change situational demands so that the focus person and close affiliates ("circle of friends") can achieve their "wishes" and avoid their "fears." Personal futures plans are not readily available as reports, because they are not usually official documents that are placed in the focus person's folder. Rather, they may be located on poster paper on a wall, to be referred to by those engaged in the planning process. There is an emerging literature describing personal futures plans, and one article contains a description of a particular plan (Vandercook & York, 1990). The description reveals the potential for a report that is designed to achieve an agenda quite different from that of traditional evaluation and progress reports. The discourse of that personal futures plan is therefore compared in this chapter with the discourse used in traditional evaluation and progress reports to further illuminate how overall agendas are closely related to how individuals in the reports are depicted.

METHOD

This study analyzes 10 evaluation reports, 10 progress reports, and a description of a personal futures plan. The evaluation and progress reports were written by different speech-language pathologists working in different professional settings (public schools, universities, hospitals). The personal futures plan was designed by a team of professionals and friends of a person with disabilities, the focus person. (The focus person also plays a large role in determining what is in the plan.)

The first analysis was of the global organization of evaluation and progress reports. Major sections of the reports were identified and their logical relations examined. The underlying logic was evaluated for how it was associated with the writers' agendas and for how it portrayed the competence of those being written about. The report sections were also compared with those located in the literature descriptions of report formats.

A second analysis was done to discover how evaluation and progress reports describe their clients and whether those descriptions reflect differing agendas between the two report types. This analysis identified statements that described the subject, and classified them as positive or negative. The prediction was that evaluation reports would contain a predominance of negative descriptions in an effort to create an argument that the individual being written about had a communication problem. In contrast, it was predicted that progress reports would be more positive so that they could best make an argument for subject improvement.

A third analysis was of the information provided in a description of a personal futures plan, a report with a very different agenda from that of evaluation and progress reports. The global structure and descriptive statements in the plan were compared with those used in standard evaluation and progress reports.

RESULTS

Organization of Evaluation Reports

The evaluation reports in this study coincided broadly with the formats laid out in professional manuals and textbooks (Emerick & Haynes, 1986; Lund & Duchan, 1993; Middleton et al., 1992; Sanders, 1972). They were organized into major subsections, usually identifiable through the use of headings that separated sections from one another. Typical headings were: identifying information, statement of the problem (reason for referral or complaint), background information (case history), assessment procedures (tests administered), results, summary (conclusions), and recommendations.

Identifying Information and Statement of the Problem. The first section of evaluation reports provided readers with what has been termed "identifying information." It included the child's name, age, birthdate, grade, address, parents' names and occupations, and phone number. Most reports included the current date (date of evaluation), name of the agency or school where the evaluation took place, the names of the referral source and of the clinician doing the evaluation. For many reports, this information was presented in a standardized listing at the top of the first page.

Evaluation reports' first paragraphs sometimes contained restatements of some of the identifying information (name, age, clinic name). These beginnings provided information about who referred the child for the evaluation and the source of concern. This information was sometimes labeled by a heading such as "complaint" or "statement of the problem." The parenthetical information following excerpts below indicates the work site—public school (PS), university (UNIV), hospital (HOSP)—the identification number of the report from which the excerpt was drawn, and whether the report was an evaluation (eval) or progress (progress) report. The names and places are changed to preserve anonymity.

> Freddie Amber, a 5-year, 6-month-old kindergarten student, was referred for a speech and language evaluation by the Child Study Team of McClain Elementary School. Concerns had been expressed by Fred's teacher, Ms. Gretta Denmore, regarding his classroom performance and distractibility. (PS, eval, 6)

Thus, the first section identified a theme—that the individual being reported about was someone who might have a problem. The focus of the rest of the report was on identifying the problem, and determining possible causes and remedies. This was the design of all the evaluation reports, even the ones in which no problem was found.

Background Information or Case History. The evaluation reports from hospitals and universities contained a case history section in which background information was presented about notable medical, social, educational, or developmental events. Most school reports did not have this section, perhaps because the referrals were from teachers who were not as likely to know the child's early history. Case history descriptions were made within the framework of causality, inviting the reader to infer what had gone wrong in the past or what was problematic about other domains of development that might be contributing to the child's current difficulties.

> Mrs. Burkhart discussed the fact that both she and her husband have articulation problems due to congenital deficits. She has micrognathia and her husband has a cleft palate. Both parents are intelligible. No other familial speech-related deficits are reported. (UNIV, eval, 2)

As indicated by their organization and focus, case histories emphasized the clients' problems more than their competencies. The histories were organized to provide significant background information that might reveal the time a problem may have originated, what might have caused it, and what other problems might be associated with it. Reports in which the children were found to have no problem also emphasized unusual aspects of medical, social, or physical history that could have produced a communication problem. The following excerpt was taken from a case history of a 4½-year-old child who was found to perform normally on all language measures:

> According to Mrs. Frankel, Carol did not sit without support until she was 1 year old. Reportedly, Carol never crawled and was over 2 years old when she began to take her first steps. No problems with sucking, swallowing or chewing were reported. Mrs. Frankel stated that Carol was a noisy baby, but that she did not say her first recognizable word until age 2 years. (UNIV, eval, 3)

Assessment Procedures (Tests Administered), Results, and Summary. Once the client was introduced in the report and the historical information of a possible problem was provided, the reports moved to a description of what was done during the assessment. This description was often combined with a results section, indicating how clients performed on the assessment tasks. The descriptions were of performance on tasks that were difficult for them. The clinicians thus followed what Hegde (1994) has called "disorder specific assessment" (p. 165).

The presentation of details in the descriptions varied, with some reports presenting a listing of scores and others presenting a list of domains in which the client's performance was found deficient. Scores were usually located in the results section. Lists often occurred in a section called "summary" that was organized something like the following:

> Formal observations support language delay. Deficits include spatial concepts, inferential reasoning, instruction sequencing, lexical development, syntactic errors, and story formulation. Patient was not able to structurally organize language to explain events or make stories. (HOSP, eval, 7)

Often clients were reintroduced in the summary section, along with the list of problem areas. There was sometimes a brief mention of areas of competence.

> Juan Escobar demonstrated a pattern of articulation and syntax typical of a speaker of English as a second language. Tests of auditory comprehension revealed moderately low understanding of vocabulary and grammatical elements. Pragmatics were most problematic for Juan. Deficits in topic maintenance and inappropriate responses to questions were noted. Voice and fluency were within normal limits. (UNIV, eval, 9)

Recommendations. The concluding section of most evaluation reports outlined ways to remedy the various problems presented in the results section. Most reports recommended individual intervention by a speech-language pathologist. Recommendations were also made for gathering additional information or evaluating a client in other areas to determine etiology or additional deficit areas. In the case of Juan in the example previously quoted, there were four recommendations:

> Juan should be enrolled in a program of speech and language management twice a week for a one-hour session; therapy should emphasize auditory comprehension and the pragmatic communicative skills necessary to support academic and social achievement; information about Juan's performance in a school setting should be acquired; hearing should be evaluated. (UNIV, eval, 9)

Organization of Progress Reports

Progress reports, as a group, were less homogeneous in their organizational structure than evaluation reports. For example, there were many instances of titled subsections that occurred only a few times: short- and long-term goals, methods, related information, and prognosis (estimated duration of treatment).

Although varying considerably from one another, progress reports were recognizable as such because of certain notable commonalities. All progress reports contained a heading with identifying information, a section on therapy methods, another section on therapy progress (sometimes these methods and progress sections were combined), and a final section on further recommendations.

Identifying Information. The section of the report headed "identifying information" contained demographic and clinical information about the client. This section was often identical with that of evaluation reports, with the possible additions of a specification of the number of times the person was seen in therapy, the period of time the therapy lasted, and the diagnostic classification of the client. This information was sometimes formatted as a list.

Background Information or History. Following the listing of identifying information, there was typically a short paragraph or two labeled "background information" or "history." This section differed from the one in evaluation reports in that it described the location and type of therapy, as well as the problem areas targeted for intervention. The background information sections of progress reports varied considerably in length and detail. Some resembled evaluation reports, describing in detail the client's medical or developmental history. Others provided only brief descriptions of the referral source and the focus of the intervention, and omitted other history related to the cause and course of the communication problem.

> Arlo Grantham has been seen for 3 X 40 (120) minutes per week speech/language services since September 14, 1994 at Murray Hill School. Services were recommended as a result of a diagnostic evaluation by Ms. Elaine Rubin completed in April, 1994. (PS, progress, 1)

Progress (Present Status). The largest section of the progress reports described the individual's change in performance over an identified therapy period. It was typically entitled "progress" or "present status." This section contained several types of information. One was a description of the goals of the intervention. A second was a description of therapy approaches used in the course of intervention. These two information types were often merged in one sentence or in the same paragraph.

> Language therapy has focused on reinforcing sound and symbol association in order to improve Arlo's ability to sound out words, increasing receptive and expressive vocabulary, and improving pragmatic skills. Pragmatic skills addressed included conversational skills and team work with a peer. Helping Arlo to recognize his strengths and take an active role in his learning as well as reinforcing classroom spelling and writing activities were also addressed. (PS, progress, 1)

A third type of information contained in the progress section of these reports was a description of the performance of the client on specified intervention tasks. The client's performance was often cast in quantitative terms, as is the following case:

> Brad was able to synthesize 3 to 5 phonemes presented verbally with 85% accuracy and minimal clinician cuing. (UNIV, progress, 2)

Sometimes progress was stated in more general terms:

> This support has contributed greatly to Benita's overall communication improvements within the areas of speaking and spelling. Benita has become more confident as a speaker and is highly motivated to become an independent speller as well. (PS, progress, 2)

Recommendations. The recommendations sections of the progress reports were brief, and often cast in a list of three or four items. All of the progress reports in this sample recommended a continuation of therapy under regimens similar to the ones described in the progress section of the report.

It is recommended that Brad continue therapy during the Fall of 1995 semester at this clinic. Continued therapy is also recommended through Brad's home school district. A combination of direct small group therapy and indirect service (collaborative consultation) with Brad's classroom utilizing Brad's academic curriculum is recommended. Direct therapy short term goals should continue to focus on attention, following directions, and auditory memory. (UNIV, progress, 2)

The Logic Underlying Evaluation and Progress Reports

The global-level analysis of evaluation reports revealed an underlying problem-based theme. The client, a person with a possible problem, is introduced with identifying information that usually includes a name, age (birthdate), names of caretakers, and address. The section that follows provides background information, including a statement of concern from a referral source. This introduces the idea that the subject of the report is someone who might have a communication problem. The third section presents irregularities in the client's family, medical, or developmental history that might have caused the possible problem. Assessment procedures and outcomes are then presented and summarized so as to specify the nature of the problem. Summary sections typically provide evidence for the problem from test results and identify problem areas. Summary sections sometimes venture a guess as to what may have caused the problem. The report then ends by recommending possible solutions to the client's communication problem, if one was found. The solutions may include further evaluations or particular types of therapy. The evaluation report becomes a coherent whole if all the components are seen as being about an aspect of a client's suspected problem (see Table 10.2).

Progress reports, while still focused on a client's problem, differ from evaluation reports in that they do not center around the question of whether or not the client has a problem. Rather, they presuppose the problem and focus on whether or not the intervention being reported has produced positive results. In progress reports, the client is introduced at the outset, often as having an already identified problem (diagnosis). The information in the background history may present the results of an evaluation report in order to establish that a problem exists, or it may presuppose

TABLE 10.2
Client's Problem as a Focus for Evaluation Reports

1. Identifying information—person with possible problem is introduced.
2. Background information (statement of the problem)—nature of the concern is explicated and possible historical origins explored.
3. Assessment procedures, results, and summary of results—problem areas are outlined.
4. Recommendations—possible solutions to the problem are presented.

that the problem exists by reporting only on prior recommendations and omitting other historical information. In either case, the emphasis is not on what caused the problem, but on its nature.

The focal theme in the organization of progress reports was intervention rather than diagnosis. Progress reports contained descriptions of what was done in therapy, the therapy goals, and the extent to which the client accomplished the therapy goals. Therapy methods were described in detail along with the individual's performance during the therapy regimens. Progress reports concluded with a description of the person's future therapy needs and recommendations related to those needs. Their primary emphasis, therefore, was to show progress and argue for the need of continuing therapy (see Table 10.3).

The logic of both evaluation and progress reports, as revealed in the global-level discourse analysis, is problem based, with the subsections of both types of reports building up an argument that the person has a communication problem and is in need of services. The reports are thereby structured to accomplish a similar purpose—to persuade the reader that the client has a problem and is in need of the additional services provided by speech-language pathologists. Thus, the global structuring of evaluation and progress reports does not lead to a difference in the construction of the client's competence. Both types of reports cast the client in a negative light—as having a possible communication problem in need of remediation.

Descriptions of Clients in Evaluation and Progress Reports

A second type of analysis was done to compare the way clients were described in evaluation and progress reports. Both types of reports contained a section summarizing the current status of the individual, based on the person's performance on particular tasks or on their presumed specific or general abilities. Descriptions were in the summary sections of evaluation reports and the progress sections of progress reports. Evaluation reports contained descriptions of the client's performance during the assessment

TABLE 10.3
Client's Problem as a Focus for Progress Reports

---

1. Identifying information—person with already identified problem is introduced. Problem is presupposed or explicitly labeled (diagnosis).
2. Background history—problem is sometimes described and medical, developmental, or social background presented. In other instances only the prior therapy recommendations from earlier reports are reviewed.
3. Progress—goals and nature of therapy are described and person's response to the intervention.
4. Recommendations—current problems are outlined and therapy recommendations are made for further work on client's deficits.

---

session. Progress reports contained descriptions of the individual's performance during the intervention period. The following paragraph is from the summary and results section of an evaluation report:

> Andrea is a 4-year, 1-month-old child with a delay in expressive and receptive language. Expressive language is characterized by use of most early developing sentence forms. Phonological and morphological errors decrease her intelligibility. Receptively she apparently grasps part of the sentence, but not the whole. Gestures and visual cues seem to augment her comprehension. (UNIV, progress, 1)

This next paragraph was located in the progress section of a progress report:

> Arthur attended 9 out of 14 scheduled therapy sessions. He made progress throughout therapy and produced more intelligible /sh/, /l/, /g/, /k/, and /s/ blends. Overall, Arthur was cooperative and motivated with activities. In addition, he was quite receptive to the clinicians and easily stimulable for productions of the target sounds. (UNIV, progress, 10)

Descriptions of clients' performance or abilities were identified in both evaluation and progress reports. They were selected from the summary sections of evaluation reports and the progress sections of progress reports. Excluded from this analysis were statements that described other aspects of the assessment or intervention procedures, such as those describing the methods used. Once identified, the performance descriptions were then classified for whether they construed the individual's ability or performance negatively or positively. Most sentences were classifiable into positive or negative categories by virtue of the language used (e.g., unable vs. able, cooperative vs. uncooperative). Some were able to be classified by examining the contextual information or through inference (inf-pos; inf-neg). A remaining minority of descriptions were indeterminate (ind). Examples of different statements and of the coding procedure are given in Table 10.4 for an evaluation report and Table 10.5 for a progress report. Words or phrases leading to the judgments of negative or positive are in bold face.

TABLE 10.4
Coding of Negative and Positive Statements in an Evaluation Report

1. Andrea is a 4-year, 1-month-old child with a **delay** in expressive and receptive language.	Neg
2. Expressive language is characterized by use of most early developing sentence forms. (Inference: 4-year-olds should have later developing forms.)	Inf-neg
3. Phonological and morphological errors **decrease** her intelligibility.	Neg
4. Receptively she apparently grasps part of the sentence, but **not** the whole.	Neg
5. Gestures and visual cues seem to **augment** her comprehension.	Pos

TABLE 10.5
Coding of Negative and Positive Statements in a Progress Report

1. Arthur attended 9 out of 14 scheduled therapy sessions.	Ind
2. He **made progress** throughout therapy and produced more intelligible /sh/, /l/, /g/, /k/, and /s/ blends.	Pos
3. Overall Arthur was **cooperative** and **motivated** with activities.	Pos
4. In addition, he was quite **receptive** to the clinicians and **easily stimulable** for productions of the target sounds	Pos

The number of positive and negative statements for each report type was calculated, and the results are presented in percentages in Fig. 10.1. Evaluation reports contained 109 independent clauses describing the client's abilities or performance. Seventy-five percent ($n = 81$) were cast negatively, 25% ($n = 28$) had a positive valence. Progress reports contained

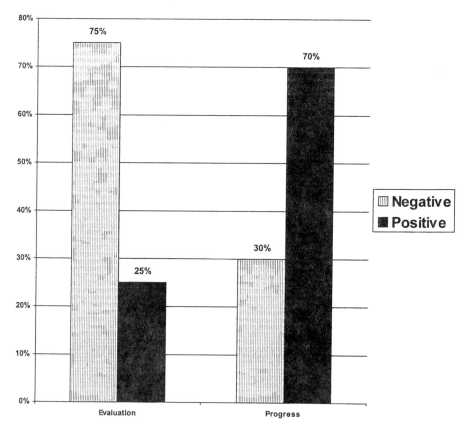

FIG. 10.1. Percent of negative and positive statements describing clients' competence in evaluation and progress reports.

196 performance statements, with 30% (58) framed negatively and 70% (138) cast positively. The results were essentially reciprocal reversals of one another.

Types of Negative Targets. The negative statements for evaluation and progress reports were categorized according to like types, based on their levels of generality and particular focus. They fell roughly into six different groupings, which are listed in Table 10.6.

The first type of negative description in Table 10.6 is of the client's overall language performance. This was sometimes cast generally (problem with receptive and expressive language) and sometimes cast as a level of performance (severe, moderate). The existence of a problem was sometimes presupposed (the etiology of the problem is unknown) and other times asserted (X has a significant delay in receptive and expressive language). There were 13 of these statements in evaluation reports and none in the progress sections of progress reports.

A second kind of negative statement targeted areas of deficits, such as domains of knowledge (sentence structures, language form) or type of processing (attending skills). The description was sometimes framed as a specified amount of delay (e.g., level of performance as indicated by test score, age equivalency) and sometimes in more general terms (e.g., mild, moderate, or severe problem in a particular area). There were 34 of these in the evaluation reports and 15 in progress reports, comprising 33% and 22% of the targets in those reports, respectively.

The most frequently found target for both evaluation and progress reports was of more specific performances. Descriptions typically cast these targets as errors, types of errors, or performance problems on particular tasks. This type differed from those identified above (overall descriptions and area of deficit descriptions) in that they pointed to a type of mistake.

TABLE 10.6
Types, Frequency, and Percent of Negative
Targets in Evaluation and Progress Reports

Target Types	Evaluation Reports		Progress Reports	
	No.	*%*	*No.*	*%*
1. Overall problem	13	13%	0	0%
2. Areas of deficit	34	33%	15	22%
3. Errors	35	34%	25	36%
4. Problem behaviors	20	19%	12	17%
5. Need/support statements	1	1%	13	19%
6. Lack of success	0	0%	4	6%
Total	103	100%	69	100%

Some of these descriptions alluded to a lack of specific knowledge (omission of consonants), others pointed to an inability (to associate behaviors), and still others indicated a lack of response (did not respond to any verbal stimuli; no symbolic play). There were 35 (34%) such descriptions in evaluation reports and 25 (36%) in progress reports.

A fourth type of problem is described as inappropriate behavior or insufficient motivation. These descriptions were also specific, in that they described a particular performance, but were not framed as errors or mistakes. There were 20 (19%) of these in evaluation reports and 12 (17%) in progress reports.

The last two categories were found in progress reports, but not in evaluation reports (with one exception). One referred to the amount of support that the individual needed to perform adequately and the second described the individual's lack of success with an intervention. There were 13 (19%) need statements in progress reports and 4 (6%) statements describing a client's lack of success with a particular intervention. Table 10.7 lists examples of each target type. The element of each statement leading to its classification is indicated in bold face.

Types of Positive Targets. Another analysis was done to compare the types of positive statements made in evaluation and progress reports for the same six categories identified in negative reports. There were a number of striking differences between positive statements made in evaluation and progress reports (see Table 10.8):

1. Overall communicative competence: There were only a few overall statements about individual's overall positive achievements in either progress or evaluation reports.

2. Areas of competence: There were a relatively large number of positive descriptions of areas of competence in the summary sections of evaluation reports (15, or 46%) but only one such description in the progress section of progress reports. This differs from the analysis of negative targets, which showed a healthy occurrence of negative references to areas of deficit in both evaluation and progress reports.

3. Particular accomplishments: This category was the reverse of the previous one in that here progress reports showed a high incidence (54 occurrences, or 61%) and the evaluation reports showed a relatively low incidence (5, or 15%). This discrepancy was not evidenced in the negative analysis. In that case, both evaluation and progress reports exhibited a high number of mentions of particular errors or performance problems.

4. Positive behaviors and motivations: This category occurred with similar frequency to the negative statements in both report types. Evaluation and progress reports contained comparable percentages of statements de-

TABLE 10.7
Types of Descriptions Containing Negative
Statements and Examples of Each

Overall communication problem
  1. Delay in **expressive and receptive language**
  2. Etiology of the **communication deficit** is not known
  3. . . . little information concerning his . . . **language deficits**
  4. . . . does not know how to handle Bob's **problem** at home
  5. . . . difficult to ascertain whether or not her **decreased language use** is related to cognitive factors.

Area of deficit
  1. use of early developing **sentence forms**
  2. very poor **articulation skills**
  3. reduced **sentence structures**
  4. **language form** appears delayed
  5. **attending skills** were impaired

Errors and specific performance problems
  1. . . . she apparently grasps part of the sentence, but not the whole
  2. . . . final consonant deletion
  3. . . . omission of auxiliaries and copulas
  4. . . . immature grasp
  5. . . . difficulty translating orally presented instructions into fine motor acts

Problems with behavior and/or motivation
  1. . . . he was . . . **unspontaneous** during these sessions
  2. . . . gave **no overt indication of his concern** with regard to his performance
  3. . . . appeared **confused** about his schedule
  4. . . . was **reticent** to come to the speech room
  5. He showed a general **lack of response** to the environment

Need statements
  1. . . . needed continued **teacher reinforcement and coaxing**
  2. . . . [to accomplish task, required] **maximum clinical support**
  3. . . . required **physical support** to attend to the task
  4. . . . did appear to **need** the voice output
  5. . . . needed **minimal cueing** with initial /sh/

Lack of success
  1. . . . although this has been of **limited success**
  2. . . . **remains extremely difficult** for Allison
  3. . . . the **changes** in productions were **not significant**
  4. . . . is **not always able** to use those skills functionally

scribing positive behaviors and motivations. The numbers and percentages for mentions of positive behavior and motivations are 6 (18%) for evaluation reports; and 12 (14%) for progress reports, as compared with the problem behaviors of 20 (19%) for evaluation reports and 12 (17%) for progress reports (see Table 10.6).

TABLE 10.8
Types, Frequency and Percent of Positive
Targets in Evaluation and Progress Reports

Target Types	Evaluation Reports		Progress Reports	
	No.	%	No.	%
1. Overall communicative competence	3	9%	3	3%
2. Areas of competence	15	46%	1	1%
3. Particular accomplishments	5	15%	54	61%
4. Positive behaviors and motivation	6	18%	12	14%
5. Needs statements	3	9%	18	20%
6. Overall successes	1	3%	1	1%
Total	33	100%	89	100%

5. Need statements: The occurrence of 18 (20%) of need statements for progress reports was comparable to the 13 (19%) negatively cast need statements in progress reports. As with negative targets, there were few need statements found in evaluation reports.

6. Overall learning success: This category, like its counterpart in negative descriptions, had only a few occurrences.

Table 10.9 provides examples of each of the six types of positive target statements. The positive element is indicated in bold face.

Summary of Results of Statements Describing Clients

The findings of this second analysis dealing with the number and types of negative and positive statements complement those of the first analysis, dealing with global-level organization of evaluation and progress reports. Both analyses offer insights as to how agendas influence discourse. The first showed how the overall agendas for evaluation and progress reports similarly influence the global structuring of the two report types. Both evaluation and progress reports reflect the view that the client is the source of the problem. They are structured negatively so as to emphasize the communication problems of the subject and the resultant need for speech-language services. The global analysis of both reports highlighted the client's communication problem and thus focused on the client's communication incompetence rather than competence.

The second analysis of statements describing clients demonstrated the influence of a subordinate agenda in the two types of reports. Evaluation reports, intended to demonstrate the need for services, are thereby designed to bring out the negative aspects of the client's performance. Progress reports, on the other hand, are intended to convey that an intervention

TABLE 10.9
Types of Descriptions Containing Positive
Statements and Examples of Each

Overall communication competence
1. Carol's **language competence**
2. . . . **potential** is there
3. Charles can orally achieve **adequate expressive language**
4. . . . demonstrate **higher level of language output**
5. Arlo shows **comprehension of material he has read** both aloud and silently

Areas of competence
1. . . . his **content** and **use** appear adequate
2. . . . adequate **attention span**
3. . . . **language comprehension** is also adequate
4. . . . **peripheral hearing mechanism** appears to be adequate
5. **Voice,** within normal limits

Particular accomplishments
1. . . . stimulability for **several test sounds**
2. . . . used a modified version of . . . **pointing to her mouth** to spontaneously communicate something she wanted
3. . . . was able to **delete 80% of the initial syllables**
4. . . . was able to **track up to three sounds**
5. . . . was able to **follow 2-step simple commands**

Positive behaviors and motivation
1. Bob's **cooperative** demeanor
2. . . . was able to make and maintain **eye-contact**
3. Aaron **came willingly** to our testing sessions
4. . . . has **imitated** as many as 20 signs in a session
5. . . . **was cooperative and motivated** with activities

Need/support statements
1. . . . his attention **can be easily diverted** to other activities of interest to him
2. . . . [accomplished X] with **maximal clinician cueing**
3. . . . [accomplished X] with **clinician support and help**
4. . . . was able to build . . . sentences **without the sentence builder** with 80% accuracy
5. . . . works best when an adult has **helped him generate some ideas**

Overall impressions of success
1. He has made **noticeable improvements** . . .
2. Brad showed **continual improvement** during the six weeks of therapy

---

program has been successful and needs to be continued. The positive accomplishments of the client are thus made more salient. This positive view, emphasizing competence, is nonetheless cast within an overarching negative view of the client as incompetent and in need of further therapy.

PERSONAL FUTURES PLANS—A REPORT
WITH A DIFFERENT AGENDA

In the last decade, a new awareness about disabilities has developed that
has led to a new type of report-writing agenda. It has been dubbed the
"personal futures plan" or "action plan" (Calculator & Jorgensen, 1994;
Mount & Zwernik, 1989; Vandercook & York, 1990; Vandercook, York, &
Forest, 1989). The agenda of the personal futures plan is to identify and
achieve the wishes of a focus person or to achieve the wishes others have
for that person. The plan contains ways to support the focus person to
achieve his or her identified life goals. The disability is taken as a given
but is not necessarily the primary focus of the report. It is but one of the
many things to be considered when eliminating blocks to accomplishing
the agenda. Mount and Zwernik (1988) and Mount (1994) describe some
of the differences between the process involved in creating a futures plan
and that behind an individualized habilitation plan (IHP):

> The Personal Futures Plan serves a different function than the IHP. It helps
> people to reflect on the quality of life of a person with a disability, to explore
> possibilities, to brainstorm strategies, and generally to reach for outcomes
> that are beyond the standard procedures and options of traditional services.
> (Mount & Zwernik, 1988, p. 41)

> A positive view of people in personal futures planning helps professionals
> come to know people with disabilities and appreciate their capacities. This
> is a discovery process because the gifts, interests, and capacities of people
> with disabilities so often are buried under labels, poor reputations, and
> fragmentation of information. (Mount, 1994, p. 99)

> Traditional forms of planning are based on the ideal of a developmental
> model, which . . . emphasizes the deficits and needs of people, overwhelming
> people with endless program goals and objectives, and assigning responsi-
> bility for decision-making to professionals. . . . The underlying values of
> traditional planning communicate subtle messages, for example: The person
> is the problem and should be fixed. (Mount, 1994, p. 98)

> The results of the futures planning process should be integrated as much
> as is appropriate into the focus person's IHP (Mount & Zwernik, 1988, p.
> 41)

A suggested way to develop a meaningful personal futures plan is for a
facilitator to pose a set of questions to be answered by a group of hand-
picked individuals who will be serving as a support group (the circle of
friends) to accomplish the stated goals (Vandercook & York, 1990). A
description of how such a plan was developed is provided by Vandercook
and York for Mary, an 8-year-old third grader who is a member of a regular

elementary school class. The group consisted of nine people who knew Mary well, and a tenth person who was the group facilitator. The group were Mary's parents, three third-grade friends, her third-grade teacher, her special education teacher, her speech-language pathologist, an exercise consultant, and the school principal. The questions answered by the group and comprising the subheadings of the report (Vandercook & York, 1990, pp. 108–111) were as follows:

1. What is Mary's history?
2. What is your dream for Mary as an adult?
3. What is your nightmare?
4. Who is Mary?
5. What are Mary's strengths, gifts, and abilities?
6. What are Mary's needs?
7. What would Mary's ideal day at school look like and what must be done to make it happen?

Unlike the evaluation and progress reports analyzed above, Mary's personal futures plan contained very few statements about Mary's particular performance abilities. While the global structure allowed for the depiction of Mary's disability and problems (e.g., What is Mary's history? Who is Mary?) the format also emphasized Mary's strengths and abilities and her future life needs (What are Mary's strengths, gifts and abilities? What is your dream for Mary as an adult? What is your nightmare? What are Mary's needs? What would [an] ideal day at school look like?)

For that section of Mary's futures plan which described her past history, the emphasis was not on what went awry in her history or what aspects of her history caused or provided evidence of her disability. Rather it described positive schooling experiences (Vandercook & York, 1990).

> This school year Mike (Mary's father) said the family had really seen Mary "opening up" and acting much more cheerful. He attributed that to Mary's classmates and the modeling they provided. In contrast, Mary's models in the self-contained classroom had been limited and consisted primarily of adults. Mike also related how nice it was for Mary to be in her home school. (p. 108)

Positive and negative descriptions of Mary had to do with character traits, life skills, and personal interests (e.g., friendly, bossy, likes to listen to audiotapes). They were made by those who knew Mary well, in contexts of everyday life situations. These descriptions thereby differ considerably from those contained in traditional reports by SLPs, who typically have limited knowledge of the person in home, community or even school contexts. The SLPs' descriptions tended to focus on the cognitive abilities, language abilities or performance exhibited by the person during the assessment or intervention sessions (e.g., cooperative demeanor, adequate attention span, delayed language form). Finally, the agenda of Mary's personal futures plan was quite different from that of traditional reports. Personal futures plans are designed to "focus upon the person's capabilities and an appreciation of his or her unique characteristics. Such a positive orientation assists in designing a hopeful future" (Vandercook & York, 1990, p. 109).

The descriptive terms characterizing Mary (Vandercook & York, 1990) were generated by the team in response to the question: Who is Mary?:

> Neat person, does what she's told, easy going, helpful, third grader, animal lover, warm smile, loves her friends, enjoys her classroom, loving, enjoys the bus, excited, screamer, enjoys Mrs. Anderson, bossy, fun, cute, headstrong, likes babies, follower, shy, stubborn, manipulator, book lover, hearty giggle, easily frightened of things she can't see, likes to eat, and a friend. (p. 109)

Lastly, the largest section of the personal futures plans was devoted to the team's description of Mary's priority needs. The team generated a listing of 30 or so needs, which then became the elements of her futures plan. This emphasis on Mary's needs is quite different from that in the SLPs' evaluation. In the case of Mary, the statements were mostly about life goals (needs love, needs more friends, needs discipline). Those that had to do with communication (needs to learn how to say more words, needs to learn more appropriate ways of initiating communication) were cast, along with the others, as a way to better achieve inclusionary practices and life goals. The casting of the communication needs as Mary's needs (and others' hopes for her) rather than as therapy recommendations invited a positive (hopes and wishes) rather than negative (deficit) interpretation of them.

OVERALL SUMMARY AND CONCLUSIONS

Several findings have emerged from this study of reports written about those with disabilities:

1. The format renditions (major sectional headings) of evaluation and progress reports in the literature were found to be broadly consistent with actual reports written by practicing speech-language pathologists.

2. The formats of the two different types of reports followed a coherent logic. Formats for evaluation reports highlighted the individual's problem and need for therapy. Subsections served to describe the problem from the referral source, historically, and according to assessment findings, and to provide recommendations for how the problem should be taken care of. Progress reports were designed to emphasized therapy progress and the need for additional therapy. They contained sections describing the nature of the problem, what was done, the results, and continuing therapy needs.

3. The similarities in global-level organization contained in evaluation and progress reports were consistent with an internal logic that reflected a common overall agenda—to identify and remediate the client's communication problem and suggest a remedy. The organization of both focused on communication incompetence.

4. The differences in the global-level organization of the two report types reflected differences in their agendas. Evaluation reports were aimed at persuading readers of the existence of a problem (concerns, background information, assessment results) and that something could be done about it (recommendations). Progress reports were aimed at persuading readers that particular solutions were successful and should be continued (progress, recommendations).

5. Differences in agendas were also reflected in the way subjects were described within each of the two report types. Evaluation reports contained high percentages of negative descriptions, in keeping with the aim of revealing a subject's problem. Progress reports contained more positive than negative descriptions, consistent with their aim of showing a subject's therapy successes.

6. The personal futures plan offered yet a third way to write a report. It did not emphasize identifying or background information, because those for whom the report was written knew the focus person well. Nor did the plan seek a historical cause for the problem, as did the evaluation report. Rather, the emphasis of the futures plan was to identify the client's needs The personal futures plan as exemplified by the Mary in Vandercook and York (1990) would include descriptions of individuals by their life and York (1990) would include descriptions of individuals by their life companions and would be about character traits rather than the impersonal performance descriptions found in the SLPs' clinical reports. The descriptions of the individuals would include both positive and negative traits, with an accentuation of the positive competencies rather than the incompetencies.

This chapter has demonstrated that the social construction of the abilities of a person with a suspected or actual communication problem depends on the circumstances in which the targeted individual is being evaluated.

This would suggest that the best way to achieve more positive renderings of an individual's competencies is to alter the agendas of those doing the rendering.

REFERENCES

Beukelman, D., & Mirenda, P. (1992). *Augmentative and alternative communication.* Baltimore: Brookes.

Calculator, S., & Jorgensen, C. (Eds.). (1994). *Including students with severe disabilities in schools.* San Diego, CA: Singular.

Emerick, L., & Haynes, W. (1986). *Diagnosis and evaluation in speech pathology.* Englewood Cliffs, NJ: Prentice-Hall.

Haynes, W., Pindzola, R., & Emerick, L. (1992). *Diagnosis and evaluation in speech pathology.* Englewood Cliffs, NJ: Prentice-Hall.

Hegde, M. (1994). *A coursebook on scientific and professional writing in speech-language pathology.* San Diego, CA: Singular.

Lund, N., & Duchan, J. (1993). *Assessing children's language in naturalistic contexts.* Englewood Cliffs, NJ: Prentice-Hall.

Meitus, I. (1983). Clinical report and letter writing. In I. Meitus & B. Weinberg (Eds.), *Diagnosis in speech-language pathology* (pp. 54–69). Baltimore: Williams & Wilkins.

Middleton, G., Pannbacker, M., Vekovius, G., Sanders, K., & Puett, V. (1992). *Report writing for speech-language pathologists.* Tucson, AZ: Communication Skill Builders.

Mount, B. (1994). Benefits and limitations of personal futures planning. In V. Bradley, J. Ashbaugh, & B. Blaney (Eds.), *Creating individual supports for people with developmental disabilities.* Baltimore: Brookes.

Mount, B., & Zwernik, K. (1989). *It's never too early, it's never too late.* St. Paul, MN: Metropolitan Council.

Neidecker, E. (1987). *School programs in speech-language: Organization and management.* Englewood Cliffs, NJ: Prentice-Hall.

Pannbacker, M. (1975). Diagnostic report writing. *Journal of Speech and Hearing Disorders, 40,* 367–379.

Sanders, L. (1972). *Procedure guides for evaluation of speech and language disorders in children* (3rd ed.). Danville, IL: The Interstate.

Vandercook, T., & York, J. (1990). A team approach to program development and support. In W. Stainback & S. Stainback (Eds.), *Support networks for inclusive schooling.* Baltimore: Brookes.

Vandercook, T., York, J., & Forest, M. (1989). The McGill Action Planning System (MAPS): A strategy for building the vision. *Journal of The Association for Persons with Severe Handicaps, 14,* 205–215.

Ward, P., & Duchan, J. (1997). *A comparison of information contained in evaluation and progress reports and its relevance for designing computerized formats for writing reports.* Unpublished manuscript.

Chapter 11

Revelations of Family Perceptions of Diagnosis and Disorder Through Metaphor

Ann M. Mastergeorge
University of California, Los Angeles

Metaphor has served as a way for a family to construct a salient explanation for some experience that is difficult to understand and interpret (e.g., Barker, 1996; Rosenblatt, 1994; Strong, 1989). Metaphoric language thus becomes a way for individuals to cope with traumatic experiences and a means used by psychotherapists to engage clients in coping with difficult life circumstances (Ferrara, 1994, p. 129). Further, metaphors can provide a bridge from an author's perspective to the thoughts and experiences of those they address.

The comprehensibility of metaphors entails viewing a topic from a particular vantage point of the author in order to connect it with what one has already thought about. For example, the metaphoric language used when a speaker says "Realizing my child was deaf was like falling in a deep, dark hole" provides a bridge so that listeners can interpret an unfamiliar experience (a diagnosis of deafness) via a more familiar one (falling in a dark hole). Lakoff and Turner (1989) describe this metaphoric bridge as "a tool so ordinary that we use it unconsciously and automatically, with so little effort that we hardly notice it. It is omnipresent: metaphor suffuses our thoughts . . . metaphor allows us to understand ourselves and our world in ways that no other modes of thought can" (p. xii).

Much of the empirical literature on metaphor (e.g., Beck, 1978; Black, 1993a; Carveth, 1984; Cormac, 1985; Lakoff & Johnson, 1980; Searle, 1993; Tourangeau, 1982) suggests that metaphoric language is used when literal language is felt to be inadequate. It serves to enhance the meaning of an

245

utterance and to convey what might otherwise be misunderstood (Crider & Cirillo, 1991).

Metaphor has been seen as a way to translate one topic or experience into another (Dent-Reed & Szokolsky, 1993). Family members may, for example, use metaphors to express what may be difficult to convey directly because of its emotional components or its unfamiliarity (Rosenblatt, 1994; Strong, 1989). Metaphor also allows an author to help a listener better understand an unfamiliar emotional experience.

Much has been written on origins of metaphor (e.g., Murray, 1931; Pepper, 1942), on metaphor and mind (e.g., Sternberg, 1993), on metaphor and thought (Cole, 1995; Olson, 1988; Ortony, 1993), on contemporary theories of metaphors (e.g., Black, 1993a, 1993b; Lakoff, 1993), and on metaphor types (e.g., Lakoff & Turner, 1989; Sternberg, 1993). More recently, metaphor has gained attention in psychotherapy (e.g., Barker, 1996; Carveth, 1984; Gonçalves & Craine, 1990; Hendrix, 1992; McMullen, 1989; Rosenblatt, 1994; Siegelman, 1990). For example, Gonçalves and Craine (1990) identified a client's use of metaphors by examining common themes in client discourse, cross-situational consistency, and process markers. These authors argue that "perhaps metaphor offers a privileged route to access structures of meaning that remain resistant to our traditional therapeutic efforts" (p. 147). Other authors argue that understanding client metaphors is a key to understanding how client realities are constructed (e.g., Atwood & Levine, 1991; Barker, 1996; Lankton & Lankton, 1989; Rosenblatt, 1994; Siegelman, 1990). Metaphors provide clients with a context for interpreting their problems and for reflecting and creating new realities.

Clinicians are also apt to use metaphors to alter client realities and influence what clients do and experience. Siegelman (1990) explored the issues of metaphor and meaning in psychotherapy by studying case examples of conventional metaphors used by both patient and therapist. One example described a client who used the conventional metaphor "I feel totally unequipped." This was later extended by the therapist to provide a metaphoric image to magnify the client's generic metaphor: ". . . And I guess that's why I have such trouble taking risks: I feel totally unequipped." The therapist responded: "It's like a person with one short leg competing in an Olympic track race." The client "brightened," ". . . You know I *am* handicapped. . . . It's a mental handicap, and that makes it harder to see than a physical handicap, but it's just as powerful" (Siegelman, 1990, p. 56).

While the use of metaphor has been studied and used extensively in psychotherapy, the role of metaphor has been virtually unexplored when examining how family members cope with the ambiguity of diagnosis and disorder. The purpose of this chapter is to explore families' use of metaphoric language and its role as a mediator in revealing family members' perceptions of diagnosis and disorder.

Ethnographic interviews were undertaken, in which family members were asked to describe their experiences with disability. In particular, they were asked to talk about having received a diagnosis. Their use of metaphoric constructions was analyzed for content themes. The analysis revealed several contexts in which metaphors were used. Metaphors were used to describe diagnoses, to describe coping, to personify experiences, and to describe feelings of ambivalence. This chapter shows that metaphors provide an all-too-often overlooked resource for understanding family perspectives on diagnoses of disability and resulting feelings of incompetence.

METHOD

Participants

Sixty families were chosen to participate in this study. All of the families were either clients or had family members who were clients at a university speech and hearing clinic. Table 11.1 depicts the client diagnosis category, the number of clients, and time since their own or their family members' diagnosis. The interviews were conducted with 37 parents of children with communication disorders and 18 spouses of adults diagnosed with aphasia and traumatic brain injury. Five adult-fluency clients were interviewed. The majority of the families interviewed had received a diagnosis within a range of 6 to 12 months preceding the interview. A few clients (those with traumatic brain injuries and language and learning disorders) were diagnosed 12 to 18 months prior to the interview. The five adult-fluency clients had received a diagnosis more than 3 years prior to the interview.

Ethnographic Interview Procedure

Family stories were collected about their experiences in coping with disabilities. Each family was interviewed twice, with each interview lasting approximately 3 to 4 hours. When possible, the families were interviewed in the privacy of their own homes by graduate students trained in ethno-

TABLE 11.1
Diagnostic Categories and Elapsed Time of Diagnostic News

Diagnostic Category	No. of Clients	Months Since Diagnosis
Developmental delay	12	6–12
Autism spectrum disorder	10	6–12
Language-learning disorder	6	12–18
Aphasia	13	12
Traumatic brain injury	9 (5 adult/4 child)	12–18
Fluency	5 (adult)	> 36
Hearing impairment	5 (child)	12–24

graphic interviewing techniques. The families were given the following information at the outset:

> I am interested in your story about [a person with a disability]. You can start wherever you like, and talk as long as you like. The content of this interview will be tape recorded and later transcribed verbatim.

Data Analysis

After transcribing the interviews orthographically, metaphoric segments offered and sustained by the family members were identified. Segments in which clinicians introduced a metaphor or made comments regarding metaphoric language were not included in the analysis.

Common themes of metaphoric construction in client discourse were identified (see Gonçalves & Craine, 1990, for details of this same methodology). In addition, a coding scheme based on Crider and Cirillo (1991) was developed to qualitatively analyze the 60 transcripts for types and exemplars of metaphor.

RESULTS

Four uses of metaphor were uncovered in the interviews of these families. Metaphors were used to describe the experience of diagnosis, to describe coping, to personify experiences, and to describe ambivalence.

Metaphor Related to Diagnosis. Metaphoric descriptions associated with diagnosis were found in the transcripts of 51 of the 60 families interviewed.

> I will never forget the day, the hour, or the room we were all sitting in waiting for some sign that everything was going to be okay. But, the doctor who gave us the diagnosis was *like a shark circling and circling our family. We were in rocky waters on a sinking ship.*

While this family member's description was unique, the use of metaphor when describing the diagnostic experience was common.

Among the common metaphoric themes used to describe the diagnostic experience were the following three: sleep states (e.g., dreams, nightmares), barrier structures (walls/doors closing), and forces of nature (e.g., storms, hurricanes, earthquakes). Table 11.2 highlights some exemplars for each. Nightmares were used quite often to describe the diagnosis and its aftermath. Use of different barrier metaphors was also highly frequent, appearing in 58 of 60 interviews. Doors shutting, slamming, locked were used to convey the despair the families were experiencing. Over half of

TABLE 11.2
Metaphors Describing Diagnosis

Metaphor Theme	Exemplar
Sleep states	"She didn't answer and didn't answer, and she didn't turn around. And I thought, 'No, this can't be.' I mean, it didn't click then that she was deaf. And then he said that she was deaf. I just blanked everything out from there. **At that moment it was like walking into a dream.** It was like 'No way. My daugher can't be deaf.' "
	"After the accident, they just took the portrait down. **It was like a parent's worst nightmare.**"
	"**It was a nightmare** . . . it was like this cannot be happening . . . or this does not happen to me . . . it happens to my neighbors or everybody else."
Barrier structures	"We knew something was wrong. We would be in the car and we'd say, 'Jay, where's your ears?' He just was not even paying attention to us. **It was like a wall.**"
	"**The doors closed.** The doctor's words will always stay with me: 'Remember he is not, nor will not be the same little boy you had eight hours ago.' And those words have always stuck in my mind. Since the accident he will forever be different and he will never be the same."
	"It's almost like **you see the light, and right before you get to it, the door closes** in your face."
	"It's just like you went to bed black and woke up white, you went to bed somebody's best friend and woke up their doctor . . . it's a tremendous change right away and there's **no light at the end of the tunnel.** You know they are never going to be what they were before."
Forces of nature	"**I must have been in a fog.** I mean it [deafness] was the furthest thing from my mind. I look back and go, 'God how did I get through it?' "
	"**It was like being hit by a tornado** and never seeing it coming. I mean, I knew he was behind, but I was not prepared for this. It was a natural disaster."
	"Hearing the news from the doctor was **like being in an earthquake.** My whole life was falling down around me, and I had no control over it. It was the worst feeling in the world."

the family interviews described the feelings after diagnosis as comparable to there being "no light at the end of the tunnel."

Forces-of-nature metaphors were quite vivid and very frequent (used in 48 of the 60 family interviews). The most common of the nature metaphors were related to fog: "I was in a fog"; "It was like being in a mist." Many families also used natural-disaster metaphors (e.g., hurricanes, earthquakes, tidal waves, sinking ships), which depicted a loss of control and impending disaster that could devastate within a few seconds. As one parent described her child's diagnosis of developmental delay: "It was like being hit by a tornado and never seeing it coming. . . . It felt like a natural disaster."

Metaphors Related to Coping. Metaphors were common in descriptions by family members of how they coped with disability (see Table 11.3). In particular, metaphors contained references to religion, journeys, and everyday routines. There was some variance in the use of these of these metaphors depending on the diagnosis. For example, the metaphors of a family dealing with late-onset disorders, such as a stroke or traumatic brain injury, were qualitatively different from those metaphors pertaining to early-onset disorders, such as when a child was diagnosed as autistic or deaf.

For most of the families interviewed, religion was mentioned as a way to cope in everyday situations. Most interesting was the way in which religious metaphors transformed their situation from hopelessness to hopefulness. While they recounted their initial responses to diagnoses of disability as ones of dismay ("why me?"), they would describe their later responses as their having been specially selected and blessed: "In the end, I am a much better parent because of this. I have God to watch over us, I have my priorities where they should be, and everything that she accomplishes is a blessing." The curse becomes the blessing; the nightmare becomes the dream from which they wake; no control becomes God's control. Many families used phrases such as "It is in God's hands"; "It is out of our hands."

A second type of metaphor related to how one copes was that involving journeys (finding a path, blazing a trail). As one parent stated, "I could either close my eyes and hope it would all go away, or I could find a door to open and walk out. It was the only way to survive for me. I opened my eyes."

Metaphors were used to highlight the need for those with problems to confront the experiences of everyday life. As one parent said, "You can't wrap him in a protective bubble all his life . . . he needs to get bumps and scrapes." Families used these kinds of metaphors as a way to re-invent some normalcy in their everyday routines as families. Everyday events that occur with young children such as bumps, scrapes, mischief (e.g., eating dirt), and discussing developmental milestones (e.g., the process of learning to walk in stages) are considered typical events. These events are ones that provide a shared context for families in that they mark some routine for coping that is common with other families with typical life events.

Finally, metaphors related to fairy tales were used to describe life stories of the family with a disability. Fairy-tale metaphors were used primarily by families of children diagnosed with autism, deafness, and traumatic brain injury. One explanation for this might be the way in which the fairy-tale structure actually mirrored their own experiences. The fairy tale begins

TABLE 11.3
Metaphors Associated With Coping

Metaphor Theme	Exemplar
Religion	"We had to put the **loss in God's hands.**"
	"I have to be real positive in my faith because that's what gets me through these hard times. I'd have to say **wherever God leads her, there is a reason.**"
	"**If you have any religion, which I do, you realize, maybe there is somebody looking out over there.** You know, looking out over the whole universe. And saying, 'You can do this' when you really think you can't. You know, maybe there is. So, looking at it from that way, I think it helps to say, 'Well, I don't really have control over this.' "
	"**I thank God everyday** for everything she can do. Eating by herself, saying a sentence, to me is **like the biggest miracle.**"
	"When you're faced with a problem like this and you're groping for ways to handle it—you just **wish there was a miracle around the next corner. And there never is, but you work toward that miracle.**"
	"It's like I look at Laura and I know that she's special for a reason. And I wanted to run from that reason for so long. But to **know that God has a plan**, and there's a reason why she is the way she is . . . I have to be real positive in my faith because it gets me through these hard times."
Journeys	"It's been a **tough road.**"
	"We've **blazed a trail** in our school district" [to get services].
	"It's been **quite a journey** with a little bit of everything in it, frustration, sadness, but more gladness and positives."
	"We're going to **stay on the same path.** It's a one day at a time thing. I can't worry about the future too much. There's too much to deal with today."
Routines; everyday events	". . . well, you can't stop. I mean it's now **become like it's the ritual of my life. Eating, sleeping, and therapy.** It's the only thing you can do to get to the other side."
	"You can't wrap him in a protective bubble all his life . . . **he needs to get bumps and scrapes. A child needs to eat dirt. It is something every little kid does. They all eat dirt.**"
	"It's almost **like . . . learning how to walk.** It's like, okay, just a little further, yes. The more they walk, your feelings of doubt get less . . . it's kinda like a crutch . . . and then with each little improvement I let go a little."
Fairy tales	"**It's like a fairy tale. It starts out so sad—like Cinderella—**and then here we go at the end and we're happy."
	"**It's like the wolf who comes and blows your house down.** You don't know how you'll ever get up and build it again."
	"**It's not a fairy tale. There will be no prince to rescue her.** Just us. We are all she will ever have."
	"**It was like the emperor has no clothes.** Everyone knew he was autistic, but no one wanted to see it. I didn't really realize how severe he was. No one ever really wants to tell you really what's wrong."

251

with typical, usual events of happily watching their child pass milestones and make discoveries. Then a disaster or unexpected turn of events takes place, leading to feelings of hopelessness. After some period of time some resolution occurs—usually with a happy ending.

Bettelheim (1977) saw fairy tales as a genre that provides a way to learn adaptive solutions. He argued that fairy tales show how struggle against a severe difficulty is unavoidable, but an unavoidable part of the human condition. If one moves ahead, so the stories go, the obstacles will be removed and the characters end up victorious—and happy. The lives of those affiliated with children diagnosed with autism, deafness, and traumatic brain injury share a similar plight. They began a life with their children without incident; a catastrophic event occurs—the discovery of the disability—and a struggle begins. Ultimately, some families develop some hope and resolution by finding a fairy-tale ending (e.g., "It starts out so sad like Cinderella . . . and at the end . . . we're happy"), while other families cast doubt on the fairy-tale ending (e.g., "It's not a fairy tale . . . there will be no prince to rescue her").

The Metaphor of Personification. Lakoff and Turner (1989) describe personification as a metaphoric concept that "permits us to use our knowledge about ourselves to maximal effect, to use insights about ourselves to help us comprehend such things as forces of nature, common events, abstract concepts, and inanimate objects" (p. 72). Three personification-like themes emerged in the data from this study: physical body metaphors, medical metaphors, and animal metaphors. Of the 60 interviews collected, 52 families used at least one of the personification metaphors quoted in Table 11.4.

Physical metaphors, likening the person's condition to that of physical breakdowns, were also common. Metaphors of broken bones, for example, were used by families perhaps as a way to help others "see" their disorder. Broken bone metaphors were often used by families who had a child with autism or developmental delays, or by a spouse of a client who had a stroke. For these families, the disorder was not visible like a broken leg, and so these metaphors might be used in this way to connect what is not visible to what is visible.

Another example of a physical metaphor was that of illness. Forty-nine of the 60 families with all types of disabilities used this metaphor. The most common example of the illness metaphor was related to cancer: "It was like hearing you had cancer." A possible explanation for the cancer metaphor might be that cancer, like a language disorder, is not always visible to the outside world. The individuals with the disability look like everyone else. But as time progresses, symptoms of the "cancer" become more visible and the outcome, "the cure" or positive outcome, is uncertain.

The animal personification metaphors were less common, occurring in 39 of the 60 interviews. Table 11.4 includes a few exemplars. One client,

TABLE 11.4
The Personification Metaphor

Metaphor Theme	Exemplar
Physical metaphors	"You know, you can tease each other, but a stroke is different. **It's not like a broken leg or a neck brace** that you can give him a hard time about . . . all these older men were nothing but a bunch of immature, cruel little first graders."
	"I think that she's aware of things that you can feel and things that you can see—not that you can hear. . . . but I don't think she really understands that she will not outgrow this. I guess, it's pretty much a permanent thing. **And I think that parents of handicapped children, like if their legs don't work or something, like they always think that as they grow, their legs will get stronger and their legs will work better** . . . I mean your mind wants them to get better, so you do have this tendency to focus on the getting better thing, even though you know it's never gonna happen."
	"It's not like you can put **a cast on her and when you take it off it will be as good as new. This is like walking around with a permanent broken bone, and no cast will make it heal. Nothing makes it go away.**"
Illness metaphors	"**It's like being anorexic.** The profile of wanting to be the perfect person and the perfect parent with your child who is far from perfect. You get blinded by it."
	"**It's finding out that your kid has cancer.** . . . All of a sudden you find out there's a problem. There may have been concerns, and it kinda progresses, but then you find out it's more serious. And there isn't necessarily a cure."
	"**It was like hearing you had AIDS** or something. It was the furthest thing from my mind. I was overwhelmed and angry . . . but I am figuring out how to live with it. What choice do I have."
Animal metaphors	"**A therapist . . . it's like on a horse,** when you ride a horse, okay, you must take command of the horse, but you must also understand the horse. A horse can teach you very much if you let it teach you. But if you keep the reins tight all the time and hold the horse's head up and jerk his head constantly you learn nothing from the horse. . . . I kept shaking my head because the reins were too tight. I taught her nothing, and she taught me nothing."
	"This thought goes in your mind and it tightens your mind like you tighten a screw . . . **for me it [stuttering] was like being a rabbit in a wolf cage.**"
	"**For my family it was like the elephant in the living room.** Everyone knew that my brother was a problem, but no one ever talked about it. He was not the same person after the accident, but everyone pretended that it didn't matter."

diagnosed with severe dysfluency, used the metaphor of a horse to describe his relationship with his therapist: "a therapist . . . it's like on a horse, when you ride a horse . . . you must take command of the horse, but you must also understand the horse." This particular metaphor provided a way for a client to create a compelling image of his client-clinician relationship. As the rider, the clinician needs to guide and understand the horse, the dysfluent client. The client felt constrained by the clinician and wanted to resist her guidance.

Metaphors Describing Ambivalence. Metaphors describing ambivalence (see Table 11.5) often included "tightropes" as a way to explain the weighing of decisions that had to be made, as well as "crutches" that would be used for a period of time and then discarded. Both tightropes and crutches involve weight and balance, and serve as an aid to staying upright. Most of these families were doing just that: trying to balance options and make decisions. Their words reflect ambivalence and issues of dilemma. As one parent stated:

> You are trying to walk this sort of line or tightrope . . . you want to keep things . . . on an even keel so that they don't feel different. But then at the same time you have to be very sensitive to the fact that they are different.

TABLE 11.5
Metaphors Depicting Ambivalence

Metaphor Theme	Exemplar
Dilemma metaphors	" . . . I don't think that it's a good idea [therapeutic companions], only because I think the child becomes dependent on that person, kinda like a crutch . . . **but on the other hand**, you know they know where they're at . . . their learning style . . . but my choice is not to have him in a special day class. I'm still not sure."
	"It has been kind of tough because it's kind of like you are **trying to walk this sort of a line or tightrope or something**. Where you don't want to make anything this really big deal so the kid thinks, oh no, there is really something wrong with me. You know like I'm really different, therefore I'm not normal like other kids. You want to keep things sort of on an even keel so that they don't feel different. But then at the same time you have to be very sensitive to the fact that they really are different."
	"I just want him to have a normal life if he can without pain. Why should he have to go through surgery just so he could run? He can walk and I am grateful that he can walk. I went to all these doctors and they all told me different things. **It was like a three-ring circus. I didn't know what to do, or when to do it [the surgery].** I went with the one who told me to do nothing."

The ambivalence metaphors were pervasive in these family interviews and were described in nearly every interview.

CONCLUSIONS

The evidence reviewed in this chapter suggests that the conceptual power of metaphor is embedded in everyday cultural understanding of disabilities. Understanding clients'/families' use of metaphor is a key to understanding how their realities are constructed. Client metaphors provide a context in which to interpret a client family's problems, reflect and create client realities, and illustrate ways in which the family comes to terms with its problems.

This chapter reveals that metaphor is a powerful vehicle through which families voice their lived experiences. The metaphors used by these families created ways to link their own understandings with listeners' understanding so as to allow others to participate in the experiences being described. The commonalities of metaphors used across families are striking and revealing. They offer clinicians ways to share in, understand, and support families as they reflect on a diagnosis, and cope with and come to understand the disability.

REFERENCES

Atwood, J. D., & Levine, L. B. (1991). Ax murderers, dragons, spiders and webs: Therapeutic metaphors in couple therapy. *Contemporary Family Therapy, 13,* 201–217.

Barker, P. (1996). *Psychotherapeutic metaphors: A guide to theory and practice.* New York: Brunner/Mazel.

Beck, B. (1978). The metaphor as a mediator between semantic and analogic modes of thought. *Current Anthropology, 19,* 83–97.

Bettelheim, B. (1977). *The uses of enchantment.* New York: Vintage Books.

Black, M. (1993a). More about metaphor. In A. Ortony (Ed.), *Metaphor and thought* (pp. 19–43). New York: Cambridge University Press.

Black, M. (1993b). *Models and metaphor.* Ithaca, NY: Cornell University Press.

Carveth, D. L. (1984). The analyst's metaphors: A deconstructionist perspective. *Psychoanalysis and Contemporary Thought, 7,* 491–560.

Cole, M. (1995). The supra-individual envelope of development: Activity, situation, and context. In J. Goodnow, P. J. Miller, & F. Kessel (Eds.), *Cultural practices as contexts for development, New Directions for Child Development, 67,* 105–118.

Cormac, E. C. (1985). *A cognitive theory of metaphor.* Cambridge, MA: MIT Press.

Crider, C., & Cirillo, L. (1991). Systems of interpretation and the function of metaphor. *Journal for the Theory of Social Behavior, 21*(2), 171–195.

Dent-Reed, C. H., & Szokolsky, A. (1993). Where do metaphors come from? *Metaphor and Symbolic Activity, 8*(3), 227–242.

Ferrara, K. (1994). *Therapeutic ways with words.* New York: Oxford University Press.

Gonçalves, O., & Craine, M. (1990). The use of metaphors in cognitive therapy. *Journal of Cognitive Psychotherapy: An International Quarterly, 4,* 135–149.

Hendrix, D. (1992). Metaphors as nudges toward understanding in mental health counseling. *Journal of Mental Health Counseling, 14,* 234–242.

Lakoff, G. (1987). *Women, fire and dangerous things.* Chicago: University of Chicago Press.

Lakoff, G., & Johnson, M. (1980). *Metaphors we live by.* Chicago: University of Chicago Press.

Lakoff, G., & Turner, M. (1989). *More than cool reason: A field guide to poetic metaphor.* Chicago: University of Chicago Press.

Lankton, C. H., & Lankton, S. R. (1989). *Tales of enchantment: Goal-oriented metaphors for adults and children in therapy.* New York: Brunner/Mazel.

McMullen, L. (1989). Use of figurative language in successful and unsuccessful cases of psychotherapy: Three comparisons. *Metaphor and Symbolic Activity, 4*(4), 203–225.

Murray, J. M. (1931). Metaphor. In J. M. Murray (Ed.), *Countries of the mind.* London: Oxford University Press.

Olson, D. R. (1988). Or what's a metaphor for? *Metaphor and Symbolic Activity, 3*(4), 215–222.

Ortony, A. (1993). Metaphor, language, and thought. In A. Ortony (Ed.), *Metaphor and thought* (pp. 1–16). New York: Cambridge University Press.

Pepper, S. (1942). *World hypotheses: A review of evidence.* Berkeley: University of California Press.

Rosenblatt, P. (1994). *Metaphors of family system theory.* New York: Guilford.

Searle, J. R. (1993). Metaphor. In A. Ortony (Ed.), *Metaphor and thought* (pp. 94–123). New York: Cambridge University Press.

Siegelman, E. Y. (1990). *Metaphor and meaning in psychotherapy.* New York: Guilford.

Sternberg, R. J. (1993). *Metaphors of mind: Conceptions of the nature of intelligence.* New York: Cambridge University Press.

Strong, T. (1989). Metaphors and client change in counseling. *International Journal for the Advancement of Counseling, 12,* 293–313.

Tourangeau, R. (1982). Metaphor and cognitive structure. In D. Miall (Ed.), *Metaphor: Problems and perspectives* (pp. 14–35). Atlantic Highlands, NJ: Humanities Press.

The Social Work of Diagnosis: Evidence for Judgments of Competence and Incompetence

Ellen L. Barton
Wayne State University

INTRODUCTION

The medical encounter is centered on diagnosis and treatment: In lay terms, people go to the doctor to find out what's wrong and what to do about it; in professional terms, the medical history and examination are the basis for the clinical reasoning that arrives at the differential diagnosis with its associated prognosis and course(s) of treatment (Wilson et al., 1991). In abstract terms, diagnosis represents the expertise of the physician, the leap to a conclusion warranted by medical education, training, and experience, and the delivery of that conclusion to the patient and/or family members (Parsons, 1951). In concrete interactions, however, diagnosis represents an interactional achievement of all the participants, not just the physician, although this achievement typically enacts and reflects the asymmetric framework characteristic of institutional encounters (Drew & Heritage, 1992).

In the literature investigating the discourse of medical encounters, considerable attention has been paid to diagnosis as an interactional achievement. Drawing on Byrne and Long's (1976) description of the generic structure of a medical encounter, Heath (1992) notes that diagnosis occupies the "pivotal position" within a medical encounter: "It marks the completion of the practitioner's practical inquiries into the patient's complaint and forms the foundation to management of the difficulties. It stands as the 'reason' for the consultation and is routinely documented in the medical-record cards" (p. 238). Heath notes that diagnosis is inter-actionally achieved in medical encounters: Physicians and patients system-atically collaborate in the production and reception of diagnosis. This interactional collaboration, however, tends to preserve the asymmetry of the institutional roles and relationships in the medical encounter. When patients do not respond or respond minimally to the delivery of diag-nostic news, for example, Heath argues that their contributions thereby preserve the physician's expertise over the professional status of the di-agnosis and its delivery (p. 262). He notes that even in more complicated cases, where the physician and patient have diverging views of the pa-tient's condition, their interaction continues to preserve asymmetry. For example, when physicians design a delivery of diagnostic news that they believe is in conflict with patients' assessment of their own status, they often preface the turn with a token of newsworthiness, like "actually" or "in fact." When patients want a reassessment of the diagnosis, they manage this goal first by nominally agreeing with the diagnosis and only later presenting new or recycled information that might call for a revi-sion of that diagnosis.

Maynard (1991a, 1991b, 1992) also describes the production and re-ception of diagnostic news in a study of diagnostic meetings between fami-lies and staff at a clinic for children with developmental disabilities. May-nard argues that physicians routinely use what he calls a perspective-display series, especially for the delivery of negative or difficult news. A perspec-tive-display series is similar to a prefacing pre-sequence in ordinary con-versations (Schegloff, 1988). In both cases, a speaker provides some op-portunity for the recipient of news to actually formulate that news him/herself. The delivery of news, especially bad news, is thereby collabo-ratively achieved rather than hierarchically imposed: In medical encounters concerning children with developmental disabilities, this ostensibly situates diagnosis as a confirmation of a family's identification of the child's prob-lem(s). Like Heath (1992), Maynard (1992) notes that this sequence ac-tually functions to preserve the asymmetry of roles and relationships in the medical encounter. Nonproblematically in cases of converging views between medical professionals and families, and more problematically in cases of diverging views, it is nevertheless the physician and clinic's view of the problem that ends up as the official diagnosis for the child (p. 337).

In the literature on social aspects of medicine, the concepts of compe-tence and incompetence are most often discussed in terms of the profes-sional knowledge, experience, and judgment of physicians (Del Vecchio-Good, 1995; Freidson, 1986, 1989; Parsons, 1951). Del Vecchio-Good calls physician competence the core symbol of the profession (p. 9). By them-selves and by the American public, the majority of physicians are assumed to be competent, delivering appropriate medical care according to the standards of contemporary medicine. The minority of incompetent physicians are supposed to be disciplined by informal and formal means (e.g., hospital credentialing committees, state licensing organizations).

When patients' and families' competence are discussed in the medical literature, however, it is most often in terms of compliance. Patients in compliance are following the prescribed treatment and advice of their medical professionals; patients out of compliance are not. (In medicine, there is a huge literature on compliance, with sources such as Gerber & Nehemkis, 1986, and Schmidt & Leppik, 1988; the journal devoted to this topic is entitled *The Journal of Compliance in Health Care: JCHC.*) But Fisher (1993) discusses competence in broader terms, suggesting that professionals view patients as more or less competent, with competence defined in part as patients' knowledge or understanding of such things as their condition, their diagnosis, their prognosis, and their treatment options.

Fisher argues that medical professionals' judgments of their patients' competence and incompetence sometimes hold very real consequences in terms of treatment decisions. In her study of women referred to university and community women's clinics, she notes that women who displayed fairly sophisticated understanding about their diagnoses were perceived as competent patients, a judgment which may have played a part in the recommendation of conservative treatment for their conditions. In contrast, women who did not display such understanding, or women who were not given the chance to display their understanding, were perceived as incompetent patients, again a judgment which may have played a part in the recommendation of radical treatment. Patients display knowledge (and therefore competence) in a variety of ways: They may provide sophisticated definitions of their diagnoses, for example, or they may ask informed questions. Patients display their lack of knowledge (and therefore incompetence) in different ways, too: They may not be able to answer questions with definitions of their diagnoses, or they may ask uninformed questions.

All of these investigations raise interesting and important questions about the discourse of diagnosis and the roles that concepts like competence and incompetence may play in the interactions of medical encounters. What all of these investigations have focused on thus far, however, is the *presentation* of diagnostic news. Maynard's (1992) data, for example, come from diagnostic meetings with families after a clinic has evaluated and tested a child but before it has begun treatment. Similarly, Fisher's (1993) data come from initial specialist appointments for patients who have received notice of an abnormal test result, and Heath's (1992) data come from general practice appointments where diagnosis and treatment are often accomplished within the same encounter. As Ainsworth-Vaughn (1994) points out, however, roles and interactions typically change in the course of long-term relationships between medical professionals and patients and/or families, especially when those relationships are based on a diagnosis of significant disease or disability. (Ainsworth-Vaughn's data came from medical encounters with cancer patients.)

The focus of this chapter, then, is the complex interconnections of *understanding* of diagnosis and judgments of competence and incompetence as they are played out in the course of extended relationships between a patient, a family, and a physician or a clinic. By looking at follow-up encounters after a diagnosis has been established, I argue that understanding of diagnosis and the linguistic display of this knowledge actually does a considerable amount of social work in the course of long-term relationships between medical professionals and families. Specifically, I argue that one aspect of this social work is its role as evidence for medical professionals as they form judgments of competence and incompetence. I show how these judgments play a role in the immediate interaction between professionals and families and how they become part of professionals' subsequent discussions of those encounters.

The data for this study come from a larger investigation of the ways that language surrounds and shapes the social experience of disability in contemporary American society. The following section of this chapter describes two cases studies drawn from the larger study. The two case studies illustrate different connections between understanding of diagnosis and judgments of competence and incompetence. In one case, a family member displays her sophisticated understanding of diagnosis and thereby provides medical professionals with evidence for their judgments of the family's competence. In another case, family members do not display a sophisticated understanding of their child's diagnosis and thereby provide medical professionals with evidence for their judgments of the family's incompetence. The data in these case studies come from two sources: transcripts of conversations between these families and the medical professionals who saw them during particular clinic appointments, plus transcripts of subsequent conversations among clinic staff. The former are fairly typical of data collected in studies of medical discourse, but the latter are less often available to researchers, even participant-observers. The two sources together provide the basis for a triangulated description of the social work of diagnosis.

BACKGROUND AND FRAMEWORKS

Diagnosis represents a linguistic moment of great import in disability: It articulates the key distinction between being abled and disabled; it labels the condition for the purposes of medical, educational, and legal institutions; and it fuses identity and disability in the social experience of the individual and those in contact with him or her (Goffman, 1963; Instad & Whyte, 1995; Lindenbaum & Lock, 1993).[1] Diagnosis (or, sometimes, the lack of one) marks the beginning of a medical career, in Parson's (1951) terms, and it comprises a central component of the background knowledge that patients and families bring to medical encounters. As noted above, researchers have examined the delivery of a diagnosis of disability (Maynard, 1991a, 1991b, 1992), so the focus of this chapter is on the role of diagnosis in follow-up encounters between medical professionals and families who have children with disabilities.[2]

The data come from fieldwork, which took place from January to December 1994, and involved collecting data through ethnographic participant-observation. One set of participant-observations took place in the urban office of a large health and welfare agency specializing in the care of children with disabilities. During the course of the research, approximately 100 follow-up appointments with a variety of pediatric specialists were observed and recorded at this site (here called the Child Care Clinic). Approximately half of the appointments observed were with White American families and half were with minority families, primarily African-American. All participant-observation sessions were recorded and transcribed in

---

[1]The disability studies literature, which addresses issues in the social experience of disability, is large and growing. In addition to the sources cited in the text of this chapter, references include L. Davis (1995); Ferguson, Ferguson, and Taylor, 1992; Fine and Asch, 1988; Hillyer, 1995; Murphy, 1987; Nagler, 1993; Phillips, 1990; and Zola, 1982. The scholarly journal in this field is *Disability Studies Quarterly*. Activist literature in disability studies, which addresses issues in the formation of a disability culture, is a growing field as well. Sources include Gallagher, 1990, 1994; Hevey, 1992; J. Morris, 1991; and Shapiro, 1993. Activist newsletters and magazines include *The Disability Rag* (see the collection edited by Shaw, 1994), *This Mouth Has a Brain*, and *Mainstream*. Other areas of academic and popular literature on disability include social histories and memoirs, such as Black, 1996, and Finger, 1991, as well as books of information and advice for patients and families (one of the best of these is Featherstone, 1980).

[2]Since the conventions of contemporary ethnograpgy require that the investigator reveal his or her situatedness (Clifford & Marcus, 1987; Geertz, 1983; Van Maanen, 1988), I note here that the focus of this project on families who have children with disabilities arises out of my personal experience as the parent of a child with cerebral palsy, making me a situated participant with an extensive background in this population. In the design and analysis of this project, I have chosen not to foreground my own experiences, but I acknowledge that my personal background was crucial in the conception of the project and in my ethnographic access to the institutions and individuals who participated in this research. I would like to thank these many participants who remain anonymous in this work, especially the staff and families of the Child Care Clinic. I also would like to thank the programs at Wayne State University that have provided support for this research, including the College of Urban, Labor, and Metropolitan Affairs, the Humanities Center, and the Career Development Chair program.

broad form, and analysis was based on these transcriptions plus brief field notes.[3]

The theoretical framework for analysis of this data comes from recent work in conversation analysis on the nature of talk in institutional encounters, particularly medical encounters (Boden & Zimmerman, 1991; K. Davis, 1988; Drew & Heritage, 1992; Firth, 1995; Fisher & Todd, 1993; Mishler, 1984; G. Morris & Chenail, 1995; Silverman, 1987). As Drew and Heritage (1992) note, within this framework, utterances are considered doubly contextual—they are shaped by the institutional context and they continually renew that context: "[T]he CA [conversation analysis] perspective embodies a dynamic approach in which 'context' is treated as both the project and product of the participants' own actions" (p. 19). In this view, institutions and institutional discourses do not exist in abstract terms alone but are enacted in interactional terms as participants jointly attend to reflecting and creating the context of their situation. Within institutional encounters, then, participants use interactional practices to enact institutional relationships and understandings—in the case of medicine, physi-

---

[3]The broad transcription of these exchanges follow a subset of conventions from Atkinson and Heritage (1984, pp. ix–xvi):

- simultaneous utterances
  left hand brackets   [What happened
                                                        [And gained
- overlapping utterances
  left hand brackets   Because [she's
                                                        [Right because
- latching utterances latched onto a previous utterance without a pause)
  equal signs   for me=
                                                        =Okay.
- incomplete utterances
  --   has it always been--
- intonation (cf. Chafe, 1993)
  .   falling tone
  ?   rising tone
  ,   slightly rising or falling tone/continuing intonation
- emphasis
  underlining   he is not right
- contextual details
  double parentheses   ((entering room))
  noticeable pauses (untimed)   ((pause))
- transcriptionist doubt
  single parentheses with a question mark   (wants?)

At this time, timing of pauses, lengthening, inhalations/exhalations, and gaze/gesture have not been systematically transcribed. I have used regularized spelling in these transcripts.

.

cians and patients or families reflexively draw on and enact the institutional discourse of medicine.

Although much conversation analysis research looks at specific linguistic features of talk, such as sequential turn design and topic transitions, Drew and Heritage (1992) suggest that researchers also look at what they call themes: "themes . . . are often generally distributed across broad ranges of conduct in institutional settings and manifest themselves in and through the features of institutional interaction" (p. 45). Themes that are typical of institutional interactions include asymmetrical social relations among participants (e.g., medical professional vs. patient or family member) and differential knowledge bases across participants (e.g., medical diagnosis vs. lay complaint). These themes can be enacted in a surprising variety of interactional practices (e.g., topic selection and development, turn design, narrative structures, etc.).

The concept of theme thus provides a bridge between the macroanalysis of ethnographic description and the microanalysis of conversational analysis as themes identified through ethnographic observation are shown to be enacted through specific interactional practices. This insistence that themes must be shown to be enacted through specific interactional practices represents a strong constraint on the contextual analyses that are possible within a conversation analysis framework. Following Schegloff (1992), Drew and Heritage (1992) note: "analysis should properly begin by addressing those features of the interaction to which the participants' conduct is demonstrably oriented" (p. 53).

In the data from this project, one such theme with ethnographic significance and interactional orientation is the understanding of diagnosis. Diagnosis played some part in every medical encounter observed in the research. Delivery of diagnostic news took place both in general and specific terms. Children might have received a general diagnosis of cerebral palsy, say, or muscular dystrophy, and they often received a set of more specific diagnoses as well; for example, a child with cerebral palsy also might be diagnosed with a seizure disorder, a speech disorder, and/or some degree of cognitive impairment. Both medical professionals and families observably attended to diagnosis at different times and to different degrees in medical encounters. Sometimes diagnosis was the central focus of an appointment, as, for example, when a child developed a new set of symptoms or a complication of a condition. At other times, diagnosis was part of the background of an encounter, as, for instance, when a child's progress or behavior was related to his or her primary or secondary diagnoses.

In order to present a situated discourse analysis of some of the different ways that diagnosis is attended to in medical encounters, this chapter presents two case studies that show different kinds of attending to diagnosis, with significantly different results. Broadly speaking, they represent different points on the continuum of success. In the first case, the family and the physician collaborate easily and successfully on their understanding of the child's diagnosis. This is especially interesting since the diagnosis is ADHD (attention deficit hyperactivity disorder), a controversial diagnosis not only in the medical domain but with the general public as well. In the second case, the family and a number of medical professionals do not collaborate successfully on their understanding of the child's diagnosis of cerebral palsy. In the discussion of each case study, I first show how the understanding of diagnosis becomes a part of the discourse of each medical encounter, enacted more or less collaboratively. I then show how the family's displayed knowledge of diagnosis played a role in the subsequent judgments that medical professionals made about the relative competence or incompetence of that family.

COLLABORATIVE RELATIONSHIPS
IN THE DIAGNOSIS OF ADHD

The existence, diagnosis, and treatment of ADHD are all controversial in contemporary America. Some individuals doubt that ADHD exists, at least as a medical (or neurological) diagnosis, pointing to its status as a clinical diagnosis based on reported behavior rather than on physical signs and/or verifiable tests; others believe that ADHD exists as a condition but is regularly overdiagnosed, blurring the distinctions between behavioral problems and neurological or psychiatric disabilities (Hancock, 1996). ADHD has an interesting, if problematic, history in medicine. Noting that the drugs to control hyperactivity were developed before the disorder was widely identified and diagnosed, Conrad and Schneider (1992) observe that what was called minimal brain damage or hyperkinesis in the 1950s and 1960s has become ADHD, the most widely diagnosed childhood psychiatric disorder of the 1980s and 1990s (p. 157). Conrad and Schneider (1992) provide the standard list of symptoms associated with the medical diagnosis of ADHD:

> Typical symptom patterns for diagnosing the disorder include extreme excess of motor activity (hyperactivity), short attention span (the child flits from activity to activity), restlessness, fidgetiness, often wildly oscillating mood swings (the child is fine one day, a terror the next), clumsiness, aggressive-like behavior, impulsivity, the inability to sit still in school and comply with rules, a low frustration level, sleeping problems, and delayed acquisition of speech. (pp. 155–156)

The treatment of choice for ADHD is stimulant drugs such as Ritalin and Cyclert, since these medications deliver the paradoxical results of slowing children down enough to control their impulsivity and increase their attention spans. Hancock (1996) notes that between 1990 and 1996, the number of children taking Ritalin increased two-and-a-half times to over 1.3 million (p. 52).

In the Child Care Clinic, a number of children are followed for ADHD, either as a primary or a secondary diagnosis. The clinic has a well-regarded ADHD clinic, where the diagnosis of ADHD is based on extensive reports from teachers and parents and a battery of physical and psychological tests for the child. The ADHD clinic is under the direction of a pediatric neurologist, here named Dr. Jonathon Brownslee (all names of physicians and family members have been changed). Dr. Brownslee has specialized in learning disabilities and related disorders such as ADHD since the late 1950s. He, too, is well regarded, with an excellent reputation in the clinic and the community. He has contributed to the pediatric literature on ADHD and other topics. He is aware of the controversial status of ADHD as a diagnosis, noting in one conversation with me:

(1) ((B: Dr. Brownslee; O: observer))

(1a) B: There's a--There's an interesting editorial in one of the-- I don't know if it was the *Journal of Well Child Medicine* or *Child Neurology*, where there was an editorial about the medicalization of behavior. You know, everything gets subsumed under the medical model. I'm not sure whether that's good or bad. I don't know whether ADHD is an entity or not. I'm still not sure.

(1b) O: You mean a culturally created, or a socially created entity, or--

(1c) B: No, like a medical entity, like- - oh, for example, uh, I think you could argue that sickle cell disease is pretty clear, it's pretty well genetically defined, we have a test for it, we can define it, we can biochemically determine it. Probably, bipolar disorder is probably somewhat uniform, it's probably genetically inherited, there's probably some biochemistry to it, you could define it once we get better machines, but I don't know whether ADHD is the same or not. Or is it just one end of the normal spectrum or caused by the environment, or caused by, you know--

((some talk about the variety of children diagnosed with ADHD))

(1d) B: That was the reason I started coming here to this institution, though, is to have a clinic for kids with that sort of problem in learning disabilities, sort of related disorders.

(1e) O: Um-hmm.

(1f) B: Not everyone in child neurology is interested in that kind of a problem.

(1g) O: Um-hm.

(1h) B: There are a few people that-- Many people in child neurology regard that as being pretty soft=

(1i) O: =Um-hm.

(1j) B: =not worthy of their attention.

Dr. Brownslee here articulates his own orientation toward the controversial status of the diagnosis of ADHD. Citing the research literature in medicine in (1a), he notes the profession's concern with the blurred line between behavioral problems and neurological or psychiatric disorders, admitting his uncertainty about *whether ADHD is an entity or not.* In (1c), he corrects the observer's orientation toward social construction by explaining exactly what ADHD would have to be in order to be considered a defined and verifiable medical entity, again raising the possibility that it is not a set of physical or psychiatric symptoms but a set of problematic behaviors *at one end of the normal spectrum.* In (1d)–(1j), he points out that the diagnosis and treatment of ADHD lacks status even among his colleagues in pediatric neurology, again noting that its lack of definition and verification as a medical entity leads some to think of it as *pretty soft, not worthy of their attention.*

Despite its controversial status in public and professional circles, the diagnosis of ADHD forms the focus or background for many encounters in the Child Care Clinic. Sometimes, the physicians and staff of the clinic and the ADHD children and families show a remarkable degree of shared understanding about this diagnosis, even its medicalized version and its controversial nature. This shared understanding can be displayed in collaborative interaction within the medical encounter, and it can become the basis for positive judgments that result in pro-active medical care. (I define pro-active medical care here as care that goes beyond treatment for the chief complaint forming the specific business of the encounter.) This first case study illustrates these positive inter-connections of shared understanding observably attended to in collaborative interaction and positive judgments underlying pro-active conse-quences. The following excerpt is from an encounter between Dr. Brownslee, a mother, and her cognitively impaired 9-year-old son, Brady, who also has a diagnosis of ADHD. The excerpt is rather lengthy, but each of its seven segments provides examples of the participants' col-laborative attending to the diagnosis of ADHD:[4]

---

[4]I use the term *segments* following Johnstone (1990), Chafe (1980), and Labov (1972), who noted that speakers divide narratives (and other extended discourses) into what researchers have called chunks, episodes, sections, or segments. Speakers have numerous resources available to indicate different chunks, or segments, in discourse, including discourse markers like *yeah* or *well*, topic continuities and changes, temporal organization, etc. In my analysis of (2), which follows, topic continuities and changes seem to underlie the major episodes: Some episodes are marked with a discourse marker (e.g., *yeah* and *and* at the beginning of Segment 3, *well* at the beginning of Segment 7); others are identified by a pause (e.g., Segment 2 and Segment 4) or a significant change in topic (e.g., specific questions about new topics from the physician at the beginning of Segments 2 and 6). Dividing a discourse into episodes is basically intuitive, and not all researchers would identify the same chunks as I did (e.g., some researchers might claim that Segments 3 and 4 or Segments 4 and 5 are actually just one segment).

(2)   ((B: Dr. Brownslee; M: Mother)
--- **SEGMENT 1**
(2a)   B: ((entering room)) Sorry to keep you waiting. How are things?
(2b)   M: Good, but we need to increase his medicine.
(2c)   B: Think so?
(2d)   M: Yeah, the school agrees, too.
(2e)   B: What do you think?
(2f)   M: ((to child)) Do you think your medicine's still working?
(2g)   B: My experience is that kids can't tell real well.
(2h)   Teachers and parents sometimes can, or ought to be able to.
--- **SEGMENT 2**
(2i)   ((pause)) So his attention span isn't real=
(2j)   M: =No=
(2k)   B: =isn't as good as it used
        to be?
(2l)   M: No. He still can't read.
(2m)   They're working with him.
(2n)   B: Uh-huh.
(2o)   M: But--you know, he don't pay attention that good.
(2p)   And his behavior is worse. You know, more fidgety and stuff.
(2q)   They think-- They said it's because he's older now and gaining
              weight and getting taller=
(2r)   B: =Could be.
(2s)   M: =or something, I don't know.
(2t)   B: Well, it makes sense if you need a certain amount of medicine
              for a certain amount of body size, then-- you know--
--- **SEGMENT 3**
(2u)   M: Yeah. And um he's got a new freedom now.
(2v)   I always kind of like kept him in the backyard.
(2w)   So now there's these little boys that live across the street.
(2x)   And he's been going 'cross the street. He'll cross the street by
              himself to play with those kids.
(2y)   Well, he does pretty good, but I have to keep a real close eye
              on him because um he gets more aggressive.
(2z)   B: Hmm.
(2aa)   M: When he first started the medicine, it's like having a different kid.
(2bb)   B: Um-hmm.
(2cc)   M: But it's not-- ((pause))
--- **SEGMENT 4**
(2dd)   ((pause)) He doesn't sleep as well, either.
(2ee)   B: Hmm. Trouble with getting to sleep or staying asleep?
(2ff)   M: Staying asleep. He wakes up easy.
              ((small talk about the end of the school year))
(2gg)   B: ((to child)) Sit up here and let me see you for a minute, OK?
(2hh)   ((to mother)) He's gaining weight OK.
(2ii)   And he's growing.
(2jj)   You're-- You're quite a bit taller than you used to be, aren't
              you? Yeah.

(2kk)   M: He eats good.
(2ll)   B: So we're not suppressing his appetite with the medicine.
(2mm) M: No.

-- SEGMENT 5

(2nn)   B: But he's taking just 5-milligram tablets.
(2oo)   M: Yeah, 'cause I didn't want him to take a high dosage.
(2pp)   Remember you thought it wouldn't be necessary either.
(2qq)   'Cause I don't want him kinda like too slow, too quiet, 'cause
             I was kinda used to him, you know.
(2rr)   I don't want it to slow him down where it's better for me, you
             know what I mean?
(2ss)   I wanted him to just have enough so he could pay attention
             and learn.
(2tt)   B: But that doesn't seem to be happening lately=
(2uu)   M: =No.
             ((some talk about time since last appointment and time until end
             of school year))

-- SEGMENT 6

(2vv)   B: Do you give it to him on the weekends?
(2ww) M: Yes.
(2xx)   B: Good. OK.
(2yy)   M: That's what you wanted me to do, right?
(2zz)   B: I think that's fine. Yeah, OK. 'Cause, you know, if he's kind of
             impulsive at home, you know, if he tends to, you know, run out
             in the street, for example, without looking for cars and stuff
             like that, if it helps in that regard, then that's good.
(2aaa) M: Um-hmm.
(2bbb) B: ((to child)) Do you think the medicine causes you any prob-
             lems? No? It makes your hair stand on end, though. Is that
             what does that?
(2ccc) M: They don't want him to go to school at all with no Ritalin.
(2ddd)   So that has to tell you somethin'.
             ((small talk about summer activities during physical exam))

-- SEGMENT 7

(2eee) B: Well, why don't we try having him take one and a half instead
             of one of the 5-milligrams. OK?
(2fff) M: OK.
(2ggg) B: He's taking it morning, lunchtime?
(2hhh) M: Eight o'clock, lunchtime, and four.
(2iii) B: OK. So instead of one, have him take one and a half.
(2jjj) M: OK.
(2kkk) B: And then we'll see how it goes, OK?
(2lll) M: All right.

What is striking about this excerpt is that the physician and the mother
collaborate in the display of their shared understanding of ADHD as a
medical diagnosis with pharmacological treatment. This shared under-

standing of the diagnosis of ADHD provides the organizing principle underlying the structure of the encounter and its discourse. That much shared background knowledge underlies this encounter is evident from its first segment, where the mother's initial utterance assumes the diagnosis of ADHD and its treatment with the stimulant drug Ritalin. In an utterance that is characteristic of long-standing relations between family members and physicians in which family members regularly act on their expertise and physicians routinely accept that expertise (Barton, 1996), the mother herself sets the goal-directed agenda for the encounter in (2b)—*we need to increase the medicine.* The physician displays his preliminary willingness to accept the mother's claim, responding with the query *think so?*, a neutral probe for more information that ratifies rather than challenges the mother's expertise. Displaying a sophisticated recognition about school as the domain of dysfunction most relevant to ADHD and a savvy understanding about the need to provide evidence for her recommendation from reliable sources, the mother offers two kinds of evidence in (2d)—her own agreement, presented minimally, and the agreement of the school.

The next sequence includes a bit of miscommunication: When the physician requests an elaboration of her own agreement, asking *What do you think?* in (2e), the mother directs the question to the child in (2f)—*Do you think your medicine's still working?* In his response in (2g)–(2h), the physician again identifies *teachers and parents* as individuals with the information and the expertise to know whether the medication dosages need adjustment. In (2a)–(2h), then, eight short utterances comprising the first segment in this encounter, quite a bit of background knowledge about the diagnosis of ADHD is displayed by both participants: knowledge about drug treatment and the need for careful monitoring and occasional adjustments, and understanding about behavior and reported behavior as the evidence for such adjustments. The physician is careful to observably attend to the expertise of both teachers and parents in school and at home, although the mother herself seems to restrict expertise to professional institutions, especially the school, a pattern that she will repeat throughout the encounter. In sum, although the specific term ADHD has not entered the conversation, the understanding of this diagnosis is the key element of background knowledge drawn on by both participants in the beginning of the encounter.

What is especially interesting about this discourse between the mother and the physician is that its major segments are systematically organized around knowledge of the symptoms and/or treatment of ADHD, sometimes with the mother taking the lead and establishing the focus and sometimes with the physician in the lead. Six subsequent segments in the encounter are organized around ADHD symptomatology and its management through medication. In (2i)–(2t)/Segment 2, the physician and mother discuss attention span and excessive motor activity in the form of fidgety behavior at school, followed by a discussion of medication dosages for a growing child. In (2u)–(2cc)/Segment 3, they discuss aggressive behavior, followed by a truncated discussion of the decreasing effects of medication. In Segment 4, the mother begins an account of sleep disturbances at home in (2dd)–(2ff), a focus on physical symptoms that continues with the doctor's discussion of growth and weight in (2gg)–(2mm). In (2nn)–(2uu)/Segment 5, the mother and the physician discuss the details of medication management, returning to the central symptoms of ADHD—behavior and attention span. In (2vv)–(2ddd)/Segment 6, the physician brings up behavioral impulsivity at home, although the mother returns the focus to behavior at school. In (2eee)–(2lll)/Segment 6, the physician actually adjusts the dosage of medicine, fulfilling the mother's original goal. In each segment, the symptoms or management of ADHD underlies the topic selection and development.

In Segment 2, the physician begins to explore some of the symptoms of ADHD in (2i), asking about the central symptom of attention span. The mother provides answers to the physician's question on two levels, first in terms of her son's primary diagnosis of cognitive impairment in (2l)–(2m)—*He still can't read. They're working with him*—and then in terms of his secondary diagnosis of ADHD in (2o)–(2p)—*he don't pay attention that good. And his behavior is worse . . . more fidgety.* In the rest of the discourse, however, she follows up the diagnosis of ADHD, focusing on her son's attention span and behavior at school and not referring again to his cognitive impairment. Specifically, the mother and physician collaborate here in (2i)–(2p) to establish two symptoms of uncontrolled ADHD—poor attention span and excessive motor behavior (fidgetiness and restlessness). In (2u), the beginning of Segment 3, the mother begins a new segment focused on another symptom of ADHD, providing some information about the child's aggressive behavior with peers in (2y). She seems to begin summing up her case for an increased dose of medication in (2aa) and (2cc), in (2aa) noting that *When he first started the medicine, it's like having a different kid* but comparing it negatively to the present in (2cc)—*But it's not-- (working anymore* is perhaps the completion of this utterance). After a pause, though, the mother begins a new segment in (2dd) by bringing up disturbances in sleep behavior, another symptom of uncontrolled ADHD. The physician continues the development of Segment 4 by discussing other physical symptoms of growth and appetite in (2hh) and (2ll).

In Segment 5, perhaps the most interesting of all the segments since it attends to the public controversy about the diagnosis of ADHD, the mother and the physician discuss the details of medication dosages, with the mother displaying her awareness of the controversial nature of her request for more medicine. In (2qq) and (2rr), for example, she notes that she has not wanted medication exclusively for behavioral control—*I don't want it to slow him down where it's better for me, you know what I mean?*—and in (2ss), she emphasizes that her use of medication is attuned to the appropriate domain—*I wanted him to just have enough so he could pay attention and learn.* As she deferred to the school's expertise in Segment 1, here she refers again to the domain of school to reassure the physician overtly that her request is not based solely on home factors. In Segment 6, however, the only segment in which the physician seems to dominate, he himself raises and pursues the topic of behavior at home in (2vv), affirming the mother's use of the medication not for the control of behavior alone but for the control of the ADHD symptom of impulsivity, which can compromise the child's safety—*'Cause, you know, if he's kind of impulsive at home . . . if it helps in that regard, then that's good.* The physician here seems to be offering the mother the ADHD symptom of impulsivity to provide an official symptom for the medical discussion of relevant home behavior. Rather than following up the physician's attention to home issues, though, the mother finishes this segment by again returning to concerns about school in (2ccc)–(2ddd). Finally, in Segment 7, the physician and the mother end the encounter by collaboratively turning to the details of increasing the child's dose of Ritalin.

It is striking that in the course of this discourse, the mother and the physician collaboratively attend to almost every one of the symptoms of ADHD as it is medically described, diagnosed, and treated: Conrad and Schneider (1992) mention attention span and hyperactivity with restlessness and fidgetiness (Segment 2); aggression and a low frustration level (Segment 3); sleep disturbances (Segment 4); and impulsivity (Segment 6). Each of these symptoms surfaced overtly in the discourse in (2), as did attention to the controversial status of a diagnosis that may be behavioral rather than physical or psychological (Segment 5). Conrad and Schneider specifically mention the domain of school and the possibility of delayed acquisition of speech and language, which was the primary concern for the mother, who was careful to emphasize repeatedly her desire for her son to be able to learn. Even though the term ADHD was not even mentioned in the discourse, both the mother and the physician attended to it throughout, using its medical description as an organizing principle for the discourse. In a display of a sophisticated understanding of the medical model of ADHD, every single piece of information the mother provided is relevant to a medical description of ADHD. Both the physician and the mother, it appears, are working with a shared understanding of the medical model of ADHD as background knowledge: The mother has displayed an expertise about ADHD that seems to be a fairly precise match with the physician's medical model of the disability. Within this high degree of shared understanding about the child, the disability, and the connection between the medication and the behavior of the child, the physician comfortably accedes to the mother's stated goal for the encounter—he increases the dose of medication in Segment 7.

After the appointment, Dr. Brownslee met the director of psychology at the clinic. He begins a conversation about Brady by summarizing the current status of medications for school and home, but the psychologist's response in (3b) is especially interesting:

(3)   ((B: Dr. Brownslee; S: Dr. Sander, psychologist))

(3a)   B: He was only getting five milligrams of Ritalin. And um, apparently it helps enough that the school told Mom he shouldn't come if he doesn't get it. She's been giving it to him on the weekends, too.

(3b)   S: She's come so far.

(3c)   B: Yeah. OK. Yeah. I wondered, have we got any spots left in the summer still, summer programs? He's going to be going to a day camp anyhow so--
       ((some talk about slots in summer programs))

(3d)   B: ((looking at chart)) He came up with an EMI, I see.
       ((EMI = Educable Mental Impairment[5]))

(3e)   S: I remember his feedback. There was a special ed teacher with her at the feedback who told us that she didn't believe it. That we were wrong. That she'd been teaching for 20 years and she [really--

(3f)   B: [Would it be useful to test him again?

(3g)   S: Sure. Is he in a regular classroom?

(3h)   B: You know, I'm-- I'm not sure. I'm sorry, I'm not--

(3i)   S: I'm not either. ((laughing)) Why should you be sorry for something on my caseload? He was in a special ed room in a temporary placement when we saw him.

(3j)   B: No, I'm not sure. Last time I saw him was in November. Why don't we have her back and I can take another look at him?

(3k)   S: OK.

---

[5]The diagnostic terms for mental impairment are roughly related to the distribution of scores on intelligence tests. The terms are often used as classifications in the special education system. In Michigan at the present time, for example, some of the diagnostic categories and definitions of mental impairment include SMI, Severe Mental Impairment, defined as four and a half or more standard deviations below the mean of intellectual assessment; TMI, Trainable Mental Impairment, defined as three to four and a half standard deviations below the mean of intellectual assessment; and EMI, Educable Mental Impairment, defined as two to three standard deviations below the mean of intellectual assessment ("Revised Administrative Rules for Special Education," Michigan State Board of Education, October 1993). In informal terms, if 100 is the mean of intellectual assessment on a given instrument such as the Stanford-Binet IQ Test, then 70–130 represents the normal range of intelligence scores; an EMI diagnosis indicates a score of 55–69; a TMI diagnosis indicates a score of 40–54; and an SMI diagnosis indicates a score of 39 or below (Geralis, 1991).

(3l) S: His scores may have come up. If he is in special ed and his scores have come up too far we just won't share them with the school so they won't decertify him.

(3m) B: ((shout of laughter))

(3n) S: It's true.

(3o) B: Dishonesty is rampant!

(3p) S: It's a private eval. It's up to them whether they'll share them with the school district. I don't want to decertify him.
((eval - abbreviation for "evaluation"))

In (3b), the psychologist makes a specific remark about the mother, offering the judgment that *She's come so far*, and the physician agrees with this judgment, using multiple agreement tokens. They then go on to discuss Brady's case in a very pro-active way, exploring the possibility of his attending a summer program at the Child Care Clinic, and even considering the possibility of repeating his psychological testing to confirm the diagnosis of cognitive impairment at the level of EMI. In a savvy awareness of the circumstances of special ed for a child with ADHD who might benefit from smaller classes and individual attention, the psychologist half-seriously suggests that Brady exists within contradictory diagnoses, especially if his diagnostic certification in the schools is jeopardized by an improved medical/psychological diagnosis. What is interesting about the sequence in (3) is that all of the pro-active efforts on behalf of the child seem to follow from a positive judgment about the mother. It is as if the performance of competence during the appointment triggers not only a successful medical encounter but also a positive judgment about the mother's parenting, which then leads to more services for the family. Although the staff does not use the expression in this particular case, this excerpt represents the expression in frequent use at the Child Care Clinic—"She's a good mom"—an expression that stands as a judgment of competence within a compliment.

In conclusion to the discussion of this case, it is interesting to speculate a bit about the hypothetical circumstances mentioned by the psychologist in (3l)–(3p): In this case there seems to be a stated willingness to go beyond categorical definitions of disability and supply services perceived as appropriate to the particular child. In particular, the medical professionals imply that they could justify entering a state of diagnostic collusion or even conspiracy with the mother, reversing the primary-secondary order of Brady's label from a cognitively impaired boy with ADHD to a boy with ADHD and related learning difficulties. The school system provides services for the first diagnostic label only, despite the obvious benefits for a child with the second label. (At this time, the state of Michigan does not recognize ADHD as a certified disability, one that would receive services from the state. Despite many attempts on the part of parents' groups to change this, the schools and state have held firm, perhaps in fear of the tremendous numbers of children who would then enter the special ed program with a diagnosis of ADHD.) The physician and psychologist here are attending to the complexities of the diagnostic label of ADHD, which can have one set of implications in a medical setting but quite another set of implications, some problematic, in a school setting. Their discussion reflects the importance and complexity of diagnostic labels in the world of disability, labels that organize not only the series of medical encounters which are part of the life of disability but also the services from educational institutions which are intended to make that life an independent and productive one.

ADVERSARIAL RELATIONSHIPS IN THE DIAGNOSIS OF CEREBRAL PALSY

The previous case study presented an exceptionally collaborative interaction and admirably positive follow-up, but relationships between medical professionals and families are not always quite so smooth. The following case study is almost the exact opposite of the previous one. Instead of a complex and sophisticated shared understanding of diagnosis, there are significantly diverging understandings about what it means to have cerebral palsy. Instead of a collaborative interaction leading to positive judgments and pro-active consequences, there is a contentious interaction leading to negative judgments and problematic consequences.[6]

The particular site for this case analysis is also the Child Care Clinic, but this case is drawn from an observation in the clinic's CMS clinic—the Children's Multidisciplinary Specialty clinic—which is funded by the state's Special Health Care Services program. The CMS clinic arose in response to a complicated set of circumstances that often occur as a result of moderate to severe disability—a necessary involvement with many medical professionals in different specialties. A child with a moderate or severe disability, such as cerebral palsy or spina bifida, routinely needs to see a neurologist, a physiatrist, an orthopedist, an ophthalmologist, and perhaps a pediatric psychologist, as well as a regular pediatrician; in addition, he or she usually has frequent evaluations and treatment sessions with physical

---

[6]The contrasting terms *collaborative* and *contentious* here are meant as general characterizations. I termed the first encounter collaborative because of the participants' lack of open conflict and their general agreement about the goals of the encounter (increasing the medicine). I termed the second encounter contentious because of the seeming disagreement about the goals of the encounter (cf. sequence (5) and its discussion) and because of the potential for conflict among the participants that arises from this lack of shared understanding. At the microlevel, it is true that even contentious encounters involve collaboration and co-construction in intricate ways (Antaki, 1994), but I do not pursue the microanalysis of collaboration within conflict here.

James Hardiman Library
Self issue receipt

Customer name: O LOUGHLIN CLAIRE
Customer ID: 06375227
Circulation system messages:
Patron in file

Title: Constructing (in)competence :
ID: 31111401176282
Due: 05/12/2009 23:45
Circulation system messages:
Loan performed

Total items: 1
11/28/2009 5:16 PM

Please take your receipt for details of return date

Pod 3

and occupational therapists and speech pathologists. This need for multiple appointments with specialists can be time-consuming and exhausting, especially for families in poverty who often have transportation problems. Even more problematically, multiple encounters with this many medical professionals can create a kind of too-many-cooks situation, where no one person seems in charge of coordinating specialty care and of communicating with family members and other institutions, such as schools and social service agencies. The CMS clinic is intended to remedy these logistical and institutional complexities by establishing a single visit with multiple specialists, resulting in a coordinated plan for medical professionals, families, and other institutions:

> Within a half-day visit, a minimum of eight different professionals evaluate the child and assess family concerns and needs. . . . An integrated treatment plan is provided to the family and their community pediatrician. ("Care for the Disabled Child," Child Care Clinic brochure)

The Child Care Clinic is rightly proud of its CMS clinic, pointing to its potential for coordinating complex health and welfare services for families.

It is important to note here that although this case study represents a particularly problematic encounter, it is an exception to what I found in the majority of my fieldwork at the Child Care Clinic. The clinic is a unique and important institution, and their CMS clinic is an innovative and effective deliverer of health care. The clinic provides services for children and families of all income levels and social classes, serving families with any insurance, including Medicaid, or with no insurance at all. Families that come to the clinic include the urban poor and working class; the median income of the families at the Child Care Clinic is less than $10,000 ("1992 Facts and Figures," Child Care Clinic brochure). Nevertheless, the medical care provided to these families is of extraordinarily high quality, and the health and welfare professionals are concerned and caring individuals. Most of the relationships between staff and families are mutually respectful and productively collaborative, as illustrated in the first case study. But adversarial relationships sometimes develop between the clinic staff and families, and the following analysis is intended not to excoriate individuals on either side but to explore some of the problematic interactions where judgments of competence come into play.

The African-American family in this particular CMS visit has a 3-year-old son named Xavier, who has been diagnosed with severe cerebral palsy. As of this visit, Xavier's physical development has been severely delayed—he does not roll, sit, crawl, stand, or walk independently. His language development is severely delayed as well—his speech consists mostly of sounds, with only one word, *Dada*. The first excerpt is from the end of a session with the therapists who are evaluating Xavier for possible referral to physical therapy (for gross motor development), occupational therapy (for fine motor development), and speech therapy (for language development). Each therapist has examined Xavier, asking about his current therapies, his adaptive equipment, and his general health and progress. At the end of the team examination, there is an opportunity for parents to ask questions, state concerns, and raise issues. The end of the interview by the team of therapists thus nominally turns control of the encounter back to the parents:

(4)   ((B: Bridgit, occupational therapist; F: father))
(4a)   B: Well, what can we do for you guys today? How could we help? You only have us for a real short time, though, today.
(4b)   F: Well, physically-wise the only problem I have is that he's just too tight. He's too-- Ought to have some type of physical therapy that could cause him to loosen. You see how relaxed he is now? He's not like this all the time. Seem like when he get excited, his whole body just tightens up.
        ((talk about tightness and about hand activities))
(4c)   B: Does Xavier-- Do you know, does he have *cerebral palsy?* Is that why he-- his muscles are doing what they're doing?
              [Is that what's happening?
(4d)   F: [Um-hmm.
(4e)   B: OK. So, uh, I'm still on the muscle thing, 'cause you guys were talking about it, and also with the hand, and it seems like there's still the muscle thing in the hand, just like there is in the legs. OK, it sounds to me, or looks to me like he's a little person who's, you know, got like an all or nothing thing, you know, he's either all, you know, relaxed, and we call that hypotonia, or low tone. And then when he wants to move, or he wants-- or he gets excited it's like too much. You know, it's--
(4f)   F: He take it overboard=
(4g)   B: =He *over*does. Right. And he can't help that.
(4h)   F: Uh-huh.
(4i)   B: You know, that happens because his brain is not-- It's not telling his muscles to grade that properly. Some of that isn't ever going to go away. In other words, there's not a physical therapy thing we can do to say it's going to get all better, you know, it's just magic. Because it's in his brain that's doing this. But there is some, you know, things we can show you that will help-- um, help you a little bit to help to reduce its-- the tone a little bit. And he also needs to work on some muscle strengthening, which is what you guys were doing in physical therapy.

The occupational therapist's turn here to the space for the parents' concerns begins in (4a) with the caution that *You only have us for a real short time, though, today*, a warning that advises the parents not to try to ask too much during their limited moments of control over the encounter.

The ensuing exchange seems to reflect significantly different understandings of Xavier's diagnosis, at least from the therapist's perspective (cf. discussion of (5) below). In (4b), the father raises a specific concern; displaying his diagnostic understanding by using a term from the vocabulary of therapy, he characterizes Xavier as *too tight*. It is interesting here that the father begins by showing a rather sophisticated knowledge of an appropriate concern for the team that is in the room at the moment: Problems with tone are exactly the domain of physical and occupational therapy (i.e., note that the father does not begin with a concern about the child's breathing, the domain of ENT specialists, or his continuing seizures, the domain of pediatric neurology). The therapist, rather than orienting her discussion of tone in terms of the father's knowledge of his child's condition, constructs an explanation of tone in (4c)–(4i) that seems to assume that the father is unknowledgeable about cerebral palsy and unrealistic in his expectations of therapy. She checks on the child's diagnosis of cerebral palsy in (4c), and she orients her remarks initially to the father's concern in (4e)—*I'm still on the muscle thing, 'cause you guys were talking about it.* She then begins to explain Xavier's state of relaxation, first in nontechnical terms—*the muscle thing [is] an all or nothing thing*—and then begins to restate this description in medical terms, saying of Xavier's state of relaxation, *we call that hypotonia, or low tone.*

In explaining that problems with low and high tone will be a consistent problem, not under Xavier's control, though, the therapist goes on to explicitly construct a representation of the father's expectations as unrealistic in (4i). But the father did not say that he expected physical therapy to make Xavier *get all better* or that he thought physical therapy was *magic*. Instead, the therapist constructs a position of ignorance for the father, rather obscurely summing up the medical understanding of cerebral palsy as permanent damage to the motor pathways of the brain by saying *Because it's in his brain that's doing this.*

The therapist continues to articulate this view of the father as uninformed in other settings. In the staff meeting after the appointment, she says of the exchange she had with the father:

(5) ((B: physical therapist))

(5a) B: The father's main concern is to come here and help the kid to crawl and walk. The father believes that this is the only thing that's wrong with the kid, he's got a normal mind but he's in a screwed-up body. I asked him what he knew, because he said when [Xavier] gets excited, he stiffens right up, so he wants us to fix that. I said, do you understand what cerebral palsy is-- ?

Again, the therapist's discourse constructs the father as ignorant about the disability and uninformed about its treatment. In (4), however, the father did not say that he expected therapy to *fix* Xavier, he actually articulated a more complex expectation, that Xavier *Ought to have some type of physical therapy that could cause him to loosen.* But the semi-sarcastic rhetorical question of the last utterance in (5)—*I said, do you understand what cerebral palsy is?*—reveals the therapist's negative judgment about the father's competence, particularly in terms of his understanding of Xavier's diagnosis.

In the excerpt in (4), the therapist may be attempting to realign the family's construct of cerebral palsy to match a medical model, but her explanations in (4e) and (4i) are problematic in several ways. First, she does not provide a comprehensive or comprehensible explanation of the relationship between cerebral palsy and muscle tone. She begins to explain low tone, or hypotonia, but she does not finish the comparison to high tone, or hypertonia, nor does she explain clearly why it is that many children with cerebral palsy alternate between hypotonia and hypertonia. Further, the therapist's explanation of the relationship between the brain damage of cerebral palsy and the amount of conscious control Xavier has over his muscles is obscure at best. In this and other exchanges the medical staff seems eager to assure the father that Xavier has no control over his tone fluctuations, but they don't offer a neurological or physiological explanation of this relationship. Instead, they concentrate on a simplistic insistence that the father not blame Xavier for his condition. The father and the therapist seem to be in a Catch-22 communicative situation here. The therapist makes negative judgments about the father's lack of diagnostic understanding, but the father is never given enough comprehensible information to develop his understanding of a medical model of cerebral palsy. The end result is that the interactional undertones in (4) are oppositional rather than collaborative—adversarial undertones that surface again in the therapist's recollection of the conversation for a meeting with her medical peers in (5).

Another exchange that is similar to the previous one occurs later in the appointment during Xavier's examination by the team pediatrician:

(6)   ((P: Pediatrician; N: Nurse; M: Mother; F: Father))
       ((talking about child's raspy breathing and his ENT specialist))
(6a)   P: Do they think that he may outgrow some of this stridor, too, with
             time?
             ((stridor = medical term for raspy breathing))
(6b)   M: [Yeah.
(6c)   F: [I do.
(6d)   P: OK.
(6e)   F: I don't know what the doctors say, but I know he is. Unless there's so
             many kids who have the signs that he has, but he is so much like a

> normal child. It's just that his muscles, it's going to take time to--
> to develop. Right now, to me, he's at a stage that a eight-month-
> old baby would be at.

(6f) P: Uh-huh.

(6g) F: And see, I looking at it like that's going to take time. By the time
he five or six, he going to be able to talk. He going to be able to
crawl, [he going to be able--

(6h) P: [At school with the right interventions, he may be able to do
some of those things. We'll have to see. Who's on your bib there,
sweetie?

((interventions = term for therapy programs))

The question-answer sequence between the pediatrician and the mother
in (6a)–(6b)/(6d) is a typical sequence in specialty medical encounters
related to disability. Family members are expected to report accurately the
opinions of other specialists who have seen their child, which the mother
does in (6b) and the pediatrician acknowledges in (6d). The father's
answer in (6c) and its elaboration in (6e)/(6g), however, complicates this
basic sequence. In (6c) he presents his own opinion—*I do*—and he then
begins his own explanation of Xavier's diagnosis and prognosis by explicitly
setting aside a medical opinion in (6e): *I don't know what the doctors say,
but. . . .* The pediatrician abruptly interrupts the father's description of
the child's prognosis, however, in (6h), perhaps enacting her judgment
that the father is unrealistic with dismissive remarks that shift the burden
of improvement to the school system rather than the medical system. The
pediatrician does not even attempt to respond to the father's contributions
here, effectively ending the conversation with the adult by turning to the
nonverbal and (apparently) noncomprehending child and using baby talk
to ask Xavier *Who's on your bib there, sweetie*. In sum, neither the therapist
in (4) nor the pediatrician here (in 6) gives any interactional credence to
the father's understanding of his child's diagnosis and prognosis, dismiss-
ing his understanding in oppositional rather than collaborative terms.

Yet another sequence like (4) occurs at the end of the pediatrician's visit.
In (7a) she nominally turns control of the encounter over to the parents,
and in (7b) the father reiterates his concern about Xavier's tightness:

(7)   ((P: pediatrician; F: father; M: mother; N: nurse))

(7a) P: What kinds of concerns do you have today that-- I want to make
sure that we address everything. What are some of your major
concerns that we can help you with?

(7b) F: My main concern is getting him to like crawl or turn over. Loosen
his body up, 'cause when he get real excited, he'll tighten his body
up. What I want, I want-- I want to have a little help with keeping
his muscles relaxed, instead of tight all the time, because if he keep

'em tight all the time, then when he get older, his body's not going to stretch out. It's gonna [be--
(7c)   P: [Have you heard the term cerebral
palsy before?
(7d)   F: [Cerebral--
(7e)   P: [Cerebral palsy?
(7f)   F: [Yeah.
(7g)   M: [That's what he has.
(7h)   P: That's what he has. Right. And [that=
(7i)   F: [Oh, I know that--
(7j)   P: [=when he gets excited, that's
part of that, 'cause he will tighten up. He will tighten up when he
gets excited because that is part of what the problem is. Now, we
hope that problem will not get worse, OK? But, and through a lot
of therapy, OK, we'll be able to work with him so that he learns how
to use those muscles, OK? The best he can, OK? We're not sure
right now how much of that he's going to be able to control.

The pediatrician here interrupts the father's discussion of Xavier's tightness
to check on the child's diagnosis in (7c)–(7h) and tries to relate Xavier's
problems with muscle tone to his diagnosis in (7j), again interrupting the
father's attempt to state what he knows about his child's diagnosis. But
like the therapist in (4), she constructs a version of the father's
understanding that represents him as uninformed about the diagnosis and
unrealistic in his expectations. When the pediatrician notes that *We're not
sure right now how much of that he's going to be able to control*, she implicitly
dismisses the father's suggestion that Xavier receive help in loosening up
so that his body can stretch out and he can learn to turn over and crawl.
But the father's concern that Xavier's body may someday not stretch out
is a legitimate one with respect to cerebral palsy: Preventing muscle
contracture through stretching is an important component of a physical
therapy regimen. And even though the father's expectation that Xavier
will learn to turn over and crawl is more problematic with respect to his
degree of impairment from cerebral palsy, his concern with Xavier's
significant physical delays is also a legitimate one.

In this exchange, though, the pediatrician does not follow up either of
the father's expressed concerns or their underlying displays of diagnostic
understanding. Instead, she presents an uncertain prognosis framed within
the medical model of treating a child with cerebral palsy with intensive
therapy so that he or she can establish control over gross and fine motor
muscle processes *the best he can*. Like the therapist in (4), the pediatrician
seems to be trying to realign the family's understanding to a medical
model, and within a medical model the prognosis of cerebral palsy is so
uncertain—*Now, we hope that problem will not get worse, OK?*—that attention
is directed to the incremental advances of a therapy program—*through a*

lot of therapy, OK, we'll be able to work with him. The interaction here nevertheless remains more adversarial than collaborative. The pediatrician seems
to oppose the father's expectations, responding to them as unrealistic and
uninformed rather than working with them as a reasonable understanding
of his child's diagnosis. Her final explanation is punctuated with tokens
of *OK*, not used as collaborative checks on understanding but as somewhat
aggressive demands for acquiescence to this particular explanation. Rather
than waiting for the father to provide back-channel OKs in an indication
of his understanding and acceptance, she provides them herself, thereby
preempting any contribution from the father. (For more on the use of
"OK" as a constraining device in medical discourse, see Beach, 1995.) In
sum, this interaction, with its interruptions, its lack of development of the
father's contributions, and its imposition of a medical model without alignment to a family model seems characteristic of an adversarial relationship
rather than a collaborative one.

That the relationship being developed here is an adversarial one is
reflected in the discussion during the staff meeting after the encounter. The
medical team's impression of the father as uninformed and unrealistic in his
understanding of his child's diagnosis and prognosis is addressed at length
by one physician at the meeting. In response to the occupational therapist's
description of the father in (5), the physiatrist who saw Xavier, says:

(8) ((Ph: physiatrist; B: occupational therapist; P: pediatrician; N: nurse))
(8a) Ph: Well, you know what? This-- It's a slow process and that. I mean,
if somebody says something like that to me, it's just showing
what he can't do over time, not what he can do. And I wouldn't
even address yes or no on that. I'd say, listen, you know, if that's
a goal you have, then we'll try to do all the little components
and see what we can get to. If that can be obtainable, that's
fine. If you want my opinion on it, you know, I'll give it to you,
but right now I'm not going to offer it.
But he's going to be casted for his AFOs, his feet have fairly
good range, he's tighter in the hamstrings. I need to prove that
they will come back, because there's some reason when I first
saw him that I didn't think he'd use them, be very compliant.
So--
(8b) B: They have bad attendance and they missed an eval.
(8c) N: [But they say it's 'cause he's always in the hospital.
(8d) P: [OK, then that's what it must have been.
(8e) P: And he has been.
(8f) N: But they need to call. I mean, the problem is--

In (8a), the physiatrist incorporates three important components of a
medical model of disability in his response (Nagler, 1993). The first aspect
of a medical model of disability that emerges from this physician's discourse

is that prognosis is uncertain. Although experience with many children with cerebral palsy can provide a background for forming an opinion about whether a given child will ever sit, crawl, stand, or walk independently, medical paternalism also dictates that it is best to treat every child's potential positively, not focusing *on what he can't do over time [but on] what he can do*. The consequent attention to progress through therapy is the second aspect of a medical model of disability that emerges from this physician's talk. Given the uncertainty of prognosis, experience shifts the focus to therapeutic goals. Even if the physician believes that the father's goals of independent crawling and walking are unrealistic, he shows his willingness to incorporate them into the therapeutic model, but operationalizing the goal as trying *to do all the little components and see what we can get to*. The long-term goal thus is subordinated to the short-term goals in a therapeutic sequence.

The final component of a medical model emerging from the discourse of the physician here, though, involves compliance. In this particular case, the physiatrist connects compliance and competence in a negative judgment: *. . . there's some reason when I first saw him that I didn't think [they'd] be very compliant.* Given the importance of a therapeutic treatment for a child to reach goals, a family's compliance with that program is essential. This family, however, is judged as not compliant or competent, first by the physician in (8a), and then seconded by a variety of staff members in (8b)–(8f). The family is finally presented as an intractable problem in (8f), one which trails off without a solution as *the problem is-- .*

One final excerpt from this encounter comes from the end of the appointment and summarizes the results of the visit:

(9)   ((N: nurse; M: mother; F: father))
(9a)   N: You'll get a report from us in a couple of weeks. OK? And it'll have
            something in it from everybody who's seen him today. And then it'll
            have recommendations at the back, OK, with, um, phone numbers,
            you know, if we've referred him somewhere, there'll be the phone
            numbers on there that you need to know. OK? And then if you have
            any problems with that-- Um, has Miss Thomas been in, the social
            worker?
(9b)   M: Uh-huh.
(9c)   N: OK. And then if you have any problems with it, you can either
            contact myself or Miss Thomas. And our phone numbers will be
            on that report, too. OK?
(9d)   F: Um-hmm.

This exchange promises that the family will receive a coordinated plan from the clinic. But whether it provides the integrated care that the clinic was designed to provide is questionable. The responsibility of the staff is to prepare a report, which the nurse promises to deliver in (9a). But no more than that is offered. The nurse offers the report with constraining *OK* tokens, not giving the family any interactional opportunity to do anything but passively wait to receive the report. Her offer of help from herself and the social worker in (9c) is in the form of a *contact* by phone only. There is no offer here to bring the family back to explain the report, to assist in fulfilling its recommendations, or to ask any questions the report may raise. The onus is now solely on the family to follow up all of the referrals recommended by the team; all the team has to deliver is phone numbers. The family is expected to rely on its own logistical skills to interpret the report and follow up on its recommendations. Given the fact that the family is already out of compliance and has been informally judged as incompetent, particularly in their understanding of their child's diagnosis and prognosis, relying on their logistical skills leaves in place precisely the situation the clinic is designed to overcome: The family is faced with an extraordinarily fragmented situation of specialty medical care, care for which they alone are responsible. The report is the designated product of the clinic; in its staff meeting, the team is conscientious about preparing its recommendations. But the simple delivery of a report, especially in comparison to the delivery of additional services in the previous (ADHD) case study, seems more reactive than pro-active, more related to duty than to active caring, and more characteristic of a distant relationship based on mutual mistrust than a close relationship based on mutual trust.

In sum, the contrasts between the two case studies presented here are dramatic. In the first case, the interaction is mutually collaborative, especially with regard to the understanding of the diagnosis of ADHD. The physician and the mother seem to draw on similar understandings of ADHD, and the physician repeatedly invites the mother to articulate her own expertise, even though the mother routinely defers to the expertise of the school and the physician. Perhaps as a result of the shared understanding displayed in this collaborative interaction, the physician's subsequent judgment about the mother is a positive one of competence (he agrees overtly with the psychologist's judgment that the mother has *come so far*), and the care that this family receives is notably pro-active (they are called back to receive more services).

In the second case, the interaction is not mutually collaborative, especially with regard to the understanding of the diagnosis of cerebral palsy. The family, particularly the father, and the medical team seem to draw on very different understandings of severe CP, and the interaction is oppositional and adversarial (the father is repeatedly interrupted, his opinions and understandings are neither solicited nor substantively incorporated into the medical team's explanations, and the medical team's explanations are delivered impositionally). Again, perhaps as a result of the lack of shared understanding displayed by the father in this contentious interaction, the medical team's subsequent judgments about this family construct the family as noncompliant and incompetent, and the care this family receives is more perfunctory than pro-active (they are delivered a report with nominal but not substantive offers of assistance).

In both cases, these judgments of competence and incompetence are formed based in part on the details of the linguistic interaction between participants, as the discourse of medicine is more or less collaboratively enacted—very successfully in the first case, but less so in the second. The actual interaction among participants then, holds significant consequences for the relationships being established and enacted by these participants, relationships that will be long-lasting ones.

CONCLUSION

This chapter has considered the understanding of diagnosis in medical discourse, arguing that the understanding of diagnosis has consequences for the relationships between medical professionals and families. Not surprisingly, in the asymmetric realities of institutional encounters, a family's display of understanding of a medical model of diagnosis is much appreciated and richly rewarded in a clinical setting. The first case study illustrated the successful enactment of shared understanding and collaborative interaction, leading to positive judgments of competence within cooperative and respectful relationships. Perhaps, again not surprisingly, a family's lack of understanding of a medical model of diagnosis, or its resistance to that model, is neither appreciated nor rewarded in a clinical setting. The second case study illustrated the problematic enactment of diverging understandings and contentious interaction, leading to negative judgments of noncompliance and incompetence within adversarial relationships.

This chapter has argued that understanding of diagnosis is an important part of long-term relationships between medical professionals and families, suggesting that the connection between understanding, interaction, and judgment is an important and complex dimension of these relationships. More specifically, it argues that the current view of compliance of patients and, especially, families may be too narrow a perspective. Competence is a broader concept, shown here to include knowledge and understanding in connection with compliance. Competence may include other aspects as well. One physician who participates in this research project as an informal consultant notes that his judgments of competence also are based on what he perceives as an appropriate emotional response to a diagnosis. The implications of this work for future research, then, point to further investigations of the interconnections between the discourse of medical encounters and the concepts of competence and incompetence.

This research also has implications for both parties in the institutional encounters of medicine for thinking about communication. For medical professionals, this research suggests how many expectations they may unconsciously hold about the knowledge and understanding they want families to have. These case studies clearly show that communication is best facilitated when both professionals and families share some degree of understanding of the medical model of a particular diagnosis of disability. These studies also show, however, that knowledge of the medical model of disability in general or of a specific diagnosis in particular is communicated obliquely and often incompletely (e.g., the physician in the first case obliquely offers the symptom of impulsivity as a way for the mother to think about ADHD-related behavior at home; the therapist in the second case begins to explain types of tone but doesn't complete her explanation). The end result can go beyond the productive asymmetry of an institution where considerable expertise is imparted to families seeking assistance. Problems emerge if physicians and other staff members do not stop to educate families about the medical understanding of a diagnosis, or if they do not guard against automatic dismissal of views of a diagnosis that are not in precise alignment with the medical view.

Similarly, for families, this research suggests that they make systematic distinctions, when necessary, between a medical model of diagnosis and their agreement or disagreement with it. Sometimes a medical model works not only for institutional encounters but for everyday life, as implied by the first case study; but occasionally diverging views of a diagnosis and its prognosis lead to significant misunderstandings with potentially negative consequences, such as the adversarial relationship being formed between the medical staff and the family in the second case study. In the case of conflict, it is important for families and for professionals to lay out their understandings and concerns explicitly so that the mismatches between models, between understandings, between priorities, and between styles of communication can be addressed directly. Social judgments, especially negative ones, are hard to overcome, and the relationships between medical professionals and families are best based on judgments of competence rather than incompetence.

REFERENCES

Ainsworth-Vaughn, N. (1994). Is that a rhetorical question? Ambiguity and power in medical discourse. *Journal of Medical Anthropology, 4*(2), 194–214.

Antaki, C. (1994). *Explaining and arguing: The social organization of accounts.* Thousand Oaks, CA: Sage.

Atkinson, J., & Heritage, P. (Eds.). (1984). *Structures of social action.* New York: Cambridge University Press.

Barton, E. (1996). Negotiating expertise in discourses of disability. *TEXT, 16*(3), 299–322.

Beach, W. (1995). Preserving and constraining options: "Okays" and "Official" priorities in medical interviews. In G. Morris & R. Chenail (Eds.), *The talk of the clinic: Exploration in the analysis of medical and therapeutic discourse* (pp. 259–289). Hillsdale, NJ: Lawrence Erlbaum Associates.

Black, K. (1996). *In the shadow of polio: A personal and social history.* Reading, MA: Addison-Wesley.

Boden, D., & Zimmerman, D. (Eds.). (1991). *Talk and social structure.* Cambridge, England: Polity Press.

Byrne, P., & Long, B. (1976). *Doctors talking to patients: A study of the verbal behaviors of doctors in the consultation.* London: HMSO.

Chafe, W. (Ed.). (1980). *The pear stories: Cognitive, cultural, and linguistic aspects of narrative production.* Norwood, NJ: Ablex.

Chafe, W. (1993). Prosodic and functional units of language. In J. Edwards & M. Lampert (Eds.), *Talking data: Transcription and coding in discourse research* (pp. 33–44). Hillsdale, NJ: Lawrence Erlbaum Associates.

Clifford, J., & Marcus, G. (Eds.). (1986). *Writing culture: The poetics and politics of ethnography.* Berkeley: University of California Press.

Conrad, P., & Schneider, W. (1992). *Deviance and medicalization: From badness to sickness* (Expanded ed.). Philadelphia: Temple University Press.

Davis, K. (1988). *Power under the microscope: Toward a grounded theory of gender relations in medical encounters.* Dordrecht, Netherlands: Foris.

Davis, L. (1995). *Enforcing normalcy: Disability, deafness, and the body.* London: Verso.

Del Vecchio-Good, M. J. (1995). *American medicine: The quest for competence.* Berkeley: University of California Press.

Drew, P., & Heritage, J. (Eds.). (1992). *Talk at work: Interaction in institutional settings.* New York: Cambridge University Press.

Featherstone, H. (1980). *A difference in the family: Living with a disabled child.* London: Penguin.

Ferguson, P., Ferguson, D., & Taylor, S. (Eds.). (1992). *Interpreting disability: A qualitative reader.* New York: Teachers College Press.

Fine, M., & Asch, A. (Eds.). (1988). *Women with disabilities: Essays in psychology, culture and politics.* Philadelphia: Temple University Press.

Finger, A. (1991). *Past due: A story of disability, pregnancy and birth.* Seattle, WA: Seal Press.

Firth, A. (Ed.). (1995). *The discourse of negotiation: Studies of language in the workplace.* Oxford, England: Elsevier Pergamon.

Fisher, S. (1993). Doctor-talk/patient talk: How treatment decisions are negotiated in doctor-patient communication. In S. Fisher & A. Todd (Eds.), *The social organization of doctor-patient communication* (2nd ed., pp. 161–182). Norwood, NJ: Ablex.

Fisher, S., & Todd, A. (Eds.). (1993). *The social organization of doctor-patient communication* (2nd ed.). Norwood, NJ: Ablex.

Freidson, E. (1986). *Professional powers: A study of the institutionalization of formal knowledge.* Chicago: University of Chicago Press.

Freidson, E. (1989). *Medical work in America: Essays on health care.* New Haven, CT: Yale University Press.

Gallagher, H. (1990). *By trust betrayed: Patients, physicians, and the license to kill in the Third Reich.* New York: Henry Holt.

Gallagher, H. (1994). *FDR's splendid deception* (Rev. ed.). Arlington, VA: Vandamere Press.

Geertz, C. (1983). *Local knowledge: Further essays in interpretive anthropology.* New York: Basic Books.

Geralis, E. (Ed.). (1991). *Children with cerebral palsy: A parents' guide.* Rockville, MD: Woodbine House.

Gerber, K., & Nehemkis, A. (Eds.). (1986). *Compliance: The dilemma of the chronically ill.* New York: Springer.

Goffman, E. (1963). *Stigma: Notes on the management of spoiled identity.* Englewood Cliffs, NJ: Prentice-Hall.

Hancock, L. (1996, March 18). Mother's little helper. *Newsweek,* 51–59.

Heath, C. (1992). The delivery and reception of diagnosis in the general-practice consultation. In P. Drew & J. Heritage (Eds.), *Talk at work: Interaction in institutional settings* (pp. 235–267). New York: Cambridge University Press.

Hevey, D. (1992). *The creatures time forgot: Photography and disability imagery.* London: Routledge.

Hillyer, B. (1995). *Feminism and disability.* Norman: University of Oklahoma Press.

Instad, B., & Whyte, S. (Eds.). (1995). *Disability and culture.* Berkeley: University of California Press.

Johnstone, B. (1990). *Stories, community and place: Narratives from middle America.* Bloomington: Indiana University Press.

Labov, W. (1972). The transformation of experience in narrative syntax. In W. Labov (Ed.), *Language in the inner city* (pp. 354–396). Philadelphia: University of Pennsylvania Press.

Lindenbaum, S., & Lock, M. (Eds.). (1993). *Knowledge, power and practice: The anthropology of medicine and everyday life.* Berkeley: University of California Press.

Maynard, D. (1991a). Interaction and asymmetry in clinical discourse. *American Journal of Sociology, 97*(2), 448–495.

Maynard, D. (1991b). The perspective-display series and the delivery and receipt of diagnostic news. In D. Boden & D. Zimmerman (Eds.), *Talk and social structure* (pp. 164–192). Cambridge, England: Polity Press.

Maynard, D. (1992). On clinicians' co-implicating recipients' perspective in the delivery of diagnostic news. In P. Drew & J. Heritage (Eds.), *Talk at work: Interaction in institutional settings* (pp. 331–358). New York: Cambridge University Press.

Mishler, E. (1984). *The discourse of medicine.* Norwood, NJ: Ablex.

Morris, G., & Chenail, R. (Eds.). (1995). *The talk of the clinic: Exploration in the analysis of medical and therapeutic discourse.* Hillsdale, NJ: Lawrence Erlbaum Associates.

Morris, J. (1991). *Pride against prejudice: Transforming attitudes to disability.* Philadelphia: New Society.

Murphy, R. (1987). *The body silent.* New York: Henry Holt.

Nagler, M. (Ed.). (1993). *Perspectives on disability* (2nd ed.). Palo Alto, CA: Health Markets Research.

Parsons, T. (1951). *The social system.* New York: Free Press.

Phillips, M. (1990). Damaged goods: Oral narratives of the experience of disability in American culture. *Social Science and Medicine, 30,* 849–857.

Schegloff, E. (1988). On an actual virtual servo-mechanism for guessing bad news: A single case conjecture. *Social Problems, 35*(4), 442–457.

Schegloff, E. (1992). On talk and its institutional occasions. In P. Drew & J. Heritage (Eds.), *Talk at work: Interaction in institutional settings* (pp. 101–136). New York: Cambridge University Press.

Schmidt, D., & Leppik, I. (Eds.). (1988). *Compliance in epilepsy.* New York: Elsevier.

Shapiro, J. (1993). *No pity: People with disabilities forging a new civil rights movement.* New York: Times Books.

Shaw, B. (Ed.). (1994). *The ragged edge: The disability experience from the pages of the first fifteen years of The Disability Rag.* Louisville, KY: Advocado Press.

Silverman, D. (1987). *Communication and medical practice: Social relations in the clinic.* Newbury Park, CA: Sage.

Van Maanen, J. (1988). *Tales of the field: On writing ethnography.* Chicago: University of Chicago Press.

Wilson, J., Braunwald, E., Isselbacher, K., Petersdorf, R., Martin, J., Fauci, A., & Root, R. (1991). *Harrison's principles of internal medicine* (12th ed.). New York: McGraw-Hill.

Zola, I. (1982). *Missing pieces: A chronicle of living with a disability.* Philadelphia: Temple University Press.

Part IV

INTERVENTION AS
SITUATED PRACTICE

The Construction of Incompetence During Group Therapy With Traumatically Brain Injured Adults

Dana Kovarsky
University of Rhode Island

Michael Kimbarow
Rehabilitation Institute of Michigan

Deborah Kastner
Wayne State University

INTRODUCTION

Language and language incompetence do not exist as independent phenomena in the heads of speakers; they present themselves in contexts of interaction. From an interaction vantage point, internal language capacities do not predict communicative proficiency:

> In order for two or more people to communicate, at whatever level of effectiveness, it is neither sufficient nor necessary that they "share" the same grammar. What they must share, to a variable degree, is the ability to orient themselves verbally, perceptually, and physically to each other and to their social world. (Hanks, 1996, p. 229)

Speakers with severely impaired language abilities are able to communicate quite effectively, given the right interactional circumstances. Goodwin (1995), for example, described how a man with aphasia, who produced only three words ("yes," "no," and "and"), was able to effect conversational meaning through the interactional work done by all participants: "Moreover, Rob's severe deficits in the production of words are not accompanied by equal restrictions on his ability to recognize, and actively participate in, the pragmatic organization of talk-in-interaction" (p. 252). The idea that language and language incompetence are situated interactionally is not a trivial one, particularly for professionals working with those suffering from brain injury. As Goodwin (1995) notes, failure to appreciate this point can have disastrous consequences:

> When Rob was in the hospital, his doctors, who had focused entirely on the trauma within his brain, said that any therapy would be merely cosmetic and a waste of time, because the underlying brain injury could not be remedied. Nothing could have been further from the truth, and medical advice based on such a view of the problem can cause irreparable harm to patients such as Rob and their families. As an injury, aphasia does reside within the skull. However, as a form of life, a way of being and acting in the world in concert with others, its proper locus is an endogenous, distributed, multiparty system. (p. 255)

Speech-language therapy is one of the contexts in which the language abilities and disabilities of those suffering from a brain injury come to interactional life. A primary goal of therapy from the speech-language pathologist's (SLP's) perspective is to improve the communicative competencies of individuals deemed to be impaired. Yet studies focusing on therapy as an interactional practice are in their infancy. For the most part, these investigations have analyzed dyadic, individualized therapy sessions involving an SLP and a child. Similar to other studies of professional discourse, particularly classrooms (Cazden, 1988; Mehan, 1985; Sinclair & Coulthard, 1975), these investigations reveal interactional asymmetries (Duchan, 1993; Kovarsky & Duchan, 1997; Panagos, 1996; Prutting et al., 1978). SLPs tend to regulate the distribution and evaluation of information, and control access to the interactional floor to achieve a set of prespecified goals and objectives (Kovarsky, 1990; Kovarsky & Duchan, 1997; McTear & King, 1991). This type of intervention has been dubbed "trainer-oriented" or "adult-controlled" (Fey, 1986).

In their strong form, "trainer-oriented approaches" consist of tightly scripted games and routines that are regulated by the SLP (Kovarsky & Duchan, 1997). Practitioners are oriented toward evaluating and repairing perceived errors in the client's communicative performance (Damico & Damico, 1997). Such repairs often manifest themselves in three-part, evaluative sequences similar to those described in the literature on classroom discourse (Cazden, 1988; Sinclair & Coulthard, 1975). Here, the SLP makes a request for known information (a quiz question), the child responds, and the clinician evaluates the appropriateness of that response. If the answer is judged appropriate by the clinician, no repair work is undertaken. If the response is considered inappropriate, repair work is initiated until the child provides the desired response. In these repair trajectories, clinicians may provide a series of hints and clues over a number of turns until the child produces the correct reply (Kovarsky, 1989a). On receipt of the appropriate response, the clinician frequently offers an overt, evaluative comment such as "good talking," "great job," or "okay." These evaluative markers may be accompanied by nonverbal gestures like smiling and vertical head nodding (Damico & Damico, 1997; Kovarsky, 1989b).

In other words, traditional therapy often revolves around correcting errors in performance of those who are perceived to have problems in communicating: "We will change anything and everything in an effort to get that ultimate plum of teaching—the correct response" (van Kleeck & Richardson, 1986, p. 25). Put another way, without errors to remediate, there would be no therapy. This error-maker expectancy pervades trainer-oriented approaches: Clients come to therapy because of perceived communicative incompetencies and participants construct therapy around remediating these mistakes (Kovarsky & Maxwell, 1992). Within this interactional framework, clinicians declare what communicative performances are to be judged as inadequate and when these errors are considered to be "fixed."

While these studies do reveal global asymmetries, they do not fully address how participants negotiate meaning during therapy. This chapter goes beyond previous investigations in two ways. First, instead of focusing on dyads with children, data involving an SLP working with a group of adults with traumatic brain injuries are examined. Second, attention is focused on how participants work to construct meaning on a turn-by-turn basis rather than being focused on interactional asymmetries. This type of analysis provides a window for viewing how competence and incompetence are negotiated in group language therapy speech events.

COLLECTING AND ANALYZING THE DATA

Group language therapy sessions involving at least one SLP and adults with traumatic brain injury (TBI) were videotaped and transcribed. Video recording took place in a large rehabilitation hospital located within an urban complex of medical facilities. The rehabilitation unit housed a variety of allied health professionals, including occupational, physical, recreational, and speech-language therapists. While a total of 20 sessions were recorded over a 5-week period, this investigation focused on the first session because it was here that particular communicative practices emerged that were sustained across subsequent meetings. On any given day, the caseload of the SLP could vary depending on the number of admissions to the TBI unit and the nature of the injuries suffered by the patients. Over the course of the entire investigation, group size varied from two to six patients. In this session, the SLP conducted therapy with five adult participants.

Individuals had to meet the following criteria established by the rehabilitation unit before being allowed to take part in group therapy: (a) mild
to moderate impairment of cognitive-communication skills; (b) the ability
to sustain dyadic interactions in conversation; (c) the capacity to recall the
content of structured interactions within therapy sessions; (d) the ability
to orient to the purpose of the therapy group; (e) the facility to initiate
social greetings; (f) the capacity to orient to person, place, and time during
an interaction; and (g) the ability to utilize compensatory strategies for
activities such as recalling information. Finally, all participants had to score
5, or better, on the Ranchos Los Amigos Scale. In other words, individuals
had to reach a certain level of environmental and communicative awareness
before being allowed to participate in group therapy.

Prior to videotaping and transcribing the group language therapy sessions, the SLP who conducted this session was interviewed. She was asked
to discuss the nature of her workday at the rehabilitation hospital, her
clinical background and interests, and the goals and objectives of intervention in this setting.

The three co-authors met on a regular basis to review the videotaped
session and the accompanying orthographic transcription. Because the
SLP who conducted the group therapy session had a full caseload, she did
not have an opportunity to participate in these videotape review sessions.
However, one of the co-authors (M. Kimbarow) who viewed the tapes was
in charge of the rehabilitation unit, familiar with the SLP who conducted
group therapy, and had over 20 years of professional experience as an SLP
with adult populations.

DESCRIBING THE INTERACTIONS

Analysis revealed that therapy consisted of a series of gamelike activities
where much of the interactional work done by the SLP was to ensure
that patients followed the rules. There were times when this focus on
the rules appeared to be at odds with the overall goals of intervention.
Furthermore, when playing these games, memory was often treated as a
static, decontextualized skill requiring individuals to generate and remember lists of items. Discussions between the SLP and the adult clients
concerning how these generated lists might be constructed or remembered, with respect to personal human experiences, were frequently
discouraged.

Together, these communicative practices served to reduce the level of
competency displayed by the patients in therapy. That is, the data revealed
a mismatch between the overall purpose of intervention—to facilitate the
communicative competencies of individuals with TBI in everyday life—and

the interactional patterning of therapy. Since intervention is a planned speech event, understanding the relationship between the agenda of the professional and the moment-to-moment unfolding of intervention is crucial. It is our contention that prevailing clinical practices and institutional constraints provide a ready resource for constructing incompetence among individuals with TBI during therapy.

The remainder of this discussion is organized as follows. First, the institutional constraints of the rehabilitation setting are considered. Next, the overall goals of intervention within the TBI unit are described, followed by a discussion of the SLP's clinical agenda within this context. It is argued that the intervention activities described by the SLP are based on models that disembed language and cognition from everyday activities. It is against this backdrop that the competency-lowering practices of the session are presented on a turn-by-turn basis through transcribed examples. Finally, the implications of these findings are discussed.

INSTITUTIONAL CONSTRAINTS OF THE REHABILITATION SETTING: PLANNING AND SCHEDULING THERAPY

The population served by the rehabilitation hospital was quite varied. Patients ranged from 20 to 60 years of age and were members of a variety of cultural and ethnic groups. The traumatic brain injuries sustained by these individuals were most often the result of assaults and motor vehicle accidents. An effort was made to serve these individuals soon after their accidents to maximize treatment outcomes. Because people came to the unit on an emergency basis, therapists often had little advance notice as to who would be joining or leaving their caseloads from one day to the next. As the SLP stated, "there is no typical day" because of the heterogeneous nature of the injuries suffered by individuals with TBI, their consequences, and difficulties scheduling therapy:

> . . . if someone's agitated, you spend a lot of time convincing them to leave the room and come to therapy . . . if my nine o'clock is ready, I'll start with that. If they're not ready, I look around and see who's free. And if they're free, I grab 'em. And that's also a good way to judge if they're flexible. Because we've got patients, that on the schedule [if] it says ten-thirty, they will say "I will NOT come see you before ten-thirty."

Given the unpredictability of scheduling and the nature of injuries suffered by individuals with TBI, planning therapy could be difficult. Beyond this, the SLP added that one of the most troublesome intervention issues was the lack of information about the personalities of individuals before their injuries:

> . . . [individuals with TBI] have all these deficits but premorbid personality, I think, plays a huge role in how the person is after the injury. And that's why I REALLY like to talk to the family. And with our population it's often not possible 'cause there isn't any family, or isn't any family who cares to be involved. And it's sad. It makes it tough because you have no baseline. You have no clue. This person's weird [but] were they weird before? There is no normal person . . . so somebody seeing me after a head injury doesn't know if maybe I didn't say a word before. They don't know.

Without background information, it was hard to intervene in a way that accounted for the individual lifeworlds of those receiving therapy. This, coupled with the lack of predictability in scheduling and the diversity of injuries, encouraged a situation where therapy games were selected and played by a set of rules that had little to do with personal human experience. In this way, there was a baseline for judging therapy performance without regard to the life histories and perspectives of those with TBI.

Finally, with respect to planning, there were issues in accountability and reimbursement from health care providers. With health care practices in the United States undergoing radical transition concerning how services will be funded, the therapists must have objective measures for demonstrating progress in order for the rehabilitation unit to receive funding. Influenced by positivistic models of science and progress, accountability translates into counting behaviors that can be measured reliably. Therapy activities that, for example, measure improved memory according to the number of listed words produced by individuals with TBI lend themselves to this kind of accountability. Perhaps what is most ironic is that although insurance companies are interested in accountability, they are also concerned with how therapy outcomes relate to the patient's social adjustment in the world. Although the memory game described in this chapter may satisfy the need for bookkeeping and numbers, it did not necessarily address concerns for ecological validity raised by some health care providers who fund therapeutic services.

PROBLEMS THAT CHARACTERIZE PATIENTS WITH TBI

The SLP summarized the types of problems characteristic of traumatic brain injury:

. . . typically, as far as the speech therapist angle, a typical TBI patient has **memory deficits**, has **attention deficits**, [and] generally has **problem solving deficits**. It's just how severe they are [that varies]. And I and I tell Mark [head of the TBI unit] you know we could make up a menu for our reports often times. With, you know, okay they have a memory problem, how severe is it you know. Pick mild, moderate, severe, profound. And uh **problem solving, thought organization, the ability to generate lists and to or to organize to complete a task**. You know what d'you do first, what d'you do second, what d'you do third.

The boldfaced portions of this passage reveal the SLP's tendency to locate TBI internally according to intrinsic, cognitive deficits suffered by individuals: "memory deficits," "attention deficits," difficulties with "problem solving," "the ability to generate lists" and "thought organization."

The comments of the SLP were consistent with published literature describing patients recovering from TBI. These characteristics include "process[ing] information inefficiently"; "shallow recent memory and poor access to knowledge"; "impaired attention, concentration, and ability to shift attentional focus"; "general inefficiency in processing information"; "inefficient retrieval of information and of words"; "poorly organized behavior and language expression"; and "relatively marked deterioration of comprehension caused by increases in the amount, complexity, and abstractness of information and in the rate of presentation" (Haarbauer-Krupa, Henry, Szekeres, & Ylvisaker, 1985a, p. 311; Haarbauer-Krupa, Moser, Smith, Sullivan, & Szekeres, 1985b, p. 287).

On the other hand, some of the concerns for patients with TBI, mentioned by the SLP, were more interactionally oriented:

Attention. . . . Are they able to follow along? When they're not being spoken to directly, are they looking out the window? . . . The ability to follow in the conversation . . . from one to another.

[The] pragmatics involved in conversation [are a problem]. You know, the body language. We've got 'em heads down on the table. [And] some of them will just push right away from the table, not say a word and leave [in the middle of a conversation]. I mean you're like wait, wait, wait, where ya' goin?

The SLP indicated that one of her biggest surprises was that individuals with TBI often did not become fully aware of their "limitations" until after they left the rehabilitation hospital:

. . . it was so surprising to me at first when people just weren't aware [of their own problems] even when you're telling them. . . . You're in a closed little world up on the unit. You generally see a transition [to greater awareness about having a problem] after they've gone for a TLOA, a therapeutic leave of absence. . . . They'll come back early because they couldn't take it. They'll say "It was too much and I was getting a headache and I just had to come back here." If they have an experience [like that] that's when I'll start to see a change, when they start to have some real awareness.

THE GOALS OF THERAPY

The overriding goal of the rehabilitation unit, with all its different therapeutic specialties, was to help TBI patients achieve their highest level of "functionality" and "independence" so that their transition back into the social world outside the hospital would be more successful. As part of realizing this goal, the SLP was aware that the therapeutic process was closely tied to issues of identity and identity transformation subsequent to traumatic brain injury. She expressed concern because the relationship between therapy and the identities and personal experiences of individuals was a difficult one to address:

> . . . we're not trying to make people back into you know high school teachers or whatever it was before . . . if I have any idea what that is. . . . You know I'm not one of those people who thinks I'm going to change this person's life. . . . [Therapy's] real **functional**. So you know if they're finishin' up their lunch or their breakfast I'll go in and you know we'll talk about what'd you have for breakfast? What'd ya have for lunch? What are ya doin'? . . . Where ya been? Where ya goin'? Where's your room. . . . Tryin' to do functional things around the unit. . . . Um things that they're gonna have to do . . . **activities of daily living**. You know if they need something who are they gonna ask if they don't know? Can they figure it out on their own? You know brushing your teeth uh . . . If they're gonna brush their teeth do they know to put the toothpaste on before they start brushing not after? . . . How is this person functioning in relationship to what they have to do for their daily life? Can they locate information? Can they problem solve? If they go into their room and there's something in the way, can they figure out what to do?

The rehabilitation was situated within a large metropolitan medical center where patients from all walks of life were constantly being admitted to the unit. Because of this, little was known about the personal life histories and experiences of these individuals prior to their injuries. This, coupled with the belief that therapy would not transform those with TBI back to their pre-injury status, meant that the goals of increased functionality and independence were reduced to a set of objectifiable "activities of daily living," which did not directly focus on the life situations and experiences of individuals.

To help patients achieve some degree of functional independence, the SLP directed her efforts toward improving memory, attending to conversation, and problem-solving. Here, memory was seen as a skill that could be treated on the periphery of interaction through drills: "We do more direct drill type things where we work on memory . . . you know that's not so much interacting with each other."

Along with these individual goals, the main purpose of group therapy was to facilitate "social interaction and pragmatics":

> I mean this person's gonna go and no matter where they're going, they're not gonna be locked in a little cell by themselves. [The purpose of group therapy is to] help them become the most appropriate at interacting that they can. I mean you've got I've got all these other individual goals. But overall, as a group therapy [goal], interaction and interaction with other people [is] important because [it] is such a part of our lives. And so many, if you watch on the unit, they isolate themselves . . . they don't know how to interact. Many of the patients have no initiation at all. [And] turn taking. Do they know when it's their turn? . . . Especially when we do a lot of games . . . do they know when it's their turn?

Analysis of the videotaped therapy sessions revealed that efforts were made to realize these different intervention goals by engaging clients in a variety of game activities: ". . . we do a lot of games . . . scavenger hunt [and] board games . . . where we work on memory . . . and we do some more direct drill type things where we work on memory." Memory drills, for example, would be nested within games where patients had to remember lists of words. A turn-by-turn description of one of these games—called Going to the Moon—is presented later.

At the same time, because the abilities of individuals with TBI to follow and sustain a conversation were seen as deficient, games provided a structure through which to build interactional coherence.

> . . . we do games [to see if] they know when it's their turn . . . turn taking is often [addressed] during the game because often times the dialogue is more directed by us. We ask a question of so and so . . . and we move from person to person to try and facilitate some interaction.

By defining successful participation according to the preestablished rules of a game, the SLP was in a position to judge the appropriateness of individual contributions to the group topic, and to intervene when necessary. Coherence could be reduced and managed according to the rules of the game, and not the personal experiences and histories that players brought to the activity.

In sum, games could thus be viewed as a means of accomplishing a complex, clinical online agenda—improving memory through drill work and building interactional coherence among individuals.

Models of Language and Cognition

The idea of treating intrinsic problems of mind through various types of drill activities is consistent with certain psychological models of language and cognition that have strongly influenced speech-language pathology as a professional discipline. From this vantage point, language and cognition are seen as internal processes of mind. These processes are like a set of tools to be pulled out of a mental folder and applied to the external, social world:

> The mind and its contents have been treated rather like a well-filled toolbox. Knowledge [language included] is conceived of as a set of tools stored in memory, carried around by individuals who take the tools out and use them . . . after which they are stowed away again without any change at any time during the process. The metaphor is especially apt given that tools are designed to resist change or destruction through conditions of their use. (Lave, 1988, p. 25)

When internal, mental processes, such as memory, break down, the practitioner seeks to repair the breakdown, or help the impaired individual compensate for it. From this perspective, games are a therapeutic means for addressing intrinsic cognitive problems caused by traumatic brain injury in areas such as attention, perception, sequencing, problem-solving and planning, and memory (Deaton, 1991):

> *Memory skills* are tapped by such games as Concentration, Memory, Numbers Up, and Enchanted Forest. These games can facilitate the acquisition and use of strategies such as rehearsal or association. They also lend themselves to teaching the use of external memory aids such as lists, as it will quickly become apparent to the client that his or her performance on the game improves dramatically when this additional tool is available to aid in recall. (p. 205)

Concerns about this type of clinical reasoning can be raised with respect to the cognitive model being applied to intervention. Conceptualizing of the mind as a set of internal tools that remain constant when applied to the external, social world overlooks the interaction between the tool and the situation of its use:

> . . . when "tool" is used as a metaphor for knowledge-in-use across settings, there is assumed to be no interaction between tool and situation, but only an *application* of the tool on different occasions. Since situations are not assumed to impinge on the tool itself, [the] theory . . . does not require an

account of situations, much less the relations among them. Knowledge acquisition may be considered . . . as if the social context of activity had no critical effects on knowledge-in-use. (Lave, 1988, p. 41)

Such a view permits improved memory, a part of the toolbox that can be isolated from those social occasions of its use, to be the goal of therapy without addressing the relationship between the game activity and how remembering is displayed in everyday contexts of interaction.

Instead of focusing on the processes in the internal mental toolbox, Lave (1988) proposes a different unit of analysis for examining cognition and learning:

. . . the whole person in action, acting within settings of that activity. This shifts the boundaries of [cognitive] activity well outside the skull . . . to persons engaged in the social world for a variety of reasons. (pp. 17–18)

. . . knowledge in practice, constituted in settings of practice, is the locus of the most powerful knowledgeability of people in the lived-in world. (p. 14)

. . . [this view] motivates a different set of problems and questions than the study of virtuoso performance and people's failures to produce such performances. (p. 15)

This situated perspective would suggest an important relationship between the display of cognitive abilities, such as memory, and the social contexts in which they occur. In the Going to the Moon activity presented subsequently, memory was accessed through an alphabetical strategy congruent with the rules of the game, but inconsistent with how the remembering of lists might surface during other types of interaction in the everyday world.

GOING TO THE MOON: MEMORY, THE ROLE OF HUMAN EXPERIENCE, AND FOLLOWING THE RULES OF THE GAME

The reliance on gamelike activities to carry the interactional work of therapy, and the treatment of memory as a skill isolated from the everyday world, were evidenced in the Going to the Moon game. During this game, each person was asked to think of an item they would want to bring to the moon. As subsequent people took their turns, they also had to repeat all the items mentioned previously and then add a new one of their own. The item selected had to begin with a letter that corresponded to successive letters in the alphabet. In other words, the first individual had to name an item that began with the letter A, the second person had to name an item that began with the letter B, and so on. The SLP was oriented toward

having the patients verbally repeat a growing list of alphabetically se-
quenced items, which could be named in successive turns by each individual. At the end of the game, the therapist indicated that the "repetitiveness
of the activity and using the alphabet [were] clues" to help the group with
remembering the list.

The therapist asked none of the patients why they would want to bring
certain items and made moves to limit such discussions if initiated by
members of the group. In the following example, Mr. Harvey (Mr. H) was
selected as the next participant and told that his contribution must begin
with the letter C (turn #121).[1]

121.	SLP:	Now Mr. HARvey your letter is C/ But you have to remember to add mine and Barry's and then yours (SLP pointing to herself, Mr. Harvey, and Barry successively)/
122.	Mr. H:	So (clears throat) my voyage is to the moon/
123.	SLP:	Mm hm/
124.	Mr. H:	On/
125.	SLP:	And you're gonna take=
126.	Mr. H:	= I'm going to take along ((pause)) writing paper ((pause))
127.	SLP:	Okay hold on/
128.	Mr. H:	Something I can make a bench with/
129.	SLP:	You're on the right track ((pause)) but what you need to do is repeat what I said ((pause))/ What did I say I was taking/
130.	Mr. H:	You was taking an apple/
131.	SLP:	Good and what was Barry taking/
132.	Mr. H:	He was taking along ((pause)) a book/
133.	SLP:	Good/ Now YOU have to think of something that begins with the letter C 'cause we're going through the alphabet/ So you need to think of someth- it doesn't have to be something you'd really take/It could be⌈ something silly/
134.	Mr. H:	⌊ Mm hmm/
135.	SLP:	But you need to think of something/ A word that begins with the letter C/
136.	Mr. H:	I see ((pause)) um ((pause)) I'll take along ((pause)) mm a ((pause)) CAMera/
137.	SLP:	Very good/ (looking at person seated next to Mr. H) Walter/

Mr. Harvey began by reiterating the experience on which his memory
was to be based: "my voyage is to the moon" (turn #122). He continued
by listing items that could be used for the purpose of writing on his journey
(turns #126 and #128). At this point, the SLP stopped Mr. Harvey and

---

[1]Transcription Key: / marks the end of an utterance; ( ) nonverbal behavior enclosed in
parentheses; ((pause)) double parentheses contain untimed pauses; = indicates latched
utterances with no gap and no overlap in between; CAPS indicate increased stress or emphasis;
heh marks laughter; [indicates point of overlap between utterances.

indicated that he was not following the rules of the game because he did not repeat items mentioned previously by other members of the group (turns #127, #129, and #131). After Mr. Harvey stated (in alphabetical succession) what other group members were bringing to the moon, the SLP indicated her approval (turn #133).

The SLP then attempted to clarify the rules of the game, indicating that Mr. Harvey must constrain his response to something "that begins with the letter C." Furthermore, his response need not be tied to anything one might want to "really take" to the moon. Instead, his reply "could be something silly," as long as the item began with the appropriate letter in the alphabet. When Mr. Harvey provided the appropriate answer, "a camera," the SLP indicated her approval (turn #137). In other words, based on the rules of the game, the appropriate display of memory was grounded in successive letters of the alphabet, as opposed to any imagined experience of going to the moon.

Later in the game, Mr. Harvey tried again, on two different occasions, to tie this memory game to the experience of going to the moon (turns #159, #161, and #197). In both instances, the SLP discouraged this type of remembering:

154.	SLP:	So/ Your turn Mr. Harvey/
155.	Mr. H:	Mm ((pause)) On this trip to the moon ((pause)) c- carema
156.	SLP:	Whoa- you have to start with A/ (SLP pointing to herself) What did I say/ What was the A=
157.	Mr. H:	=Got your apple/
158.	SLP:	Uh huh/ And ((pause)) what did Barry
		⌐say (SLP pointing to Barry)/
159.	Mr. H:	└I didn't want to leave it
		expose⌐d/
160.	SLP:	└Heh
161.	Mr. H:	Might be chemical reaction could destroy your apple (Mr. H smiles)/
162.	SLP:	Well we're not really
		⌐going to the moon/ This is this is just practice
163.	Barry:	├Heh heh
164.	Mr. H:	└I know I know (smiling)/
165.	SLP:	Okay I said an apple/ What had Barry said that first time/

.
.
.

196.	SLP:	He had H ((pause)) and you're next/ What letter do you have now/
197.	Mr. H:	Um ((pause)) well I would like to carry along ((pause)) limited vitamins or something/
198.	SLP:	Okay hold on a minute though/ It has his began with the letter H/ What letter comes after H in the alphabet/

199. Mr. H: I/
200. SLP: I/ So your word has to start with an I/
201. Mr. H: Oh/
202. SLP: Heh heh heh you got the hard one heh heh heh/

In turns #159 and #161, Mr. Harvey indicated that he did not want to leave the apple "exposed" because there "might be chemical reaction that could destroy your apple." The SLP responded, "Well we're not really going to the moon" and "This is . . . just practice." As Pomerantz (1983, p. 72) notes, "well" is one way of "prefacing [a] disagreement . . . thus displaying reluctancy or discomfort." In this instance, "Well" prefaced a statement that served to minimize Mr. Harvey's continued efforts to tie memory to personal experience without respecting the rules of the game.

Finally, in turn #197, Mr. Harvey indicated that he would like to bring along some vitamins, presumably because nutrients would be a concern to someone experiencing space travel. The therapist responded by saying "okay." As a discourse marker, one of the functions of "okay" is to release a participant from a prior turn at talk (Schiffrin, 1987). In speech-language therapy, these markers may simultaneously hold an evaluative function, indicating whether the prior contribution is judged to be appropriate or inappropriate (Kovarsky, 1989b, 1990). In turn #198, the SLP indicated that Mr. Harvey's contribution was not correct by saying "hold on a minute," and then redirected him to provide an appropriate contribution based on the next letter in the alphabet.

In all of the cases above, Mr. Harvey attempted to address how the personal experience of going to the moon would relate to those items he would want to bring on the trip. Indeed, memories often surface in interaction as a way of relating personal experiences through the presentation of particularistic details and concrete images (Tannen, 1989). Yet the therapist indicated that this was not how remembering was to be achieved. Instead, the task of remembering was disembedded from personal experience and rooted in a list of words based on the alphabetical ordering of items.

Strict adherence to the rules of this game could be viewed as a competency-lowering communicative practice. By not allowing memory tasks to be grounded in experience, either real or imagined, participants were prevented from using a potential resource for remembering: a resource that some individuals with TBI were clearly able to draw upon in other contexts. Before a different group therapy session began, Larry (a patient) was explaining to a fellow patient about insurance benefits. This description, which related to Larry's previous experience in the rehabilitation hospital, contained remembrances of prior interactions:

Larry: Did you talk to the social worker yet about all your bills or stuff on
        whatever your benefits/ Did you get the benefits/ You will be able

to right/ If you get in an accident you'll be able to get'em/ That's what she told me/ That's what the lady told me/ She says "you're in an accident buddy"/ "you're you're you're somebody's gonna give you money"/ That's what she told me/ Maybe not your car insurance but through state/

Larry effectively recounted a prior experience that contributed to the overall point of the interaction: that his listener needs to find out about insurance benefits.

There are also instances in which lists may present themselves in interaction (Tannen, 1989). In the following example, a woman is recalling information about an office coworker:

And he knows Spanish,
and he knows French,
and he knows English,
and he knows German,
and he is a gentleman.
(Tannen, 1989, p. 50)

The listed items contributed to the evaluative point being made by the speaker: that she "finds the length of the list impressive—and so should the listener" (Tannen, 1989, pp. 50–51).

The Going to the Moon game is not rooted in experience and the word list does not emerge as part of a larger conversational point. Rather, the list is generated for its own sake during therapy. In this way, memory is isolated from experience and disembodied from larger segments of talk-in-interaction in which remembrances may present themselves. In other words, the particular gamelike practices of this therapy activity provided a context in which communicative incompetencies were more likely to surface, as in the case of Mr. Harvey.

On the other hand, as long as participants were playing by the rules of the game, there were instances of more supportive communicative practices. Below, a misunderstanding about the meaning of the word "edge" becomes a resource for Jay's successful recounting of what objects he would take to the moon:

139. Jay: Goin' to the moon/ Taking a apple a book ((pause)) camera a dock and an edge to practice some of my golf/
140. SLP: An edge okay (heh heh heh)/
141. Pam: An edge/
142. Jay: Um hmm/
143. SLP: Edge/
144. Pam: What is an edge/
145. Jay: It's a golf club/

146.   Pam: Oh okay/

Jay indicated that "an edge" was a "golf club." While the term "edge" fits
the rules of the game because it begins with the appropriate letter of the
alphabet, it represents a mistake. The golf club Jay referred to is actually
called a "wedge." However, no one in the group mentioned this error.
When asked about this error after the session, the SLP laughed and said
she had no knowledge of golf and no idea whether or not an "edge" was
a club. Furthermore, when Jay stated he would use the "edge" to practice
golf (turn #139), he was not admonished by the SLP for relating his
contribution to the list to a personal experience. It would seem that as
long as the alphabetical rule for participation was not violated, therapy
participants could discuss their internal motivations for bringing certain
items to the moon.

Later, when Mr. Harvey had trouble recalling Jay's contribution to the
list, the SLP provided a hint by pointing to Jay (turn #337) and mentioning
that the item was "a golf club" (turn #339):

337.   SLP: There you go/ And after that came ((pause)) the one that
                begins with an E (SLP points to Jay)/
338.   Mr. H: ((pause)) Mm E ((pause)) E E E I can't exactly get that
                one/
339.   SLP: It's a ((pause)) golf club
340.   Mr. H: Somethin' (shakes head sideways) I know nothing
                abo⌈ut
341.   SLP: ⌊Or you might
                say this is th⌈ree ((pause)) (SLP patting to edge of table))
342.   Pam: ⌈Something of night/
343.   Mr. H: ⌊E-   Edge/
344.   Pam: The edge of night/
345.   SLP: Yeah/
346.   SLP: So edge/ What was F/

In turn #340, Mr. Harvey indicated he knew nothing about golf. The SLP
then changed the nature of her clue by pointing to the edge of the table
which signaled the conventional referent for the word "edge." At the same
time, Pam provided a hint, saying "Something of night" (turn #342), in
reference to the soap opera "The Edge of Night" (turn #344). Subsequent
to the clues provided by Pam and the SLP, Mr. Harvey produced the
appropriate response. In other words, within the confines of this activity,
"edge" became a homonym for both a golf club and its conventional concrete
definition. To a degree, as long as the players adhered to the rules of the
game, word meaning could be appropriated to facilitate memory.

As Jacoby and Ochs (1995) suggest: "relying only on the informational,
semantic, and propositional content of words and utterances will fail to

get at what utterances might be doing as actions in a sequence of detailed interactional events" (p. 176). Providing clues that were not tied to golf, something outside Mr. Harvey's claimed realm of experience, was a supportive move within the confines of the game. This example illustrates that word meaning could be brought into play during therapy, as long as the rules of the game were not violated.

DISCUSSION

Ways of remembering tied to personal experience were sanctioned negatively when they violated the alphabetical, listing rules of the game. Because this activity was divorced from how memories surface in other communicative contexts, it had the potential for constraining the display of memory during therapy. In this sense, the manner in which the Going to the Moon game was played could be viewed as a competency-lowering practice. When remembered lists do appear in interaction, they contribute to the overall point of the interaction and are not an end in themselves (Tannen, 1989). During therapy, however, a list was generated for the sole purpose of taxing an area of presumed deficit (i.e., memory) among individuals with TBI. The point of this therapy activity was to recall a list of items according to successive letters in the alphabet, irrespective of relevant personal experience.

This session appeared to be at odds with the overall purpose of intervention. Although the long-term goal of therapy and of the whole rehabilitation unit was functional independence in the social world, activities like playing Going to the Moon disembedded both language and cognition from the communicative practices of everyday life. In doing so, therapy participants were at greater risk for displaying incompetence because they were not allowed to draw upon important resources and purposes for communicating memory found in everyday interaction.

Several facets of therapy provide a ready set of resources for the construction of incompetence. First, in this rehabilitative setting, numerous patients were seen on an emergency basis and little or no information on their premorbid status was available. It becomes easy to overlook personal life experience in planning and implementing intervention when such information is not readily accessible. Second, it would be naive to suggest that individuals with traumatic brain injury have no intrinsic problems. In fact, models of language and cognition within the discipline of speech-language pathology have traditionally led practitioners to remediate these internal deficits by fixing or correcting errors in performance through extended repair sequences. Third, the gamelike activity, which was based on a currently established set of rules, provided a context for (a) building interactional coherence among group members without necessarily having to account for their personal life histories, (b) practicing memory through drill activities like remembering a sequence of words, and (c) divorcing memory from everyday life. In these ways, problems in remembering a list of words could be attributed to the intrinsic propensities of individuals with TBI and not to the rules of the game.

In sum, the particular models of language and cognition that influence the discipline of speech-language pathology—the error-maker expectancy, the complex clinical agenda, and the manner in which intervention is planned and scheduled—all contribute to therapy practices where games like Going to the Moon are constructed. Taken together, these facets of intervention may have provided the resources for divorcing therapeutic interaction from the communicative life experiences of individuals with TBI: a context in which the display of personal experiences and motivations does not help constitute competent performance. This was particularly problematic, given that the overall goal of intervention within the rehabilitation unit was functionality and independence in the social world.

All this is not to imply that both practitioners and researchers within the discipline of communicative disorders are unaware of such contextualization problems. There has been a growing concern that the way in which practitioners have been trained to locate and address problems serves to isolate (or, according to Kent, 1990, fragment) language and cognition from their interactive contexts of use:

> Based on a fragmentation orientation, we were trained in speech-language pathology to segment and decontextualize the communicative behaviors we observe and immediately attempt to find deficits within a client's internalized psychological/linguistic system rather than focus on the full and complex array of variables and behaviors that make up the communicative process. It is this narrow focus . . . and its resulting orientation toward fragmentation of human behavior that has caused our professional difficulties. Because of this narrow focus, our attempts to address the complex phenomenon of communicative discourse with a superficial and modular approach to description, assessment, and remediation are naive and insufficient. (Damico, 1993, p. 93)

The results of fragmentation have also been discussed with respect to traditional language intervention practices, which:

> . . . emphasize output and quantifying performance (e.g., counting various linguistic structures elicited, arranging reinforcement schedules for target behaviors, etc.). In other words, the essence of therapy is getting the client to do something so that the clinician can say, "I saw it, I counted it, and I reinforced it." How "it" is elicited and what "it" really means to the client

(important questions from a pragmatic perspective) have not been critical issues. (Dejoy, 1991, p. 18)

Realizing that mismatches can exist between the overall goals of intervention and what happens in therapy has led some students of language disorders to call for theories and framewords that are more attuned to language as a communicative practice (see Damico, 1993; Duchan, 1997; Duchan, Hewitt, & Sonnenmeirer, 1994; Kovarsky & Crago, 1991; Kovarsky & Maxwell, 1997; Maxwell, 1993). One common theme they share is echoed by Jacoby and Ochs (1995): "things allegedly in people's heads—such as cognition and attitudes, linguistic competence, or pragmatic and cultural knowledge—are made relevant to communication through social interaction" (p. 175).

Competence with respect to language and cognition cannot be predicted simply by noting the presence of an internal, traumatic brain injury. Indeed, as the Going to the Moon data demonstrated, therapeutic situations may be constructed in ways that serve to lower the competencies displayed by patients. The manner in which language disabilities are constituted in patterned ways through interaction should be a vital concern for both researchers and practitioners who seek to understand language disorders. It is important for practitioners to recognize that the process of defining a language problem is itself an interactional achievement shaped by the emergent context: a context that includes a number of resources which participants draw on to construct meaning. Failure to recognize this can lead professionals to narrow frameworks for judging the communicative abilities of those who are deemed impaired. On a theoretical plane, models of language that do not address social interactions as a primary concern do little to enhance our understanding of the human world where "people go about managing their identities, their relationships, and their lives" (Jacoby & Ochs, 1995, p. 179).

REFERENCES

Cazden, C. B. (1988). *Classroom discourse: The language of teaching and learning.* Portsmouth, NH: Heinemann.

Damico, J. S. (1993). Establishing expertise in communicative discourse. *ASHA Monographs, 30*, 92–98.

Damico, J. S., & Damico, S. K. (1997). The establishment of a dominant interpretive framework in language intervention. *Language, Speech, and Hearing Services in Schools,* 288–296.

Deaton, A. V. (1991). Rehabilitating cognitive impairments through the use of games. In J. S. Kreutzer & P. H. Wehman (Eds.), *Cognitive rehabilitation for persons with traumatic brain injury* (pp. 201–213). Baltimore: Brookes.

Dejoy, D. (1991). Overcoming fragmentation through the client-clinician relationship. *National Student Speech, Language, Hearing Association Journal, 18*, 17–25.

Duchan, J. F. (1993). Clinician-child interaction: Its nature and potential. *Seminars in Speech and Language, 4*, 53–61.

Duchan, J. F. (1997). A situated pragmatics approach for supporting children with severe communication disorders. *Topics in Language Disorders, 17*(2), 1–18.

Duchan, J. F., Hewitt, L. E., & Sonnenmeier, R. M. (1994). *Pragmatics: From theory to practice.* Englewood Cliffs, NJ: Prentice-Hall.

Fey, M. (1986). *Language intervention with young children.* San Diego, CA: College-Hill Press.

Goodwin, C. (1995). Co-constructing meaning in conversations with an aphasic man. *Research on Language and Social Interaction, 28*(3), 233–260.

Haarbauer-Krupar, J., Henry, K., Szekeres, S. F., & Ylvisaker, M. (1985). Cognitive rehabilitation therapy: Late stages of recovery. In M. Ylvisaker (Ed.), *Head injury rehabilitation* (pp. 311–341). San Diego, CA: College-Hill Press.

Haarbauer-Krupa, J., Moser, L., Smith, G., Sullivan, D. M., & Szekeres, S. F. (1985). Cognitive rehabilitation therapy: Middle stages of recovery. In M. Ylvisaker (Ed.), *Head injury rehabilitation* (pp. 287–310). San Diego, CA: College-Hill Press.

Hanks, W. F. (1996). *Language and communicative practices.* Boulder, CO: Westview Press.

Jacoby, S., & Ochs, E. (1995) Co-construction: An introduction. *Research on Language and Social Interaction, 28*(3), 171–183.

Kent, R. (1990). Fragmentation of clinical services and clinical science in communication disorders. *National Student Speech, Language, Hearing Association Journal, 17*, 4–16.

Kovarsky, D. (1989a). *An ethnography of communication in child language therapy.* Unpublished doctoral dissertation, University of Texas at Austin.

Kovarsky, D. (1989b). On the occurrence of *okay* in child language therapy. *Child Language Teaching and Therapy, 5*(2), 137–145.

Kovarsky, D. (1990). Discourse markers in adult-controlled therapy: Implications for child-centered intervention. *Journal of Childhood Communication Disorders, 13*, 29–41.

Kovarsky, D., & Crago, M. (1991). Toward the ethnography of communication disorders. *National Student Speech, Language, Hearing Association Journal, 18*, 44–55.

Kovarsky, D., & Duchan, J. F. (1997). The interactional dimensions of language therapy. *Language, Speech, and Hearing Services in Schools, 28*, 297–308.

Kovarsky, D., & Maxwell, M. (1992). Ethnography and the clinical setting: Communicative expectancies in clinical discourse. *Topics in Language Disorders, 12*(3), 76–84.

Kovarsky, D., & Maxwell, M. (1997). Rethinking the context of language in schools. *Language, Speech, and Hearing Services in Schools, 28*, 219–230.

Lave, J. (1988). *Cognition in practice.* New York: Cambridge University Press.

Maxwell, M. (1993). Introduction: Linguistic theories and language interaction. *ASHA Monographs, 30*, 1–9.

McTear, M. F., & King, F. (1991). Miscommunication in clinical contexts: The speech therapy interview. In N. Coupland, H. Giles, & J. M. Wiemann (Eds.), *"Miscommunication" and problematic talk* (pp. 195–214). Newbury Park, CA: Sage.

Mehan, H. (1985). The structure of classroom discourse. In T. Van Dijck (Ed.), *Handbook of discourse analysis* (Vol. 3). London: Academic Press.

Panagos, J. M. (1996). Speech therapy discourse: The input to learning. In M. D. Smith & J. S. Damico (Eds.), *Childhood language disorders* (pp. 41–63). New York: Thieme Medical Publishers.

Pomerantz, A. (1983). Agreeing and disagreeing with assessments: Some features of preferred/dispreferred turn shapes. In J. Maxwell Atkinson & M. Heritage (Eds.), *Structures of social action* (pp. 57–101). New York: Cambridge University Press.

Prutting, C. A., Bagshaw, N., Goldstein, H., Juskowitz, S., & Umen, I. (1978). Clinician-child discourse: Some preliminary questions. *Journal of Speech and Hearing Disorders, 43*, 123–139.

Ripich, D., & Panagos, J. M. (1985). Accessing children's knowledge of sociolinguistic rules for speech therapy lessons. *Journal of Speech and Hearing Disorders, 50,* 335–346.

Schiffrin, D. (1987). *Discourse markers.* New York: Cambridge University Press.

Sinclair, J. M., & Coulthard, R. M. (1975). *Towards an analysis of discourse: The English used by teachers and pupils.* Oxford, England: Oxford University Press.

Tannen, D. (1989). *Talking voices: Repetition, dialogue, and imagery in conversational discourse.* New York: Cambridge University Press.

van Kleeck, A., & Richardson, A. (1986). What's in an error? Using children's wrong responses as teaching opportunities. *National Student Speech, Language, Hearing Association Journal, 14,* 25–50.

Chapter 14

Social Role Negotiation in Aphasia Therapy: Competence, Incompetence, and Conflict

Nina Simmons-Mackie
Southeastern Louisiana University

Jack S. Damico
University of Southwestern Louisiana

Speech-language therapy is a complex, goal-directed activity undertaken to improve an individual's communication. Interestingly, by traditional design speech-language therapy harbors an inherent paradox. The goal of therapy is to build communicative competence, yet the assumptions required for treatment demand that the client be incompetent. That is, the therapist expects the client to demonstrate problems with communication. Thus, both parties act in accordance with a presupposition of deficit in the individual targeted for therapy (Damico & Simmons-Mackie, 1996; Kovarsky & Maxwell, 1992; Panagos, 1996; Ripich, 1982; Simmons-Mackie, Damico, & Nelson, 1995). In keeping with this presupposition, the clinician and client implicitly adopt necessary roles as competent expert and incompetent patient in order for therapy to proceed in an orderly and efficient fashion.

The social contract that establishes these roles of competent helper and incompetent person in need of help is instilled through a variety of means. Physical aspects of the setting establish the speech-language pathologist as an expert (Kovarsky, 1989a; Simmons, 1993; Simmons-Mackie, Damico, & Nelson, 1995). For example, characteristic architectural layout, furnishings, and modes of dress dictate an obvious authority hierarchy. This recognizable context dictates prescribed discourse patterns in much the same manner as the authority-biased context of the courtroom (Panagos, 1996). In addition, verbal and nonverbal interactive dynamics of therapy reinforce the social contract between the helper and the one in need of help (Damico

& Damico, 1997; Damico & Simmons-Mackie, 1996; Simmons-Mackie, Damico, & Nelson, 1995). For example, components of discourse, such as elicitation of known information, challenge questions, and therapist evaluations, reinforce these roles (i.e., Silvast, 1991; Simmons-Mackie, Damico, & Nelson, 1995; Wilcox & Davis, 1977).

Assumption of the roles of expert and patient is a necessary aspect of the therapy encounter. In order to fulfill the mediational goals of therapy and proceed forward in an orderly and efficient manner, both parties in therapy conform to standardized routines. However, rigid role casting and an inflexible adherence to the structure of therapy can blind the "expert" to the remarkable competence displayed by clients. In such instances, the imposition of the initial social roles of the helper and the one in need of help may prevent the emergence of other social roles that reveal greater competence in the client during therapy. Thus, a paradox occurs when rigid compliance with designated roles (a) prevents the therapist from appreciating highly competent aspects of a client's communicative behavior, and (b) places the client in the position of adhering to the role of incompetent patient (Kovarsky & Maxwell, 1992).

The remarkable stability of these social contracts adopted in therapy is illustrated through a conversational analysis of an argument between a person with aphasia and her speech-language therapist. The argument provided an interesting contrast with a standard therapy session. The comparison reveals several ways that social interaction in therapy is determined, highlighting the established roles of therapist and patient. Furthermore, the session provided an opportunity to view the person with aphasia both as "incompetent patient" and, in an alternative role, as "competent consumer" within one situation. Such an opportunity emphasizes the complexity of the collusion that takes place within therapy to create social roles.

PARTICIPANTS AND DATA

C, a 50-year-old woman, sustained a left-hemisphere CVA in May 1991. Prior to her stroke, C had been an office manager. She was divorced, self-supporting, and lived alone. Her friends described her as outgoing and independent. After her stroke, C was diagnosed with severe aphasia and apraxia of speech. Initially, her auditory comprehension was moderately impaired and verbal communication was virtually nonexistent. C was enrolled in speech-language therapy in a hospital-based rehabilitation center. She slowly improved until she was able to communicate in single words and short phrases accompanied by gesture and some writing. Scores on the *Porch Index of Communicative Ability* (Porch, 1981) administered in July 1992 placed C in the 72nd percentile of individuals with aphasia, with a mean score of 12.63. Verbal communication was nonfluent and agrammatic; she primarily produced content words (e.g., nouns, verbs) with a mean length of utterance (MLU) at about 3.5 word forms. During the spring of 1992, C became increasingly concerned about her slow progress in therapy. Her concerns also related to her poor insurance coverage for speech services, and her inability to pay for the services herself.

L was C's speech-language pathologist. L was a certified speech-language pathologist with over 5 years of experience with adult aphasia. She was well respected by her peers as an aphasia clinician.

The first video-recorded therapy session occurred in January 1992, approximately 8 months after C's stroke and 2½ months after L and C had started working together. The session was 56 minutes long and yielded 229 turns. There were two treatment tasks. One task focused on auditory comprehension of two-step commands. The other task involved verbal and written picture descriptions. According to the participants, this was a typical treatment session.

The second recorded session occurred in April 1992. This session lasted 11 minutes and comprised 108 turns. Therapy in the second session focused on written and verbal descriptions of commercially available picture cards using an adaptation of Response Elaboration Training (Kearns, 1985). For this task the therapist directed the client to describe a picture, elaborate on the description, then write the elaborated description. This session ended with an argument between L and C.

Both sessions took place in L's office/treatment room in a hospital clinic. L and C were seated directly across from each other at a table. Sessions were videotaped, transcribed using an adaptation of the Jefferson transcription system (Sacks, Schegloff, & Jefferson, 1974), and analyzed via conversational analysis procedures (i.e., Goodwin & Heritage, 1990; Psathas, 1995). The transcription of the argument is included in the Appendix.

THERAPY AS AN INSTITUTIONALIZED ROUTINE

It is from within the routinized therapeutic context, with its well-defined and expected roles, that the changes discussed in this chapter are most apparent. In the data examined, several aspects of the therapy interaction appeared to be standard features, which served to reinforce the underlying social contract and therapeutic goals.

Establishing the Structure of Participation

Both aphasia therapy sessions began with a period of casual conversation that conformed to textbook recommendations of an initial phase of adjustment and rapport building (Brookshire, 1992; Porch, 1994). The casual conversation consisted largely of the therapist asking questions and the client providing simple answers (primarily yes–no). The therapist effectively controlled and promoted turn sharing (albeit somewhat asymmetrical), which guaranteed continued talk. C provided simple responses and accepted allotted time slots. In effect, the participants cast a casual conversation into a loose form of elicitation sequence in which L asked and C responded. While both L and C participated in this repartee, C did not introduce topics, expand on topics or attempt to demonstrate complex language competence. Rather, L provided "slots" for C to fill with simple answers. As Panagos (1996) suggests, it is the role of the therapist to keep the session moving forward. L successfully moved the conversation along with no difficult repair sequences or misunderstandings typical of C's nontherapy conversational interactions. The impression was that of a casual conversation controlled and facilitated by the therapist. Thus, the therapist controlled the participation structure of therapy and promoted the flow of activities. In these ways the social contract between therapist and client was clearly negotiated during this opening phase.

Establishing the Therapeutic Framework

After the opening phase of both sessions, therapy tasks were introduced by the therapist using a specific structural framework. The task introduction in the first session is shown in Example 1.

Example 1
63   L: Okay. I'm gonna put 10 pictures out.
64   Awright. These are our pictures that we work with off and on
65   and I'm gonna ask you to point to two things for me.
66   Okay. Remember how much better you did with this on Monday?
67   C: Yeah
68   L: All right. Show me the chair and the brush.
69   C: ((points to the chair and brush))

A similar introduction to the second session is found in Example #2.

Example 2
32   L: Okay. All right. Let's run through ((clears throat))
33   and look at our pictures.
34   Remember we had pulled 10 pictures out?
35   I'm gonna kind of mix 'em up a little bit.
36   Um::: I want you to tell me in as many words
37   as you can, tell me what's happening in the picture.
          ((places picture on table))
38   C: The c couple is bed in. What isy:: ((points to picture))

Although the therapy tasks in each session are different, the similarity in basic format and style are revealed in the therapist's introduction. Each introduction begins with a discourse marker ("Okay," "Okay. All right"), which signals a shift from the opening phase to the beginning of a treatment task (Kovarsky, 1989a, 1989b, 1990). The therapist, not the client, establishes this shift to the treatment task.

Next, the therapist employs several alignment strategies to enlist the client's cooperation with the task. First, the therapist joins herself with the client pronominally as in Example 2, lines 32–34 (let *us, our* pictures, *we* had pulled). This brings therapist and client together as an established team with a joint past. The therapist further capitalizes on their joint history with "*remember we* had pulled 10 pictures out" and orients the client to the task. This royal "we" reinforces the roles already established and reminds C of her past cooperation with the task and acquiescence with the format of therapy. In effect, the structure and content of this introduction grounds the activity in a background of past cooperation in keeping with the social contract.

Having marked a shift in structure and established a basis for alignment and cooperation, the therapist moves on to request performance by the client: "I'm gonna ask you to point to two things for me" (Example 1, line 65) and "I want you to tell me" (Example 2, line 36). The therapist, in effect, requests displays of client performance. Such behaviors signal that the therapist has the right or power to dictate; a clear signal of her authority role (Maxwell, 1993). C's heightened attention, compliance with requests, and virtual absence of counterrequests signals collaboration in this distribution of control, and willing assumption of the "patient taking the cure" role. L's use of personal pronouns in the directives (*I want, for me, tell me*) creates another strong solicitation for cooperation with the social contract. These "do it for me" constructions by the expert authority are powerful exhortations for C's fulfillment of L's expectations. In addition, the wording "I want you to" (expressed as a desire) and "I'm going to ask you to" (a plan of action) are softer and less imperious than a raw command. Research suggests that speakers often temper requests using polite constructions, or cast requests as opinions (I think you should . . .), in order to minimize the chance of a refusal (Brown & Levinson, 1978; Button & Lee, 1987; Schiffrin, 1990). Furthermore, these constructions, when used in a routinized manner, signal the beginning of a familiar series of turn constructional units allowing C to prepare for her standard part in the interaction. Thus, the discourse shapes, and is shaped by, the social roles associated with aphasia therapy.

Finally, the heart of the treatment task is characterized by a triad of adjacency units initiated by a therapist request or question. This usually takes the form of a directive, such as "Show me the chair," or a question,

such as "What is the name of this?" Both directives and questions constitute
requests to perform. For example, the intent of the question "What is the
name of this?" is to request labeling performance.

In nontherapy discourse there are several possible responses to a request
(Schiffrin, 1994). The person who receives the request can comply with
the request (or attempt to comply), refuse to comply with the request, or
derail the request (such as asking for clarification or changing the topic).
The following adjacency units are typical of natural discourse: (a) request–
fulfill request (or attempt to fulfill request); (b) request–reject request; or
(c) request–derail request.

During speech-language therapy, however, the only option available to
the client is the first—to fulfill the request. A therapist's request is followed
by a client's attempt to comply with that request. The client's response is
then followed by the therapist's evaluation of the response. This produces
an adjacency triad consisting of request-response-evaluation (RRE).

If the client is unable to perform the task due to deficit or does not
understand the task, then a side sequence ensues in which the therapist
offers help to insure that the client performs the task successfully, ultimately
completing the RRE sequence as follows:

```
Therapist:   ┌ Request
Client:      │      ┌Help request
Therapist:   │      └Help
Client:      ├ Response
Therapist:   └ Evaluation
```

Although the content of RRE sequences varies considerably, the structure of this three-part adjacency sequence is relatively invariable. Once
initiated, each party is constrained to fill the slot for the next part of the
triad. Several researchers have identified the presence of request (initiation)-response-evaluation sequences in child therapy and classroom discourse (i.e., Bobkoff, 1982; Duchan, 1993; McTear & King, 1991; Mehan,
1979; Ripich et al., 1984). This pattern of request-response-evaluation
(RRE) is pervasively evident in C's language therapy, as in Example 3 from
the first session:

Example 3
```
┌ Request      93   L:   Show me money and watch
├ Response     94   C:   ((Points to money and watch))
└ Evaluation   95   L:   Mhm.
┌ Request      96        Show me bed and car.
├ Response     97   C:   ((points to bed and car))
└ Evaluation   98   L:   Mhm. good.
```

The therapist makes the request, the client performs, the therapist evaluates the performance. This predictable structure, along with the routinized phrase ("Show me . . ."), serves as a resource to the participants allowing them to stay on track efficiently, maintain the flow, and complete the work of instruction in an organized fashion.

During the second session, this format is initiated and proceeds with each triad ending with an evaluation and model of the target sentence, followed by the next request.

Example 4

⌈ Request	37	L:	. . . tell me what's happening in the picture.
⊦ Response	38	C:	The c couple is bed in. What isy:: ((pts to picture))
⌊ Evaluation/Model	39	L:	Okay. Okay. The couple is <u>IN</u> the bed.
⌈ Request	40		What are they doing?
⊦ Response	41	C:	Sleep.
⌊ Evaluation/Model	42	L:	Mhm. The couple is in bed <u>SLEEPING.</u>
⌈ Request	43		Can you try to say that whole sentence for me?
⊦ Response	44	C:	The couple is bed is sleep.
			((looking at card then looks steadily at L))
⌊ Evaluation/Model	45	L:	Mhm (pause) ngkay
	46		The couple is in bed <u>SLEEPING.</u> Okay.

Throughout these sequences L and C fulfill the expected therapy discourse format. Talk during tasks is directed toward fulfilling the current RRE sequence relative to the specific stimulus item chosen by the therapist. Side sequences are initiated only to repair misunderstandings or assist the client in obtaining the correct response. A topic change by the client or a client's refusal to perform the task are not permitted within the context of therapy, and such behaviors are not observed in either session (until the argument ensues).

C is an active collaborator in the construction of this discourse pattern. While L presents the request portion of the RRE sequence, C attends carefully and gazes at L. As soon as L completes the instruction, C begins her designated, expected response. The give-and-take is orderly and swift. When C is unable to respond accurately, she signals a need for help (such as gazing steadily at L, verbally requesting help). The following sequence from the first session is an example:

Example 5

⌈ Request	83	L:	Show me cup and chair.
Help request	84	C:	((looks at cards)) [I don't know ((nods no))
			((hand out, palm up; gazes at L))
Continuer	85	L:	[Mhm
Help request	86	C:	Is here ((points to card)) I don where?
			((holds hand out))

Help	87	L:	Listen (pause) CUP and CHAIR
Response	88	C:	Thank you ((points to cup and chair))
Evaluation	89:	L:	Mhm. Okay

C recognizes that her job is to provide the correct answer. However, difficulty providing the correct answer is not unexpected. When C encounters difficulty, she solicits the help of L, who provides cues or prompts. Both parties participate in this enactment of the helper–helpee relationship in order to fulfill therapeutic goals. C accepts the subordinate position and signals her appreciation for the help with a polite "Thank you." Once C performs the requested behavior, C looks up at L and awaits the evaluation phase of the adjacency triad. In order for this structure to proceed, both parties must accept that L is an expert equipped to help C, the incompetent speaker.

Thus, routine therapy interactions between C and L simultaneously manifest and construct the social roles as therapist and patient. These roles are reflected in the structure of the session and the talk-in-interaction. The norms of therapy conduct are created cooperatively. Here we see a typical example of resources jointly enacted by therapist and client to maintain therapist control, organize the session, and promote cooperation. The client not only adheres to the interactive routines, but looks to the therapist for completion of the adjacency triad. Within the therapeutic context both parties know their place and keep their place, consistent with their negotiated social roles.

CONFLICT WITHIN THE THERAPY ENCOUNTER

At times, however, there is the need or desire for a shift in a participant's social role—even within the rigid structure of the therapeutic context. In such instances there is a dynamic interplay between the norms of therapy conduct, the expected social roles, the stability of established routines, and the competence required to shift role. This interplay can result in conflict between participants within the therapeutic encounter. The talk involved in negotiating the conflict can be examined, providing insight into these institutionalized routines, social roles, and interactive competencies. Such was the case with L and C. In the second therapy session, which is detailed in the remainder of this chapter, C attempts to shift her social role from that of "a patient in need of help" to the role of "a consumer concerned about the therapy services." That is, within the session, C begins to allude to her lack of progress and the repetitious therapy task. This requires a shift in C's social role, but it is a shift that apparently is not accepted by L. Consequently a conflict arises. This conflict is examined to determine how the interaction is structured and advanced, to determine what conflict reveals about the power of talk-in-interaction, and to highlight the communicative competency exhibited by C.

The session containing the conflict of interest begins characteristically with an opening phase and introduction to the task involving joint focus, establishment of common ground by referring to previous tasks and sessions, and requests to perform. The task consists of Response Elaboration Therapy (Kearns, 1985), in which C is asked to verbally describe a picture, progressively expand her descriptions, and write the picture description. This task had been repeated in several past sessions using the same set of pictures.

Signaling the Onset of Conflict via Affective Shift

As the therapy activity unfolds, both L and C adhere to the expected structure and therapy proceeds as usual. Then the trouble begins. The first hint of conflict is apparent in Example 6, line 49, when C displays an affective shift that marks the onset of the conflict between the therapist and client.

Example 6

⌈ Request	43	L:	Can you try to say that whole sentence for me?
⊢ Response	44	C:	The couple is bed is sleep.
			((looking at "sleeping" card then looks up steadily at L))
⌊ Evaluation	45	L:	Mhm (pause) ngkay.
	46		The couple is in bed <u>SLEEPING</u>. Okay.
	47		If I can give you a tablet here.
			((putting a tablet and pencil before C))
Request	48		All right. I want you to write that sentence for me.
→ Reject	49	C:	hhhhhh ((audible sigh)) ((clears her throat))
	50		(pause) ((downward gaze, shakes head no))
	51		I don't know ((quiet voice, rapid, clipped rate))
	52	L:	(hhhhh) ((hissing laughter sound))
Encourage	53		You can do it. You can do it. You can do that.

At this juncture L makes a request (line 48) and C appears to express unwillingness to respond to the request (line 49). The contextualization cues offered by C in line 49 are highly uncharacteristic of her usual response to a request. Unlike prior responses to requests, C does not immediately perform the task nor does she employ the customary signals requesting help. In fact, C shifts her gaze away from L, sighs, and shakes her head as though she is rejecting the request itself.

L recognizes the failure to perform as evidenced by her laugh (line 52) and encouragement to C to perform the task (line 53). It appears that L interprets C's response as difficulty due to language deficit—a lack of competence to perform the task. This is gleaned from L's prompt to perform: "You can do it." L invokes her expert authority to persuade C that the task is within her ability in spite of the language deficit. In other words, L interprets C's uncharacteristic rejection by employing her stable therapeutic expectation and her interpretation of C's actions as an "incompetent patient." In effect, these assumptions construct L's interpretive framework.

Within this framework, L's interpretation bears on the local context (a focus on the task) and L's belief that C would willingly perform the task if able (the social contract). Thus, C's rejection is interpreted by L within the context of therapy discourse structure and the roles of therapist–patient. Given this interpretation, one would expect that the expert's encouragement would help C perform the task—obtain the correct answer—then L and C would resume the routine. In fact, the encouragement does result in C's performance of the task as follows:

Example 7

→ Response	54	C:	((Writes)) hhhhhh ((sighs loudly)) ((stops writing))
	55		(pause) ((writes then drops pencil))
	56		((C pushes the tablet toward L and lifts eyes to L))
	57		((looks down; leans back with downward gaze))
Evaluation	58	L:	Goo:d. Very good.
Request	59		Can you read that sentence for me now?
	60		Read that whole sentence.

Escalation of Affective Signaling

In Example 7, line 54, C again registers discontent. Although C writes the sentence as requested, she sighs loudly, frowns, audibly drops the pencil, and shoves the completed work at L in an obvious display of dissatisfaction and anger. C's affect is incongruent with her cooperative performance. However, L ostensibly directs her next turn (line 58) to the cooperative task performance rather than the negative affect by maintaining the request-response-evaluation (RRE) sequence with "Good. Very good." Although L maintains the integrity of the therapy RRE structure rather than diverge to address C's affect, it is interesting that L's evaluation of C's begrudging performance is considerably more positive than her prior evaluations. L switches from "Okay" and "Mhm" to "Good. Very good." Possibly this special reward serves several purposes—to reinforce a correct sentence, to reward C's return to appropriate therapy behavior (fulfilling a request), and to rebuild affective alignment, which has eroded with C's anger display. L fulfills her role in maintaining the RRE therapy structure in spite of trouble brewing, and crafts her evaluation to insure continuation of this format.

As noted, L does not disrupt the RRE sequence to address C's affective shift. Rather, she continues with the therapy structure by moving into another request sequence, as follows:

Example 8

Request	59	L:	Can you read that sentence for me now?
	60		Read that whole sentence.
	61	C:	(pause) ((downward gaze, leans forward))
	62		((clears throat, eyes closed))
→ Counterrequest	63		Is <u>NE:::W</u> please ((lifts "sleeping" card)) ((looks at L, then down, then up and down rapidly))

Signaling Conflict via Rejection

Clearly, C has not conformed to the expected RRE adjacency triad. Rather, C nonverbally rejects L's request and offers a counter request (lines 61–63). C's intent to request is apparent from her intonation and politeness tag "please." Although retrospectively it is apparent that C is requesting a new task or new picture cards, L expresses confusion over C's behavior and responds to C's request with a long repair sequence, which in effect derails C's request for a new task.

Example 9

64	L:	New? [What ya mean?
65	C:	[Yeah, plea::se ((tense voice))
66		I don know ((nods "no" rapidly))
67		is is alu ((gestures stop))
68		((writes "enough"))((loudly drops pencil))
69		<u>PLEA:::SE</u>
70	L:	Enough?=
71	C:	Yeah.
72	L:	=What ya mean?
73	C:	Isy ((pointing to "sleeping" card))
74		is is is good ((speaks rapidly, points to tablet then to card))
75		is <u>NE:::W</u> ((points to L))
76	L:	What's new?
77		What ya [mean it's new?
78	C:	[Is is too
		((leans forward and sweeps hand across cards on L's side of table))
79	L:	You want anoth[er one?
80	C:	[Yeah, plea::se.

After this extended repair sequence, L finally interprets C's request as a request for a "new card." However, rather than immediately fulfill C's request, L repeats the general instructions characteristic of task introductions.

Example 10
81   L: What I'd like you to do is go through
82   and [read it after you've written it.

Thus, L refuses to fulfill C's request. Instead she appears to interpret C's utterance as a symptom of misunderstanding of the task requirements, and reverts to the "introducing the task" structure in an attempt to restart the therapy routine and re-enter the RRE sequence. This results in an affective display by C, as follows:

Example 11
83   C: [I know (pause) I don kno::w ((gaze down))
84   O::h o:h no:::: ((grabs head))
85   L: Too frustrating today?
86   C: Yeah— ((clipped, terse))
87   L: Okay. The couple is sleeping in bed.
88   That was good. Perfect sentence.
89   Nothin' wrong with it ((singsong intonation))
90   Awright, let's look at this one.
91   Tell me in as many words as you can
92   what he is doing.

In line 85 L again interprets C's affect as anger and frustration with inability to perform—aphasic incompetence (as in Example 6, line 53). In contrast, there is a decidedly sarcastic tone in C's response of "yeah" to L's query "Too frustrating today?" (lines 85, 86). Clearly, L refers to frustration performing the task due to aphasia. C refers to frustration with L's failure to acknowledge C's request for a new task; frustration over not being heard as a "competent consumer." The misunderstanding reflects two different role orientations. L continues to cast C as the frustrated and incompetent "aphasic patient." C is now casting herself as the "competent consumer" who wants to move on to new material in treatment.

After L expresses sympathy with C's frustration, the therapist moves to preserve the outline of the RRE sequence in spite of C's failure to perform. In effect, L makes a request (Example 10, line 81) that C rejects (Example 11, lines 83, 84); then L evaluates (Example 11, lines 87–89) as though C has performed the task, filling the last slot of the three-part sequence and providing a structural entree to continue the session. In Example 12 (a reformat of Examples 10 and 11), the attempt to preserve the RRE structure can be seen.

Example 12
┌ Request   81   L: What I'd like you to do is go through
│   82   and [read it after you've written it.

```
            83   C:   [I know (pause) I don kno::w ((gaze down))
  ?         84        O::h o:h no:::: ((grabs head))
            85   L:   Too frustrating today?
            86   C:   Yeah— ((clipped, terse))
  Evaluation 87  L:   Okay. The couple is sleeping in bed.
            88        That was good. Perfect sentence.
            89        Nothin' wrong with it ((singsong intonation))
  Request   90        Awright, let's look at this one.
            91        Tell me in as many words as you can
            92        what he is doing.
```

L maintains the RRE sequence by evaluating a "ghost" response; that is, L continues as though the patient has fulfilled the request. Once the evaluation slot is filled with a positive evaluation (lines 87–89), the therapist is free to proceed to the next therapy item (line 90). Again L has used a routinized structure to get treatment back on track and disregard C's attempt to derail the task. The structure of talk repositions C into the patient role and reinforces the therapy contract.

From the first sign of trouble in Example 6, L has interpreted the interaction in terms of C's frustration with performance of a particular therapy item. Initially (Example 6, line 53), L interprets C's negative affect as difficulty performing the task—an expected symptom of incompetence. Later, L repeats the general instructions (Example 10, line 81), suggesting that C has failed to understand the task overall—a symptom of incompetence. Finally, in Example 11, line 85, L again interprets C's behavior as a display of frustration in performing the task—a symptom of incompetence. Throughout the interaction L responds to C within the confines of therapeutic role. That is, L is the expert who makes requests; C is the patient who performs requests. If C does not perform, it is due to aphasia (incompetence). L adopts a discourse structure that maintains L's position in control. Thus, L stays firmly in role and responds to C within the narrow role definitions of therapist and patient.

C, on the other hand, has clearly attempted to extricate herself from addressing the therapy task and is, in fact, questioning L's control and L's treatment plan. C adopts the role of a consumer of services who has evaluated the service and found it deficient. She wants a new task and attempts to communicate this request to L.

Maintaining the Therapeutic Focus

Over the next several turns C and L negotiate to maintain the interaction and to avoid conflict. C complies with L's requests, although C's affect continues to reflect anger and frustration and she derails the flow of the session with repeated requests for clarification. C appears to struggle not to completely reject her role as patient; however, the session does not proceed as smoothly and seamlessly as usual.

Example 13

	88		That was good. Perfect sentence.
	89		Nothin' wrong with it ((singsong intonation))
	90		Awright, let's look at this one.
Request	91		Tell me in as many words as you can
	92		what he is doing.
	93	C	((holds head, hand over left eye; gazes down))
	94		((moves hand to cheek and rests head on fist))
	95		((clears throat, then looks up))
	96		Is what?
	97	L:	Tell me in as many words as you can
	98		what he is doing?
Response	99	C:	A MAN IS IS IS READ ((angry voice)) (pause) ((gazes at card))
	100		IS BOOK ((points to picture)) ((loud, tense, terse)) ((looking up, lips tight, staring at L))
Evaluation	101	L:	Mhm, a ma:n is rea:ding a boo:k.
	102	C:	[Yeah—
	103	L	[That's right
Request	104		Where is he?
	105	C:	Is what? ((staring at L and leaning forward))
	106	L:	Where is he?
Response	107	C:	E:::z s::: ((staring at L and leaning forward))
Evaluation	108	L:	Mhm. You're going to tell me he's sitting, huh?
	109	C:	Is what? ((staring and leaning forward))
Request	110	L:	What is he sittin' in?
Response	111	C:	(pause) ((leans forward)) Is blue ((rapid))
	112		.hhhhhhhh ((inspiration through clenched teeth))
Evaluation	113	L:	It is blue, huh? Mhm
	114	C:	[(((leaning forward gazing steadily at L))]
	115	L:	The ma:n is rea:ding a BOO:K in a CHAI:R, huh ((slow and exaggerated speech))

C complies with requests, but her performance is characterized by clarification requests and incomplete responses. L appears to interpret this behavior as difficulty performing the task, and adjusts the discourse structure to facilitate C's task performance. The session continues in this manner with L simplifying requests and accepting approximate responses in deference to C's frustration. This therapist's behavior is entirely consistent with the recommendation of aphasia therapy texts to simplify tasks to promote successful performance and reduce frustration (e.g., Davis, 1993). Thus, L continues to judge C's affect as evidence of "deficit frustration" or incompetence, and consequently reduces the demands.

Shifting the Focus From Therapy to Conflict

Up until this point in the interaction, both C and L have maintained their focus on therapy activities. As seen in Example 14, however, the precariously maintained RRE sequence entirely degenerates when C begins to cry (line 125).

Example 14

124 L: Is that what you were going to tell me?
125 C: I don know is is
        ((crying, looking down at lap, body turned to side))
126 L: Is it frustrating today?
127   (pause) C———, it's okay (pause) All right? ((said in soft voice))
128   ((pause)) Just take it each day as it comes
129   ((places a box of tissues directly in front of C))
        and we just do as much as you can do, okay?

L continues to craft utterances suggesting that the problem with the session is C's incompetence (line 126). L interprets the interaction within their social contract as therapist and patient, without recognizing that C has attempted to shift out of this role. L reinforces her authoritarian role by giving C permission to be frustrated ("it's okay") and offering alternatives ("we just do as much as you can do"). Although L is genuinely attempting to console and encourage C, in effect, L is addressing her as an incompetent person. L maintains control of the session and fails to hear the voice of the competent consumer.

At this time C appears to collaborate with L's participation frame in a variety of ways. She has continued to fulfill requests (lines 99, 107, 111) suggesting that "therapy continues." Filling the response slots constitutes an implicit acknowledgment of her patient role. After starting to cry, C apologizes for her behavior in a subservient manner; this bolsters L's power position. Thus, C's discourse exposes C's difficulty shifting out of her dependent patient role.

C's anger is not appeased by L's "pardon" of her behavior in line 127. Instead the conflict generalizes beyond the therapy task. Note in the following sequence that L has provided a box of tissue (line 129); C abruptly rejects the offer of tissue by roughly returning the box to its original position (line 135). This nonverbal power struggle parallels the verbal argument.

Example 15

126 L: Is it frustrating today?
127   (pause) C———, it's okay (pause) All right? ((said in soft voice))
128   ((pause)) Just take it each day as it comes

→ 129   ((places a box of tissues directly in front of C))
               and we just do as much as you can do, okay?
130   C: ((Turns to L, leans forward)) So:::rry
131   L: So[rry?
132   C: [Yeah
133   L: Don't apologize. No need to apologize.
134   [No reason to say you're sorry
→ 135   C: [(((C grabs tissue box, abruptly puts it aside, looks down))
136   L: Okay? (pause) Want to skip the writing part today?
137   You tell me what you feel up to [doing, okay?

Having nonverbally demonstrated that the conflict continues, C makes another request for a new task as follows:

Example 16
138   C: [NO IS IS
                     ((leaning forward, speaking loudly, rapidly))
139   IS IS IS NEW ((gestures writing))
140   PLEA:::SE ((holds up picture card))
141   CARD IS (pause) [I don know isy=
142   L: [Mhm
144   C: Is PLEA::SE NE:W (pause) ah CARD
         ((pleading intonation))
145   L: Oh, you want different [pictures?
146   C: [PLEA:SE! YES ((nods))
147   L: O:::::H. Oh. Okay
148   Well, remember last time we talk[ed=
149   C: [hhhhhhhhh
         ((sigh and downward gaze))
150   L: =and we went through the pictures
151   and I just picked 10 out and said
152   we'd [work with these a few times?

L recognizes C's request for new pictures; however, L defends her continued use of this task (lines 148, 150). In effect, L's utterance serves as an implicit rejection of C's request since it is an accounting of why the task is appropriate. Through this implicit rejection, L is acting to defuse C's concerns and requests. Consequently, C escalates her demands and meets this rejection with a threat to leave (I don know. Bye bye) in the following sequence (line 159):

Example 17
153   C: [I know I know ((looking away and shaking head "no"))
154   ((raises hand as in stop gesture))
156   No, I don know is ((hand to forehead)).
157   L: I know (soft voice)

```
    158   C:   Isy I don know ((hand up)) where
→   159        I don know. Bye-bye
                 ((looking down, waves bye, nodding no))
    160        is me ((points to self)) [isy ((looking at L))
    161   L:                            [Well, I'll try to find
    162        some different pictures but remember
    163        when I found some that wer- had more to them
    164        and it got you frustrated 'cause
    165        you tried to write so much? (pause)
    166        Ya remember that?
    167        So we said we'd back up and try these again.
```

In response to C's threat, L makes an offer to find different pictures
("Well, I'll try. . . ."). It is remarkable that at this point in the conflict L
continues to struggle for control. Her use of the marker "Well" suggests
continued disagreement with C's request and potential noncompliance
with the request (Schiffrin, 1987). This is reinforced by her use of the
qualifier "I'll try," suggesting that she might *not* find different pictures. L
then provides another accounting for the task based on C's history of
difficulty performing other, more difficult tasks (lines 162–167). This accounting also reinforces the patient role by reminding C of her past incompetence.

In response to L's defense of the task, C defends her request by repeating
her threat to leave ("Is bye bye") and providing an explanation of her
motive for the request—financial concerns (line 170: "Is money"). Apparently, C is referring to her limited funds; as a consumer she no doubt
wants to make "every minute count." Thus, C appears to be arguing that
doing the same task repeatedly is not cost effective.

Example 18
```
    168   C:   ((looking down, looks up and then down))
    169        Isy, I don know isy. Is bye-bye
                 ((waves with rapid expansive gesture))
    170        Is MONEY ISY ((gestures grasping money to self))
    171        BYE-BYE ((waves))
    172   L:   About money?
    173   C:   YEAH::: IS ME. PLEA::SE
    174        IS NEW ((leans forward; stares at L))
    175   L:   OKAY, OKAY. IT'S AWRIGHT!
    176        I'll find some new ones.
    177        Can we use these today then
    178        [since I haven't picked any new ones out?
```

At this point the conflict is clearly the focus of the interaction. For most
of the session, both parties have attempted to maintain their roles and

avoid entirely shattering the structure of therapy. L has repeatedly pulled the interaction back into the RRE framework of a therapy interaction. She has responded to C based on an expectation of patient behavior and patient frustration, and has altered the task difficulty to reduce C's frustration with her distressing deficit. C's assertion of herself as "consumer" was contaminated by continued fulfillment of L's expectations (performing requests). Thus, both L and C continued to fulfill the social contract between therapist and patient until the conflict became the central focus of the interaction. Once the argument became the central focus, the routines of therapy were abandoned and a power struggle ensued. C was furious that her consumer request went unheeded. L was confused and distraught that C's aphasic frustration could not be mitigated through therapeutic control. The struggle continued until C finally walked out of treatment.

DISCUSSION

The Complexity of Discourse

Conversational analysis of therapy sessions between L and C revealed remarkable interactive complexity and structure hidden beneath what appeared to be simple activities.

Routine Therapy Discourse. The structure of therapy discourse proved a powerful resource for constructing and maintaining routines of therapy and social roles of competent expert and incompetent patient. For example, the adjacency triad of request-response-evaluation (RRE) was a key feature marking the interaction as a therapy routine. Both L and C knew their part in the RRE sequence and constructed a seamless give-and-take characteristic of an efficient therapy session. As long as this structure was maintained, therapy proceeded and associated social roles were enacted. When trouble was encountered, the therapist played her part flawlessly by employing methods of modifying the talk to insure that C filled the middle slot of the RRE sequence. L simplified requests, rewarded incomplete responses, and even rewarded a "ghost" response in order to continue therapy. Therapy discourse constituted a recognizable, routinized global structure, which both participants enacted in order to achieve remedial goals. Therapy discourse shaped, and was shaped by, the social roles played by each participant.

The Discourse of Argument. Once the routine structure of therapy dissolved, the argument became the discourse focus and the competing roles of competent consumer and incompetent aphasic became readily visible.

C's rejection of the RRE triad and replacement of it with the nontherapy adjacency pair of "request–reject" resulted in a shift into conflict. The argument constituted a negotiation in which the therapist attempted to get back into therapy routines, while C attempted to make her request understood. Both parties participated in the give-and-take of the conflict with competing adjacency pairs of "therapist request–client rejection" and "client request–therapist rejection." Each participant employed discourse strategies typical of "normal" arguments in an effort to get her way. For example, both used "accountings" for rejecting the other's request and reasons why their request should be honored. In Example 19, lines 162–167, L provides a reason to continue with the current task:

Example 19

```
161   L:                        [Well, I'll try to find
162         some different pictures but remember
163         when I found some that wer- had more to them
164         and it got you frustrated 'cause
165         you tried to write so much? (pause)
166         Ya remember that?
167         So we said we'd back up and try these again.
```

C accounts for her request based on finances ("Is money") and adds a threat to leave if her request is not fulfilled:

Example 20

```
169   C:   Isy, I don know isy. Is bye-bye
                ((waves with rapid expansive gesture))
170         Is MONEY ISY ((gestures grasping money to self))
171         BYE-BYE ((waves))
```

Another characteristic of nontherapy argument found in L and C's interaction is the tendency for conflict to override the original argument topic. Thus, the conflict generalizes from the topic of new pictures to C's rejection of the tissue offer (lines 129–135) and later disagreement regarding the video camera (see Appendix, lines 181–199). Thus, in the "tissue box interaction" C abruptly pushes the box aside, physically demonstrating the power struggle. L is acting as "helper" providing tissues, C rejects help and acts independently. Similarly, at the end of the interaction, L and C "argue" about the best method to turn off the video camera. In other words, the power struggle born within the treatment task overflows into other aspects of the relationship. C no longer plays the role of patient; L continues to treat C as a patient. This negotiation of power and identity across several topic areas is a typical characteristic of argument (Goodwin & Goodwin, 1990; Varenne, 1987).

An additional characteristic of the argument session, which is consistent with nontherapy discourse, is the preference for agreement and avoidance of conflict (Brown & Levinson, 1978; Pomerantz, 1984; Sacks, 1987). This was apparent in the slow onset of the argument. Initially, C uses affective signals to alert the therapist to her dissatisfaction. In effect, C's early affective displays represent a slow leakage of her consumer role into her role as the patient. As typical of nonaphasic speakers, she avoids open disagreement and upsetting the power balance by delaying an overt demand for a new task—an overt and sudden shift of role. The affective signals identifying her as a "dissatisfied customer" might have been adequate to alert the therapist, if the therapist had not been biased by her own expectations. That is, the therapist expected negative affect to signal "frustration with aphasia" not "consumer dissatisfaction." Thus, an agreeable solution was not negotiated despite C's relatively subtle attempts to express her "consumer voice."

The conflict between C and L constituted an orderly, though sometimes angry, give-and-take proceeding across 80 turns. Although C's turns were characterized by telegraphic utterances, she employed legitimate speech acts and discourse devices to negotiate turn-taking and to construct meaning. Both C and L moved slowly into the argument as they initially made efforts to avoid disagreement and confrontation. Finally, the argument erupted, proved irreconcilable, and the interaction terminated.

Therapeutic Insights

This conversational analysis of therapeutic interaction provided two insights into the institution of therapy as experienced by L and C. First, their argument provided a window into the rigid social roles constituted by therapy and exposed routinized features of the institution of therapy that hinder the enactment of multiple social roles.

Second, the argument provided an excellent example of a language-disordered individual demonstrating remarkable interactive competence as she negotiated the talk to maintain a difficult interaction. Furthermore, the analysis demonstrates the "creation" of incompetence via expectation. That is, the therapist expected C to be incompetent, and interpreted the talk in light of this expectation. The expert failed to recognize the interactive competence of her client.

Argument as a Window to Social Role. The finding that argument provided a window into the rigid social roles associated with therapy is consistent with prior research demonstrating that arguments can effectively display social organization and reveal how participants situate themselves in particular types of social contracts (Goodwin & Goodwin, 1990; Maxwell, 1993). This is clearly apparent as this argument session demonstrates the strongly established social roles associated with the institution of aphasia therapy. The analyzed therapy session involved an unstated social contract, which cast the participants into designated roles as expert and patient. The argument exposed the conflicting roles as the participants struggled to negotiate an agreeable interaction. The implied social contract and resulting roles were visible in the discourse structure and content—the talk-in-interaction. In fact, the talk both created and was shaped by these roles.

The drive to maintain the social contract and avoid disagreement was very strong as evidenced in C's initial vacillation between "performing" and "rejecting" requests, and L's persistent adherence to the RRE structure. The roles were rigidly wrought and interpretation of talk inconsistent with role expectations proved difficult—in fact, impossible. Thus, the rigid role casting prevented the participants from succeeding in communicating outside of therapeutic expectations. Ultimately, the interaction dissolved and the therapy relationship terminated.

Argument as a Window to Competence. Research has demonstrated that argument in human discourse is a highly complex and organized activity requiring "a process of very intricate coordination between the parties who are opposing each other" (Goodwin & Goodwin, 1990, p. 85; Grimshaw, 1990). Argument entails not only competition, but also cooperation (Schiffrin, 1990). There is a need to collaborate in order to follow some organized and agreed-on sequence that allows both parties to participate and proceed in an orderly, albeit conflicting, fashion (Goodwin & Goodwin, 1990; Schiffrin, 1990). The argument between L and C is an excellent example of an intricate and complex negotiation. From the beginning to the end of the session, L and C engage in an orderly give-and-take of talk. Early on, the discourse conforms to "therapy" routines. While C attempts to communicate her displeasure with the choice of task, this is initially accomplished through affective displays, but the structure of the session is preserved. As the conflict proceeds, C begins to disrupt the RRE routines by rejecting and derailing requests. These are legitimate discourse options available to participants in nontherapy discourse; thus, C uses her "discourse competence" to remove herself from the "therapy options" and perform options permitted to competent speakers. L attempts to keep C on track by reverting to routines of therapy and casting C as a "frustrated patient."

Both L and C employ normal interactive resources for arguing. They take turns. They threaten. They defend. They raise their voices. Thus, C demonstrates her competence as a discourse partner. Not only has she expertly conformed to the institutionalized discourse routines of therapy, but she also demonstrates the capacity to shift successfully and easily into another discourse genre. In spite of this finely tuned negotiation demonstrating C's competence as a communicator, C remains cast in the role of the incompetent patient. Which returns us to our first observation: The institution of therapy brought with it a fixed role for C—that of the incompetent patient. The rigid role masks C's potential as a competent communicator and a competent consumer, able and willing to make decisions regarding her future.

Thus, the argument not only exposes the strong drive of both participants to maintain established therapeutic identities and shape talk to fulfill these roles, but it also reveals competence that has been masked by the institution of aphasia therapy. The therapist was "blind" to the fact that the difficulty encountered with the session was due to a competent human being struggling to extricate herself from a dependent social role. As in all conversation analysis, it is easy to be insightful retrospectively. The reader will appreciate that the transcribed argument, although taking pages to transcribe and analyze, occurred in a matter of minutes; the therapist did not have the luxury of deeply analyzing each utterance. As a caring person who genuinely wanted to improve C's communication, she was surprised and bewildered by the conflict. We question the institution of traditional therapy, not the therapist. Panagos (1996) raised the possibility that structured therapy, with rigid role casting, can have undesirable side effects. We believe that these data provide an example of potential problems associated with institutionalized therapy routines: specifically, the failure to appreciate potential communicative competence in our clients, the undermining of a client's communicative confidence, and the potential dissolution of therapeutic relationships. Even though routines of therapy have evolved in order to support the therapist's position as a mediator and facilitator, these routines can create an atmosphere that fails to foster a client's competence, confidence, and well-being.

Analysis of this aphasia therapy session raises interesting questions about traditional therapy as an institution. Does the institution of therapy overenforce nonegalitarian role casting as a means to mediate communication change? Does rigid role casting deprive our clients of an opportunity to successfully experience a variety of communicative roles? Does the institution of therapy prevent us from viewing the interactive competence of individuals cast as "disordered"? What is the effect on communicative competence of such practices?

Further research is needed on the discourse of traditional aphasia therapy. In addition, study of alternative aphasia interventions could provide important insights. Alternatives to traditional aphasia therapy (such as conversation groups focused on social interaction) have been suggested in order to build increased social participation and foster communitive confidence (e.g., Elman & Bernstein-Ellis, 1996; Kagan & Gailey, 1993; Simmons-Mackie, 1997). Research comparing the interactive dynamics of these interventions to traditional therapy discourse might reveal methods of mediating communication change while, at the same time, reinforcing and expanding a variety of social roles. Perhaps further study of the interactions between therapists and clients can increase our understanding of this complex but extremely important aspect of therapeutic effectiveness and help us hear the "other voices" of our clients.

APPENDIX

Argument Session Transcript

Setting: Aphasia therapy session between L (speech-language pathologist) and C (client). L and C are seated across from each other at a table in a therapy room.

1	L:	Your weekend was okay?
2	C:	Is what? ((leans forward, gazes at L))
3	L:	Your weekend was okay?
4	C:	Is sleep ((gestures sleep)) yeah. ((smiles))
5	L:	Did you sleep a lot?
6	C:	Oh, yeah ((nods))
7	L:	Did you sleep a lot during the day?
8	C:	Yeah.
9	L:	Me too with my cold.
10	C:	Oh, is is bad?
11	L:	It's better. Yeah. It's better.
12	C:	Yeah? ((nods yes))
13	L:	Yeah. I had the flu
14		when I missed you last Wednesday
15		but it was all gastrointestinal.
16	C:	O::h
17	L:	Then I came— I woke up Friday morning
18		and I had this bad cold.
19	C:	O::h ((nods no))
20	L:	But it's getting better.
21		I'm taking stuff.
22		But the medicine is making me sleepy (pause) too.
23		I don know.
24		Did you get your physical therapy
25		schedule straightened out?
26	C:	I don't know ((shrugs)) is yeah.
27		I don't know ((hand out, shrugs))
28		(pause) later see.
29	L:	They're gonna try and keep it the same
30		I understand.
31	C:	Yeah ((shrugs))
32	L:	Okay. All right. Let's run through ((clears throat))
33		and look at our pictures

34		Remember we had pulled 10 pictures out.
35		I'm gonna kind of mix 'em up a little bit.
36		Um::: I want you to tell me in as many words
37		as you can, tell me what's happening in the picture.
		((places picture on table))
38	C:	The c couple is bed in. What isy:: ((points to picture))
39	L:	Okay. Okay. The couple is IN the bed.
40		What are they doing?
41	C:	Sleep.
42	L:	Mhm. The couple is in bed SLEEPING.
43		Can you try to say that whole sentence for me?
44	C:	The couple is bed is sleep.
		((looking at "sleeping" card then looks up steadily at L))
45	L:	Mhm (pause) ngkay.
46		The couple is in bed SLEEPING. Okay.
47		If I can give you a tablet here.
		((putting a tablet and pencil before C))
48		All right. I want you to write that sentence for me.
49	C:	hhhhhh ((audible sigh)) ((clears her throat))
50		(pause) ((downward gaze, shakes head no))
51		I don know ((quiet voice, rapid, clipped rate))
52	L:	(hhhhh) ((hissing laughter sound))
53		You can do it. You can do it. You can do that.
54	C:	((Writes)) hhhhhh ((sighs loudly)) ((stops writing))
55		(pause) ((writes then drops pencil))
56		((pushes the tablet toward L and lifts eyes to L))
57		((looks down; leans back with downward gaze))
58	L:	Goo:d. Very good.
59		Can you read that sentence for me now?
60		Read that whole sentence.
61		C: (pause) ((downward gaze, leans forward))
62		((clears throat, eyes closed))
63		Is NE:::W please ((lifts "sleeping" card)) ((looks at L, then down,
		then up and down rapidly))
64	L:	New? [What ya mean?
65	C:	[Yeah, plea::se ((tense voice))
66		I don know ((nods "no" rapidly))
67		is is alu ((gestures stop))
68		((writes "enough")) ((loudly drops pencil))
69		PLEA:::SE
70	L:	Enough?=
71	C:	Yeah.
72	L:	=What ya mean?
73	C:	Isy ((pointing to "sleeping" card))
74		is is is good ((speaks rapidly, points to tablet then to card))
75		is NE:::W ((points to L))
76	L:	What's new?

77		What ya [mean it's new?
78	C:	[Is is too
		((leans forward and sweeps hand across cards on L's side of table))
79	L:	You want anoth[er one?
80	C:	[Yeah, plea::se.
81	L:	What I'd like you to do is go through
82		and [read it after you've written it.
83	C:	[I know (pause) I don kno::w ((gaze down))
84		O::h o:h no::::: ((grabs head))
85	L:	Too frustrating today?
86	C:	Yeah— ((clipped, terse))
87	L:	Okay. The couple is sleeping in bed.
88		That was good. Perfect sentence.
89		Nothin' wrong with it ((singsong intonation))
90		Awright, let's look at this one.
91		Tell me in as many words as you can
92		what he is doing.
93	C:	((holds head, hand over left eye; gazes down))
94		((moves hand to cheek and rests head on fist)
95		((clears throat, then looks up))
96		Is what?
97	L:	Tell me in as many words as you can
98		what he is doing?
99	C:	A MAN IS IS IS READ ((angry voice)) (pause) ((gazes at card))
100		IS BOOK ((points to picture)) ((loud, tense, terse))
		((looking up, lips tight, staring at L))
101	L:	Mhm, a ma:n is rea:ding a boo:k.
102	C:	[Yeah—
103	L:	[That's right
104		Where is he?
105	C:	Is what? ((staring at L and leaning forward))
106	L:	Where is he?
107	C:	E:::z s::: ((staring at L and leaning forward))
108	L:	Mhm. You're going to tell me he's sitting, huh?
109	C:	Is what? ((staring and leaning forward))
110	L:	What is he sittin' in?
111	C:	(pause) ((leans forward)) Is blue ((rapid))
112		.hhhhhhhh ((inspiration through clenched teeth))
113	L:	It is blue, huh? Mhm
114	C:	[(((leaning foward gazing steadily at L))]
115	L:	The ma:n is rea:ding a BOO:K in a CHAI:R, huh?
		((slow and exaggerated speech))
116		((C sits back))
117		He's sittin' in a chair, huh?
118	C:	Yeah.
119	L:	What do you call that famous chair

120   you guys have at home?
121   C: ((frowns)) [Is what?
122   L: [The easy chair, huh?
123   C: Yeah
124   L: Is that what you were going to tell me?
125   C: I don know is is ((crying, looking down at lap, body turned to side))
126   L: Is it frustrating today?
127   (pause) C————, it's okay. (pause) All right? ((said in soft voice))
128   ((pause)) Just take it each day as it comes
129   ((places a box of tissues directly in front of C))
           and we just do as much as you can do, okay?
130   C: ((Turns to L, leans forward)) So:::rry
131   L: So[rry?
132   C: [Yeah
133   L: Don't apologize. No need to apologize.
134   [No reason to say you're sorry
135   C: [(((C grabs tissue box, abruptly, puts it aside, looks down))
136   L: Okay? (pause) Want to skip the writing part today?
137   You tell me what you feel up to [doing, okay?
138   C: [NO IS IS
                                          ((leaning forward, speaking loudly, rapidly))
139   IS IS IS NEW ((gestures writing))
140   PLEA:::SE ((holds up picture card))
141   CARD IS (pause) [I don know isy=
142   L: [Mhm
144   C: Is PLEA::SE NE:W (pause) ah CARD ((pleading intonation))
145   L: Oh, you want different [pictures?
146   C: [PLEA:SE! YES ((nods))
147   L: O:::::H. Oh. Okay.
148   Well, remember last time we talk[ed=
149   C: [hhhhhhhhh
                                           ((sigh and downward gaze))
150   L: =and we went through the pictures
151   and I just picked 10 out and said
152   we'd [work with these a few times?
153   C: [I know I know ((looking away and shaking head "no"))
154   ((raises hand as in stop gesture))
156   No, I don know is ((hand to forehead)).
157   L: I know (soft voice)
158   C: Isy I don know ((hand up)) where
159   I don know. Bye-bye ((looking down, waves bye, nodding no))
160   is me ((points to self)) [isy ((looking at L))
161   L: [Well, I'll try to find
162   some different pictures but remember
163   when I found some that wer- had more to them
164   and it got you frustrated 'cause
165   you tried to write so much? (pause)

166		Ya remember that?
167		So we said we'd back up and try these again.
168	C:	((looking down, looks up and then down))
169		Isy, I don know isy. Is bye-bye ((waves with rapid expansive gesture))
170		Is <u>MONEY ISY</u> ((gestures grasping money to self))
171		<u>BYE-BYE</u> ((waves))
172	L:	About money?
173	C:	<u>YEAH:::: IS ME. PLEA::SE</u>
174		<u>IS NEW</u> ((leans forward; stares at L))
175	L:	<u>OKAY, OKAY. IT'S AWRIGHT!</u>
176		I'll find some new ones.
177		Can we use these today then
178		[since I haven't picked any new ones out?
179	C:	[hhhhhh ((sighs, gazing down))
180		((puts hand to head over left eye))
181		(pause) ((points to video camera)) is bye-bye ((stop gesture))
182		isy ((points to camera)) Please
		((low voice, quiet and terse; chin resting on fist))
183	L:	I'm not understanding.
184		You want me to turn that off?
185	C:	Yes please.
186	L:	I don't really know how to do it.
187	C:	uh well, bye-bye isy ((gestures pulling plug))
188		Isy is good.
189	L:	Oh, unplug it? hhhha ((breathy laugh))
190		Well, I don't want to damage it C———. ((L stands up))
191		Let me come around and see if
192		I can unplug it or stop it.
193	C:	I don know isy ((standing up and moving toward camera))
194	L:	I'm not very good with these. O::h
		((standing at camera looking at it))
195		You rather Nina not tape you today?
196	C:	No, is bye-bye ((turning to leave))
197	L:	Hang on, let me go get Nina to undo it.
198		I don't want to break it. Okay?
199	C:	((Reaches for cane and continues to leave))
200	L:	C——— it's okay ((places hand on C's shoulder))
201	C:	<u>I DON KNOW ISY IS MONEY. IS</u> ( ) ((high pitch and voice breaks))
202	L:	C——— ((pleading tone as C leaves))
203	C:	((Leaves room))

REFERENCES

Bobkoff, K. (1982). *Analysis of the verbal and nonverbal components of clinician-client interaction.* Unpublished doctoral dissertation, Kent State University, OH.

Brookshire, R. H. (1992). *An introduction to neurogenic communication disorders.* St. Louis, MO: Mosby.

Brown, P., & Levinson, S. (1978). Universals in language usage: Politeness phenomena. In E. Goody (Ed.), *Questions and politeness* (pp. 58–189). Cambridge, England: Cambridge University Press.

Button, J., & Lee, J. (Eds.) (1987). *Talk and social organization.* Clevedon, England: Multilingual Matters, Ltd.

Damico, J. S., & Damico, S. K. (1997). The establishment of a dominant interpretive framework in language intervention. *Language, Speech and Hearing Services in the Schools, 28,* 288–296.

Damico, J., & Simmons-Mackie, N. (1996). *Maintaining impairment in aphasia therapy: The co-construction of deficit via talk-in-interaction.* Paper presented at the International Pragmatics Association Conference, Mexico City.

Davis, G. A. (1993). *A survey of adult aphasia and related language disorders.* Englewood Cliffs, NJ: Prentice-Hall.

Duchan, J. (1993). *The IRE structure as viewed ethnographically.* Presentation at the First International Round Table of Ethnography and Communication Disorders, Urbana, IL.

Elman, R., & Bernstein-Ellis, E. (1996). *Effectiveness of group communication treatment for individuals with chronic aphasia.* Presentation at the American Speech-Language-Hearing Association Annual Convention, Seattle, WA.

Goodwin, C., & Goodwin, M. (1990). Interstitial argument. In A. Grimshaw (Ed.), *Conflict talk* (pp. 85–117). Cambridge, England: Cambridge University Press.

Goodwin, C., & Heritage, J. (1990). Conversation analysis. *Annual Review of Anthropology, 19,* 283–307.

Grimshaw, A. (Ed.). (1990). *Conflict talk.* Cambridge, England: Cambridge University Press.

Kagan, A., & Gailey, G. (1993). Functional is not enough: Training conversational partners for aphasic adults. In A. Holland & M. Forbes (Eds.), *Aphasia treatment: World perspectives* (pp. 199–226). San Diego, CA: Singular.

Kearns, K. (1985). Response Elaboration Training for patient initiated utterances. In R. Brookshire (Ed.), *Clinical aphasiology conference proceedings* (pp. 196–204). Minneapolis, MN: BRK Publishers.

Klippi, A. (1991). Conversational dynamics between aphasics. *Aphasiology, 5,* 373–378.

Kovarsky, D. (1989a). *An ethnography of communication in child language therapy.* Unpublished doctoral dissertation, University of Texas, Austin.

Kovarsky, D. (1989b). On the occurrence of okay in therapy. *Child Language Teaching and Therapy, 5*(2), 137–145.

Kovarsky, D. (1990). Discourse markers in adult-controlled therapy: Implications for child centered intervention. *Journal of Childhood Communication Disorders, 13*(1), 29–41.

Kovarsky, D., & Maxwell, M. (1992). Ethnography and the clinical setting: Communicative expectancies in clinical discourse. *Topics in Language Disorders, 12*(3), 76–84.

Maxwell, M. (1993). Conflict talk in a professional meeting. In D. Kovarsky, M. Maxwell, & J. Damico (Eds.), *Language interaction in clinical and educational settings* (pp. 68–91). Rockville, MD: American Speech-Language-Hearing Association.

McTear, M. F., & King, F. (1991). Miscommunication in clinical contexts: The speech therapy interview. In N. Copeland, H. Giles, & J. M. Weimann (Eds.), *Miscommunication and problematic talk* (pp. 195–214). London: Sage.

Mehan, H. (1979). *Learning lessons.* Cambridge, MA: Harvard University Press.

Panagos, J. (1996). Speech therapy discourse: The input to learning. In M. Smith & J. Damico (Eds.), *Childhood language disorders* (pp. 41–63). New York: Thieme, Inc.

Pomerantz, A. (1984). Agreeing and disagreeing with assessments: Some features of preferred/dispreferred turn shapes. In J. Atkinson & J. Heritage (Eds.), *Structures of social action: Studies in conversation analysis* (pp. 57–101). Cambridge, England: Cambridge University Press.

Porch, B. (1981). *The Porch index of communicative ability.* Palo Alto, CA: Consulting Psychologists Press.

Porch, B. (1994). Treatment of aphasia subsequent to the Porch index of communicative ability. In R. Chapey (Ed.), *Language intervention strategies in adult aphasia* (pp. 178–183). Baltimore: Williams & Wilkins.

Psathas, G. (1995). *Conversation analysis: The study of talk-in-interaction.* London: Sage.

Ripich, D. N. (1982). *Children's perceptions of speech therapy lessons: A sociolinguistic analysis of role-play discourse.* Unpublished doctoral dissertation, Kent State University, OH.

Ripich, D. N., Hambrecht, G., Panagos, J. M., & Prelock, P. A. (1984). An analysis of articulation and language discourse patterns. *Journal of Childhood Communication Disorders, 7*(2), 17–26.

Sacks, H. (1987). On the preferences for agreement and contiguity in sequences in conversation. In J. Button & J. Lee (Eds.), *Talk and social organization* (pp. 152–205). Clevedon, England: Multilingual Matters, Ltd.

Sacks, H., Schegloff, E., & Jefferson, G. (1974). A simplest systematics for the organization of turn-taking for conversation. *Language, 50,* 696–735.

Schiffrin, D. (1987). *Discourse markers.* London: Cambridge University Press.

Schiffrin, D. (1990). The management of a cooperative self during argument: The role of opinions and stories. In A. Grimshaw (Ed.), *Conflict talk* (pp. 241–259). Cambridge, England: Cambridge University Press.

Schiffrin, D. (1994). *Approaches to discourse.* Cambridge, MA: Blackwell.

Silvast, M. (1991). Aphasia therapy dialogues. *Aphasiology, 5,* 383–390.

Simmons, N. (1993). *An ethnographic investigation of compensatory strategies in aphasia.* Unpublished doctoral dissertation, Louisiana State University, Baton Rouge, LA.

Simmons-Mackie, N. (1997). *Adult aphasia: Alternatives to traditional approaches.* Presentation at the Southwest Conference on Communicative Disorders. Albuquerque, NM.

Simmons-Mackie, N., Damico, J., & Nelson, H. (1995) *Interactional dynamics in aphasia therapy.* Presentation at the Clinical Aphasiology Conference, Sunriver, OR.

Varenne, H. (1987). Analytic ambiguities in the communication of familial power. In L. Kedor (Ed.), *Power through discourse* (pp. 129–152). Norwood, NJ: Ablex.

Wilcox, J., & Davis, G. A. (1977). Speech act analysis of aphasic communication in individual and group settings. In R. Brookshire (Ed.), *Clinical aphasiology conference proceedings* (pp. 166–174). Minneapolis, MN: BRK Publishers.

Chapter 15

The Social Construction of Language Incompetence and Social Identity in Psychotherapy

Kathleen Ferrara
Texas A&M University

INTRODUCTION

Recent work in the dialogical or conversational version of social constructionism (Coulter, 1979; Gergen, 1994; Shotter, 1993) advances the notions that reality is interpersonally negotiable and that the social setting and its participants are primary in the ascription and ratification of mental states. McNamee and Gergen's (1992) treatise *Therapy as Social Construction*, along with the work of Labov and Fanshel (1977), *Therapeutic Discourse*, and Ferrara (1994), *Therapeutic Ways With Words*, call attention to the discursive realities created within the setting of the psychotherapy session. Ferrara (1994) examines how language and self are mutually constructed in therapeutic discourse as people interweave pieces of their own and others' sentences, metaphors, and narratives. The individual psychotherapy hour, actually 50 minutes, is a powerful force in the lives of hundreds of thousands of individuals as they work through problematic aspects of their lives with degree-holding and trained professionals, such as clinical psychologists and psychiatric social workers. Because language is both the method of diagnosis and the means of treatment in the so-called talking cure, it is surprising that so little is known about language use in psychotherapy.

Although the bulk of psychotherapy sessions are constructive events in the lives of clients, this chapter examines five discourse practices within the mental health community that contribute to the creation of client feebleness or linguistic incompetence, paying particular attention to the

343

complex ways in which this role is responded to and sustained throughout the therapy session by the self- and other-appraisals of a multi-voiced community. It uses an ethnographically enriched discourse analysis to investigate language of the therapist, the absent but invoked mental health community, the client, and the client's voice to self and others. The data are drawn from 48 hours of tape-recorded consecutive psychotherapy sessions, with special focus on the talk between three therapists and three clients in individual sessions in private practice in the American Southwest. Each client was audio recorded for six hour-long sessions over the course of 6 to 8 weeks. Both male and female clients and therapists are represented.

BACKGROUND

The seeds of a quiet revolution are currently being planted within the mental health community in the change from a modernist approach to a postmodern approach. Within the newer framework there is a healthy questioning of the premises generated from within the mental health community. As McNamee (1992) observes, "the modernist reliance on the individual as the primary organizing principle of society is replaced in postmodernism by a communal, relational, interactive attention to understanding the social order" (p. 191). Specifically, according to Fruggeri (1992, p. 41), therapists are beginning to question the medical model on which psychotherapy was developed and are attempting to demystify the therapist's transformative skills and stance as expert.

The medical model relied on diagnosis of a disorder, a cure, and an expert knower who could administer a solution. This expert knower was able to navigate between the world of trained psychotherapists and the mind of the client. In fact, in an influential paper, Anderson and Goolishian (1992) have advocated what they call a "not-knowing approach to therapy." In this approach the client is the expert. Taking the client as the expert involves the "abnegation of the role of the therapist as a superior knower, standing above the client as an unattainable model of the good life" (Gergen & Kaye, 1992, p. 74) and, instead, a shift toward "viewing the therapeutic encounter as a milieu for the creative generation of meaning." In this framework the "client's voice is not merely an auxiliary device for the vindication of the therapist's pre-determined narrative, but serves . . . as an essential constituent of a jointly constructed reality" (p. 74). A small but growing number of scholars and practitioners share the view of Anderson and Goolishian (1992) that "human action takes place in a reality of understanding that is created through social construction and dialogue" (p. 26), and see that "meaning and understanding are socially constructed by persons in conversation, in language with one another. Thus, human action takes place in a reality of understanding that is created through social construction and dialogue" (p. 29).

However, as Gergen and Kaye (1992) admit, the vast majority of therapy still retains "significant vestiges of the modernist view" (p. 175). In short, the quiet revolution is in its earliest stage. Fewer than several dozen researchers are championing this approach to psychotherapy, and the filtering into the ranks of everyday practitioners has barely even started. We can compare the progress to the uphill battle for acceptance of the notion of "communicative competence" in another applied realm, that of language learning.

For that reason, we look in this chapter at specific ways in which psychotherapy, as actually practiced, falls short of the goals advocated by workers such as Gergen and Kaye, McNamee, Fruggeri, and Anderson and Goolishian. This chapter traces ways in which the context, or structure, of psychotherapy "furnishes the client a lesson in inferiority" (Gergen & Kaye, 1992, p. 171). All too often, "the client is indirectly informed that he or she is ignorant, insensitive, woolly-headed, or emotionally incapable of comprehending reality. In contrast, the therapist is positioned as all-knowing and wise" (Gergen & Kaye, 1992, p. 171).

Gergen and Kaye (1992) state that

the therapeutic process must inevitably result in the slow but inevitable replacement of the client's story with the therapist's. The client's story does not remain a free-standing reflection of truth, but rather, as questions are asked and answered, descriptions and explanations are disseminated by the therapist, the client's narrative is either destroyed or incorporated—but in any case replaced—by the professional account. (p. 171)

These views present a rather harsh picture so I invite the outside observer to be the judge, using examples from the corpus to form the basis for assessment. The large majority of client–therapist sessions are extremely therapeutic, often yielding lifelong benefits (see Ferrara, 1994). However, we can still ask if the darker side of therapy is that many therapists do not encourage people to accept themselves as they are, for who they are, but rather encourage clients to change by denigrating their language skills and sense of self.

FIVE GENERAL WAYS IN WHICH THERAPISTS REINFORCE THE SELF-PERCEPTION OF LANGUAGE INCOMPETENCE

In this chapter I identify five general practices, or strategies, in the mental health community and their role in reinforcing clients' self-perception of language incompetence:

1. THE CREATION OF THE EXPERT-TO-NOVICE STANCE
2. METALINGUISTIC COMMENTARY ON THE PROPER USE OF LANGUAGE at the client's expense
3. REAUTHORING EMOTIONS, squelching the Client's Voice
4. THE MANUFACTURE OF HYPOTHETICAL DIALOGUE, in which the therapist speaks as if he/she had entered the mind of the client and were voicing his or her words
5. RECYCLING EPISODES OF COMMUNICATIVE FAILURE

Each of these practices is examined in turn in an attempt to appreciate the magnitude of the problem. Specific examples from actual discourse contain salient utterances indicated by arrows, boldface, or dots.

Strategy 1: The Expert-to-Novice Stance

The first strategy is creation of the expert-to-novice stance, in which the therapist draws on and the client accepts the medical model of a pathology or problem in need of a 'cure' and an expert practitioner. Three items play a part: (a) overt instruction, (b) the use of professional "we," and (c) jargon (e.g., "fixation," "project onto"). In Example 1, for instance, the male therapist tells a female client, "I want you to do some homework," and "I want you to start learning how to have more control." His stance is that of a professor, in charge of learning and giving a homework assignment, which he calls in the last line "a very clever assignment."

Example 1 (Overt instruction)

    Therapist: There's something I'd like you to do.
    Client: Okay.
→ Therapist: I want you to do some homework. Uh I want you to (4) take uh 10 important relationships to you . . . and I want you to uh like in one column put their name and in the second column I want you to put which part of you is most in (.) uh (3) most there in that relationship. Is it the cold aloof part or is it or is it the soft, warm-hearted.
             . . . . . .
→ Therapist: I want you to start learning how to have more control.
    Client: Okay.
    Therapist: 'Cause I think as soon as you learn how to (.) learn that you do have more control than you think you do, that you won't feel great but that you'll feel better. (2)
    Client: Okay.
    Therapist: So it's really a very clever assignment from that angle.

The client puts up no objection and actually completes three fifths of the assignment for the next session held a week later.

In Example 2, the therapist appropriates the pronoun "we," drawing on her affiliation with an entire learned body of practitioners, from Freud on, when she instructs the client "We don't believe you forget anything. . . . It's all in there," referring to the unconscious. The client attempts to dispute the therapist's interpretation three times with "no" or *not*, then falls silent after a feeble "Well" in the face of the vociferous claim to science by the therapist.

Example 2 ("We")

Client: I thought most of today that I had so much to tell you. . . . Now I'm here! I don't have much else to (.) tell you.
Therapist: Do you think it's the tape?
Client: No: I had forgotten about the tape.
Therapist: Hm.
Client: No. I <u>had</u> forgotten about it.
→ Therapist: But you see, we don't believe you forget. Remember. . . . We've worked together long enough. You ought to know what I believe about the unconscious. The unconscious doesn't forget. It's all in there.
Client: My conscious didn't know it.
Therapist: Well, I think it probably does have something to do with why you feel funny about what's to say. That's my guess.
Client: Well (6).

Examples 3 and 4 illustrate the role of jargon in giving therapists the upper hand. Although every specialized field has its jargon, it is notable that psychology has penetrated the popular culture to such an extent that the person on the street is familiar with dozens of major psychology concepts. My data indicate that clients from both the working and middle class utilize psychological jargon adroitly in their sessions. Nonetheless, there is a proprietary tendency by therapists to define and explain concepts even when their clients avow knowledge of the terms. Notice in Example 3 that the male therapist defines the term *autistic* even though the client says, "Yeah," he knows the term. Recorded discourse previous to this extract reveals that both the client and the therapist know that the client is fixated on pedophilic fantasies and has been treated by a psychiatrist in another state. Nevertheless, the therapist defines the two underlined terms *autistic* and *fixated*.

Example 3 (Jargon)

Therapist: Um it's as if the kiddie porn um represents uh metaphorically (.) some of your feelings about yourself(.) uh some of your more childlike or regressive desires but uh (.) with a considerable tendency to involve a (.) how shall I say (.) a self-limiting or a a (.) a self-blaming side (.) when you're into that. It's like you're pulling in (.)

Client: Mmh
Therapist: You're not, you're not growing (.) somehow
Client: Mmhm See well [the reason I haven't been]
Therapist: [That's what I think]
Client: growing for a while (.) and I have noticed that this thing,
             this fascination has kept me from uh entering in a relation
             with other people
→ Therapist: With people (.) Yeah. More autistic. You know the term
             autistic?
Client: Yeah
Therapist: Uh, more withdrawn. So that's I guess what I was trying to
             indicate by this (.) uh pulling in=
Client: =unhuh=
Therapist: =yourself. (3) Maybe (.) you're also less powerful because if I
→   understand some of the literature on (.) on men that are
             (.) fixated (.) is the term for it— Fixated means that they've
             never been able to (.) have any fantasies of sexual relations
             with adults (.)
Client: Yeah
Therapist: either heterosexual or homosexual. The individual tends
             to be seen as seeing themself as very powerless. Uh very
             impotent. So, wanting to have the fantasy of the child be-
             cause that's the only one that that can be controlled.
Client: Yeah.

Gergen (1994) observes that a host of psychological items are "no longer professional property but are part of 'what everybody knows' in the cultural vernacular"; he gives the examples, "stress, depression, split personality, identity crisis, midlife crisis, PMS" (p. 158). More frighteningly, as the culture absorbs the argot of the profession, Gergen (1994) points out:

> the role of the professional is both strengthened and threatened. If the
> client has already identified the problem, in the professional language, and
> is sophisticated about therapeutic procedures (as is true in many cases),
> then the status of the professional is placed in jeopardy. (p. 16)

When a psychological term becomes common sense, professionals must reclaim knowledge, couch it in science, and technologize the term in order to reassert the authority and justification for their claim to specialized knowledge. Gergen (1995, p. 153) gives the example of the development of technical definitions of *depression* in order to reconstitute depression as an object of professional knowledge. We can see this at work in Example 4, which is examined again later in another context. Here the therapist is at pains to define depression, although she is speaking to a client with a Ph.D. who has read widely in psychology.

Example 4 (Jargon)

Client: I can't get out of my system how angry I am at them.
Therapist: Good! That's what I want you to recognize, that this is all connected up with anger. You are furious.

. . . . . .

            And it makes you so angry that you get— I think I think you hurt yourself is what I think happens when you get angry.
→   ((sniff)) (5) Maybe to save them? (1) See, that's essentially what depression is: is it's hurting oneself to spare others, taking it in, letting it eat you, corrode you from the inside out so that you can still be nice to others out there in the world. They won't hurt to be. You will not visit your grief on them. Well, I think you try so hard to do that. When it comes out here now, so we're getting somewhere.

Strategy 2: Metalinguistic Commentary on the Proper Use of Language

The second practice that contributes to the construction of language incompetence is the therapist's metalinguistic commentary on the proper use of language. This strategy is particularly troubling for its implications of inferiority and language deficiency. Frequently, therapists complain about ambiguity; or implicitly invoke the Sapir–Whorf hypothesis (the belief that language influences thought) with undereducated clients; or deny the labeling of the clients, forcing them to abandon their words and accept the "correct" form provided by the therapist. When therapists offer metalinguistic commentary on the client's use of language it sends a critical message that they are superior and the client is somehow less capable. Consider Example 5. Here the therapist accuses the client of using pronouns in an ambiguous way, something that all speakers do. This client is blue-collar with aspirations for upward mobility, and may be particularly vulnerable to claims of superiority in language.

Example 5 (Proper use of pronouns)

Client: Cause cause I had that [her own beauty parlor] uh before I was divorced from the kids' dad. I—well when we were divorced that's what I was doing and that's the reason Mother had me go on to (.) Union Carbide because my income there— you couldn't tell from one week to the next what it'd be and uh ((sniff)) insurance and all the basics. (2) So I guess I felt like I was (.) you know, like it was a necessity for me to do it.
→ Therapist: To do what? Uh when you— you use a lot of pronouns that I don't know what you mean, like "it," ["that:" and]

Client: [Okay] Well I felt like it was a necessity for me to go <u>get</u> that other job (.) uh (.) because uh financially it was for me and the kids ((sniff)). It really wasn't a hard one to do. I just, I didn't care for it when I had to work out on the floor there. Uh I enjoyed it in the office.

Therapist: What were you doing in ( ).

Client: Well out on the floor was where they made batteries. I was just workin' line (.) and it was pretty good [money (.) for] back then.

Therapist: [Production line?]

Client: Unhuh and then for two years I worked in the accounting office. Then I had to go back to the floor to make more money because Teddy and I got a divorce.

In Example 6, the therapist, dealing with the same working-class client, implicitly invokes a notion familiar to many readers but not necessarily to the average person, the Sapir–Whorf hypothesis. He does not name the hypothesis but instructs the client that he would like her to ask her lover about his reactions to her weight. He says at the first arrow, "I'd like you to ask it verbatim." After a 1-second pause he paraphrases *verbatim*, "you know, like I'm saying," indicating his doubt about her lexicon. He then says, "In fact, I think I'm gonna write it down so I can have you ask it in the exact words."

That there is a metalinguistic gap present becomes apparent when the client interprets the reason for his giving written instructions as "so I don't forget it." The mismatch in intentions for the "exact words" is negotiated in an exchange when the therapist explains, at the second arrow, "sometimes a single word can make a difference." His assumption, implicitly the Sapir–Whorf hypothesis that language may affect thought, is not fully appreciated by the client even by the end of the hour. At the third arrow the therapist scolds the client for speaking "in a rather vague manner" and again points out that her pronouns don't seem clearly related to anything, providing a lesson in language inferiority.

Example 6 (Implicit Sapir–Whorf hypothesis)

GW6 (16)

(prior talk about weighing 170 lbs. and a recent gain of 40 lbs.)

Therapist: Well there's something I'd like you to ask Martín.

Client: Okay.

→ Therapist: And I'd like you to ask it verbatim (1) you know, like I'm saying. In fact I think I'm gonna write it down so I can have you ask it in the exact words.

Client: Okay, so I don't forget it.

Therapist: Huh?

Client: Just so I don't forget it.

→ Therapist: Well, yeah, cause the words, sometimes a single word can make a difference. And I'd like you to look him straight in the eye and say, "Martín, you told me that sometimes you want me to be fat. (2) What would be too fat?" (2) And I'd like you to ask him (.) to have him describe what "too fat" would be. And not to let him get away with, for example, something you commonly do with me (.) is to uh answer
→ things in a rather vague manner or (.) use pronouns that don't really seem to be clearly uh related to anything. So have him describe in great detail what too fat would be. . . . What's his cut off point?

Strategy 3: Reauthoring of Emotions

Coulter (1979) points out a phenomenon called reauthoring of emotions and observes that we can "intelligibly suggest to people that they abandon certain emotions on rational grounds, that we can argue them out of their anger, shame, embarrassment, disappointment, fear, etc." (p. 129). A particularly lucid and compelling account of how multiple voices attempt to reauthor the emotion of fear is Capps and Ochs' (1995) account of *Constructing Panic*. Observe in Example 7 how reality is personally negotiable through the relabeling of emotions. The therapist asks at the arrow, "Are there any other words . . . that would describe the feeling?" He wants the female client to relabel "weaker" as "caring" but, as shown at the first dot, the client expresses her reticence and objects that to her the two feelings are similar. The therapist insists on his view that the two are quite different. This example is especially notable if we examine the client's five feeble attempts to maintain her own point of view. As shown with dots, she objects with two turns of "I don't know," one "but," and two "wells," along with stating that "weaker" and "caring" are the same. Given Pomerantz' (1984) well-supported findings of the preference for agreement, these five prefaces to disagreement are considerable and suggest coercion. Here again the notion that a single word can make a difference is expressed.

Example 7 (Sapir–Whorf and reauthoring)

Client: . . . I felt myself slipping (.) after I got my divorce. It just seemed like (.) maybe after each tra— every time something happened ((voice quaver)) I felt myself getting weaker. (3)

→ Therapist: Weaker. (4) Are there any other words that you could put on that piece, I mean, any other words that would describe (.) the feeling?

Client: •1) Mm I don't know. They're confused so I don't know ((upset)).

Therapist: I'm just, you know, it may be "weaker" but it might be a different feeling too, and I I've found that when people (.)

put the wrong label (.) on a feeling, well ah then it ends up in<u>cr</u>easing the negative feelings a great deal 'cause then they're not only, they not only <u>feel</u> something that doesn't <u>feel</u> good, they feel they can't make sense out of it either.

Client: •<u>May</u>be it's "caring." I don't I don't know.
Therapist: Right. [Yeah] it sounds real different than "weaker."
Client: •[but]
Client: •Well, I guess I feel "weaker" and "caring" are the same.
Therapist: Do you? (2) How come? (1) you [mean-] They don't strike me— I
Client: •[well]
Therapist: I guess there're some similarities but they don't strike me as being the same kind of feeling at all.

In contrast, Anderson and Goolishian's (1992) proposed "not-knowing approach" means, according to Shotter (1993) an

adoption by the therapist of both a way or method of listening to what clients say and also a special way of responding to it, a sustained attitude which "invites" clients to try to say what their world is like to them rather than as in everyday life where we struggle to institute our form of life in the face of other peoples'. (p. 120)

Therapists who silence the clients' realities, effectively coercing rather than coaxing them to disown their feelings, constrain the clients' ability to know themselves as they attempt to change. By privileging their own perceptions and legitimizing only their notions, therapists may fail to recognize the power of interpersonally negotiating lived realities and different ways of knowing.

Strategy 4: Use of Hypothetical Dialogue, Speaking for the Other

We turn now to a fourth way in which the therapist authors the words and thoughts of the client in a critical manner. In this section we examine the creation of hypothetical dialogue, in which the therapist speaks as if he were the client, literally putting words in the client's mouth, taking on a presumed voice and taking away the voice of the client. This may serve the purpose of allowing the client to become an observer of her own linguistic functioning, splitting the self into an experiencer and an observer. The therapist appropriates the client's own internal voice for the purpose of public appraisal. This appraisal is invariably negative, holding the client's words up for critique, thus adding to linguistic incompetence.

In Example 8, the therapist and client have been discussing the topic of the client's warring sides, her strong/weak dichotomy. At the first arrow, the therapist takes on the voice of the client and expresses aloud his assessment of what her thoughts are. He takes on her presumed thoughts: "I'm not sure when one's gonna pop up or." At the second arrow he speaks for the client as if he were inside her head when he says, "So that rather than saying, 'Golly this is really interesting, I have . . . these two different parts of me' . . . you kinda go, 'Oh no: I'm acting weird again and it means I'm crazy.'" The client's response to this, prefaced by "Well," shows less than ready acceptance of the therapist's appropriation of her voice.

Example 8 (Hypothetical dialogue)

Therapist: (6) I think (.) that part of the problem here is not that you have (.) these two different sides (.) or these two different aspects (.) but that you don't feel like you have any control over them.

Client: Uh

Therapist: (6) Is that true?

Client: Uh (1) I I we:ll, yeah and no. Yeah, most of it. [That is true]

Therapist: [But it it is] sort of like a Jekyll and Mr. Hyde sort of thing.

Client: Mmhm mmhm.

→ Therapist: "I'm not sure when when one's gonna pop up o:r"

Client: Yeah, cause one minute I can be (.) the more cocky a:nd (.)I don't=

Therapist: =and probably what you've never really thought about in a very organized way is (2) the fact that you at some level make a decision about what you— how you're gonna act. But you don't really think about THAT part. You just think that sometimes you're feeling (1) you know, cocky and aloof, and sometimes you end up feeling like uh you gotta go hide in the closet.

Client: Mmm. (1) Yeah cause I I have— like I have said, told Martín before, you know, I I can be in one mood one time and the next minute I'll be right back out of that mood. Well that's what it is, uh the feeling (1) he calls me Milly whenever I'm feeling ((softly)) . . . cause I told him one time I feel like a Milly Mouse.

Therapist: (( ))

Client: Yeah the little country bumpkin, you know.

Therapist: He had a— how do you take that when he says it? Does that feel like a (.) caring kind of statement or [does it] make you become more aloof and cold?

Client: [Oh he] ((sigh))

Therapist: Or do you respond to it now?

Client: Well, like, if he's on the phone or something he'll say, "Who's this?" And I'll say, "Well, it's Milly" And he said,

"Milly?" And I said, "Yeah." And he says, "Well what kind
of day did you have, and I'll say, "Same old thing." So it's
not just him that uses Milly, it's me too.

Therapist: See my, my guess is that you ((noise)) end up not learning
a lot about yourself when that kind of stuff starts happening
because you get worried about it.

Client: Mmhmm.

→ Therapist: So that rather than saying, "Golly, this is really interesting,
I have, uh I have these two different parts of me and uh,
boy they're really different and in one situation I can act
like (.) this and in another situation I act like this. Uh. And
I'm probably gonna learn a lot about how I do this, I mean
uh 'cause I could learn a lot" you kinda go, "Oh no: I'm
acting weird again and it means I'm crazy."

Client: Well I I was talking about this thing. I had said before I
think I've hit on things more than what I really I was,
because I have said there's no middle of the road for me,
you know, either black or white.

Therapist: Yeah Yeah I can see that. But I also think the two parts that
you're dealing with are helpful parts, Wilma, that it would
be useful for you to learn something about how to integrate
them. (4).

In Example 9, taken from a different dyad, the female therapist expresses
aloud what she assumes the client was thinking at a particular juncture when
she wanted to call her therapist after hours but was afraid of becoming a
nuisance.

Example 9 (Hypothetical dialogue)

Client: But I did catch you at a bad time. I'm sure, Monday. (2)
Ah (6) (It was I guess) this was Wednesday that I talked to
you.

Therapist: So again you're wrestling with some real mixed feeling
about me. You think of me and turn to me when you're
feeling some stress. You want to make a call, want to have
a word with me

→ about some things. You fight off that. "I should learn to (.)
steel myself and if I just wait a little longer this impulse will
pass."

Client: Yeah because I don't know whether you're gonna get mad
or not. . . .

Similarly, in Example 10 the same therapist speaks the presumed inner
thoughts of the client, "They didn't really want to know. See, I tried," at
the third arrow. In this segment the therapist also uses the fifth strategy
(to be discussed) to connect past and present situations in which commu-

nication was problematic for the client. The client's family and present bosses all communicate badly. At the first and second arrows in Example 10, the therapist voices a presumed family motto, speaking for the client and her parents, "Don't tell me anything personal" and "Don't want to know." At the third arrow the therapist follows by appropriating the inner voice of the client, speaking as if she were the client.

Example 10 (Hypothetical dialogue and recycling communicative failure)

      Client: . . . What I felt that Tom started doing after that conversation was what I saw going on in my family. They don't argue openly, they don't criticize openly, they don't do anything openly, just just simply don't deal. You know, whether it's not have time to make assignments or not have time to critique them (.) um.

      Therapist: They avoid feelings.

      Client: Yeah, they avoid (.) them.

      Therapist: They avoid FEELINGS. They avoid uh sexual feelings, close

→   feelings, personal revelations. "Don't tell me," you know, is is the message in your family. "Don't tell me anything personal."((laugh))

      Client: Might as well be.

→ Therapist: "Don't want to know." And you <u>told</u> him. (3) Told him, and he's coming on like your family. And maybe you picked (.) well (.) I think you were caught tsk ((noise next door))

      Client: What? Maybe I picked what?

      Therapist: Maybe you picked well who you would tell. He confirms the whole dynamic for you (.) so nicely (.) by turning away from

→   you when you do tell. How depressing. We're back there. "They didn't really want to know. See, I tried." Uh. It's uh. They didn't come through very well for you, that's for sure.
              . . .

Strategy 5: Recycling of Episodes of Communicative Failure

Last, a frequent theme of therapy clients is to recite past communicative failures with significant others. Therapists seize on these portrayals of inadequacy and recycle the topic of failures, resulting in a reinforcement of language inadequacy and the view of the therapist–client dyad as a way to learn more appropriate models of language use. This subtle conveyance of linguistic incompetence serves to sustain the client dependence on the therapist as a means to gain communicative competence.

In Example 11, three of the strategies previously discussed can be seen at once. We can observe (a) hypothetical dialogue; (b) jargon defined, perhaps unnecessarily; and (c) emphasis on poor communication as a recurrent theme. At the first arrow, the therapist gives voice to what the client has never uttered as if it were spoken aloud. She releases the pent-up frustration and resentment by giving it a linguistic basis in the privacy of the therapy hour. At the second arrow, the therapist draws parallels between maladjusted communication patterns at home and work with her comment, "Does this all sound like you know the the the synopsis of what went on in your house? (7) Poor communication." At the third arrow, the therapist defines depression, as we have seen.

Example 11 (Showing hypothetical dialogue; jargon defined, perhaps unnecessarily; and emphasis on poor communication as a recurrent theme)

Therapist:	. . . What I'm uneasy about is that you are you seem to be taking it so to heart
Client:	((deep breath))
Therapist:	about what it says about your essential basic character. And now I hear you projecting onto me that I'm saying it must be
→	something about your attitude, and then you angrily say, "Goddammit I'm not gonna do the lousy filing and yes I didn't have any enthusiasm to get in there on time." (1) I know that and I
Client:	At least for the last month
Therapist:	I am not attacking you on that basis.
Client:	(8) I can't get out of my system how angry I am at them.
Therapist:	Good! That's what I want you to recognize, that this is all connected up with anger. You are furious. And I do want to sort of sidestep my being involved in it ((laugh)). I will not betray you but I think you are furious that once again you've been betrayed. (2) And you tried to do your best and they didn't use you well. Indeed they misused you. [They seem to be promoting] dullards and (.) jerks
Client:	[And somebody else decided.]
Therapist:	and overlooking your assets. Does this all sound like you know
→	the the the synopsis of what went on in your house? (7) Poor communication. Heaps of blaming. Not recognizing what you could do. Taking for granted what you did. And giving lots and lots of attention to people who didn't deserve it. Or who manipulated with them, played games with them. And it makes you so angry that you get— I think I think you hurt yourself is what I think happens when you get angry. ((sniff)) (5) Maybe to save them? (1) See, that's essentially
→	what depression is: is it's hurting oneself to spare others, taking it in, letting it eat you, corrode you from the inside out so that you can still be nice to others out there in the world. They won't hurt to be. You will not visit your grief on them. Well, I think you try so hard to do that. When it comes out here now, so we're getting somewhere.

Example 12 is a segment that provides another instance of a therapist's pointing out patterns of communicative failure. This extract illustrates the social construction of language incompetence by a multivoiced community. In it the client reveals that first his mother, then teachers, then fellow graduates from a deaf school (all references highlighted by boldface) contributed to the composite picture of language inadequacy, providing a lesson in inferiority. It is the case that the client has difficulty getting the timing right to interrupt or ask for clarification. However, as the literature in conversation analysis reveals (Sacks, Schegloff, & Jefferson, 1974), turn taking is hard not only for the hearing impaired but for everyone. Nonetheless, the facts are that this client is able to participate fully in psychotherapy, the talking cure. He is not so inadequate after all. By concentrating on the 5% language failures rather than reassuring the client, the therapist is perhaps underemphasizing the fact that the client has achieved numerous communicative successes, even in the face of disability—graduating from college, maintaining a job, having friends, and engaging in psychotherapy.

Example 12 (Patterns of communicative failure)

Client: Well I would always feel extremely uncomfortable around people, uh very ((throat clear)) like I am not really ((throat clear)) capable of sharing. I guess my being hard of hearing has a lot to do with that, because it really is hard for me to understand other people, especially when there're three or four following around. An uh (2) I suppose very early in my life I was taught that it's very rude to interrupt when someone is talking. Uh I remember **my mother** would put up her hand like this in the form of a three,* which means "Be quiet. I am talking."

Therapist: How did she get that?

Client: I haven't the vaguest idea. But she did that only— ever since when I was very young, very young, so I haven't even given it a thought (.) to that. But she always said "Be quiet. I am talking." "Now be quiet. Mother is talking."

Therapist: Hm.

Client: I remember one time that I— see more than a few times I got I used to get. I wanted to say something. She would hold up my hand like this. I wanted to reach out and just grab her fingers.

Therapist: Very very angry about that. Yes, telling you to shut up in a sense. And you were just trying to understand what people were saying to you.

Client: Yeah.

---

*The sign or hand gesture referred to (the thumb and little finger bent to touch with 3 middle fingers held erect) is widely used by Brownies and Girl Scouts to signal respectful turn taking. It is perhaps a gesture more familiar to females than males.

Therapist: And that's what— by interrupting you would be able to get some clarification on what they were saying.
Client: Yeah
Therapist: Now you seem to do that with me quite okay.
Client: Oh yeah. I don't. I think like I can do that fairly well, not nearly as crippling as it used to be.
Therapist: Mmhm.
Client: But I remember when I was uh (.) I used to have **teacher** tell me uh, "Don't be afraid to tell me to uh speak up louder if you can't read, uh hear me. So I'd say, well then I'd interrupt to tell her to speak up louder and after a while they get very irritated
Therapist: yeah
Client: because you're doing it. So the teachers, they don't figure. And I've got more than a few negative feedbacks.
             . . . . .
Therapist: Hm but I can see how you were crippled and very very hurt by that.
Client: Just recently though uh a bunch of **kids who are X [deaf institute] alumni** I uh met over at Christy's place, just about, oh yeah, this Sunday. And uh I was uh X, graduated from X but anyway, alumni. So she invited me over there. They were all manually responding and something like that. And uh I just sat there on the edge of the group and watched their hands. Several times Christy asked me, "Uh, can you understand all this?"
Therapist: Mmhm.
Client: I said, "yeah, yeah" But I'm not really. I wasn't really understanding all this. And (1) finally after the meeting was over and everybody got up, went away, you know, Christy said she was just trying to do me a favor. She noted that I had a lot of good ideas for the uh alumni. But I didn't enjoy. She was disappointed I didn't get very much involved
Therapist: Mm
Client: uh and with the group, you know. I didn't seem too worried about that. I just stayed away. You know, the're all manual.
Therapist: Why were you holding back?
Client: Uh (2) I guess I was still a little afraid of them. You know, they were, all communicate manual. My manual sign is very bad. So just try to listen. I didn't want to seem like an ass, uh, dumb cluck, you know like that.
Therapist: **Well, that's the kind of feeling you had when you were a child with the people that were uh (.) normal in hearing.**
Client: Yeah
Therapist: **And now you have it with the people who are deaf— who use the manual sign.**
Client: Right.
Therapist: Same phenomenon. Different uh aspect. ((laugh))
Client: Extreme kind of reverse now.

Therapist:	Reversed, yes. Uh huh. But you didn't want to speak up and tell them uh you didn't want to express yourself that you had trouble with your confidence of uh your manual signs.
Client:	uh huh

The preceding example illustrates that we live in and through the discursive identities we develop in conversation with one another. One purpose of psychotherapy is to explore the relativity of these realities.

SUMMARY

In summary, the field of psychotherapy, as practiced in the foregoing examples, has sufficient opportunity to reexamine its tenets and to question its role in contributing to the discursive construction of language incompetence. Exemplified above are five practices that diminish clients and their language abilities. These are:

1. The creation of the expert-to-novice stance
2. Metalinguistic commentary on the proper use of language at the client's expense
3. Reauthoring of emotions
4. The manufacture of hypothetical dialogue where the therapist speaks as if he/she had entered the mind of the client and were voicing his or her words
5. Recycling episodes of communicative failure.

HOPEFUL SIGNS FOR THE FUTURE

To conclude on a positive note and demonstrate that there is hope, we can report several signs of change on the horizon. If therapists do not yet fully recognize their role in the social construction of language incompetence, we can still draw inspiration from two facts: A few researchers/practitioners have begun lecturing, publishing, practicing and demonstrating discursive psychology (see Edwards & Potter, 1992) and their influence is growing. Another point is that clients themselves are being educated in the role that social construction plays in their lives. Some are also voicing their concern about the social construction that may devalue them, characterize their words as scarcely adequate, and move them to silence (Gergen, 1995, p. 153) while others assert their superiority and justify their role as models of the good life.

An encouraging illustration of the second point can be seen in Example 13, in which the client, in her own words, explains to her therapist what social construction is and how she sees herself as possibly contributing to the picture others may have of her. We can hope that if clients are this enlightened about the role that a culture and its members, as well as the individual self in interaction, play in the construction of reality and the social self, then therapists will not be far behind.

Example 13 (Client's view of social construction, in her own words)

Therapist: . . . And, so; it's hard for you to know with whom, under what conditions, when are things safe. When can you be less guarded, when can you not. I think that's brand new to you. Terra incognito.

Client: (2) Although I remember a lot of examples of uh uh young adulthood, especially, where I was <u>not</u> guarded. And that's what got me in trouble.

Therapist: Hmm. Give me an example.

Client: Oh, I can always say things that can be used against me later. And it's uh [whether it's a self]

Therapist: [What are you think]ing of when you said that? What what?

Client: Well, sometimes it's a self-criticism. Um sometimes the jokes that I make are taken seriously at some point but it's usually— I like to think a lot about uh (1) some of what I read in sociology. It was a literature generally called **the social construction of reality** and it's where (.) uh a situation is ambiguous but becomes important to <u>some</u>body to be able to define a person *or* a situation. And you start looking for all those little bitty things and and you put them into whatever mixture you've already got going yourself and come up with a definition of this person. And sometimes I think that some people had, have a picture of <u>me</u> and when I really stop to think I can think of ways that I (.) pro<u>mo</u>ted that picture. But it was maybe a joke that I made at my own expense or uh (.) you know, when I answer the question very specifically without elaborating on it to give some of the (.) more positive or rosier details (.) whatever [uh]

Therapist: [Mmhm] (5) So you— you're wondering more what role you play in the=

Client: =Yeah, I think I do my own. I do myself some damage sometime.

The therapist here shows interest in understanding what the client has to say about social construction.

CONCLUSION

Finally, we can agree with Gergen (1994, p. 147) that the "ways we talk" are intimately intertwined with patterns of cultural life. They sustain and support certain ways of doing things and prevent others from emerging.

Representatives of institutions, in particular, have a responsibility to recognize the role of social construction of reality and to actively use this force for self-enhancing rather than self-denigrating purposes. Rather than stifling and supplanting clients' voices or moving them to silence, therapists should acknowledge to themselves and their clients their mutual complicity in the complex construction of self through language. With the "not-knowing approach" advocated by Anderson and Goolishian (1992), therapists can facilitate a climate for change in which receptivity to explore multiple viewpoints underscores the acceptance of the relativity of meaning. The present study furthers the small but growing tradition of discursive psychology, underscores concepts of the co-construction of social realities, and contributes to a discourse-centered ethnography of communication by elucidating practices in a little-studied discourse community, psychotherapy.

REFERENCES

Anderson, H., & Goolishian, H. (1992). The client is the expert: A not-knowing approach to therapy. In S. McNamee & K. J. Gergen (Eds.), *Therapy as social construction* (pp. 26–39). Newbury Park, CA: Sage.

Capps, L., & Ochs, E. (1995). *Constructing panic.* Cambridge, MA: Harvard University Press.

Coulter, J. (1979). *The social construction of mind.* Totowa, NJ: Rowan & Littlefield.

Edwards, D., & Potter, J. (1992). *Discursive psychology.* Newbury Park, CA: Sage.

Ferrara, K. W. (1994). *Therapeutic ways with words.* New York: Oxford University Press.

Fruggeri, L. (1992). Therapeutic process as the social construction of change. In S. McNamee & K. J. Gergen (Eds.), *Therapy as social construction* (pp. 40–53). Newbury Park, CA: Sage.

Gergen, K. J. (1994). *Realities and relationships: Soundings in social construction.* Cambridge, MA: Harvard University Press.

Gergen, K. J., & Kaye, J. (1992). Beyond narrative in the negotiation of therapeutic meaning. In S. McNamee & K. J. Gergen (Eds.), *Therapy as social construction* (pp. 166–185). Newbury Park, CA: Sage.

Labov, W., & Fanshel, D. (1977). *Therapeutic discourse: Psychotherapy as conversation.* New York: Academic Press.

Maynard, D. W. (1991). Interaction and asymmetry in clinical discourse. *American Journal of Sociology, 97,* 448–495.

McNamee, S. (1992). Reconstructing identity: The communal construction of crisis. In S. McNamee & K. J. Gergen (Eds.), *Therapy as social construction* (pp. 186–199). Newbury Park, CA: Sage.

McNamee, S., & Gergen, K. J. (Eds.). (1992). *Therapy as social construction.* Newbury Park, CA: Sage.

Pomerantz, A. (1984). Agreeing and disagreeing with assessments: Some features of preferred/dispreferred turn shapes. In J. M. Atkinson & J. Heritage (Eds.), *Structures of social action* (pp. 57–101). Cambridge, England: Cambridge University Press.

Sacks, H., Schegloff, E. A., & Jefferson, G. (1974). A simplest systematics for the organization of turn-taking in conversation. *Language, 50,* 696–735.

Searle, J. (1995). *The construction of social reality.* New York: The Free Press.

Shotter, J. (1993). *Conversational realities: Constructing life through language.* Thousand Oaks, CA: Sage.

AUTHOR INDEX

A

Abrahams, R., 200, 202
Adelman, H. S., 172n.4
Agar, M., 145
Ainsworth-Vaugh, N., 259, 260
American Psychiatric Association, 30
Anderson, H., 344, 345, 352
Anderson, R., 166n.6
Antaki, C., 274n.6
Asch, A., 261n.1
Astington, J., 5
Atkinson, J. M., 193, 262
Atwood, J. D., 246
Au, K. H., 198

B

Baber, C. R., 200, 201, 204, 207, 208
Bagshaw, N., 292
Barker, P., 245, 246
Baron-Cohen, S., 30
Barton, E., 269
Bates, E., 36
Beach, W., 281
Beck, B., 245
Bedrosian, J. L., 57
Bellah, R., 138
Bereiter, C., 198
Bernstein-Ellis, E., 334
Bettelheim, B., 252
Beukelman, D., 225
Biber, D., 8
Bierce, A., 125
Birge, J., 149
Black, B., 111, 112
Black, K., 261n.1
Black, M., 245, 246
Bliss, L., 111, 112

Bobkoff, K., 318
Boden, D., 262
Bogdan, R., 78
Boggs, S. T., 198
Braunwald, E., 257
Braverman, M., 30
Brinton, B., 19, 113
Brody, J., 149
Brooks, C. I., 36
Brookshire, R.H., 315
Brown, H. D., 84
Brown, P., 317, 332
Bruner, J., 85–86, 108, 109
Bryan, T., 111, 112
Bryce, J., 126
Button, J., 317
Buzolich, M. J., 70
Byrne, P., 257

C

Calculator, S., 240
Capps, L., 351
Carbaugh, D., 4, 5, 144, 145, 146, 147
Carveth, D. L., 245, 246
Cazden, C. B., 292
Chabon, S. S., 31
Chafe, W., 266n.4
Chen, 113
Chenail, R., 262
Church, M. A., 36
Cicourel, A. V., 171, 193
Cirillo, L., 246, 248
Clark, H., 9, 50–53, 55, 61, 69
Clifford, J., 261n.2
Coie, J., 111, 112
Cole, M., 246
Cole, P. A., 31
Coles, G. S., 172n.4

Collings, J., 198
Conrad, P., 264, 270
Cormac, E. C., 245
Coulter, J., 343, 351
Coulthard, R. M., 175 n.9, 292
Coupland, J., 6
Coupland, N., 6
Courchesne, E., 30, 45
Crago, M., 309
Craig, H., 114, 199
Craine, M., 246, 248
Creech, R., 54–58
Crider, C., 246, 248
Culatta, R. A., 31
Cupach, W., 84

D

Dalby, D., 200
Damico, J. S., 292, 293, 313, 314
Damico, S. K., 292, 293, 309, 313, 314
Dandy, E. B., 204, 207
Danforth, S., 13
Davis, G. A., 314
Davis, K., 262
Davis, L., 261 n.1
Dawson, G., 30, 45
Deaton, A. V., 300
Dee, K. M., 204
Dejoy, D., 309
Del Vecchio-Good, M. J., 258
Denham, S., 111, 112
Dent-Reed, C. H., 246
Dodge, K., 112
Drew, P., 176 n.10, 180, 257, 262, 263
Duchan, J. F., 6, 212–213, 224, 226, 292, 308, 309, 318
Duranti, A., 149
Dweck, S., 201, 202

E

Edwards, D., 359
Eggins, S., 5, 8
Eisenberg, A. R., 198
Elman, R., 334
Emerick, L, 224, 226
Englemann, S., 198
Ervin-Tripp, S., 198

F

Faici, A., 257
Fanshel, D., 343
Fasold, R., 209
Featherstone, H., 261 n.1
Fein, D., 30
Feinberg, H., 149
Ferguson, D., 261 n.1
Ferguson, P., 261 n.1
Ferrara, K. W., 245, 343, 345
Fey, M., 292
Fine, M., 261 n.1
Finegan, E., 8
Finger, A., 261 n.1
Firth, A., 262
Fisher, S., 259, 262
Fogel, A., 36
Forest, M., 240
Fox, B., 158
Frankel, R. M., 30–31, 44
Fraser, L., 36
Friedson, E., 258
Frith, U., 30
Fruggeri, L., 344, 345
Frye, D., 5
Fujiki, M., 19, 113
Furman, R., 111, 201

G

Gailey, G., 334
Gallagher, H., 261 n.1
Galpert, L., 45
Gannon, J., 138
Garfinkel, H., 173, 180, 190, 193
Garretson, M., 139
Geertz, C., 146, 261 n.2
Geralis, E., 259, 272 n.5
Gerber, K., 259
Gergen, K. J., 4, 84, 85, 86, 108–109, 343, 344, 345, 348, 359
Gertner, B., 113
Giles, H., 6
Glickman, K., 138
Goffman, E., 9, 11, 12, 13, 150 n.3, 166, 261
Goldstein, H., 292
Gonçalves, O., 246, 248
Goode, D., 13

Goodwin, C., 149, 173, 192, 193, 291, 292, 331, 332, 335
Goodwin, M. H., 150, 192, 315, 331, 332, 335
Goolishian, H., 344, 345, 352
Graham, S., 113
Grandin, T., 30, 45
Greenspan, S. I., 30
Grice, H., 8
Griffin, P., 175n.9
Grimshaw, A., 179n.13, 335
Grumet, G. W., 36
Guess, D., 47
Gumperz, J., 149

H

Haager, D., 113
Haarbauer-Krupar, J., 297
Hadley, P., 113
Halliday, M. A. K., 5
Hambrecht, G., 318
Hancock, L., 264, 265
Hanks, W. F., 145, 291
Harris, M. A., 201
Harris, P., 5
Hatfield, F., 19
Hayashi, M., 158, *168*
Haynes, W., 224, 226
Hazen, N., 111, 112
Health, S. B., 198
Heap, J. L., 171
Heath, C., 174, 183, 257, 258, 259
Hegde, M., 224, 228
Hendrix, D., 246
Henry, K., 297
Heppner, C., 142–143
Heritage, J., 193, 315
Heritage, P., 257, 262, 263
Hertweck, A., 171, 191
Hevey, D., 261n.1
Hewitt, L. E., 309
Higginbotham, D. J., 65, 70
Hill, D., 45
Hill, J., 149
Hillyer, B., 261n.1
Hoag, L. A., 57
Holmes, V., 134
Holstein, J. A., 171
Holt, R., 111, 112
Howard, D., 19
Hudley, C., 113

Hudlin, R., 201
Hudlin, W., 201
Humphries, T., 128n.4
Hymes, D., 5, 7–8, 83, 149

I

Instad, B., 261
Isselbacher, K., 257
Ivey, M., 201, 202

J

Jacobson, L., 18, 192
Jacoby, S., 306, 309
Jasperson, R., 158, *168*
Jefferson, G. N., 52, 150, 152, 153, 163, 173, 175n.8, 176n.10, 193, 315, 357
Jennings, K. H., 171, *194*
Jennings, S. H. M., 171, *194*
Joesting, A. K., 198
Johnson, D. E., 57
Johnson, M., 19, 245
Johnstone, B., 266n.4
Jordan, B., 193
Jordan, C., 198
Jorgensen, C., 240
Juskowitz, S., 292

K

Kagan, A., 334
Kane, B. D., 204
Kaye, J., 344, 345
Kaye, K., 36
Kearns, K., 315, 321
Kendon, A., 6
Kent, R., 308
Kernan, K., 113
King, F., 292, 318
Kleinke, C. L., 36
Klippi, A.
Kochman, T., 200, 202, 203, 215
Kovarsky, D., 10, 123, 292, 293, 304, 309, 313, 314, 317
Kreckel, M., 10

L

Labov, W., 9, 198, 214, 266n.4, 343
Lakoff, G., 19, 245, 246, 252
Langer, E., 18

Lankton, C. H., 246
Lankton, S. R., 246
Lavation, L., 134
Lave, J., 300, 301
LaVesque, J., 141
Lee, J., 317
Leiter, K. C. W., 171, *194*
Lentz, E., 138
Leppik, I., 259
Lesham, T., 113
Leslie, A. M., 30
Levine, L. B., 246
Levinson, S., 317, 332
Levitt, M., 201
Lindenbaum, S., 261
Livingstone, E., 180
Lloyd, R., 180n.17
Lock, M., 261
Logan, A., 112
Long, B., 257
Lorendo, L. C., 31
Lovaas, O. I., 45
Lund, N., 212–213, 224, 226
Lynch, M., 172n.3, 175, 180, 180n.15, 180n.17, 193

M

MacKay, R., 171, *194*
Madsen, R., 138
Maehr, M. L., 192
Majors, K., 46
Marcus, G., 261n.2
Markowitz, P., 30
Marlaire, C. L., 171, 173n.5, 179, 180, 180n.16
Martin, J., 5, 257
Masters, 111
Mathy-Laikko, P., 70
Mattes, L., 211
Maxwell, M., 10, 127, 293, 309, 313, 314, 317, 332
Maynard, D. W., 5, 12, 171, 175n.8, 179, 180n.16, 258, 259, 261
Mazeland, H., 176n.10
McCormick, L., 199
McDermott, R., 50, 76
McHoul, A., 175n.9, 176, 180n.16
McIntosh, A., 5
McMullen, L., 246
McNamee, S., 343, 344, 345
McTear, M. F., 292, 318

Mehan, H., 171, 175n.9, 191, *194,* 292, 318
Meihls, J. L., 171, 191
Meitus, I., 224
Mercer, J., 18
Merrell, K., 113
Michaels, S., 198
Middleton, G., 224, 226
Miller, P., 113
Mirenda, P., 225
Mishler, E., 262
Mitchell-Kernan, C., 113, 198, 201, 202–203
Moerman, M.
Molineux, B., 57
Moore, C., 5
Morris, G., 262
Morris, J., 261n.1
Moser, L., 297
Mount, B., 225, 240
Mundy, P., 30, 45
Murphy, R., 261n.1
Murray, J.M., 246

N

Nagler, M., 261n.1, 281
Nehemkis, A., 259
Neidecker, E., 224
Nelson, H., 313, 314
Niemenen, R., 143

O

Ochs, E., 149, 306, 309, 351
Olson, D. R., 5, 246
Omark, D., 211
Ortony, A., 246
Owens, R., 200

P

Padden, C., 128n.4
Panagos, J. M., 292, 313, 316, 318, 334
Pannbacker, M., 224, 226, 244
Parsons, T., 257, 258, 261
Pennington, B., 30
Pepper, S., 246
Percelay, J., 201, 202
Petersdorf, R., 257
Philips, S., 150
Philipsen, G., 147
Phillips, M., 261n.1

Pindrozola, R., 224
Poeppelmeyer, D., 126, 127n.3
Pollner, M., 179, 190
Pomerantz, A., 7, 304, 318, 332, 351
Pop, S. C., 202
Porch, B., 314, 315
Potter, J., 359
Prelock, P.A., 318
Priel, B., 113
Prutting, C. A., 30, 292
Psathas, G., 315
Puett, V., 224, 226, 244

R

Raimondo, D., 127
Rank, K., 202
Rice, M., 113
Richard, B., 112
Richardson, A., 293
Ripich, D.N., 313, 318
Robillard, A. B., 50, 54, 58–64, 74, 79
Root, R., 257
Rose, T., 204
Rosenblatt, P., 245, 246
Rosenthal, R., 18, 192
Roth, D. R., 171, *194*
Rubin, 113
Rubin, R., 84
Rubovits, P. C., 192
Rutherford, S., 138

S

Sacks, H., 5, 12, 52, 150, 152, 153,
    175n.8, 176n.10, 179, 179n.13, 192,
    315, 332, 357
Sacks, O., 44
Saenz, T., 114, 117
Said, K., 151n.4
Saitoh, O., 30, 45
Sanders, K., 224, 226, 244
Sanders, L., 224, 226
Savigon, S., 84
Schaeffer, N. C., 191, 193
Scheflen, A., 9
Schegloff, E. A., 5, 12, 12n.2, 52, 150,
    152, 153, 175n.8, 176n.10, 177, 189,
    192, 258, 263, 315, 357
Schenkein, J., 175n.8
Schieffelin, B. B., 198
Schiffrin, D., 304, 317, 318, 329, 333

Schmidt, D., 259
Schneider, W., 264, 270
Schuler, A. L., 46
Scollon, R., 9
Scollon, S., 9
Searle, J. R., 245
Seligman, M., 18
Sexton, A., 204
Seymour, H. N., 212
Shapiro, J., 261n.1
Sharrock, W., 166n.6
Shaw, B., 261n.1
Sherman, T., 30, 45
Shotter, J., 343, 352
Shuy, R. W., 175n.9
Siegel-Causey, E., 47
Siegelman, E. Y., 246
Sigman, M., 30, 45
Silvast, M., 314
Silverman, D., 262
Simmons, N., 313
Simmons-Mackie, N., 313, 314, 334
Sinclair, J. M., 175n.9, 292
Slade, D., 5, 8
Smith, E., 201
Smith, G., 297
Smitherman, G., 200
Sonnenmeier, R. M., 309
Spencer, A., 45
Sperry, L., 113
Spitzberg, B., 84
Steinsalt, A., 167n.7
Sternberg, R. J., 246
Stevens, L., 111, 112
Stillman, R., 32, 46
Stockman, I. J., 199
Stoller, P., 214
Strevens, P., 5
Strong, T., 245, 246
Suchman, L., 193
Sullivan, D. M., 297
Sullivan, W., 138
Sun, 113
Sweidel, G. B., 78
Swidler, A., 138
Szekeres, S. F., 297
Szokolsky, A., 246

T

Tannen, D., 9, 150, 158n.5, 304, 305, 307
Taylor, S. T., 78, 261n.1

Tench, P., 9
Terry, R., 111, 112
Terry, S. E., 31
Tipton, S., 138
Todd, A., 262
Todd, C., 113
Tourangeau, R., 245
Townsend, J., 30, 45
Trix, F., 156, 167
Tur-Kaspa, H., 111, 112
Turner, M., 245, 246, 252

U

Umen, I., 292
Ungerer, J., 30, 45

V

Van Kleeck, A., 198, 200, 206, 208, 293
Van Maanen, J., 261 n.2
Vandercook, T., 225, 240, 241, 243
Varenne, H., 331
Vaughn, S., 113
Vekovius, G., 224, 226, 244
Ventola, E., 9
Verenne, H., 50, 76

W

Ward, M., 198
Ward, P., 6

Washington, H., 114, 199
Waterhouse, L., 30
Watson, L., 45
Watson-Gegeo, K. A., 198
Weiner, B., 18
Weismer, S., 19
Wellman, H., 5
Wetherby, A., 30
Whyte, S., 261
Wiemann, J. M., 70
Wilcox, J., 314
Wilkins, D. P., 65
Williams, C., 32, 46
Wilson, J., 257
Wolfram, W., 209
Wyatt, T. A., 197, 199, 205, 208, 209

Y

Ylivisakar, M., 297
Yoder, D. E., 70
York, J., 225, 240, 241, 243
Ysseldyke, J. E., 172 n.4

Z

Zimmerman, D., 262
Zola, I., 261 n.1
Zwernik, K., 225, 240

SUBJECT INDEX

A

Abdal, Pir Sultan, 163–164
Acceptance, 4
of children, 112, 113–114, 118
desire for, 39, 42, 44, 47
Action plan, *see* Personal futures plan
Addressees, 53
ADHD, *see* Attention deficit hyperactivity disorder (ADHD)
Adjacency triad, see Request-response-evaluation (RRE)
Adjectives, 8
Administrativeness, 174, 181
Adult-controlled intervention, 292
Adverbs, 8, 14
Adversarial relationships, 274–284
African-American English (AAE), 197, 209
African-American speech events, 200–201
copping a plea/gripping, 214
playing the dozens, 201–202, 205, 207, 214, 215–216
preschoolers, 205–206
rapping, 203–204, 206, 207, 215
signifying, 202–203, 214
tomming, 214
African-Americans
cultural identity and language, 198–201, 207
language testing in children, 198–200, 206–213
Agendas, report writing and, 22–23, 224–225, 238–242, 243
Aggression studies, 113
Albanians, 155
ALDA, *see* Association for Late-Deafened Adults (ALDA)
Alexander Graham Bell Association, 131

Alienation, 4, 12, 17, 21, 42
of nonmembers, 127, 128–130, 133–134
Alignment, 187–190
Alphabet boards, 50, 59, *see also* Augmentative communication devices
constraints of, 60–62
gender and use of, 63, 64
nurse/patient interaction with, 62–64
Ambivalence metaphors, 254–255
American culture, compared with Ottoman, 151
American Sign Language (ASL), 128, 139, 142, *see also* Sign language
American Speech-Language-Hearing Association (ASHA), 31
Animal metaphors, 252, 253t, 254
Aphasia therapy, 20
asymmetrical roles in, 313–314, 316–317
conflict within, 320–335
institutional practices of, 315–326, 330, 334
Appraisal, 5
Argument, discourse of, 330–335
Ascribed identities, 145–146
ASL, *see* American Sign Language (ASL)
Association for Late-Deafened Adults (ALDA), 133
Assumptions, 44
incorrect, 30–31
Asymmetries, 23, 149
physician/patient, 258, 263, 284
therapist/client, 313–314, 316–317, 345
Asynchronous movement, 9
Attention deficit hyperactivity disorder (ADHD), 17

collaborative diagnosis, 264–274, 283
controversial diagnosis, 264–266
Attitude, 5, 9
Attribution theory, 18
Audiences, 20, 21
Audiologically deaf, 133
Augmentative communication devices, 51, 55, 65, 72, see also under individual device
limitations of, 78
selective use of, 75–76
Augmented communication, 4, 55
communication rates, 66–70
constraints in, 54–62, 69, 70–72, 77, 78
suggestions/strategies for, 56, 57, 72, 74, 76
Authentic nurses, 62–64
Authority hierarchies, see Asymmetries
Autism, see Children with pervasive developmental disorders (PDD)

B

Baba Rexheb, 152, 156–157
Back on the Block (album), 204
Barrier structure metaphors, 248, 249*t*
Bebe's Kids (film), 201, 215–216
Behavior
cultural construct of, 113
popularity and, 112
Behavioral cues, 60, 74
Bektashi
cultural beliefs, 155–156
practices of repair, 150, 152–167
Belongingness, see Acceptance
"Birdland," 204
Blending, sound, 16
Blending subtest, 171–172, 173, 174*n*.7
Body movements, see also Gaze behaviors; Nonverbal behaviors
child during educational testing, 183–187, 189, 192, 293
clinician during educational testing, 180–183, 192
constraints in, 59–60
evaluation and, 9–10
Brigance Diagnostic Inventory of Early Development, 171*n*.2
Broken bone metaphors, 252, 253*t*

C

Call and response, 207
Cancer metaphors, 252
Casual conversations, 315–316
CHAT, 136*n*.11
Children
ADHD diagnosis in, 264–265
African-American
language testing, 198–200
speech events, 205–206
educational placement, 19–20, 272*n*.5, 273
social rules for, 121
Children with pervasive developmental disorders (PDD), 29, 30
desire for acceptance from, 39, 42, 44, 47
eye gaze, 36–37, 44–45, 47
focus on objects, 36, 37–38, 46, 47
judgment standards of, 34–36
perceived rejection from, 40–41, 44, 46, 47
verbalizations of, 42
Children with specific language impairment (SLI)
evaluating social competence (approaches to), 111–114, 122
evaluating social competence (study), 114–122
perceived incompetence of, 114
Claiming, 117
Clear communication, 141, 143
Clerc, Laurent, 139
Clerc Day, 139
Clients, see also Patients
asymmetries with therapist, 313–314, 316–317, 345
incompetence construction of, 15, 23, 62, 343–344, 345–359
role in psychotherapy, 13, 344
Co-construction of conversation, 56, 57–58, 66–68, 70, 77
Co-orientation, in testing, 173–174, 181, 184, 187, 189
Cognition and language, models of, 300–301
Cognitive scientists, 5
Cogswell, Alice, 139
Collaborative conversation, see Co-construction of conversation

Collapsed test sequences, 176–177, 187, 191
Common ground, 53, 57, 68, 79
Communication
clear, 141, 143
real, 141, 144, 146
Communication boards, 65, 75, see also
Augmentative communication devices
collaborative use of, 67–68, 70
selective use of, 75, 76
Communication competence, definition of, 83–84
Communication rates, of augmented communicators, 66–70
Communicative failure, recycling, 355–359
Competence, see also Incompetence; Social competence
classifications, 19
communication, 5, 83–84
comparisons, 16–17
components of, 19
as containment, 18–20
feelings of, 5, 102, 105–106, 107
conversational partners and, 94–97, 100, 103
loss of/lack of. see Incompetence, feelings of
patient, 259
perceived, in SLI children, 118, 122–123
physician, 258–259
testing, 19
Competence construction, 5–6
components of, 7–18
Competence judgments, 5–6, see also
Gaze behaviors; Negative evaluations; Positive evaluations
conditional, 17
hidden factors influencing, 20–21
of patients, 12, 259, 269, 284
of PDD children, 34–36
reports and, 6, 231–238
Competency-lowering, in TBI patients, 294–295, 303–304, 307–308
Compliance, patient, 17, 259, 282, 284, 318
Computerized communication devices, 55, 65
Conditional judgments, 17

Confidence, see Competence, feelings of
Constructing Panic (Capps & Ochs), 351
Container view, 18–20
Context, 18
histories and, 9, 10
language and, 197–198
Contextual constraints
augmented communication, 57–58, 62, 72, 74
rehabilitation therapy for TBI patients, 308–309
Conversation, see also Conversational partners casual, 315–316
interlocutors' co-construction of, 56, 57–58, 66–68, 70
tracking, 5–6
Conversational Analysis
aphasia therapy, 314–315, 332
Bektashi practice, 150, 152–154, 157–159, 161, 164–166
medical encounters, 262–263
turn taking, 357
Conversational partners, 98–99
feelings of competence/incompetence, 94–97, 100, 103
importance of, 144
Coordination devices, 58
Coping, metaphor and, 245–246, 250–252
Copping a plea, 214
Correction, 152, see also Repair
distinguished from repair, 150
embedded, 153, 158–159, 164–165
exposed, 153, 157–158, 160, 161–164, 164–165
master-initiated master-correction, 159
master-initiated repair of other-initiated other-correction, 163–164
other-correction, 152
other-initiated other-correction, 158–159, 163–164, 165
other-initiated self-correction, 153, 154, 157
self-correction, 154, 156, 164
self-initiated self-correction, 158, 160
student-initiated self-correction, 160–161
Crutches metaphor, 254

Cues
  behavioral, 60, 74
  helper-helpee relationships, 320
  importance of, 60, 74
  repair and, 293
  in testing, 173–176, 179, 180
Cultural agencies, 146
Cultural constructs, 50, 145
  behavior and, 113
  competence judgments and, 5, 20
  language disorders and, 22,
    208–213
Cultural identities
  deaf communities, 127–128,
    133–137, 140–142, 144,
    146–147
  disabled, 261 n.1
  effective communication and,
    63–64, 79, 144
  language and, 198–201, 207
Cultural pragmatics, 146, 147
Culturally hearing, 133
Culture, shared, see Cultural identities
Cyclert, 264

D

Deaf, see also Sign language
  among hearing parents, 125, 138,
    141, 144
  audiological, 133
  hard-of-hearing, 128, 133
  oral, 128, 131 n.8, 132
  real, 128, 147
  signing, 127, 147
Deaf American Monograph, 139
Deaf Comedy Club, 135
Deaf communities
  cultural identities of, 127–128,
    133–137, 140–142, 144,
    146–147
  nonmembers, 127, 128–130, 132,
    135, 142, 146
  alienation, 133–134
Deaf Life, 135
Deaf Way, 137, 140
"Deaf way, the," 137
Deafies, 138
Deafness
  as communication, 140

  as ethos, 140
  as history, 138–140
  paradox of, 127–128, 133–134
  as territorial, 137
Deficit frustration, 326
Delayed communication, 60, 69, 70–71,
    78
Delayed speech, 50, 52, 53
Diagnosis, 19–20, 257–258, 260, 263,
    see also Evaluation reports
  adversarial relationships in,
    274–284
  controversial (ADHD), 264–266
  emotional impact of, 23
  metaphor and, 248–250
  physician/patient collaboration in,
    264–274, 283
  significance of, 259–260, 273–274
  as situated practice, 22–23
Diagnostic and Statistical Manual of Mental
    Disorders, 30
Diagnostic evaluations, see Diagnosis
Diagnostic reports, see Evaluation reports
Dilemma metaphors, 254 t
Directives, 317–318
Disability Rag, 261 n.1
Disability Studies Quarterly, 261 n.1
Disabled identities, see Identities, disabled
Disattention, of interlocutors, 69, 78
Discourse markers, 163, 258, 266 n.4,
    293, 304, 317, 329
Domains of evaluations, 15–16
Door metaphors, 248
Dozens, see Playing the dozens
Dynavox, 65, 68–69, 70–72, see also
    Augmentative communication
    devices
  picture of, 82 f
  selective use of, 75–76

E

Ebonics, see African-American English
    (AAE)
Echolalia, 30, 31
Ecological assessments, 199–200
Educable Mental Impairment (EMI),
    272 n.5
Educational placement, 19–20, 272 n.5,
    273
Educational testing

children during, 183–187
clinicians during, 180–183
examiner/examinee interaction,
    171, 172, 173–174
feedback during, 191–192
instructional sequences, 174–175
interactional substrate, 172, 174,
    177–178, 184, 190, 192, 193
learning during, 190–191
recipiency and alignment, 187–190
repair in, 176, 178–180
smiling sequences, 192
testing instruments, 171 n.2, 172 n.4
testing sequences, 171, 172, 175–177,
    187, 191
local history of, 178–180
Elaborated testing sequences, 176
Eliciting language, 208
Embedded corrections, 153, 158–159,
    164–165
Embodied behaviors, *see* Body move-
    ments
Emotional impact, of diagnosis, 23
Emotional reactions, judgments based
    on, 45–46
Emotions, reauthoring of, 351–352
English language
    African-American English (AAE),
        197, 209
    learning & importance of conversa-
        tional partners, 94–97,
        98–99, 100, 103
    speaking & feelings of incompe-
        tence, 90–97, 103–104,
        106–107
    Standard American English (SAE),
        197
Environmental stimuli, failure to
    respond to, 37–38
Epithets, 8
Ethnomethodologists, 5
Evaluation reports, 15, 223, 224
    compared with progress reports,
        12, 22–23, 231–239,
        242–243
    organization of, 226–229
Evaluations, 3–4, *see also* Competence
    judgments
    competence comparisons and,
        16–17
    effects of, 12, 17–18

interactant positions and, 11–14
locally determined, 14–15
resources for expressing, 7–11
scope & domain of, 15–16
situated, 17–18
Evaluative markers, see Discourse markers
Evaluative standards, 10
    of children with PDD, 34–38
Evaluative terms, 8
Evidentials, 14
Expectancy theory, 18
Expectations, 13, 16–17
    and evaluation of PDD children,
        34–36
    identity and, 146
    time, 21
Expert-to-novice stance, 346–349
Exposed correction, 153, 157–158, 160,
    161–164, 164–165
Eye contact, *see* Gaze behaviors
Eye rolls, 10

F

Face, *see* Saving face
Face-to-face interaction, 6, 77
    through lip movements, 59
Fairy tale metaphors, 250, 251 t, 252
Feedback, *see also* Negative feedback;
    Positive feedback
    boosting self-image, 99
    diminishing self-image, 99, 100,
        102, 106
    disbelief in, 92–93, 96
    during educational testing, 191–192
    as a learning tool, 102, 105
Fitzgerald, Edward, 156
Flying nurses, 62–64
Fog metaphors, 249
Footing, 11, 13, 166
Fragmentation orientation, 308

G

Gallaudent University, 127, 135, 137, 139
Game metaphors, 174 n.7
Games for TBI patients, 299–300
    Going to the Moon, 301–307, 308
    rules of, 294, 299, 304, 305–306

Gaullaudet, Thomas, 139
Gaullaudet Day, 139
Gaze behaviors, 9–10
    aversion, 36, 44–45
    educational testing and, 181–187,
        189
    effect on competence judgments,
        20–21, 36–37, 44–45, 47
Gaze membership, 79
Gender (non-disabled), use of alternative
    communication, 63, 64
Gestures, *see* Nonverbal behaviors
Ghost responses, 325
Going to the Moon, 301–307, 308
Good (discourse marker), 14, 15, 179, 191
"Good Organizational Reasons for Bad
    Clinic Records" (Garfinkel), 173
Grammar, 8–9
Gripping, 214
Grounding, 53
Group membership, 79–80, *see also*
    Common ground; Cultural
    identities
Groups, problems of, 130–133
Guessing, 68, 70

H

Habits of the Heart, 138
Hard-of-hearing, 128, 132, 133
Hasidic communities, 149, 155
Head-mounted pointers, 55
Health care insurance, patient concerns
    of, 315, 329, 331
Health care providers, 296
Hearie, 130
Hearing, culturally, 133
Hearing loss, 128, 142, *see also* Deaf
    communities, nonmembers
Helper-helpee relationships, 320
Heuristics, 52
Hidden factors, competence judgments
    and, 20–21
Hirka, 153
History
    context and, 9, 10
    of deafness, 138–140
    testing sequences and, 178–180
Hyperkinesis, 264
Hypothetical dialogue, 352–355

I

Identities, *see also* Alienation; Competence;
    Cultural identities; Incompetence,
    feelings of
    ascribed, 145–146
    augmented communication and, 78
    construction of, 84, 85, 86, 92, 108
    disabled, 6, 133–134
    effect of evaluations on, 17–18, 20
    as evaluative, 4
    expectations and, 146
    footing shifts, 166
    reconstruction of, 90–94, 97, 98,
        99, 100–102, 106, 107, 109
    social participation and, 126, 144,
        145, 146
    TBI patients', 298
    watershed experiences and, 90,
        100–102, 104
Illness metaphors, 252, 253t
Iman Ali, 153
Immediacy premise, 52, 53–54
Implicatures, 8
Incompetence, *see also* Competence;
    Competency-lowering; Repair(s)
    construction of client, 15, 23, 62,
        343–344, 345–359
    construction of patient, 277–284,
        321–330
    feelings of, 4, 5, 6, 17, 18, 98,
        103–104
    augmented communicators, 56
    conversational partners and,
        94–97, 100, 103
    negative feedback and, 99, 100,
        102, 106
    speaking English, 90–97,
        103–104, 106–107
    speech-language pathology
        students, 35, 38, 39
    patient, 259
    perceived, 90, 92, 114
    public construction of, 151,
        163–164, 166
    record keeping, 173
    reports & construction of, 231–236
Individualized habilitation plan (IHP),
    240
Inheritance, 145

Institutional practices, 6, 17, 23, 262
    constraints of, 295–296, 314, 334
    failed communication and, 59–60
    of interaction, 50
    of therapy, 295–296, 315–326, 330
Instruction, overt, 346
Instructional sequences, 174–175
Insults, exchange of, see Playing the
    dozens; Signifying
Insurance, see Health care insurance
Interactants, positioning of, 11–14
Interactional substrate, 172, 174, 177–178,
    184, 190, 192, 193
Interjections, 8
Interlocking of sequences, 177
Interlocutors, 51
    alphabet boards and, 60, 61
    co-construction of conversation,
        56, 57–58, 66–68, 70
    disattention and, 69, 78
Internet, see World Wide Web (WWW)
Interpretation, 9, 11, 21, 85–86, see also
    Assumptions; Social construc-
    tionism
    of evaluations, 12–13
    of social competence, 122–123
Intersubjectivity, 30
Intervention, as situated practice, 23–24
Intonation, 9–11
Islamic Ottoman culture, 155
    compared with American, 151, 167
Isolation, see Alienation

J

Jargon, 346, 347–349, 355–356
Joint actions, 51–52, 53, 55, 56, 77
    with communication boards, 70
    faileed, 59
Jones, John W., 139
Jones, Quincy, 204
Journal of Compliance in Health Care
    (JCHC), 259
Journey metaphors, 250, 251t
Judgments, see Competence judgments

K

Khayyam, Omar, 156

L

Label quests, 198–199
Labeling theory, 18
Labels, diagnostic, 273–274
Languaculture, 145
Language
    as an object of play, 200–204,
        214–216
    eliciting, 208
    joint actions. see Joint actions
    metaphoric. see Metaphors
    social context of, 197–198
    speech events. see African-Ameri-
        can speech events
    testing in African-American chil-
        dren, 198–200, 206–213
Language and cognition, models of,
    300–301
Language competence, 19
Language disorders
    cultural considerations and, 22,
        208–213
    measuring social competence in
        children with, 112–113
    testing based on Standard American
        English (SAE), 197
Language incompetence, reinforcement
    of, 345–359
Language therapy, 23
Late-deafened adults, 133
Learned-helplessness, 18
Learning disorders, 112–113
Lexicon, 8
"Life as a Spectator Sport" (Heppner), 143
Linguistics, 8–9, see also Metalinguistics
Linguists, systemic, 5
Lip movements, 59
Lists, 305
Logic of Nonstandard English (Labov), 198
Loudness, 9

M

Mainstream, 261 n.1
Markers, see Discourse markers
Master-initiated master-correction, 159
Master-initiated repair of other-initiated
    other-correction, 163–164

Master-student relationships, *see* Student-master relationships
Medical metaphors, 252, 253*t*
Medical model of disabilities, 281–282, 284, 344
Membership
  gaze, 79
  group. *see* Group membership
Memory games, *see* Games for TBI patients
Memory skills, 300
Men (non-disabled), use of alternative communication, 63, 64
Mental status exams, 180*n*.15, 180*n*.17
Metapragmatics, 206
Metacommunicative devices, 207
Metalinguistics, 200, 206, 207, 349–351
Metaphor(s), 8, 15, 23
  clinicians' use of, 246
  container view, 18–20
  coping and use of, 245–246, 250–252
  describing ambivalence, 254–255
  diagnosis and use of, 248–250
  game, 174*n*.7
  personification, 252–254
Mindlessness/mindfulness theory, 18
Minimal brain damage, 264
Mishearings, 179*n*.13, 180
Miss Deaf America, 135
Misunderstanding, of PDD children, 30–31, 44
Mo' Yo' Mama! (Pop & Rank), 202
Mockery, 14
Modification, 152
Modifiers, 8
Mouth-speech communication, 54, 66*n*.6
Movements, *see* Body movements
Muhammad, 153
Muslim traditions, 151, 155
  Bektashi. *see* Bektashi
Mutual sense-making, 30, 31

N

Nachman, Rabbi, 167*n*.7
"Name that Tune," 151, 167
Natural disaster metaphors, 249–250
Nature metaphors, 248, 249, 249*t*
Neck rolls, 10

Negative evaluations, 12, 20
  of clients, 15
  of patients, 274, 278–283, 284
  of PDD children, 41, 44–45
  in reports, 23, 233–236, 243
Negative feedback
  diminishing self-image, 99, 100, 102
  as a learning tool, 102
Negative judgments, *see* Negative evaluations
Negative politeness, 150*n*.3, 152, 153
Neurobehavioral exams, 174–175, 180
Nightmares, 248
Nominals, 8
Nommo, 200
Non-face-to-face interaction, 6
Nonverbal behaviors, 9, 47, 65, *see also* Body movements; Gaze behaviors
  children during educational testing, 183–187, 192, 293
  clinicians' during educational testing, 180–183, 191–192
  and social acceptance of children, 114, 117–118
Nonmembers, *see* Deaf communities, nonmembers
Normal development, as a judgment standard, 34–35
"Not-knowing approach," 344, 352
"Not now," 14, 61, 62
Noun phrases, 8
Nouns, 8
Nurses, interacting with Robillard, 62–64

O

Object-oriented thinking, 46
Objects
  PDD children's focus of, 36, 37–38, 46, 47
  strategies for obtaining, 117–118
Okay
  constraining device, 281, 283
  discourse marker, 15, 179, 191, 304, 317
Ongoing Developmental Assessment Tool, 171*n*.2
Oral deaf, 128, 131*n*.8, 132
Ostracism, *see* Alienation
Other-correction, 152

Other-initiated other-correction,
    158–159, 163–164, 165
    master-initiated repair of, 163–164
Other-initiated self-correction, 153, 154,
    157
Ottoman culture, 155
    compared with American, 151, 167
Overt instruction, 346

P

Parables, 157–158, 165
Paralinguistic signals, 9–11
Partial understandings, 179n.13
Participation possibilities," 192
Passive voice, 9
Patient/physician asymmetries, see
    Physician/patient asymmetries
Patient/physician collaboration, see Phy-
    sician/patient collaboration
Patients, see also under individual disorder
    competence judgments of, 12, 259,
        269, 284
    competency-lowering in, 294–295,
        303–304, 307–308
    compliance of, 17, 259, 282, 284,
        318
    as the expert, 344
    health insurance concerns, 315,
        329, 331
    incompetence construction of,
        277–284, 321–330
    interpretation of evaluations, 12–13
Pauses, 52
PDD, see Children with pervasive devel-
    opmental disorders (PDD)
PDD-NOS, see Children with pervasive
    developmental disorders (PDD)
Peer acceptance, see Acceptance
Peer-rating studies, 112, 113
Perception, self, see Identities
Personal futures plan, 225, 240–242, 243
Personification, 252–254
Perspective-display series, 258
Pervasive developmental disorders, see
    Children with pervasive develop-
    mental disorders (PDD)
Pervasive developmental disorders not
    otherwise specified (PDD-NOS),
    see Children with pervasive
    deevelopmental disorders (PDD)

Physical body metaphors, 252, 253t
Physical distance, 9
Physician/patient asymmetries, 258,
    263, 284
Physician/patient collaboration, 258,
    259–260
    in ADHD diagnosis, 264–274, 283
Physicians
    competence of, 258–259
    judging patients' competence, 12,
        259, 269, 284
Pitch, 9
Playing the dozens, 201–202, 205, 207,
    214, 215–216
Popularity, 112
Porch Index of Communicative Ability, 314
Positive evaluations, 11, 12, 23
    of patients, 273, 284
    in reports, 23, 233–235, 236–238,
        243
Positive feedback
    boosting self-image, 99
    disbelief in, 92–93, 96
Positive judgments, see Positive evalu-
    ations
Positive politeness, 150n.3, 152, 153, 157
"Postmodern turn," 84
Pragmatics, 207
    cultural, 146, 147
Pre-stored utterances, 72, 74
Preconceptions, 44
Preposed adverbials, 8
Previous evaluation, impact of, 12
Progress reports, 12, 22, 223, 224–225
    compared with evaluation reports,
        12, 22–23, 231–239,
        242–243
    organization of, 229–231
Prompt (in three-part turn), 14
Pronouns, proper/improper use of,
    349–350
Prophet Muhammad, 153
Psychoeducational Profile, 171n.2
Psychotherapy
    clients' role in, 13, 344
    construction of client incompe-
        tence, 15, 343–344,
        345–359
    language use in, 343
    "not-knowing approach," 344, 352
"Pygmalion effect," 18, 192

Q

Questions, 317–318
Quincy Jones, 204
Qur'an, 153, 155

R

Rabbi Nachman of Bratslav, 167n.7
Ranchos Los Amigos Scale, 294
Rappin' and Stylin' Out (Kochman), 200, 215
Rapping, 203–204, 206, 207, 215
Rates, augmented communication, 66–70
Ratified position, 11
Reading, evaluations and, 12
Real communication, 141, 144, 146
Real deaf, 128, 147
Real time, 50, 59, 61, 77
Recipiency, 6, 174, 183–184, 187–190
Recipient design, 5, 12
Reconstructed perception, 90–94
Record keeping, incompetent, 173
Recycling communicative failure, 355–359
Redundancy, 204
Rejection
    of nonmembers, 130
    perceived, 40–41, 44, 46, 47
    of requests, 321, 323–325, 328
Religious metaphors, 250, 251t
Remote evaluations, 12
Repair(s), *see also* Correction
    augmented communication, 70, 71, 78
    Bektashi practices of, 150, 152–154
    construction of incompetence in, 163–164
    defined, 150, 152
    forms of, 157–164
    opportunity space in, 165
    recognition of, 154
    in testing, 176, 178–180
    tikkun, 167
    "trainer-oriented approaches" and, 292–293
    turn taking, 153–154, 175n.9
Repertoire, 7
Repetition, 9–11, 204

Reports, *see also* Evaluation reports;
    Personal futures plan; Progress reports
    agendas and, 22–23, 224–225, 238–242, 243
    comparison of, 12, 22–23, 231–239, 242–243
    competence judgments and, 6, 231–238
    prescriptive formats in, 224–225, 242–243
    types of, 223–225
Request-response-evaluation (RRE), 318–320, 322–325, 330
Requests, 317–318
    rejection of, 321, 323–325, 328
Response
    call and response, 207
Response Elaboration Therapy, 321
Response Elaboration Training, 315
Responses
    constructed, 6
    ghost, 325
    negotiated, 22
    of PDD children, 41–42
    to requests, 318, 321
    in testing. *see* Cues, in testing
    three-part turn, 14
Rhyme, 201, 204
Rhythm, 201, 204
Ritalin, 264–265
Roles, social, *see also* Asymmetries
    evaluation and, 12, 20, 21
    shifting of, 320–330
    subordinate, 16–17
    violation of, 13, 331–333
Routine event metaphors, 250, 251t
Royal "we," 317, 346, 347
Rules
    game. *See* Games for TBI patients, rules of
    for children, 121, 122, 123

S

Sampling, 204
Sapir-Whorf hypothesis, 349, 350–352
Saving face, 20, 21, 150n.3, 154
Scope, of evaluations, 15–16
Self, situated, 5, 6, 7, 108
Self-correction, 154, 156, 164

Self Help for the Hard of Hearing
    (SHHH), 131, 132
Self-identity, see Identities
Self-initiated self-correction, 158, 160
Seminal events, see Watershed experiences
Sequences
    instructional, 174–175
    interlocking of, 177
    request-response-evaluation
        (RRE), 318–320, 322–325,
        330
    testing, 171, 172, 175–177
    local history of, 178–180
Severe Mental Impairment (SMI),
    272n.5
Shared culture, and effective communi-
    cation, 63–64, 79
Shared knowledge, and effective com-
    munication, 268–271, 283, 284
Sharing, see also Cultural identities
    as a social rule, 121, 122, 123
Shehadah, 155
Shyness and sensitivity studies, 113
Sign language, 142–143, 144, 146
    American Sign Language (ASL),
        128, 139, 142
Signal-messages, 57, 58
Signifying, 202–203, 214
Signing deaf, 127, 147
Silent pauses, 52
Situated evaluations, 17–18
Situated practice
    diagnosis as, 22–23
    intervention as, 23–24
Situated self, 5, 6, 7, 108
Sleep state metaphors, 248, 249t
SLI, see Specific language impairment
    (SLI)
Smiling, 192, 293
Snaps, 202
Snaps (Percelay et al.), 202
Social acceptance, see Acceptance
Social competence
    evaluating children with SLI (ap-
        proaches to), 111–114
    evaluating children with SLI
        (study), 114–122
    interpretation of, 122–123
Social constructionism, 149
    psychotherapy and, 343–360
    suppositions of, 84–86, 107–109

Social context, of language, 197–198
Social incompetence, see Incompetence
Social roles, see also Asymmetries
    evaluation and, 12, 20, 21
    shifting of, 320–330
    violation of, 13, 331–333
Social rules, 121, 122, 123
Social stigmatization, 78
Socially consensual "real time," 50, 59,
    61, 77
Sociocultural factors, in interaction,
    62–64, 79
Solitariness, see Alienation
Sound blending, 16
Speaker initiation, 6
Speakers, 5, 51
Speaking, act of, 51
Special education
    assessment tests, 171n.2
    placement categories, 19–20,
        272n.5, 273
Specific language impairment (SLI), 113
    evaluating social competence of
        children (approaches to),
        111–114, 122
    evaluating social competence of
        children (study), 114–122
    perceived incompetence of chil-
        dren with, 114
Speech, delayed, 50, 52, 53
Speech communities, 149
    African-American, 200–201
Speech events, African-American, see
    African-American speech events
Speech-language pathologists (SLPs),
    29, 223, 292, 313
Speech-language pathology students,
    29, 31, 47
    desire for acceptance, 39, 42, 44, 47
    evaluation of PDD children, 34–43
    feelings of incompetence, 35, 38,
        39
    perceived rejection of, 40–41, 44,
        46, 47
Speech-language therapy, 292, 313
Speech synthesizers, 55, 65
Spiraling of stories, 165
Spiritual master-student relationships,
    see Student-master relationships
Standard American English (SAE), 197
Standardized tests, 19, 190

Standards, evaluative, 10, 34–38
Stanford-Binet IQ Test, 272n.5
Stigmatization, 78
Stimulus-response model, 171
Stowe, Harriet Beecher, 214
Student-initiated repair of the master, 161–163
Student-initiated self-correction, 160–161
Student-master relationships, 149n.2, 150, 152, 156–157, 158, 165, 166–167
    master-initiated master-correction, 159
    master-initiated repair of other- initiated other-correction, 163–164
    student-initiated repair of the master, 161–163
    student-initiated self-correction, 160–161
Students, see also Speech-language pathology students
    evaluation of, 12
    interpretation of teacher's evaluation, 13
    prompt-response-evaluation exchange and, 14–15
Sufi traditions, 155
Symbols, 145
Synchronous communication, 53
    with communication boards, 70
    inhibitors of, 60
Synthesized speech output, 55, 65
Systemic linguists, 5

T

Talk-in-interaction, 320, 321, 333
TBI, see Traumatic brain injury (TBI)
Teachers, evaluation of, 6, 12
Tempo, prompt-response-evaluation exchange and, 15
Temporal constraints, 61–62, 69, 71–72, 77, 78
Temporal coordination, 70
Temporal imperative, 9–11, 14, 20, 49–50, 51, 52, 54, 56, 58, 66–67, 69, 77, see also Timing
Temporal order, see Time orders
Testers, 14–15
Testing

competence, 19
educational. see Educational testing
    negotiated responses in, 22
    three-part turn in, 14–15
Testing sequences, 171, 172, 175–177
    collapsed, 176–177, 187, 191
    local history of, 178–180
Themes, of institutional interactions, 263
Therapeutic Discourse (Labov & Fanshel), 343
Therapeutic Ways with Words (Ferrara), 343
Therapy, see also Psychotherapy
    asymmetrical roles in, 313–314, 316–317
    conflict within, 320–335
    goals of rehabilitative, 298–301, 314
    institutional practices of, 295–296, 315–326, 330, 334
    language, 23
Therapy as Social Construction (McNamee & Gergen), 343
This Mouth Has a Brain, 261n.1
Three-part turns, 14–15, 175–176, 175n.9, 191, 292
    elimination of, 176–177, 184
    request-response-evaluation (RRE), 318–320, 322–325, 330
Tightrope metaphors, 254
Tikkun, 167
Time expectations, 21
Time orders
    alternative, 69, 77
    conversation, 50, 52, 64, 69
    failed communication and, 60
    "real time" distinguished from, 61
Timing, 9–11, see also Temporal imperative
    constraints, see Temporal constraints
    defined, 55–56
Timing strategies
    pre-stored utterances, 72, 74
    word prediction display, 65
Tomming, 214
Tracking, 5–6
Trainable Mental Impairment (TMI), 272n.5
"Trainer-oriented" intervention, 292–293
Traumatic brain injury (TBI), 20, 23

Traumatic brain injury (TBI) patients,
    see also Games for TBI patients
    characteristic problems of, 296–298
    competency-lowering in, 294–295,
        303–304, 307–308
    institutional constraints in therapy,
        295–296
    therapy goals, 298–301
Triple Snaps (Percelay et al.), 202
Turn taking, 54, 153–154, 165, 357, *see
    also* Three-part turns
    two-part, 175*n*.9

U

Uncle Tom's Cabin (Stowe), 214
Utterances
    guessing, 68
    pre-stored, 72, 74

V

Verbal assertiveness studies, 113

Verbal intentions, for obtaining objects,
    117
Verbalization, of PDD children, 42
Verbs, 8
Visual cues, importance of, 60, 70
Visual modalities, 128

W

Watershed experiences, 16, 17
    self-identity and, 90, 100–102, 104
Web pages, *see* World Wide Web
    (WWW)
Women (non-disabled), use of alterna-
    tive communication, 63, 64
Woodcock Johnson Blending Subtest,
    173
Woodcock Johnson Psychoeducational
    Battery, 171, 191
Word prediction display, 65
World Wide Web (WWW), 135
Writing, report, *see* Reports
WWW, *see* World Wide Web (WWW)